Believers Church
Bible Commentary

Elmer A. Martens and Willard M. Swartley, Editors

Believers Church
Bible Commentary

1 and 2 Thessalonians

Jacob W. Elias

To Bill Klassen
with gratitude
+ best wishes.
Jacob W. Elias

HERALD PRESS
Scottdale, Pennsylvania
Waterloo, Ontario

Library of Congress Cataloging-in-Publication Data

Elias, Jacob W., 1941-
   1 and 2 Thessalonians / Jacob W. Elias.
     p. cm. — (Believers church Bible commentary)
   Includes bibliographical references and index.
   ISBN 0-8361-3698-5 (Kivar-bound squareback : alk. paper)
   1. Bible. N.T. Thessalonians.—Commentaries. I. Title. .
II. Title: First and Second Thessalonians. III. Series.
BS2725.3.E45 1995
227'.8107—dc20
                                                  94-23408
                                                    CIP

The paper used in this publication is recycled and meets the minimum requirements of American National Standard for Information Sciences—Permanence of Paper for Printed Library Materials, ANSI Z39.48-1984.

BELIEVERS CHURCH BIBLE COMMENTARY: 1 AND 2 THESSALONIANS
Copyright © 1995 by Herald Press, Scottdale, Pa. 15683
   Published simultaneously in Canada by Herald Press,
   Waterloo, Ont. N2L 6H7. All rights reserved
Library of Congress Catalog Number: 94-23408
International Standard Book Number: 0-8361-3698-5
Printed in the United States of America
Cover by Merrill R. Miller

04 03 02 01 00 99 98 97 96 95 10 9 8 7 6 5 4 3 2 1

To Lillian,
my companion
in faith and life

BELIEVERS CHURCH BIBLE COMMENTARY

(Volumes available to 1995)

Old Testament

Genesis, by Eugene F. Roop
Jeremiah, by Elmer A. Martens
Ezekiel, by Millard C. Lind
Daniel, by Paul M. Lederach

New Testament

Matthew, by Richard B. Gardner
Acts, by Chalmer E. Faw
Colossians, Philemon, by Ernest D. Martin
1 and 2 Thessalonians, by Jacob W. Elias

Contents

1 THESSALONIANS

*The Text in Biblical Context
+The Text in the Life of the Church

2 THESSALONIANS

Series Foreword

The Believers Church Bible Commentary Series makes available a new tool for basic Bible study. It is published for all who seek more fully to understand the original message of Scripture and its meaning for today—Sunday school teachers, members of Bible study groups, students, pastors, and other seekers. The series is based on the conviction that God is still speaking to all who will listen, and that the Holy Spirit makes the Word a living and authoritative guide for all who want to know and do God's will.

The desire to help as wide a range of readers as possible has determined the approach of the writers. Since we have chosen not to provide the biblical text from a published version, readers may continue to use the translation with which they are most familiar. The writers of the series use the *New Revised Standard Version*, the *Revised Standard Version*, the *New International Version*, and the *New American Standard Bible* on a comparative basis. They indicate which text they follow most closely, as well as where they make their own translations. The writers have not worked alone, but in consultation with select counselors, the series' editors, and the Editorial Council.

Every volume illuminates the Scriptures; provides necessary theological, sociological, and ethical meanings; and in general, makes "the rough places plain." Critical issues are not avoided, but neither are they moved into the foreground as debates among scholars. Each section offers explanatory notes, followed by focused articles, "The Text in Biblical Context" and "The Text in the Life of the Church." This commentary aids the interpretive process but does not try to supersede the authority of the Word and Spirit as discerned in the gathered church.

The term *believers church* has often been used in the history of the church. Since the sixteenth century, it has frequently been applied to the Anabaptists and later the Mennonites, as well as to the Church of the Brethren and similar groups. As a descriptive term, it includes more than Mennonites and Brethren. *Believers church* now represents specific theological understandings, such as believers baptism, commitment to the Rule of Christ in Matthew 18:15-20 as crucial for church membership, belief in the power of love in all relationships, and willingness to follow Christ in the way of the cross. The writers chosen for the series stand in this tradition.

Believers church people have always been known for their emphasis on obedience to the simple meaning of Scripture. Because of this, they do not have a long history of deep historical-critical biblical scholarship. This series attempts to be faithful to the Scriptures while also taking archaeology and current biblical studies seriously. Doing this means that at many points the writers will not differ greatly from interpretations which can be found in many other good commentaries. Yet basic presuppositions about Christ, the church and its mission, God and history, human nature, the Christian life, and other doctrines do shape a writer's interpretation of Scripture. Thus this series, like all other commentaries, stands within a specific historical church tradition.

Many in this stream of the church have expressed a need for help in Bible study. This is justification enough to produce the Believers Church Bible Commentary. Nevertheless, the Holy Spirit is not bound to any tradition. May this series be an instrument in breaking down walls between Christians in North America and around the world, bringing new joy in obedience through a fuller understanding of the Word.

The Editorial Council

Author's Preface

As a pastor I preached most frequently on the Gospels and Acts. When I turned to the epistles for sermon material, I apparently found other letters to be more relevant to the needs of the congregation than Paul's two letters to the first-century church in Thessalonica. As I reviewed my sermon files from that period of my ministry, I realized that I had rarely preached from 1 and 2 Thessalonians.

I "discovered" 1 and 2 Thessalonians in 1980. Congregations in Hillsboro, Kansas, and Rosthern, Saskatchewan, each invited me to come for a week of Deeper Life meetings. While discerning content and direction for these worship services, I meditated on several of Paul's letters. I was especially impressed by the way 1 Thessalonians seems to address issues still facing our churches. The fact that this letter is short also helped! The progression of themes in the letter could readily be adapted for a series of inspirational congregational Bible studies.

Since that time I have had the privilege of preaching and teaching from the Thessalonian epistles in a variety of congregations and other settings in both Canada and the United States. At Associated Mennonite Biblical Seminary (AMBS), I developed a course entitled "The Early Paul," focusing on Galatians as well as 1 and 2 Thessalonians. By the time I began writing this commentary, I had profited from the cumulative experience of prayerful engagement around these biblical texts along with Christian brothers and sisters from many congregations and in several seminary classes. I gratefully acknowledge the gifts of inspiration and insight which I gained in their company.

In pursuing my calling as a preacher and teacher of the Word, I have been shaped by many pastors, teachers, and colleagues. I mention two formative beginnings and two institutional settings. My first Bible teacher was my father, John Elias, who obtained permission to begin the first Sunday school class in the Bergthaler Mennonite Church near Rosthern. A few years later, when I was enrolled as a student at the University of Saskatchewan, my roommates invited me to join a Bible study group. As a student at Mennonite Biblical Seminary during the 1960s, I became increasingly interested in biblical studies under the dedicated tutelage of Howard H. Charles, William Klassen, Jacob J. Enz, Millard C. Lind, and others. During my doctoral studies at Toronto School of Theology, I pursued scholarly work in New Testament under such scholars as Richard N. Longenecker, John C. Hurd, Jr., and Joseph Plevnik, S.J.

These teachers and mentors—and the writings of many others—gave me the tools and the background for the writing of this commentary. However, the life and mission of the congregations where I have been nurtured in the faith have provided the drive and the motivation. I often reflect on the fact that 1 and 2 Thessalonians, likely the earliest of all the letters in the New Testament, can be considered a primer in the Christian faith. Written by missionary pastors to a newly formed community of believers, these letters can still inspire, encourage, and warn faith communities in our day.

I am grateful for the support, encouragement, and counsel which I have received during the writing of this commentary. For the academic year 1992-93, AMBS gave me a welcome sabbatical, during which I completed the initial draft. The Believers Church Bible Commentary Editorial Council gave constructive feedback and enthusiastic support. The New Testament editor, my colleague Willard M. Swartley, read the manuscript in several stages and gave me invaluable advice throughout the project. S. David Garber, Book Editor at Herald Press, attended diligently to the detailed editing of this manuscript, often suggesting areas of improvement.

Several others also read the commentary in process and offered their critique and suggestions: Mary Klassen, a fellow member of Hively Avenue Mennonite Church and a staff colleague at AMBS; Ashish Chrispal, former dean at Union Biblical Seminary, Pune, India, and a visiting professor at AMBS during the spring semester 1993; and Robert Jewett of Garrett-Evangelical Theological Seminary, Evanston, Illinois, whose scholarship in Pauline studies generally and the Thessalonian correspondence specifically has stimulated my own ongoing attempt to understand the apostle Paul. My father-in-law, William Bartel of Winnipeg, also read the whole text—a moving gesture of interest and support! I say "Thank you!" to all of these partners who have contributed toward the completion of this commentary-writing project.

My deepest appreciation goes to Lillian, my companion in life and faith, to whom I dedicate this commentary. For many of our morning meditation times, she read portions of this material and then lovingly shared both her affirmations and her suggestions for improvement.

Jacob W. Elias
Associated Mennonite Biblical Seminary
Elkhart, Indiana

Cross-References

[Grammatical Analysis, p. 350.]   Sample cross-reference to essay at the back of this book that explains the sentence-flow diagrams in the Explanatory Notes. Other back-of-book essays will be cross-referenced in this style and enclosed by square brackets—all in italics.

(Metzger, 1992:3-4)   Sample reference to source listed in the Bibliography: author's name if not already given outside the parentheses, date of publication if needed to distinguish it, and page numbers—all enclosed by parentheses.

notes   Explanatory Notes for each section

TBC   The Text in Biblical Context, after notes in each section. These essays are cross-referenced in quotation marks and roman type and enclosed by parentheses as in these samples: ("in Faith, Love, and Hope" in TBC below); ("Peace and Grace" in TBC for 2 Thess. 3:16-18).

TLC   The Text in the Life of the Church, after TBC in each section. These essays are cross-referenced in quotation marks and roman type and enclosed by parentheses as in this sample: ("The Holy Kiss" in TLC below).

Other Common Abbreviations
LXX   Septuagint
NT   New Testament
OT   Old Testament

See pages 343-344 for a longer list of abbreviations.

Paul and the Thessalonians

Listening In

One who discovers and then reads a personal letter addressed to someone else can feel invited into an imaginative exploration of an otherwise unknown world of relationships. A reader of the NT who discovers "the first letter of Paul to the Thessalonians" also enters such a world. In particular, such a reader becomes attuned to the relational interaction between several missionary pastors and the people among whom they have worked. Both 1 and 2 Thessalonians beckon the readers to listen in. By listening in, readers not earlier on the scene become able to catch echoes of a truly dynamic event—the formation and the shaping of the earliest Christian community in ancient Thessalonica.

Those who move beyond the thrill and excitement of reading through someone else's mail, however, grasp the challenge of making connections with the modern world. A historian may not look for such points of contact. But a believer struggling with questions similar to those addressed in these letters often longs for relevance. Yet an understanding of how the message of 1 and 2 Thessalonians relates to life requires that one first try to listen attentively to the interaction that previously occurred between these pastors and their people.

Several dimensions of this dynamic interaction between pastors and people require some preliminary attention. A framework of understanding is helpful as one seeks to "listen in." The bare fact that a *letter* serves as the vehicle of communication here deserves atten-tion. Furthermore, some basic data about the authors and the recipi-ents of the letters might cast light on the message. Some initial reflec-tions on the purpose of these epistles will also clarify our reading.

Fortunately, the modern reader need not rely only on 1 and 2 Thessalonians for background information. The narrative in Acts 17 provides Luke's summary of events as well as his perspective on them. To this story we now turn.

Some Background from Acts

In Acts 17:1-9, Luke tells us about the birth of the church in Thes-salonica. This account contains vital data otherwise not available. A reading of this story in the context of the rest of Luke-Acts reveals that, in addition to reporting selected events, Luke accentuates cer-tain theological and missionary themes important to him. These Lukan emphases shape both the selection of the episodes and his telling of this whole story.

According to Acts 17:1, Thessalonica had a synagogue, which Paul visits first, "as was his custom" (cf. Luke 4:16, which shows that Jesus' ministry also begins in the synagogue). Before his Thes-salonian ministry, Paul has announced a change from this customary mission strategy of going to the Jews first. When the gospel was re-jected by Jews in Antioch of Pisidia (Acts 13:13-52), Paul declares, "We are now turning to the Gentiles" (13:46). Despite that decision to focus on a mission to the Gentiles, Paul continues his earlier pat-tern. In every community he begins his ministry in the synagogue by announcing the good news to Jews and God-fearers gathered there (14:1; 17:1).

For three Sabbaths, Paul enters the synagogue and argues with them from the Scriptures (Acts 17:2). In subsequent narratives, Luke frequently depicts Paul's activity in similar terms. For city after city, Luke describes Paul's debates with the Jews and his attempts to per-suade them to accept Jesus as the awaited Messiah: in Athens (17:17), Corinth (18:4), and Ephesus (18:19; 19:8-9). These con-frontations reach their climax in Paul's testimony before leaders in the major centers of the Jewish and Roman worlds: in Jerusalem (22:1-21; 23:1-10), Caesarea (24:1-21), and Rome (28:17-28).

Two participles further portray this vigorous evangelistic activity in the local synagogue in Thessalonica: "explaining and proving" (Acts 17:3). Luke thus underscores the strength of Paul's efforts to win the Jews and God-fearers. The substance of Paul's message is summarized in a fashion reminiscent of the way in which Luke elsewhere (for example in Luke 24:26) conveys the divine necessity "for the Messiah to suffer and to rise from the dead" (Acts 17:3). Paul emphatically highlights his claim that Jesus is the Messiah who fulfills Scripture by suffering and rising from the dead: "This is the Messiah, Jesus whom I am proclaiming to you" (17:3).

How do the people in Thessalonica respond? Some believe this message, others do not. Were the converts Jewish or were they Gentile? On this question, scholars have often noted a difference between Acts and the Thessalonian correspondence. In his first letter to Thessalonica, Paul implies that the recipients are converts who had come out of paganism: *You turned toward God from idols* (1:9). No clue of the existence of a synagogue or a Jewish community can be found in Paul's letters to the Thessalonian church. In Acts, the picture is different. After Luke describes Paul's active dialogue in the synagogue, he indicates that some Jews are persuaded and join Paul and Silas (Acts 17:4). Others responding positively to the gospel include the God-fearers: "a great many of the devout Greeks and not a few of the leading women" (17:4). However, other Jews become jealous and provoke a public outcry against the evangelists. As a result, "the people and the city officials were disturbed" (17:8). Luke therefore depicts a separation within both the Jewish and the Gentile communities between those who accept and those who reject the gospel.

Luke reports that Jewish leaders, accompanied by a mob, make their way to the home of Jason in an attempt to catch up with Paul and Silas (Acts 17:5). It appears that Jason has extended hospitality to Paul and his companions. Apparently other Christians are congregating there as well. Malherbe suggests,

> We should understand Jason's house as having been the base for Paul's work among the Gentiles after the separation from the synagogue, as Titius Justus's house would be in Corinth (cf. Acts 18:6-7). (Malherbe, 1987:13-14)

Jason is a man of some means and social standing in the community. He posts bond for the evangelists (17:9) so they can leave the city (17:10).

At first Jason and the congregation gathered in his home bear the brunt of the suspicion and antagonism provoked by the message which Paul has preached (17:6). Since Paul and Silas cannot be located, Jason and some other believers are brought before the city officials to hear the accusations.

> These people who have been turning the world upside down have come
> here also, and Jason has entertained them as guests. They are all acting
> contrary to the decrees of the emperor, saying that there is another king
> named Jesus. (17:6-7)

The charges leveled against Paul and Silas sound a familiar note
within Luke's writings. According to Luke's passion narrative, similar
charges were brought against Jesus during his hearing before Pilate:

> We found this man perverting our nation, forbidding us to pay taxes to
> the emperor, and saying that he himself is the Messiah, a king.
> (Luke 23:2)

As in the case of Jesus' own ministry, so within the expanding Christian movement, Luke portrays a climate of political nervousness. The notion of a rival king upsets the powers-that-be. According to Luke, the Jewish leadership in Thessalonica capitalizes on this apprehensiveness by getting the city authorities and the mob to vent their anger against these missionaries (Acts 17:8).

That night Paul and Silas are escorted out of Thessalonica and taken to Beroea (17:10). Here they continue their evangelistic ministry in the synagogue. Many receive the word "eagerly and examined the scriptures every day to see whether these things were so" (17:11). In addition, once again Greek women of high standing and not a few men join this group of believers (17:12). When the Thessalonian Jews hear what is happening in Beroea, they come and stir up trouble against the missionaries. Paul soon leaves by sea for Athens, while Timothy and Silas stay in Beroea (17:15).

What contribution can Luke's account of church beginnings in Thessalonica make to our understanding of 1 and 2 Thessalonians? Luke's story makes us aware that the Jews, though they likely are a minority group in Thessalonica, play a significant role in the emergence of this predominantly Gentile congregation in their city. However, we need to recognize that Luke does not tell the whole story. His "orderly account" (cf. Luke 1:3) features episodes which illustrate the church's expanding witness from the beginnings in Jerusalem "to the ends of the earth" (Acts 1:8). Yet the story in Acts 17 alerts the reader to important aspects of the social and political climate in Thessalonica. This information, supplemented by archaeological, historical, and social data, helps us gain a picture of the circumstances facing the new Thessalonian believers. These two letters need to be read in light of this background. *[Historical and Political Context, p. 357.]*

Why Letters?

Though the answer may seem self-evident, the question still deserves to be addressed. Why did Paul and his missionary companions write letters? Luke's sketch of the turbulent events in Thessalonica makes it clear that their opponents forced Paul and his party to leave town. Even though the letters to the Thessalonian church do not give details about the evacuation of the missionaries, there are hints. Paul and his colleagues even allude to that experience by suggesting that they felt orphaned when they were separated from the Thessalonians (1 Thess. 2:17). A return visit to Thessalonica by Paul seems out of the question, despite his keen desire to come back. The writers of the letter seem eager to impress on their readers that their abrupt departure and delayed return should not be read as lack of interest or desire: *We wanted to come to you—certainly I, Paul, wanted to again and again—but Satan blocked our way* (2:18).

Letters provide a vehicle for continuing a relationship between people while they are apart from each other. The two letters addressed to the church at Thessalonica certainly have that function. As Paul himself asserts in the first of these letters, *For this reason, when I could bear it no longer, I sent [Timothy] to find out about your faith* (3:5). When unable physically to be present with them, Paul employs a letter as a substitute for another personal visit.

Letters in antiquity conveyed more than information. When interpreting the Thessalonian epistles, we need to keep in mind that the letter form functioned in the world of that day in a wide variety of ways. Letters might be written to initiate, maintain, restore, or end a relationship with a person or group. Similarly, a letter might offer praise, express thanks, evoke shame, or convey honor. Thus these letters need to be read for more than the information or the doctrines which they contain. The letter form had become a convenient medium of communication whereby interpersonal relationships were continued while the parties were absent from one another.

Research on NT letters has been enhanced in recent years through discoveries of numerous ancient letters. Many of them were written on sheets made from papyrus plants, which flourished in the shallow water of the Nile delta (cf. Job 8:11; Isa. 19:5-7). Pith from foot-long sections of the plant's triangular stem was cut into thin strips. On a flat surface, a layer of strips with fibers running parallel was covered by another layer with fibers at right angles to the first. The layers were pressed into one fabric and dried to become writing material almost as strong as modern paper (Metzger, 1992:3-4). The word *paper* is derived from *papyrus*.

Because of extremely dry conditions in desert areas of Egypt outside the delta, such papyri were preserved in the sand until discovered many centuries later, brittle with age. Papyri carrying personal and business letters from NT times have been analyzed carefully to gain insights into letter-writing conventions of that day (Stowers: 1986). Comparative studies of the papyri from the Greco-Roman era have yielded useful information, including some insights into the standard letter form:

> Letter opening (sender, addressee, greeting)
> Thanksgiving, or a wish for the recipient's health
> Letter body (formal opening, then discussion of business at hand)
> Letter closing (greetings, wishes expressed in behalf of other people, final greeting, wish or prayer)

Paul follows this basic letter form of his day, but he adapts, modifies, and expands it in several ways. In Paul's letters, an opening thanksgiving section usually serves notice concerning the major content of the rest of the letter. Paul also introduces exhortation as part of the main letter body, to give specific pastoral and ethical counsel. Other adaptations in a given letter often reveal something about the writer's particular purpose. First Thessalonians features an unusually lengthy thanksgiving section; the opening in 1:2-10 seems to be resumed in 2:13. A reader of this letter might well ask what this unusual characteristic of the letter reveals about the author's main intent.

The following chart identifies the main epistolary features of both 1 and 2 Thessalonians (adapted from Roetzel: 71, and expanded to include 2 Thessalonians):

Letter Structure	1 Thessalonians	2 Thessalonians
Salutation	1:1	1:1-2
A. Senders	1:1a	1:1a
B. Recipient	1:1b	1:1b
C. Greeting	1:1c	1:2
Thanksgiving	1:2-10	1:3-12
Body	2:1—5:22	2:1—3:15
A. Thanksgiving	2:13; 3:9-10	2:13
B. Wish Prayer	3:11-13	2:16-17; 3:5
C. Exhortations	4:1—5:22	3:1-15
Closing	5:23-28	3:16-18
A. Peace Wish	5:23-24	3:16
B. Greetings	(5:26)	3:17
C. Kiss	5:26	
D. Apostolic command	5:25, 27	
E. Benediction	5:28	3:18

[Epistolary Analysis, p. 348.]

These Letters Also Preach!

Paul's letters to the congregation at Thessalonica were shaped not only by the epistolary conventions of the day. The fact that Paul and his co-workers were preachers also shows in these letters. In a real sense, Paul's letters substitute not only for his personal presence but also for his preaching. Just as Paul utilized but also adapted the standard letter format of his day, so he undoubtedly also preached in ways that he had been taught and seen modeled. Even his letters, therefore, reflect contemporary rhetorical forms. Readers of the NT letters can benefit from understanding this rhetorical dimension.

Rhetorical analyses of literature in general focus on ways in which writers attempt to persuade their readers. Like orators addressing their audiences, so ancient authors used a variety of rhetorical strategies to move their readers. Three species of rhetorical speech have been discerned in Greek rhetoric, each with different settings or occasions (Mack: 34): A *judicial* speech at a trial seeks to persuade a judge and jury concerning the legality of an event in the past. A *deliberative* speech in a public debate tries to persuade the audience to take a particular course of action in the future. And an *epideictic* (e-pi-DĪK-tik: demonstrative) speech commemorates an event or memorializes a person; a memorial speech of this type often focuses on questions of honor or of grounds for praise or blame in the present.

Judgments vary among interpreters concerning the nature of the rhetoric in 1 and 2 Thessalonians. However, some consensus appears to be emerging. Jewett suggests that 1 Thessalonians best fits the epideictic genre, because the writers address the community primarily on the basis of their present status. Basically they are on the right path. The letter therefore offers pastoral encouragement based on the progress these new believers have already made (Jewett, 1986:71-72; so also Wanamaker: 47). Second Thessalonians has a different tone, however. This second letter appears to employ deliberative rhetoric. It seeks to persuade the readers to think or behave differently in the future. Paul and his companions are especially eager to challenge and correct the eschatological views and the lifestyle which some members of the Thessalonian congregation have adopted (Jewett, 1986:82; Wanamaker: 48).

Readers of these two letters to the Thessalonian congregation will benefit from being alert to their persuasive impact. Using the rhetorical modes available to them, Paul and his companions framed these letters quite intentionally. The initial letter first praises and commends the faith and life of this community of new believers and then urges them *to do so more* (4:10; cf. 5:11). The follow-up letter appears to be more reserved in its commendations and considerably more directive concerning the desired changes in their beliefs and practices. Listening carefully to these letters will let the reader hear the passion and power of Paul's continued preaching to these new believers. *[Rhetorical Analysis, p. 352.]*

Focusing In

Having begun a process of listening for the echoes of the dynamic ongoing conversation between the missionaries and their people, we now focus on some introductory issues. There are several basic questions about these two NT letters: Who wrote them? To whom? When? Why? In some cases the answers need to be quite preliminary. The overall picture will become more clear as we deal with specific passages in the main body of the commentary.

Who Wrote These Letters?

In both 1 and 2 Thessalonians, the opening salutation identifies three persons as the senders: Paul, Silvanus, and Timothy. Actually, all of the letters in the Pauline collection, except Romans and the Pastoral epistles (1 and 2 Timothy and Titus), name multiple senders. Yet 1 and 2 Thessalonians are unusual among Paul's letters in their dominant use of the first-person plural subject, *we*. Paul draws attention to himself as distinct from his colleagues by using the first-person singular subject, *I*, on three occasions in 1 Thessalonians—2:18; 3:5; 5:27; and twice in 2 Thessalonians—2:5; 3:17. We conclude that in writing to the congregation at Thessalonica, Paul says *I* when he wants to speak for himself and *we* when they speak as a team (Collins, 1984:176-180).

The order in which the names are given in the salutation is significant. Paul serves as the primary initiator of this pastoral intervention. His co-workers, Silas (Silvanus is the Latin form of this name) and Timothy, who have been involved with Paul during the evangelistic visit and/or the follow-up visit, are named as co-senders with Paul, perhaps to express their solidarity as a team and their common concern and love for the Thessalonian church.

In my exposition of these two letters, I sometimes mention only Paul when referring to the writers, since it is simpler to do so, and since Paul is the primary writer. However, as a reminder that Paul sees himself as part of a team, my language often reflects the corporate authorship of these letters.

Who are these writers? According to Acts, Paul and Silas worked together in missionary endeavors from Antioch through Asia Minor to Troas and across the Aegean Sea to Macedonia (Acts 15:3—17:15). Timothy, whose partnership in the gospel is explicit in the first letter (1:1; 3:1-2), also appears in Luke's narrative as Paul's missionary companion both before and after the mission to Thessalonica (Acts 16:1-6; 17:14-15). Thus Timothy was also involved in Thessalonica. *[Chronology of Paul's Life, p. 369.]*

It would appear therefore that the question about authorship has a straightforward answer. Silas and Timothy both worked with Paul in the evangelistic outreach to the cities of Macedonia, including Thessalonica. A letter written by Paul in behalf of himself and his missionary colleagues seems like a natural next step. Numerous NT scholars have raised doubts, however. Even though 1 Thessalonians is almost universally acknowledged as a genuine Pauline letter, serious questions have surfaced about the authorship of 2 Thessalonians.

Interpreters of 1 and 2 Thessalonians have long been puzzled by two phenomena when comparing these two letters: they are so similar, and they are so different. First and 2 Thessalonians display great similarities both in words, phrases, and concepts, as well as in their structure, which differs in some respects from the standard Pauline letter form. Yet 2 Thessalonians seems to be less personal and intimate than 1 Thessalonians, and it has been seen as teaching a different eschatology. So how does one explain both these major linguistic and structural similarities and these differences in tone and content?

Several allusions in 2 Thessalonians to a previous letter (2:1-2, 15; 3:14) can most naturally be taken to refer to 1 Thessalonians. Yet a problem arises when we try to understand the reference in 2:2 to the *letter, as though from us,* a letter identified as a possible source of eschatological views upsetting people in Thessalonica. Surely Paul would not describe his first letter in this way! Might this be a fraudulent letter? Or is it perhaps an indication that some are interpreting 1 Thessalonians wrongly?

Debate on these issues continues. My operating assumption is that Paul was responsible for both of these letters. A change in the circumstances in Thessalonica, or new information about the situation there, led to the need for a follow-up letter. It is also possible, though this cannot be documented, that one of the co-senders had a more active role in writing the second letter. One or both of these factors would adequately account for the similarities and the differences between these two letters addressed to *the church of the Thessalonians. [Relationship between 1 and 2 Thessalonians, p. 374.]*

To Whom Were These Letters Written?

Both letters specify the addressee as *the church of the Thessalonians.* A few words about the city of Thessalonica will help us to envision this congregation and its relationship to its environment.

During the time when this congregation emerged, Thessalonica was a major urban center in the Roman province of Macedonia. The Via Egnatia, a road running from the Adriatic Sea to the Black Sea, passed right through Thessalonica, connecting it with other cities in the Roman world. A fine natural harbor put the merchants and artisans of Thessalonica in a good position to pursue their commercial activities throughout the Mediterranean region. All of these business opportunities created a demand for a significant pool of manual laborers, both skilled and unskilled, who manufactured the goods sold locally or shipped elsewhere. The Thessalonian believers likely came from this working class. That would account for Paul's reminders that he worked for his own support (1 Thess. 2:9; 2 Thess. 3:7-8) and his admonitions that the Thessalonians should work with their own hands (1 Thess. 4:11; cf. 2 Thess. 3:9). [*Social and Economic Context, p. 368.*]

As the capital of Macedonia, Thessalonica had major political importance. The Roman proconsul resided there, but the city itself was governed by officials called "politarchs" (NRSV note to Acts 17:6). In order to maintain cordial relationships with Rome, the politarchs sought to ensure that the populace demonstrate their loyalty toward the emperor. They arranged for the construction of a temple dedicated to Caesar. Coins were minted, featuring the heads of Caesar Augustus and his great-uncle Julius Caesar, both identified as divine. These manifestations of the civic cult in Thessalonica illustrate that any group unwilling to show homage to the emperor could be in trouble with the city and provincial authorities. In such a political climate, any talk about "another king named Jesus" (Acts 17:7) or about a God who calls people *into his own kingdom and glory* (1 Thess. 2:12; cf. 2 Thess. 1:5) would sound subversive, especially if it came from an otherwise restless working class.

Ethnically, the population of Thessalonica was largely of Greek descent. However, when Macedonia became a Roman province in 146 B.C., some Italians soon made themselves at home here as well. As already noted, Acts 17 informs us about the existence of a Jewish community there. Archaeologists have not yet found evidence of a synagogue from the first century A.D., but it is known that by this time Jews had settled into many of the major cities of Asia Minor and the whole Mediterranean region. According to Bruce, a militant messianism was spreading among Jewish communities throughout the Roman empire (Bruce, 1977:224-227). In about A.D. 49 the emperor Claudius issued an edict expelling Jews from Rome because of this kind of political unrest (Acts 18:2). This casts additional light on the situation in Thessalonica. Jewish expectations of the coming of a messianic deliverer had in recent history created an upheaval elsewhere in the Roman empire. An announcement of a rival Caesar would assuredly provoke Roman officials in Thessalonica to take strong measures to quell any politically embarrassing uprisings in their region. [*Judaism in the Diaspora, p. 363.*]

Religious life expressed itself largely in customary Greek forms, although the traditional religions had lost their vitality. Several mystery religions had made significant inroads into the community. For example, some of the Thessalonian converts might have been previously involved in the cult of Dionysus with its sensual orgies (cf. 1 Thess. 4:3-8). Other converts probably had a previous history in a cult of the Cabiri, which identified with the working class but had increasingly been drawn into the civic cult of the Roman establishment. [*Religions in the Greco-Roman World, p. 365.*]

When Were These Letters Written?

There is a remarkable consensus among scholars that 1 Thessalonians was written in the year 50. Those who accept 2 Thessalonians as a letter written by Paul usually date it a short time later, perhaps in 50 or 51.

Some debate has surfaced about the relative sequence of 1 and 2 Thessalonians. Some biblical scholars suggest that 2 Thessalonians was written first. The recent commentary by Wanamaker proceeds from that premise (Wanamaker: 37-45). It is generally agreed that Paul's letters in the NT are not arranged in their chronological order, but rather on the basis of some other criteria, such as length. In the case of the Thessalonian epistles, however, the traditional sequence is still the most plausible. The references in 2 Thessalonians to a previous letter (2:2, 15; 3:17) make most sense if they are taken to refer to 1 Thessalonians. Furthermore the extensive rehearsal of the founding mission (1 Thess. 1—3) is more likely in the first letter to that community rather than in a subsequent one (Jewett, 1986:26-30). [*Relationship between 1 and 2 Thessalonians, p. 374.*]

Both 1 and 2 Thessalonians were probably written from Corinth, where, according to Acts 18:11, Paul spent a total of eighteen months in a teaching ministry. [*Chronology of Paul's Life, p. 369.*]

Why Were These Letters Written?

Simply stated, the Thessalonian letters were written to continue the relationship between the missionary pastors and their people. Their letters also served as a vehicle for addressing several situations which emerged in the Thessalonian congregation following the initial preaching ministry by Paul and Silas in Thessalonica. What were these circumstances? We can discern several stages in the ongoing interaction between the missionary pastors and their people.

The first stage was the initial evangelistic visit in Thessalonica. Both epistles refer back to that time, often using statements such as *you know* or *you remember* (1 Thess. 1:5, 9-10; 2:1-12; 2 Thess. 2:5).

Another phase begins during the journey away from Thessalonica, when Paul decides to send Timothy back to that city as his emissary (1 Thess. 3:1-5). In due time, Timothy returns to Paul in Corinth with a report about his visit in Thessalonica (1 Thess. 3:6). Might he also have delivered a letter to Paul from the Thessalonian believers? The phrase *now concerning* (4:9; 5:1; as in 1 Cor. 7:1; 8:1; 12:1; 16:1) has been taken as a hint that the Thessalonians also wrote a letter to Paul (Faw, 1952). Whether communicated orally or in written form, concerns and questions from the believers in Thessalonica are communicated back to Paul.

The third stage in this ongoing relationship would then be Paul's writing of 1 Thessalonians. In the thanksgiving section (1:2-10), we learn that the missionaries are basically gratified at the dynamic *faith*, *love*, and *hope* of the Thessalonian believers. However, they are also concerned about several matters, some of which may already have been in evidence while the missionaries were still in that city. Judging from the issues which this letter addresses, several situations must have provoked Paul and his companions to write. These circumstances include:

1. Persecution and suffering as a threat to their continuing faithfulness (1:6; 3:1-10; 5:15).
2. A case of sexual immorality or the risk of slipping back into previous habits and patterns (4:3-8).
3. A group of idle and unruly people needing to be called to responsible and loving behavior (4:9-12; 5:14).
4. The believers' response to the death of members of their faith community (4:13-18).
5. Questions about the timetable for the day of the Lord and how to ensure readiness for that event (5:1-11).
6. Some conflict about the role of congregational leaders and the exercise of spiritual gifts in the congregation (5:12-22).
   (adapted from Jewett, 1986:91-109)

The fourth stage in this "conversation" between the missionaries and these converts cannot be reconstructed with confidence. It is also difficult to ascertain how much time elapsed between the first letter and the follow-up letter. Likely it was less than a year. In any case, further news from Thessalonica somehow comes to Paul, and some of the news is not good. Persecution has continued, and it apparently has become worse (2 Thess. 1:3-4), leading some to doubt the justice of God (1:5-10). Most disturbing, however, is the fact that some radicals in Thessalonica have taken their extremism one step further; they claim that the day of the Lord has already come (2:1-12). Also distressing is the fact that the group of idle and unruly people has become even more so (3:6-15).

During the fifth stage, Paul and his co-workers write 2 Thessalonians. A thankful attitude comes through again (1:3-4; 2:13). Yet, perhaps letting their exasperation show, the writers are more reserved in expressing their thanks. Some of the previous teachings, both those given in person while in Thessalonica and those included in the first letter, need to be repeated or further clarified. Since 1 Thessalonians has been written relatively recently, Paul naturally uses some of the same words and phrases, as well as a similar structure. Some new instruction also needs to be transmitted:

1. The experience of aggravated persecution leads to the need for some teaching on vindication and judgment (1:5-10).
2. The mistaken belief that the day of the Lord has already arrived elicits elaborate proofs showing that this day is still future (2:1-12) and assurance that believers already do experience salvation (2:13-17).
3. The worsening situation with the unruly and idle in the congregation calls for disciplinary action (3:6-15).

Why Listen In?

Though the reasons may be self-evident to most readers, the question still merits pondering: Why should we listen in to these letters? Why should these first-century missionary letters to a remote Mediterranean congregation be of interest to us?

The short answer: By God's grace and through the inspiration of God's Spirit, these letters are part of the Christian canon, the Holy Scriptures. Throughout the history of the church, 1 and 2 Thessalonians, along with other letters, the Gospels and Acts, and the book of Revelation, have guided and nurtured individuals and congregations in their faith, life, and practice as followers of Jesus Christ.

Already during Paul's lifetime, his letters to local congregations came to be recognized as relevant to the wider church. The first letter to the congregation in Thessalonica includes instructions regarding the public reading of this letter to the whole community of faith (1 Thess. 5:27). In the letter to the church in Colossae, Paul becomes quite specific:

> And when this letter has been read among you, have it read also in the church of the Laodiceans; and see that you read also the letter from Laodicea. (Col. 4:16)

Eventually Paul's letters were gathered together into a corpus of epistles for widespread use in the church. This collection of letters, along with the Gospels and Acts, the general epistles and Hebrews, and the book of Revelation, came to constitute the NT. Along with the OT, these writings make up the church's Scriptures.

Throughout this commentary, this canonical aspect of the interpretation of 1 and 2 Thessalonians will be kept in mind. Under "Text in Biblical Context," we seek to highlight the connections between the particular passages in 1 and 2 Thessalonians and the rest of Scripture. Under "Text in the Life of the Church," we note how some of these themes have echoed throughout the history of the church, particularly within the believers church family, and we attempt to make some application to the present life of the church.

We listen in to these letters addressed to the church at Thessalonica because we want to hear the same God speak to us today.

1 Thessalonians

The Salutation

PREVIEW

Gathered for a public reading of the letter from Paul and his co-workers, the believers in Thessalonica immediately hear the reassuring themes of *grace and peace*. They will hear the same themes when the letter ends.

First Thessalonians begins like other letters of its time, with a salutation (1:1) followed by a thanksgiving section (1:2-10). The salutation identifies the senders, names the addressee, and extends a greeting. By means of the greeting, Paul and his co-workers express a prayer whose themes resurface at the end of the letter. The greeting, *Grace to you and peace*, echoes in the twofold concluding benediction: *May the God of peace himself sanctify you to be whole* (5:23, author's translation; see note on copyright page), and *The grace of our Lord Jesus Christ be with you* (5:28). Prayers for *grace* and *peace* form a bracket around the whole letter!

EXPLANATORY NOTES

Paul led the initial mission in Thessalonica, and he takes the initiative in their ongoing pastoral intervention by writing this letter. In the salutation, he names as co-senders his co-workers, Silvanus (Silas) and Timothy, who have been involved with Paul during the evangelistic visit and/or the follow-up visit. The salutation also identifies the addressee and conveys a greeting:

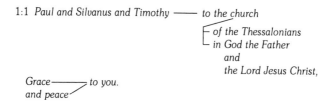

1:1 *Paul and Silvanus and Timothy* ——— *to the church*
  of the Thessalonians
  in God the Father
  and
  the Lord Jesus Christ,

Grace ——— *to you.*
and peace

This letter is addressed *to the church of the Thessalonians.* As capital of the Roman province of Macedonia, Thessalonica had become a prominent political, cultural, and commercial center. When choosing Thessalonica as a setting for evangelism and church planting, Paul followed his customary urban strategy. Roman roads and communication links served the missionaries well in moving from one urban center to the next.

Some attention deserves to be given to the word *church* (*ekklēsia*). Why *ekklēsia?* Originally this term simply connotes an assembly or gathering, as, for example, in Acts 19:32, 39, 41. In the Septuagint (LXX, the OT in Greek), it usually translates the Hebrew word *qahal,* meaning *assembly.* Yet this secular term becomes the distinctive title for the Christian community, employed in the NT for both the local congregation (so here; also in 1 Cor. 1:2; Rom. 16:1) and the universal church (1 Cor. 10:32; 12:28; Col. 1:18, 24).

Perhaps in part because this word normally points to any assembly or gathering, Paul appends a qualifying phrase: *in God the Father and the Lord Jesus Christ. Already in the Septuagint, assembly* occasionally takes on sacred dimensions, through the added phrase, "assembly of the Lord" (as in Deut. 23:2-3). In the OT, *assembly* also becomes associated with Israel as a people called together by God and therefore assembled as God's people. When addressing the Thessalonians as *the church in God the Father and the Lord Jesus Christ,* Paul is therefore making a radical claim. Jewish believers in Jerusalem and elsewhere in Judea are known as *the churches of God which are in Judea in Christ Jesus* (2:14). Now this community of Gentiles and Jews in Thessalonica is similarly recognized as belonging to God's chosen people.

God the Father and *the Lord Jesus Christ* are here linked with the conjunction *and.* Some understand this as synonymous parallelism, implying that in Paul's mind to be "in God" means also to be "in Jesus Christ." So F. F. Bruce: "God and Christ are entirely one in the salvation of believers and in their maintenance in a spiritual fellowship" (Bruce, 1982:7). Others suggest that the sequence shows that Jesus

Christ is the instrument through whom God creates the church: "To be a member of the Christian community is to participate in the salvation which has been achieved by God through Christ" (Best: 62). In the mystery of God's working, both affirmations are true!

The greeting, *Grace to you and peace,* may be an adaptation of the traditional salutation used in Hellenistic letters, *chairein* (greetings), expanded under the influence of the normal Jewish greeting, *shalom, peace.* This brief greeting forms the central wish which recurs in expanded form in Paul's later letters and becomes the model for the salutations in other NT epistles.

Did Paul create this greeting, which so strikingly blends both Greek and Jewish elements? Both *grace* and *peace* play central roles in Paul's theology. A greeting of this nature may have emerged quite spontaneously within the life and worship of a bicultural Christian community such as Antioch of Syria, which included both Messianic Jews and Gentile Christians (Acts 11:19-25). However, there are also noteworthy precedents in the OT and in other Jewish literature for combining the notions of *peace* and *grace* or mercy (Mauser: 106-109). Jewish blessings, such as the priestly benediction of Numbers 6:24-26, illustrate this rich theological heritage ("Peace and Grace" in TBC for 2 Thess. 3:16-18).

1 Thessalonians 1:2-10

Work of Faith: You Turned Toward God

PREVIEW

The letter to the church at Thessalonica opens with a long-distance pastoral embrace! Separated from the Thessalonians by circumstances beyond their control, Paul, Silvanus, and Timothy use a letter to express gratitude toward God and communicate their deep affection toward these new believers.

The thanksgiving section (1:2-10) briefly traces the story of the conversion of the Thessalonians and their emergence as a community characterized by *faith, love,* and *hope*. Rhetorically, this section functions as the beginning of a narration detailing the grounds for thanksgiving. The behavior of the persons being addressed is lifted up for commendation.

Beginning with the fact that God loves and chooses, Paul refers to the witness through both the inspired words and deeds of him and his co-workers in Thessalonica. The thanksgiving section concludes with the grateful acknowledgment that the Thessalonian group also has became a model for their own immediate and more distant neighbors. While reporting the testimony of others regarding the Thessalonians' response to the gospel, Paul summarizes what they as missionaries have preached during their initial visit. Their preaching has invited the people of Thessalonica to turn *away from idols* and *toward God*, to *serve the living and true God*, and to *await his Son from heaven*.

A characteristic feature of the thanksgiving section is that it sounds themes later developed in the letter. Especially important is the triad of qualities and commitments which Paul and his companions list as reasons for their thanksgiving: *your work of faith and labor of love and steadfastness of hope* (1:3). *Faith, love,* and *hope* appear together prominently elsewhere in Paul's letters, notably in 1 Corinthians 13:13, though in a different order. In 1 Thessalonians this is also the case, most explicitly in 3:10-13 and 5:8.

The three themes of *faith, love,* and *hope* appear to signal the structure of the letter as a whole. The salutation (1:1) and the letter closing (5:23-28) provide the characteristic epistolary framework. The remainder of the letter can be viewed as follows:

Work of faith	1:2-10
Labor of love	2:1—3:13
Steadfastness of hope	4:1—5:11

The last section (5:12-28) presents summary admonitions concerning life and leadership in the community in which *faith, love,* and *hope* need to become even more evident.

OUTLINE

Thanksgiving for Faith, Love, and Hope, 1:2-3
God Has Chosen You! 1:4
How the Gospel Came, 1:5
Imitators of Us and the Lord, 1:6-8
Turned Toward God to Serve and Await, 1:9-10

EXPLANATORY NOTES

The body of Paul's letters generally opens with thanksgiving (2 Thess. 1:3-10; 1 Cor. 1:4-9; 2 Cor. 1:3-7; Phil. 1:3-11; Rom. 1:8-17). In this too, Paul follows the customary epistolary form of his time. One exception is Galatians, where Paul appears to have been too upset to express gratitude. In 1 Thessalonians the theme of thanksgiving begins with 1:2-10 but then resumes in 2:13 and again in 3:9.

The leading assertion, *We give thanks,* sets the tone and establishes the direction for this entire paragraph. Grammatically 1:2-10 can be considered as one rather unwieldy sentence which first states the reasons for thanksgiving (1:2-4) and then narrates the underlying story of the emergence of the Christian community in Thessalonica (1:5-10).

Thanksgiving for Faith, Love, and Hope 1:2-3

We can visualize the message of the first part of this paragraph through a sentence-flow diagram. *[For an explanation of this way of presenting the text, see Grammatical Analysis, p. 350.]*

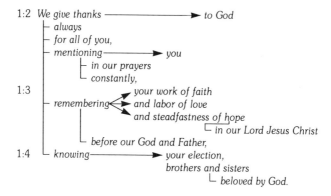

Apparently taking to heart their own later admonition (*in everything give thanks*: 5:18), Paul and his co-workers here openly express their gratitude to God: *We give thanks to God.* Use of the present tense underscores the active character of prayerful thanksgiving, both ongoing, *always*, and all-encompassing, *for all of you.* Following their premature exit from Thessalonica, Paul and his companions find that these new believers are never far from their thoughts and their prayers.

As the sentence diagram above illustrates, the leading verb *we give thanks* is modified by three participial phrases: *mentioning, remembering,* and *knowing.* Grammatically it is not clear whether the adverb *constantly* modifies *mentioning* (RSV) or *remembering* (NRSV). Either way, this sentence vividly demonstrates the prayerful attitude of the missionaries in their continuing relationship with the church which they had founded.

What do the missionaries remember when they mention this Christian community in their prayers? Three things: *your work of faith, labor of love,* and *steadfastness of hope.* As noted above, the themes of *faith, love,* and *hope* form a familiar trio in Paul's letters. These three themes can also be recognized as having provided the broad structure for this letter. In view of the fact that Paul and other NT writers have so much to say about *faith*, *love*, and *hope*, one gains a clear impression of the theological weight of this threefold statement ("Faith, Love, and Hope" in TBC below).

One interpretive matter, which has evoked debate, arises from the three prepositional phrases: *of faith*, *of love*, *of hope*. Some commentators find the notion of *work of faith* to be opposed to Paul's clear insistence elsewhere that salvation comes by grace and is received by faith rather than by works or the law (Rom. 3:21-26; Eph. 2:8-9). These interpreters suggest that Paul here means *work* (which consists) *of faith* (and similarly also for *love* and *hope*). Others point out that for Paul *faith* and works are not in opposition. Even in Galatians, where some texts (such as 2:16) articulate the primacy of faith over works, Paul also stresses that faith results in works (5:6). According to these interpreters, therefore, Paul here prayerfully remembers the Thessalonians' *work of* (which proceeds from) *faith*, *labor of* (which comes out of) *love, and steadfastness of* (which derives from) *hope*.

This latter interpretation rings true to the way in which the entire letter repeatedly invites the Thessalonians to experience a dynamic *faith*, which expresses itself in *love* and *hope* (especially 1 Thess. 5:8). Clearly the evangelists' gratitude results from an awareness of the way in which the Thessalonians have already expressed their newly discovered *faith*. What Paul and his companions recall is an active *faith*, which has already been tested by affliction (cf. 1:6). Even though their *faith* has deficiencies needing to be remedied (as noted in 3:10), the Thessalonian believers are remembered for their *faith*, *love*, and *hope*. This triad therefore identifies the fruit-bearing nature of *faith*, *love*, and *hope*. Beginning a life of *faith* requires more than an act of passive acceptance. Life for the believer requires a dynamic faithfulness which expresses itself in acts of *love* and a stance of *hope*. It should be noted that *hope* has the climactic position here, perhaps because this is the evangelists' primary area of concern as they address these new believers.

The fruit-bearing character of *faith*, *love*, and *hope* may also have a more concrete connection with the situation in Thessalonica. Both *work* and *labor* appear elsewhere in the letter, as both verb and noun, notably in the references to the evangelists' model of hard work (1 Thess. 2:9; 3:5; 5:12-13; 2 Thess. 3:8), the general exhortations to follow this example (1 Thess. 4:11; 2 Thess. 1:11; 2:17), and the specific admonitions directed to the *unruly* who were unwilling to work (2 Thess. 3:10-12).

Jewett proposes that the community of faith in Thessalonica has instituted communal sharing of their resources with each other and with the poor in their midst. Love feasts provide the main vehicle for such "love communalism" (Jewett, 1994: ch. 6). In the opening thanksgiving of this first letter, Paul and his missionary partners articulate their gratitude for the Thessalonians' active sharing. Not all is well, however, as 4:11 hints and 2 Thess. 3:6-18 makes clear. The generous spirit of brotherly/sisterly love is not evidenced by everyone in the community. At this point in the first letter, however, the missionaries articulate their thanksgiving for the active *faith, love,* and *hope* already being expressed.

The phrase *in our Lord Jesus Christ* can be construed as defining the object of the believers' hope. More likely it describes the dynamic source and goal of their *faith, love,* and *hope.* Also the phrase *before our God and Father,* which in the original text comes after this reference to Jesus Christ, appears to be linked to the word *remembering.* In prayer before their God and Father, Paul and his co-workers remember the active *faith, love,* and *hope* already evident in this newly formed congregation.

God Has Chosen You! 1:4

The third participle modifying the verb *we give thanks* illustrates a foundational theological conviction:

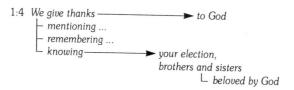

1:4 *We give thanks* ──────────────► to God
     ├ *mentioning ...*
     ├ *remembering ...*
     └ *knowing* ──────────► *your election,*
                             brothers and sisters
                                └ *beloved by God*

Here for the first time in the letter, the readers are addressed with the intimate family term, *adelphoi, brothers and sisters,* which occurs so frequently in all of Paul's letters. Although *adelphoi* literally means *brothers,* the larger context within Paul's letters as a whole clearly shows that this word is to be understood in an inclusive sense. Hence it is highly appropriate with the NRSV to read *brothers and sisters.*

This affectionate note is further deepened by the phrase *beloved by God.*

Paul and his companions here let the Thessalonians know that their thanksgiving basically arises from the fact of their election:

knowing your election (*God . . . has chosen you*, NRSV). The Thessalonians hear a moving reminder concerning God's love and call. God loves and God chooses! Without the prior activity of God before their proclamation of the gospel at Thessalonica, there would be no *faith, love*, or *hope* for which to give thanks. Paul and his co-workers do not thank the Thessalonians; they thank God (see "Election" in TBC below).

How the Gospel Came   1:5

Having declared that they continually thank God, who loves and chooses people through whom *faith* and *love* and *hope* become living realities, the writers tell the story of the way the Thessalonian church came to be:

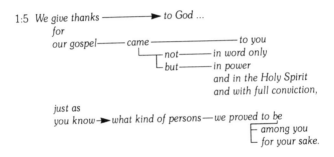

The gospel came to Thessalonica through messengers, who themselves had accepted and incarnated it. Hence they could refer to *our gospel* (similarly also 2 Thess. 2:14; 2 Cor. 4:3; Rom. 2:16; 16:25; 2 Tim. 2:8), not in the sense that they had exclusive rights to the gospel, but to recall their vigorous proclamation of the good news. It is their gospel because they have preached it and appealed to the Thessalonians to receive it. And yet the gospel is conveyed in more than words. The gospel *came*. The gospel is an event, a happening!

Rehearsing this dynamic and transforming event, Paul recalls: *our gospel came to you in power and in the Holy Spirit and with full conviction. Power* (*dunamis*) could refer to miraculous signs and wonders (*the power of signs and wonders*, as in Rom. 15:19) or to the message itself as the transforming power of God (1 Cor. 1:18). This power is intimately linked with the *Holy Spirit*, through which divine power is channeled to believers. *Full conviction* speaks about the inner confidence with which the gospel has been powerfully proclaimed.

But the integrity of the proclaimed word is linked to the authenticity of the lifestyle of the messengers. The conjunction *just as* introduces a reference to the living model which they have left in the memories of these people. The evangelists appeal to the Thessalonians' memory of their initial visit and they dare to remind their readers: *You know what kind of persons we proved to be among you for your sake.* They say even more concerning this matter in 2:1-12. The parallelism here between word and deed is noteworthy. The authenticity of the message (*our gospel*) is corroborated by the behavior of the messengers.

Imitators of Us and the Lord   1:6-8

At this point in the narration, the attention shifts from the evangelists' preaching and lifestyle to the Thessalonians' response. With the Spirit's empowerment, the gospel came to Thessalonica as word proclaimed and dynamic witness lived. Now the coauthors of the epistle report that their hearers have imitated them, and these new converts in turn have become examples to others:

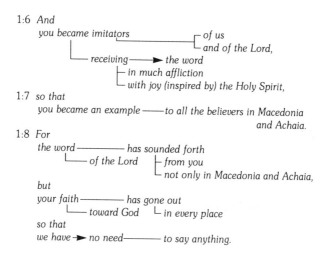

Imitation functions crucially in Paul's letters, as this early occurrence attests. Elsewhere Paul frequently enjoins his converts to become imitators of himself (2 Thess. 3:7, 9; 1 Cor. 11:1; Phil. 4:9).

Here he reports that the Thessalonian converts have become imitators *of us and of the Lord.* To what does he refer? The Thessalonians' imitation of the evangelists and the Lord consists of *receiving the word in much affliction, with joy (inspired by) the Holy Spirit* (1:8). Their readiness to accept the gospel with joy despite bitter opposition has made them imitators of Paul, indeed imitators of Jesus Christ himself.

What was the nature of their *affliction (thlipsis)?* Luke tells the story about the opposition faced by both the missionaries and the believers in Thessalonica (Acts 17:5-9). Information in the Thessalonian letters is quite general. On the basis of Stoic and Cynic parallels, Malherbe argues that this affliction was internal in nature:

> It is reasonable to understand *thlipsis* in 1:6 as the distress and anguish of heart experienced by persons who broke with their past as they received the gospel. (Malherbe, 1987:48)

However, in 2:14, where the imitation motif recurs, the Thessalonians' suffering at the hands of their own compatriots is compared to that experienced by the churches in Judea from their own people. Suffering here appears to be physical and social rather than internal or psychological. Soon after their conversion, the Thessalonian believers apparently faced social or political persecution from among their own people. In this way, therefore, their experience parallels that of Paul and of Jesus Christ himself. Paul also attests that paradoxically the Holy Spirit inspires joy among believers, despite their persecution or other suffering (cf. also Rom. 5:3).

As a consequence of their joyous acceptance of the word of the Lord in the midst of affliction, the Thessalonian church has become *an example (tupos,* literally *a type)* for others. Daniel Patte concludes that Paul uses the term *imitator* in a sense quite different from its modern meaning:

> What makes the Thessalonians "imitators" of others is not that they follow their example (although they also do this) but that the same things *happened* to them. When they received the word, two things happened to them: they were in affliction, that is, other people inflicted suffering upon them; and they were joyful, but this joy was a gift from the Holy Spirit and not their own doing. (Patte: 133-134; emphasis his)

The impact of their acceptance of the gospel under duress, yet with deep joy, is felt both nearby in their home province of Macedonia and further away in Achaia, where this letter is being written. The experience of others also has followed the same pattern: *You be-came an example to all the believers in Macedonia and in Achaia.* Believers throughout these two provinces in Greece gain strength from the active *faith, love,* and *hope* which the Thessalonian believers exemplify under trying circumstances. As the next statement suggests, this witness also influences those who are not yet participants in the newly established churches in these regions.

For the third time within the thanksgiving section, Paul mentions *the word,* in this case specifically *the word of the Lord* (1:8). Even though the gospel came to the Thessalonians *not only in word* (1:5), they *received the word* despite the suffering which came with it (1:6). Receiving the word involves more than internal assent. It requires a commitment through which this message is authentically modeled in their lives: *You became an example* (1:7). Here the letter continues by declaring to the Thessalonians that, as a result of their faithfulness, *the word of the Lord has sounded forth from you* (1:8). Two parallel assertions help Paul to make his point emphatically:

> *the word of the Lord*——*has sounded forth*——*from you*
> *your faith toward God*——*has gone out*

We cannot help but be impressed by the way in which *the word of the Lord* and *your faith toward God* are correlated. Just as in the case of the missionaries, whose spoken word and lived witness has complemented each other (1:5), so also with the Thessalonian believers, both their words and their deeds give powerful testimony to the people around them. *Faith* here is defined in terms of goal and direction, namely, *toward God,* implying an active life commitment rather than mere mental assent ("Faith" in TBC for 2:17—3:10).

With reference to *the word of the Lord,* Paul employs a verb used nowhere else in the NT, *has sounded forth,* perhaps with the connotation "like a trumpet blast." Similarly, their faith toward God *has gone out,* perhaps like waves in a pond emanating in concentric circles from the place where the stone breaks the surface of the water. To underscore what both of these verbs already convey, Paul includes two geographical references, the first one echoing what has already been said in 1:7, *in Macedonia and Achaia,* and the second adding *in every place.* With dramatic flair Paul lets his Thessalonian readers know that he delights in the way their acceptance of the gospel is being reported in their own region and beyond.

What is the upshot of the fact that their faith toward God has gone out in every place? The evangelists do not need to boast about this community of *faith, love,* and *hope: We have no need to speak about it.* News of their faith and faithfulness has traveled!

Turned Toward God to Serve and Await   1:9-10

Paul and his fellow evangelists continue by noting that the way the Thessalonians welcomed them and responded to their message is being widely reported. Circulating in Corinth or other parts of Achaia at the time when he wrote this letter, Paul himself might have been hearing via the grapevine about recent events in Thessalonica. At this point in the letter, Paul takes the occasion to summarize how the Thessalonians have responded to their initial evangelistic mission:

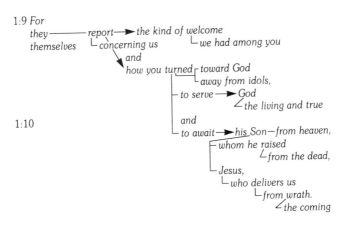

This summary deserves special attention. It recalls for the Thessalonians what they already know, but other readers of this epistle normally do not know—their crucial decision to turn from idols to the God who has raised Jesus from the dead. The distinctive vocabulary, style, and Christology in this summary strongly suggest that Paul here echoes the language and themes of a traditional credal statement (Collins, 1984:253-261).

Scholarly discussion of the tradition history of this passage has resulted in a number of different suggestions (Collins, 1984:20-23). First, Paul might have been a Jewish missionary before he became an apostle of Christ; in its earliest form this statement could have been a summary of a Hellenistic Jewish missionary sermon. Second, this credal formulation reflects early Christian missionary preaching, somewhat reminiscent of Paul's preaching to Gentiles as reported by Luke (to the people of Lystra [Acts 14:15] and Athens [17:22-31]). Third, this passage could reflect a hymn or confession perhaps used for baptismal celebrations.

Some interpreters reject the idea that 1:9-10 came from a pre-Pauline source, suggesting instead that this is Paul's summary of his thought which is then further developed in the rest of 1 Thessalonians. Wanamaker (85) challenges the notion of "pre-Pauline missionary material," since Paul's missionary activity went back to the earliest days of the Christian faith.

Ultimately, of course, whether Paul is quoting a traditional creed or composing his own summation may not make much difference. For Paul and his co-workers, this statement definitely conveys the profound import of what has transpired among the believers in Thessalonica. Each phrase in this summary deserves careful scrutiny.

In rehearsing the Thessalonians' experience, Paul begins with the words, You turned toward God. The underlying verb turn (epistrephein) is used frequently in Acts to describe conversion (as in Acts 3:19; 9:35; 11:21; 14:15). Paul employs this verb in only two other places: in 2 Corinthians 3:16 (a reference to Exod. 34:34) to describe the act of turning to the Lord; and in Galatians 4:9, of turning away from the Lord. In 1:8, Paul describes the Thessalonians' faith as faith toward God, perhaps because of the spatial imagery utilized in this part of the summary. Having turned toward God, the Thessalonians' lives are oriented in active faithfulness toward God.

In turning to God, the Thessalonians turned away from idols. This language displays the typical Jewish and Jewish-Christian perspective on non-Jewish religions as idol-worship. Similar language is employed in Acts 14:15 in the missionaries' appeal to the people of Lystra. This passage clearly implies that the Thessalonian church is predominantly Gentile, although it does not prove (as some commentators allege) that there are no Jews in this early Christian community.

Two infinitives of purpose define the desired outcome of the Thessalonians' decision to turn to God. First, the Thessalonians have repented so that they might serve God: to serve the living and true God. In contrast to dead and false idols, God is described as the living and true (or real) God. Both as Creator and as Redeemer, the living God lives and gives life. Such a God ought to be served! The verb serve connotes not only worship but also a lifestyle characterized by service.

Second, having turned to the living and true God, the Thessalonians also look into the future with expectant hope: *to await his Son from heaven.* The infinitive *to await (anamenein)* occurs nowhere else in Paul's letters nor the rest of the NT. However, the expectation expressed here recurs frequently (1 Cor. 1:7; Phil. 3:20; Rom. 8:19). What shines through here, of course, is the fervent hope cherished by the early Christian community that Jesus Christ would come soon to consummate his reign as triumphant Lord. *[Eschatology, p. 355.]* The place of Jesus' post-resurrection role is *heaven* (literally, *the heavens*), from which he will be revealed (so 2 Thess. 1:7).

The one awaited is God's *Son.* Even though this title for Jesus does not recur in Paul's letters to the Thessalonians, it appears elsewhere in the Pauline epistles, often rather specifically in material which shows Jesus as God's agent for bringing about eschatological salvation (Gal. 4:4-5; Rom. 5:8-11).

At this point the credal summary seems complete. However, Paul adds a relative clause, which further identifies God's Son as the one *whom he raised from the dead.* The grammatical awkwardness of this appended portrait of Jesus testifies to the importance which Paul attaches to what it says. This may be the oldest written testimony to the resurrection of Jesus. Note that God is the subject and Jesus the object of this extraordinary reversal: God raised Jesus from the dead!

Yet another clause provides supplementary data concerning Jesus, whom God raised from the dead (past), and whom the believers await from heaven (future). This Jesus also has a ministry in the present: *Jesus, who delivers us from the coming wrath.* The personal name *Jesus* reminds the readers that *the Lord Jesus Christ* (1:1, 3), *the Lord* (1:6, 8), *his [God's] Son* (1:10) is none other than Jesus of Nazareth, crucified yet raised to life again. This Jesus himself, having been delivered from the clutches of death, now also *delivers us from the coming wrath.*

But what does Paul mean by *deliver* and *wrath*? The root meaning of *deliver (rhuomai)* is to rescue, save, deliver, or preserve. More frequently Paul uses the verb *save (sōzein)* to describe God's saving activity through Jesus (2:16; 2 Thess. 2:10; Rom. 5:9-10; 10:9, 13; and many more). Deliverance and salvation seem to be largely synonymous, and both can refer to either a past experience, a present reality, or a future hope. Here we find the present tense, *delivers.* This could have one of several possible meanings. In the midst of present peril, Jesus rescues the believer. In the face of an imminent future crisis, the assurance of deliverance leads to confidence in the present.

Believers confront both present and future wrath trusting that Jesus the delivered Deliverer will sustain and rescue them ("Jesus Delivers" in TBC below).

Commentators generally argue that here *deliver* communicates the hope of future salvation on the day of judgment, as made explicit in the phrase *from the coming wrath*. End-time deliverance may be the dominant motif here. However, also prominent is the conviction that those who have turned from idols to serve the living God and to await God's Son from heaven experience divine rescue in their present historical circumstances. In his first letter to the Thessalonians, Paul refers to *wrath* on two other occasions, neither of which specifically defines this *wrath* as God's eschatological judgment. The enigmatic assertion in 2:16 refers without further explanation to *wrath which has come upon them [the Judeans] until the end*. In 5:9 Paul contrasts *wrath* and *obtaining salvation* and reassures the *children of the day* (5:5) that God clearly intends for them to experience salvation, both present and future ("Wrath" in TBC in 2:13-16).

THE TEXT IN THE BIBLICAL CONTEXT
Faith, Love, and Hope

The triad *faith, love,* and *hope* (1:3) reappears in several passages in 1 Thessalonians, notably in the wish-prayer of 3:10-13 and in the metaphor of the breastplate and helmet in 5:8, and similarly also in 2 Thessalonians 1:3-4, where *steadfastness and faith* substitute for *hope*. Paul also frequently links these three aspects of the Christian experience in other letters. A number of other NT letters, both Pauline and others, reflect this triad (with some variation in the order: Rom. 5:1-5; Gal. 5:5-6; Eph. 4:2-5; Col. 1:4-5; Heb. 6:10-12; 10:22-24; 1 Pet. 1:3-8, 21-22). A notable example in Paul's letters is 1 Corinthians 13:13: "Now faith, hope and love abide, these three; and the greatest of these is love." Here love has the climactic final position, likely because the discord in the Corinthian congregation concerning spiritual gifts could be resolved only if they learned the true meaning of love (*agapē*). When addressing the Thessalonians, Paul and his fellow evangelists consistently list hope as the last member of the triad, since uncertainty and confusion about eschatology seems to be a problem in this community. In 3:6 Paul reports that Timothy came back from Thessalonica with good news about their *faith and love*, but *hope* is not mentioned.

The triad of *faith, love,* and *hope* witnesses to the dynamic character of Christian experience with its past, present, and future dimensions. Jesus' preaching and teaching about the kingdom of God also conveys an all-embracing reality in which past, present, and future come together. Jesus began his public ministry saying, "The time is fulfilled, and the kingdom of God has come near; repent, and believe in the good news" (Mark 1:15). Through parables and miracles and confrontations with religious leaders, Jesus taught about God's reign and its values, including love as the key to wholesome relationships between people (12:28-30). Jesus also urged his followers to be watchful in anticipation of the coming of the Son of Man in power (13:26). Life within the kingdom of God therefore involves *faith, love,* and *hope.* Rooted in the choice to repent and believe, committed in an ongoing fashion to the way of love, and enlivened by the Christian hope, the disciple of Jesus knows that past, present, and future fit together in a dynamic way from the vantage point of God's reign.

Yet this comprehensive view of a commitment embracing the whole of life with its movement from the past into the future does not begin with Jesus. In the OT, the people of Israel frequently hear the reminder that God had acted decisively to deliver their ancestors from bondage in Egypt. One can illustrate from the book of Deuteronomy. The declaration of God's past saving activity potentially elicits responses of faith and trust:

> "I am the Lord your God, who brought you out of the land of Egypt, out of the house of slavery; you shall have no other gods before me."
> (Deut. 5:6-7)

With this reminder and requirement, the Ten Commandments invite loyalty and obedience. This invitation is often repeated: "The Lord your God you shall fear; him you shall serve" (6:13). To serve God is to "love the Lord your God with all your heart, and with all your soul, and with all your might" (6:5). This stance of trust, faithfulness, and loving service is elicited and sustained by the promise and threat of God's present and future covenant faithfulness:

> Know therefore that the Lord your God is God, the faithful God who maintains covenant loyalty with those who love him and keep his commandments, to a thousand generations, and who repays in their own person those who reject him. (7:9-10)

In thanking God for the active *faith*, *love*, and *hope* already evidenced by the Thessalonian converts (1 Thess. 1:3), Paul asserts that they belong to the community which confesses that their past, present, and future rest with God. Essentially the same claim comes through in the concluding summary: *You turned to serve and await* . . . (1:9-10).

Election

An atmosphere of family intimacy surrounds Paul's startling claim that the Thessalonian believers have been chosen by God. Literally translated, this assertion, which further defines the grounds for thanksgiving, reads: *knowing, brothers and sisters, your election* (1:4). In 2 Thess. 2:13, also a thanksgiving statement, the same message comes through, even though the word is different: *God chose you as first fruits.* What lies behind this confident declaration that God has chosen these Gentiles and Jews in remote Thessalonica?

The OT repeatedly asserts and variously interprets the election of Israel as a people specially chosen by God. In Deuteronomy, the motif of God's special choice frequently accompanies reminders of God's saving activity, consequent requirements, and assurance of God's covenant faithfulness:

> You are a people holy to the Lord your God; the Lord your God has chosen you out of all the peoples on earth to be his people, his treasured possession. (Deut. 7:6)

God's choice of Israel came to be misunderstood, when the people lost sight of the goal of their election—to participate in God's redemptive mission, which has the whole earth in view.

The global scope of God's intention when choosing Israel shines through clearly in the Exodus version of the giving of the law at Sinai, where Moses receives the divine word for Israel:

> Now therefore, if you obey my voice and keep my covenant, you shall be my treasured possession out of all the peoples. Indeed, the whole earth is mine, but you shall be for me a priestly kingdom and a holy nation. (Exod. 19:5-6)

Election therefore does not give privileged status to one ethnic group but designates a particular people as a channel for service and witness to all the world.

Unfortunately Israel often forgot this fundamental reality. The prophets therefore called the people back to the basic premise behind their election. Addressing Israel as a servant called by God, Isaiah reminds these people of God's declared intent: "You are my servant, Israel, in whom I will be glorified" (Isa. 49:3). The prophet continues, "I will give you as a light to the nations, that my salvation may reach to the end of the earth" (49:6).

In the NT, the apostle Peter addresses "the exiles . . . chosen and destined by God" (1 Pet. 1:1-10) and picks up the election theme by using the language of Exodus 19:5-6: "You are a chosen race, a royal priesthood, a holy nation, God's own people" (1 Pet. 2:9). Peter hastens to clarify the purpose behind this divine choice. God chooses the church as a channel for proclaiming God's mighty acts (2:9b).

The theological problems often raised in attempts to think systematically about election do not appear to have bothered the biblical writers. Is human freedom violated by God's choice? Are the nonelect predestined to be condemned? These questions and others reflect an abstract and highly individualized notion of election which is foreign to the dominant biblical understanding. The people of God are called to share the good news of salvation by word and deed among all peoples of the earth! The fact that the recent converts in Thessalonica quite spontaneously and effectively have become channels for sounding forth the word of the Lord in Macedonia and Achaia and beyond (1:8) provides vivid proof that they have indeed become members of God's chosen people!

Jesus Delivers

According to the confession of the early church, as cited here by Paul, Jesus has an ongoing ministry as one who *delivers* (1:10). The same credal statement also asserts that Jesus had himself been rescued: *whom (God) raised from the dead.* Even though the *wrath* from which Jesus *delivers* is still said to be future, the term *delivers* here appears in Greek as a present-tense participle. How is this divine deliverance to be understood? as present? or as future?

If one examines Paul's other writings, one realizes that he testifies to deliverance both as an experience within history as well as something still anticipated at the consummation of history. A search of the other occurrences of *deliver* (*rhuomai*) in other Pauline letters points that out. In 2 Thessalonians 3:2 Paul invites prayer in behalf of himself and his mission partners, *that we may be delivered from perverse and evil persons* (cf. also Rom. 15:31; 2 Cor. 1:10; 2 Tim. 3:11; 4:17-

18). When facing historical perils or the opposition of enemies, Paul looks for deliverance to the same God who has raised Jesus from the grips of death.

Yet this deliverance also has the more distant future in view. One gains the impression, for example, that, in his outburst in Romans 7:24, Paul has ultimate deliverance in mind: "Who will rescue me from this body of death?" He proceeds immediately to answer his own question: "Thanks be to God through Jesus Christ our Lord!" Similarly in Colossians 1:13, the reader catches a glimpse of the believer's eschatological transfer from one realm, "the power of darkness," to another, "the kingdom of [God's] beloved Son." In both Romans and Colossians, one immediately senses, however, that, while full deliverance awaits the future climactic consummation of God's redemptive work, the believer can know and experience this divine rescue already within circumstances in the present.

Jesus therefore is presented as the delivered Deliverer. This could mean that in the midst of present peril, Jesus rescues the believer. Or it could imply that in the face of a future crisis, the assurance of deliverance leads to a believer's confidence in the present. Likely both are included. Believers confront both present and future *wrath*, trusting that Jesus the delivered Deliverer will sustain and rescue them.

THE TEXT IN THE LIFE OF THE CHURCH
How Christian Communities Emerge

The *Martyrs Mirror* (365-367) has preserved memories of some contacts between sixteenth-century Anabaptists and Christians in Thessalonica. A hymn in the *Ausbund*, still used by the Amish, has been inspired by these accounts. The story has a seventeenth-century Dutch source. According to this information, in the 1530s the Turks captured some Moravian Anabaptists (Hutterites) and took them as prisoners from Moravia to Thessalonica, where they became acquainted with some local Christians. To their mutual joy these Anabaptist prisoners and the Thessalonian Christians discovered a remarkable kinship of spirit. This led to a delegation from Thessalonica going to Moravia for a visit with the Anabaptists there. Recognizing each other as brothers and sisters in Christ, they joyfully celebrated the Lord's Supper together. The Thessalonians declared the Anabaptists to be "the true church of God." Furthermore, they reported that "the church of God at Thessalonica had remained unchanged in faith from the time of the apostles."

According to Friedmann, the details in this narrative cannot be verified historically (ME, 4:708-709). We are left to wonder about the eventual fate of the original Christian community in ancient Thessalonica. The possibility that a sectarian group in that city might have connected with Moravian Anabaptists in the midsixteenth century sounds intriguing. My visit to modern Thessaloniki in 1986 proved disappointing because of the sparse archaeological remains and the apparent lack of vitality, at least in churches the tourist brochures identified as having historical significance.

What are some connections between the life of the church today and the opening of the first letter to the Thessalonians? The recital of events in Thessalonica which evoked Paul's gratitude creates resonance with anyone involved in the ministries of evangelism and church planting. What this text provides is not a strategy but rather a theological framework for understanding the key stages which lead to the conversion of a people and the formation of a community of committed disciples. Some reflection on these stages follows. Illustrations come from the writings of Peter Riedemann, a sixteenth-century Moravian Anabaptist, who may or may not have met the alleged delegation from Thessalonica.

First, God loves and God chooses! In fact, God's love precedes all human response. Those not yet within the community of faith are nonetheless also people whom God loves. They need to hear the story of God's love, especially as revealed in Jesus Christ, and be invited to appropriate God's love for themselves. Quarrels with Calvinism or other theological traditions which espouse predestination should not blind heirs of the Anabaptists to biblical understandings of election. As Riedemann says:

> We confess also that God has, through Christ, chosen, accepted, and sought a people for himself, not having spot, blemish, wrinkle, or any such thing, but pure and holy, as he, himself, is holy. (Rideman: 38)

Second, the church has been called to proclaim and live out God's message of love. Unless congregations share this message in words reinforced by their actions, the good news remains hidden, like a treasured heirloom which is hoarded rather than shared. The dynamic witness by living word and loving deed invites repentance and personal acceptance of the good news. Turning toward God requires a corresponding movement away from cherished idols. The genuineness of that step of faith expresses itself in a deep joy which transcends outer circumstances. Riedemann articulates some of this:

According to the words of Paul, this faith comes from a diligent hearing of the preaching of the word of God, which is proclaimed by the mouth of God by means of those whom he sends. Here, however, we speak not of the literal, but of the living word that pierces soul and spirit, which God has given and put in the mouth of his messengers. The same word makes wise unto salvation, that is, it teaches to know God; and from the knowledge of God faith springs up, grows and increases, and with faith knowledge. (47-48)

Finally, this personal step of receiving the gospel involves more than just the individual choice to accept Jesus. Personal decisions to affirm the good news will lead to the formation and growth of communities of believers characterized by *faith, love,* and *hope.* As the experience of the church in Thessalonica demonstrates, groups of believers sometimes face persecution. This calls for both conversion and a genuine transformation of life, even when the surrounding society rejects Christian values. After reading the above quotations from Riedemann, Ashish Chrispal, former dean of Union Biblical Seminary, Pune, India, raised a concern in one of our conversations. Ashish lamented that present-day preaching often "proclaims the gospel as a medicine for inner turmoil" rather than as the way of life for the faith community as it follows Jesus and is empowered by the Spirit. The ancient church in Thessalonica, the Anabaptists of the sixteenth century, and this brother from India all speak to us about the need for faithful discipleship lived out in the world through Spirit-empowered communities of believers.

South African missiologist David Bosch eloquently describes the Christian community living within the world:

We live within the creative tension between the already and the not yet, forever moving closer to the orbit of the former. We Christians are an anachronism in the world: not anymore what we used to be, but not yet what we are destined to be. We are too early for heaven, yet too late for the world. We live on the borderline between the already and the not yet. We are a fragment of the world to come, God's colony in a human world, his experimental garden on earth. We are like crocuses in the snow, a sign of the world to come and at the same time a guarantee of its coming. (Bosch: 85)

Catching this beautiful vision of an experimental garden, of crocuses in the snow, present-day missioners can join Paul and his companions in proclaiming and living out the gospel of Jesus Christ in today's world. Such ministries will bear fruit in the emergence of Christian communities whose identifying marks are *faith, love,* and *hope.*

1 Thessalonians 2:1—3:13

Labor of Love: The Story of Pastors and People

OVERVIEW

A letter sometimes rehearses the history of the relationship between the writer and the reader. The first letter to the Christian community at Thessalonica includes such a review of past associations and friendships between the missionaries and these people.

Paul and his companions vigorously appeal to what they insist their readers already know. This signals the transition from the thanksgiving section (1:2-10) to the main body of the letter: *You yourselves know, brothers and sisters, that our coming to you was not in vain* (2:1). In letter structure, this constitutes the beginning of the letter body, which extends through 3:13. With reference to rhetorical conventions, 2:1—3:13 resembles the narration in a persuasive speech, where a story is retold not primarily to inform the audience but to cultivate or renew a friendship and to influence the hearers to accept the speaker's point of view. [*Rhetorical Analysis, p. 352.*]

Whose story is it? Basically, the story line features the missionary pastors, Paul, Silvanus, and Timothy, and their strategies during their initial evangelistic ministries in Thessalonica (2:1-12). Yet the story focuses centrally also on the Thessalonian believers, whose conversion introduces them to suffering (2:13-16). But Paul also eagerly brings the readers up to date concerning his desire to pay a return visit (2:17-20), his decision to send Timothy instead (3:1-5), and then the welcome report that Timothy eventually brings back (3:6-10).

A pastoral prayer (3:11-13) draws this narration to a close and provides a fitting transition into the exhortation section of the letter (4:1—5:22).

OUTLINE

2:1-12	Gentle Nurse and Encouraging Father
2:13-16	Imitators in Suffering
2:17—3:10	Orphaned Yet Reassured
3:11-13	Pastoral Prayer

1 Thessalonians 2:1-12

Gentle Nurse and Encouraging Father

PREVIEW

Already in the thanksgiving section, Paul asks the Thessalonians to call to memory how the gospel came to their community (1:5). In fact, the expression, *You know*, launches the telling of that exciting story of *faith, love,* and *hope*, a story which provides grounds for the thanksgiving with which the letter opens.

In 2:1 this story continues, but in a different mood. Even though in 1:5 Paul already comments about the dynamic power of the message and their integrity as messengers, he now transposes this theme to another key. In the review of their missionary activities in 2:1-12, the authors of this letter make some positive statements concerning their past ministry. However, they also issue a series of disclaimers, often with the formula *not . . . but . . .* (2:1-2, 3-4, 5-7). Furthermore, Paul frequently appeals to the Thessalonians' awareness of what has happened during their initial visit. Following the emphatic opening assertion, *You yourselves know* (2:1), the phrase *as you know* (2:2, 5, 11), supplemented by *you remember* (2:9) and *you are witnesses* (2:10), functions as a refrain throughout this recital. On two occasions God is even called in as a supplementary witness: *God is our witness* (2:5, 10). Clearly the tone has changed from thanksgiving to a spirited retrospective look at what has transpired in Thessalonica.

A further link between 2:1 and what precedes comes in the word visit (RSV) or *coming* (NRSV). In 1:9 the reference is to *what kind of welcome we had among you.* The same Greek word *eisodos* lies behind both *welcome* and *visit/coming.* The character of that visit and the nature of that welcome are described in more detail here in 2:1-12.

The recital opens with a glance backward at the rough treatment which the evangelists endured in Philippi before coming to engage in the same type of ministry in Thessalonica (2:2). What follows are several rounds of denials and assertions: first, regarding their motivation for preaching the gospel in Thessalonica (2:3-4); and second, concerning their behavior and strategy during that time (2:5-8). One of several kinship metaphors occurs here: Paul as nursing mother (2:7).

The story continues with the reminder that Paul supported himself while preaching the gospel in Thessalonica (2:9). Another reference to the model behavior of the evangelists introduces a second kinship metaphor, in which Paul's role is likened to that of an encouraging father (2:10-12). These intensely personal family images (mother and father) suggest that Paul here speaks primarily for himself, though he continues to represent his partners as well.

In concluding this review of their evangelistic mission in Thessalonica, Paul provides a glimpse into what appears to be at the heart of his concern—his longing that these people might *walk worthy of God* (2:12). This ethical agenda will be elaborated later in the letter, especially in 4:1—5:22.

OUTLINE

From Philippi to Thessalonica, 2:1-2
Motivations for Preaching the Gospel, 2:3-4
Behavior and Strategy: Like a Nursing Mother, 2:5-8
Strategy and Goals: Like an Encouraging Father, 2:9-12

EXPLANATORY NOTES

From Philippi to Thessalonica 2:1-2

Two signals reveal the importance which the writers ascribe to the material now being introduced. First, they issue an emphatic appeal for the Thessalonians to retain awareness of what happened during their initial visit: *For you yourselves know.* As noted above, variations of this opening declaration echo like a refrain throughout this section. The second signal is the personal address, *brothers and sisters (adelphoi),* which appears frequently in Paul's letters to mark transitions and to underscore the point being made. In 1:4 this affectionate term, accented further with the phrase *beloved by God*, accompanies the solemn declaration concerning God's choice of the Thessalonian believers. In the present passage the intimate address, *brothers and sisters*, adds to the persuasive impact of the plea for a sympathetic hearing of the story of what had transpired during the time Paul and his co-workers spent in Thessalonica:

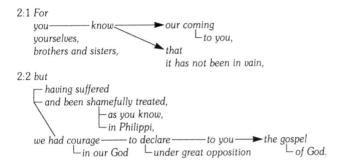

The opening plea recalls that initial visit by the missionaries. In regard to *our coming to you*, Paul asks for the recognition that *it has not been in vain*. As already indicated, one of the links between 2:1-12 and what precedes is provided by the word *eisodos*. In 1:9 Paul mentions that the *welcome* which the Thessalonians showed the evangelists is being widely reported. Here in 2:1 Paul begins to review the story of their *coming* (or *visit*, RSV) to Thessalonica. Both the reception which the Thessalonians gave the evangelists and the evangelistic visit as a whole appear to be in view.

That visit *has not been in vain*, Paul insists, likely meaning that their mission was fruitful and effective. Later in the letter, Paul also expresses the hope that this evangelistic labor might not turn out to have been in vain (3:5). The Greek *gegonen*, a verb in the perfect tense, implies not only that their ministry has been fruitful then but that the results still remain. A similar confidence is expressed eloquently throughout the opening thanksgiving.

Paul continues by reminding the Thessalonians that before they came to Thessalonica, he and his companions were persecuted and humiliated at Philippi (2:2). Details are not provided. Presumably the original readers already know about the abuse which these missionaries suffered during their earlier ministry in that neighboring Macedonian city. According to Luke's rendition in Acts 16:19-40, Paul and Silas experience both physical suffering and moral outrage, especially during the public flogging which they as Roman citizens received without the normal due process. Such harsh and illegal treatment must be in their minds when the writers of this letter mention *having suffered and been shamefully treated in Philippi.*

Despite this rough and unfair treatment, Paul and his co-workers proceeded to Thessalonica: *We had courage in our God to declare to you the gospel of God.* The verb here translated *we had courage* has a rich background among Cynic philosophers of that day; it conveys the notion of speaking freely and by extension also speaking boldly, even when ridiculed or persecuted (Malherbe, 1989:35-48). This same word appears frequently in the NT, especially in Acts, to describe the boldness of Paul and others when they proclaim the gospel. For example, following his experience on the Damascus road, Saul was "speaking boldly in the name of the Lord" (Acts 9:28). Such courage is not a human character trait. As Paul readily testifies, this boldness springs from beyond the missionaries themselves: *We had courage in our God.* Paul and his colleagues also recognize that, even though the message which they preached could be called *our gospel* (1:5), fundamentally it needs to be acknowledged as *the gospel of God.*

The proclamation of the gospel of God in Thessalonica came in the face of *great opposition.* What was the nature of this opposition (*agōn*)? *Agōn* is a motif borrowed from the world of athletic contests. It takes on metaphorical meaning to describe deep struggles in pursuing a goal or in facing external conflict or inner personal distress. Several suggestions have been put forward in attempting to understand this particular struggle. Some take their cue from the account in Acts 17:5-9 (similarly Phil. 1:30), which reports the public agitation stirred up against the missionaries (Bruce, 1982:25). Others see this as a reference primarily to the inward anxiety which Paul and his companions felt because of the way they had been treated in Philippi (Malherbe, 1987:48). Likely external dangers and internal anxiety both played a part in their agony.

Motivations for Preaching the Gospel   2:3-4

Paul proceeds with a series of disclaimers and then an affirmation concerning the nature of their proclamation:

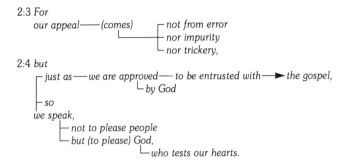

2:3 *For*
   our appeal —— *(comes)*   ┌ *not from error*
                               ├ *nor impurity*
                               └ *nor trickery,*

2:4 *but*
   ┌ *just as* —— *we are approved* —— *to be entrusted with* ——▶ *the gospel,*
   │   └ *by God*
   ├ *so*
   we speak,
        ├ *not to please people*
        └ *but (to please) God,*
                      └ *who tests our hearts.*

The term *appeal* (*paraklēsis*) communicates the fact that their preaching was not just a lecture about Jesus but an invitation person-ally to accept the gospel of Jesus Christ, an exhortation to believe in Jesus and live worthily (cf. 2:12-13). But how was this *appeal* made? A few disclaimers define how this invitation was extended: *not from deceit* (RSV: *error*), as those who either willfully wander off the path of truth or innocently become deceived or deluded in their thinking; nor with *impure motives* (RSV: *uncleanness*), succumbing to moral failure either generally or specifically in sexual relationships (cf. 4:7, where this same word surfaces in a discussion of sexual morality); nor with *trickery* (RSV: *guile*), the use of deceptive or dishonest or cun-ning tricks to lure people into believing the message or joining the movement.

A positive declaration follows (2:4). Instead of refuting charges, however, Paul refers to his qualifications as one tested and approved by God. Without overtly saying so, Paul here lays claim to an apostol-ic calling for himself and likely also for his two colleagues (cf. 2:6). Elsewhere in his writings, Paul vigorously asserts his apostolic cre-dentials (Gal. 1) and defends his authority as an apostle (2 Cor. 10-13). In the letters to the Thessalonian believers, however, the pre-script (1:1) does not identify Paul or the other senders as apostles. Nor do these letters exhibit the passion to establish or defend apos-tolic authority. Instead, Paul gives testimony to his sense of vocation as one *approved by God to be entrusted with the gospel* (2:4). Divine approval for a specific task, therefore, rather than an eagerness to please people, instills the primary driving motivation for preaching the gospel: *we speak not to please people but to please God who tests our hearts* (2:4). Human verdicts concerning inner motivation for engaging in ministry ultimately need to yield to God's judgment.

The verbs *approved* and *tests* in this verse derive from the same underlying Greek word *dokimazō*. *Approved* (perfect tense) conveys the inner conviction that God has examined Paul and granted him a positive approval rating and the divine mandate to preach the gospel. *Tests* (present tense) communicates the fact that divine scrutiny continues even after approval has been granted. In the cases of Silvanus and Timothy, not much can be known about their inner reflections concerning their calling. However, Paul's self-reflections are generously known to us. Paul knows the grace of God, who chose him despite his past activity as a persecutor of the Christian community (Gal. 1:22-24; 1 Cor. 15:8-10). Knowing himself to be approved (2 Cor. 13:5-10), Paul nevertheless still serves in the hope that he will ultimately pass the test (1 Cor. 9:24-27). Such assurance of divine calling and approval leads to a humble assertion of leadership authority rather than to an arrogant exercise of power.

Paul knows himself to be *entrusted with the gospel*. When he writes to the Galatians, Paul provides the story behind this claim, first giving a robust denial: "The gospel which I preach is not a human gospel, I'll have you know!" (Gal. 1:11, author's paraphrase). This leads to the assertion that this gospel came "through a revelation of Jesus Christ" (1:12). Paul's personal story follows, as he describes this revelation and narrates his call to preach the gospel to the Gentiles (1:13-16). Later in the same letter, Paul notes that he has been "entrusted with the gospel for the uncircumcised" (2:7). Paul views the gospel as a precious trust, not to be treasured selfishly but to be shared generously with others. Paul also knows that the gospel as sacred trust must not be preached in ways that will sully or tarnish it. The actual speaking of the gospel needs to be motivated not by the desire to please people but by an eagerness to please God.

Behavior and Strategy: Like a Nursing Mother   2:5-8

With another connecting *for*, Paul begins to discuss missionary behavior and strategy. Specifically, he outlines ways in which philosophers or other preachers speaking their messages in public settings might be tempted to try to please people (diagram on next page).

Calling once more on the Thessalonians' personal awareness (*as you know*), Paul continues with a description of their behavior as evangelists during their initial visit in Thessalonica (2:5-6). Again there are disclaimers followed by a positive statement. What behavior does Paul repudiate? *We came not with flattering speech*, he says. *Flattering speech* tickles the ears of the hearers, perhaps giving them something that they want to hear, so that the speaker gains an advantage over the audience. Second, summoning God as witness, Paul also denies having come *with a cloak of greed*, namely, using ministry as a cover-up for the real agenda of lining his own pockets. Third, he disavows having come to Thessalonica *seeking honor* (*doxa*). *Doxa* can mean *praise*, or *glory* (RSV), but the better translation here is *fame* or *honor*, since Paul has in mind the human desire for recognition and fame within society. Paul asserts that he and his companions have not come to Thessalonica either to seek fame or to demand recognition or honor, whether from the Thessalonians themselves or from anyone else.

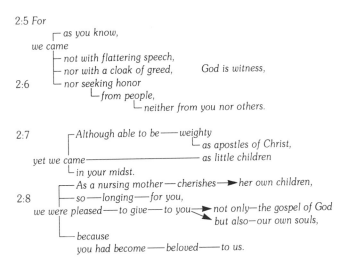

Note the tone in this part of the letter. Here and repeatedly elsewhere throughout this section, Paul invites the Thessalonians to verify what he says by checking their own memories. In addition to employing the recurring phrase *as you know* (2:1-2, 5, 11) Paul even reminds the readers that *God is witness* (2:5, 10).

What moves Paul to write in this way? At first hearing, Paul appears to be defending himself by refuting charges leveled by his opponents. Reading between the lines, one might judge that serious accusations and misunderstandings about Paul's ministry (and that of his co-workers) have surfaced after they left. By a process of "mirror reading," the nature of these accusations can then presumably be reconstructed. According to such a "mirror reading," Paul, following his departure, is being depicted as a deceitful and immoral trickster (2:3) who flatters his audience, lines his pockets, and seeks fame and fortune for himself (2:5-6). That kind of caricature would surely call for response!

But was 1 Thessalonians written in self-defense? In his study of the autobiographical passages in Paul's letters, George Lyons questions the validity of the "mirror reading" approach. He argues for an awareness of Paul's motives at the rhetorical level:

> Paul's autobiographical remarks function not to distinguish him from his converts nor to defend his person or authority but to establish his ethos as an "incarnation" of the gospel of Jesus Christ. He highlights his "autobiography" in the interests of this gospel and his readers. He is concerned that, by imitating him, they too should incarnate the gospel. (226)

Rather than defending himself against opponents, Paul highlights his own motivation and behavior as a model for the believers to follow. By calling on the Thessalonians to remember how he and his companions conducted themselves while they were in their community, Paul implicitly also urges that their conduct conform to this same pattern. In 1:6 the Thessalonians have already been told: *You became imitators of us and of the Lord.* Lyons suggests that the detailed reflections concerning motivations and strategies of the missionaries serve to encourage these new believers in their imitation.

Paul's extended characterization of his ministry in 2:1-12, especially the disclaimers and the affirmations, does differentiate him from other popular preachers of philosophy and religion of his day. A study of Paul and the Cynic philosophers by Malherbe (1989:45-48) demonstrates striking parallels between this description of Paul's ministry and the way in which the orator-philosopher Dio Chrysostom (A.D. 40-c.120) depicts the ideal Cynic. According to Dio, ideal Cynic philosophers speak boldly without resorting to flattery, with purity and without guile, not for the sake of material gain but genuinely, and out of good will toward their audience. In this portrayal of the good Cynic, therefore, Dio employs both disclaimers and positive statements, thereby distinguishing the genuine philosopher from the huckster. *[Philosophies, p. 364.]*

Paul's review of his mission motivation and method is markedly similar in approach. One can therefore conclude that Paul employs the language and rhetoric of his day to depict his own ministry and that of his partners in a way that encourages their spiritual offspring in Thessalonica to follow their example.

We return to a more specific analysis of this text. The sequel to the disavowals of flattery, greed, and desire for honor (2:5-6) comes in two vivid word pictures designed to help the listeners visualize a sharply contrasting model characterized by apostolic gentleness and motherly tenderness (2:7-8).

The first word picture portrays Paul and his co-workers as *apostles of Christ* (2:7). Even though in 2:4 Paul has made an implicit claim to apostolic authority as one tested and approved by God, this is the first and only time that the term *apostle* occurs in the Thessalonian letters. What might the term *apostle* have meant to the authors and the readers of this letter? *Apostle* can have a general meaning: *sent one, messenger, missionary.* However, Paul understands his own role as *apostle* more specifically. He has experienced a revelation of the risen Christ and the commission to preach the gospel to the Gentiles (Gal. 1:1-2, 15-17).

In an effort to understand how Paul interprets his apostolicity in this letter to the Thessalonians, a few grammatical and translation challenges need to be addressed. For one thing, English versions differ on the placement of the verse division. Some have 2:7 begin before the clause about apostles (RSV), whereas others, as suggested here, start 2:7 after this clause (NIV, NRSV). More significant are the questions of where the thought in this clause should be connected and what this clause actually says. Our rather wooden translation reads: *although able to be weighty as apostles of Christ.*

The phrase translated *weighty* (*en barei*) has been understood in two main ways: a financial burden, since apostles have the right to be financially supported by their converts (cf. 1 Cor. 9:3-12); or the moral or spiritual authority to demand honor or compliance. Those who argue for the former can point to the fact that in 2:9 Paul mentions that they were self-supporting as missionaries during their stay in Thessalonica (thus NIV: *could have been a burden*). Those interpreting the phrase as a reference to their spiritual authority as apostles often connect it with the previous statement, in which Paul denies demanding honor or recognition. Most translations simply evade the issue (as *weighty* does as well); *demands* (RSV) could be interpreted either way. The best case can be made for this latter more general meaning, which then can also include within it the apostolic right to expect material support.

However, where does this thought connect? Likely it links most closely not with what precedes but with what follows: *Although able to be weighty as apostles of Christ yet we came as little children in your midst* (2:7).

Note the rendering *children* instead of *gentle*, which is in almost all English versions, although RSV and NRSV have *babes* and *infants* respectively as footnoted minority readings. This uncertainty arises from a textual problem. The earliest ancient manuscripts of 1 Thessalonians read *little children* (*nēpioi*); some of these oldest manuscripts were "corrected" by scribes to read *gentle* (*ēpioi*). Since the previous word in the sentence ends in an *n*, one can guess either that the word was lengthened to *nēpioi* (*little children*) or that it was shortened to *ēpioi* (*gentle*) by association with the preceding word (Metzger, 1971:629-630). Most translators and commentators opt for the less-supported reading (*gentle*), since the thought flows more naturally with *gentle* than with *little children*. After all, how can Paul compare himself to a little child and then immediately in the same verse refer to himself as a mother?

However, if the sentence structure unfolds as proposed here, this jarring transition of metaphors becomes understandable. Paul is quite capable of inverting his imagery even midsentence. For example, in Galatians 4:19, a pregnant Paul is in labor, giving birth again to Galatian believers; and the Galatians also, Paul hopes, have become pregnant, with Christ being formed again within them! *[Textual Analysis, p. 346.]*

What kind of apostle had Paul been during their initial visit? In this first of several family metaphors, the missionaries portray their activity and attitudes as humble and childlike rather than as domineering or demanding. As it turns out, therefore, the meaning expressed metaphorically by *nēpioi* is very close to *ēpioi*. Their posture has been that of gentle and childlike apostles ("Brothers and Sisters, Child, Mother, and Father" in TBC below).

Another family metaphor develops this characterization even further. This next thought then continues to the end of 2:8 with an intimate portrait of motherly tenderness: *As a nursing mother cherishes her own children, so longing for you we were pleased to give to you not only the gospel of God but also our own souls because you had become beloved to us.* Their pastoral care as apostles compares to the way a mother nurses her own children. With feelings of deep affection, like those of a mother toward her infant, they were ready to share not only the gospel but also themselves. *Soul* (*psuchē*) refers to the innermost person, the self. In other words, the message of the gospel of God came most powerfully through the motherly affection of the messengers, who did not hesitate to give deeply of themselves.

The root motivation for such self-giving is love (*agapē*). Not much is said in the Thessalonian correspondence about God's *agapē* love as expressed supremely in Jesus' self-giving death on the cross. However, it is significant that Paul verbalizes the depth of his affection by calling the Thessalonians *beloved* (*agapētoi*), using that special word for sacrificial self-giving love.

Strategy and Goals: Like an Encouraging Father   2:9-12

Yet another *for* introduces one more aspect of the missionaries' model of behavior while in Thessalonica. Their exemplary behavior is both described further and also illustrated with another family metaphor—that of an encouraging father. A futuristic glimpse into the ultimate goal of their ministry wraps up this section of the letter:

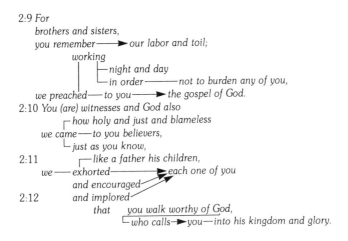

Once more the believers hear the endearing address, *brothers and sisters* (2:9). There is also another rapport-building appeal to their common awareness, in this case the memory of how Paul and his companions supported themselves while preaching the gospel in Thessalonica: *You remember our labor and toil.* The words *labor* and *toil* occur together again in 2 Thessalonians 3:8, a passage which appeals to the Thessalonians to imitate the example of the hard-working evangelists rather than join the ranks of the *unruly*. In 2 Corinthians 11:27 the list of hardships which Paul endured during his ministry includes these same two words. Evidently the accent here falls on the harshness and drudgery of the work in which Paul and his companions chose to be engaged as a way of providing for their own needs. In another catalog of his harsh experiences, Paul notes: "We labor, working with our own hands" (1 Cor. 4:12, RSV). Manual labor in that culture was viewed as debasing. By working as an artisan (a tentmaker, according to Acts 18:3), Paul identifies himself with the working class. Artisans typically worked long days, as Paul himself testifies: *We worked night and day. [Social and Economic Context, p. 368.]*

Along with hard physical labor came the ministry of proclamation: *We preached to you the gospel of God* (2:9). By necessity the workshop became a significant context for this evangelistic activity. This also turned out to be a good opportunity for spreading the good news, since some persons, who would normally not gather in a synagogue or a home or other more public settings where the gospel might be preached, did come to the workshop (Hock: 26-49).

Another motive for working for their own support is also stated: *so that we might not burden any of you.* No further elaboration of this motive is offered. Perhaps part of the motivation was to differentiate themselves from popular philosophers or other preachers who fattened their own purses through their persuasive speeches (cf. 2:5). More importantly, however, this purpose statement appears to echo the earlier phrase in 2:7, which contrasts the apostolic right to make demands with their actual gentle and childlike practice. Here in 2:9 one application of this principle appears. The missionaries waived their apostolic right to receive material support, thereby also demonstrating a central dimension of the gospel. Instead of demanding their own rights, they modeled the self-giving love demonstrated in Jesus' ministry through his life and his death ("Ministry and Support" in TBC for 2 Thess. 3:6-15).

A solemn aura surrounds the next affirmation (2:10). Both human and divine witnesses are invoked: *You are witnesses and God also.* At the end of this same verse there is another *just as you know.* These somber reminders that both the Thessalonians and God know the truth bracket another listing of the personal qualities which characterized their behavior toward the new believers: *holy, just, and blameless.* Their demeanor has been *holy,* as God could attest; their relationships *just,* as the Thessalonians themselves have seen; and their conduct *blameless,* so as to provide an example for the believers to imitate.

In support of this rather strong (some might say arrogant) claim concerning his behavior and that of his companions among the Thessalonian believers, Paul employs yet another family metaphor (2:11-12). After underscoring the childlike and maternal qualities of gentleness and nurturing love (2:7), Paul now adds to this portrait by using the image of the father: *like a father with his children* (2:11). The father metaphor occurs frequently elsewhere in Paul's writings (notably 1 Cor. 4:14-16) to depict his relationship with his converts ("Brothers and Sisters, Child, Mother, and Father" in TBC below).

Three action words (all participles acting like verbs) characterize Paul's fatherly ministry among the Thessalonians: *we exhorted, encouraged, and implored each one of you.* As other occurrences in 1 Thessalonians show, to *exhort* (*parakalein*) can include both the dimension of comfort or consolation (3:7; 4:18; 5:11) and of ethical admonition (3:2; 4:1, 10; 5:14). Similarly, the verb *encouraged* (*paramuthoumenoi*) has both connotations, as illustrated in 5:14, where it describes the admonition and comfort needed by *the fainthearted* in Thessalonica. The third word, *implored* (*marturomenoi;* RSV: *charged*), expresses the ethical appeal most insistently, without a corresponding softening. However, the overall picture shows these missionary pastors offering their ethical guidance in a firm yet affectionate fatherly manner.

At this point in the letter, Paul does not yet issue any specific instructions. In 4:1 the exhortation section begins. Here the desired outcome of Paul's fatherly encouragement is articulated in general terms: *that you walk worthy of God, who calls you into his kingdom and glory.* Paul frequently employs *walk* (*peripateō*) in a metaphorical sense, something like the expression "the Christian walk," to refer to the way in which a Christian commitment expresses itself in life: 4:1, 12; 2 Thessalonians 3:6, 11. In this way Paul perpetuates the Hebraic notion of halakah, the legal material which offers guidelines for how the covenant people should *walk*, in other words, how they should live. Paul urges the Thessalonians to live in a manner *worthy of God.*

Instead of distinguishing between specific worthy and unworthy kinds of behavior, Paul reminds the Thessalonians that God *calls you into his kingdom and glory.* The conduct of believers needs to be shaped by the eschatological framework within which they live: within God's *kingdom/reign* (*basileia*) *and glory* (*doxa*). *Reign* better conveys the dynamic character of the biblical concept of God's *basileia; kingdom* tends erroneously to suggest a territorial understanding. Since *basileia* appears in the Thessalonian letters only here and in 2 Thessalonians 1:5, it will be necessary to explore the meaning of this concept from within a broader biblical base ("Kingdom of God" in TBC below). The reference to *glory* (*doxa*) provides additional insight into the futuristic point of view which informs Paul's reflections. Both their ministry as evangelists and the Thessalonians' actual and desired responses can best be viewed from the perspective of God's glory. A doxology brings this narration to a close!

THE TEXT IN THE BIBLICAL CONTEXT
God Is Witness

Psalm 139 gives eloquent testimony to the awareness that God sees and knows all things, including also the personal worlds of each mind and heart. This psalm begins by confessing: "O Lord, you have searched me and known me." It ends with the petition: "Search me, O God, and know my heart; test me and know my thoughts." Embedded within this confession lies a harshly worded appeal for rescue from enemies. Knowing that God knows and searches the inner motives of the heart, the psalmist pleads for deliverance. A similar perception informs both Paul's repeated declaration, *God is witness* (2:5, 10), and his affirmation that *God tests our hearts* (2:11). Paul testifies to his settled sense of having been approved by God. Then he confidently discloses his motives and methods in sharing the gospel of God, knowing that human criticism matters less when God approves.

Similar themes recur frequently in the story of Israel. The selection of the shepherd boy David as king over Israel calls for an explanation of such an unlikely choice: "The Lord looks on the heart" (1 Sam. 16:7). According to the Chronicler, near the end of his reign, David reminded his son Solomon: "The Lord searches every mind, and understands every plan and thought" (1 Chron. 28:9). The sages and prophets also announce that God knows and tests the human heart (as in Ps. 7:9; Prov. 17:3; Jer. 12:3; 17:10).

In Luke's story of the early church, the prayer before the appointment of Matthias and Peter's testimony at the Jerusalem Conference both include the recognition that the Lord knows the human heart (Acts 1:24; 15:8). In Romans 8:27 Paul asserts that God "searches the heart." On several other occasions Paul calls on God as witness (Rom. 1:9; 2 Cor. 1:23; Phil. 1:8), and he even invokes a solemn oath: "Before God, I do not lie" (Gal. 1:20; cf. 2 Cor. 11:31). One wonders whether Paul might be dangerously close to the kind of oath prohibited by Jesus (Matt. 5:33-37; cf. James 5:12).

In light of this larger biblical picture, we suggest two reasons why Paul highlights God's omniscience. In this way Paul expresses his confidence in God's calling, approval, and protection in his own life. But Paul also prepares the Thessalonians for the exhortations later in the letter (4:1—5:22) by reminding them that God knows their hearts.

Brothers and Sisters, Child, Mother, and Father

Fifteen times in this short letter the Thessalonians are directly addressed as *brothers and sisters (adelphoi)*. As noted earlier (at 1:4, where *adelphoi* first occurs), the larger context within Paul's letters clearly shows that *adelphoi* needs to be understood in an inclusive sense, as embracing both *brothers and sisters* (as in NRSV).

However, Paul also utilizes other family images in this letter, especially here in 2:1-12. What light does the rest of the Bible cast on this use of kinship metaphors?

One might begin with the parent-child metaphor. Strikingly, Paul portrays himself as both mother and father to the Thessalonians (2:7, 11). Does this have biblical precedent? The book of Proverbs opens by picturing a parent-child relationship between the wise sage and those being instructed in wisdom:

> Hear, my child, your father's instruction,
> and do not reject your mother's teaching. (Prov. 1:8)

According to this picture, wisdom is transmitted to the children by both father and mother. The image of father appears more frequently in the OT to define various human relationships. For example, Job in his defense says, "I was a father to the needy" (Job 29:16). The biblical maternal metaphors are less common and sometimes overlooked. In the wilderness, when Moses becomes weary of the complaints of the people, he angrily asks God,

> Did I conceive all this people? Did I give birth to them, that you should say to me, 'Carry them in your bosom, as a nurse carries a child,' to the land that you promised on oath to their ancestors? (Num. 11:12)

In his self-portrait, Paul welcomes a role which is like that of a nursing mother tenderly caring for her children (2:7). The father metaphor occurs more often. To the Corinthians Paul writes, "In Christ Jesus I became your father through the gospel" (1 Cor. 4:15). Yet, despite the biological fact that Paul is a male, he also compares his relationship with the people in the churches to that of a mother nursing her child.

If the believers in Thessalonica or Corinth or elsewhere have a common spiritual father/mother, it is natural for them also to recognize each other as brothers and sisters in the faith. Yet the frequent occurrences of *brothers and sisters* in both 1 and 2 Thessalonians underscore another aspect of the relationship between the missionary pastors and their people. Within the family of faith, pastors and people are all brothers and sisters in Christ. This acknowledgment that the evangelists and their spiritual progeny are sisters and brothers in the same family has its roots in their view of God as their common parent.

Though portrayed more often as a father, in Scripture God is also viewed by the use of maternal images. Hosea pictures God as a loving and nurturing parent:

> When Israel was a child, I loved him, and out of Egypt I called my son. . . .
> It was I who taught Ephraim to walk, I took them up in my arms; . . .
> I was to them like those who lift infants to their cheeks. I bent down to
> them and fed them. (Hos. 11:1, 3-4)

Hosea's portrait does not make clear whether God is pictured as father or as mother. However, maternal imagery for God comes through clearly in several passages in Isaiah where the prophet speaks the word of the Lord:

> For a long time I have held my peace, I have kept still and restrained myself; now I will cry out like a woman in labor, I will gasp and pant. (42:14)
> Can a woman forget her nursing child, or show no compassion for the child of her womb? Even these may forget, yet I will not forget you.
> (49:15)
> As a mother comforts her child, so I will comfort you. . . . (66:13)

Whether or not Paul consciously recalls these or other texts depicting a motherly God, it is clear that he wants the Thessalonians to hear the gospel of God not only through his words but also by his relationships with them. Having fathered and mothered them into the faith, Paul and his companions now acknowledge that before God (identified here only as *the Father,* 1:1, 3), they are all sisters and brothers.

But Paul paradoxically also represents himself to the Thessalonians as an infant or little child (2:7). As background for this rather startling word picture, we might recall Jesus' dramatic action after he predicted his suffering and death. Sensing that his disciples in their distress do not understand, Jesus calls a child into their midst and says, "Unless you change and become like children, you will never enter the kingdom of heaven" (Matt. 18:3). True greatness is best illustrated by childlike gentleness and trust. This dramatic action can help us comprehend why Paul would characterize his role as apostle by using the child metaphor. However, we are also reminded of the mystery of the incarnation. The Gospel of John helps us grasp the truth of the incarnation theologically: "The Word became flesh and lived among us" (1:14). The nativity narratives in Matthew and Luke give us a glimpse of the baby Jesus, *"Emmanuel, . . . 'God is with us' "* (Matt. 1:23). Paul's child metaphor therefore suggestively draws the readers into the depth of God's identification with humankind in Jesus Christ, who "emptied himself, taking the form of a slave, being born in human likeness" (Phil. 2:7).

Kingdom of God

A glimpse into the future concludes the retrospective glance back on the initial visit by Paul and his colleagues in Thessalonica: *God calls you into his kingdom and glory* (2:12). Even though the concept of God's kingdom/reign *(basileia)* surfaces in the Thessalonian epistles only here and in 2 Thessalonians 1:5, an understanding of this theme will enhance our interpretation of the major eschatological passages in these letters (especially 1 Thess. 4:13-18; 5:1-11; 2 Thess. 2:1-12).

The expression *kingdom of God* does not occur in the OT. However, the Psalms show that in their worship the people of Israel confessed, "The Lord is king!" (Ps. 93:1; 96:10; 97:1; 99:1). In fact, when the Israelites asked that Samuel anoint a king to reign over them, this request was interpreted as a rejection of God as king (1 Sam. 8:7).

According to Mark 1:14-15, Jesus opens his public ministry by announcing the imminence of the kingdom of God:

> The time is fulfilled, and the kingdom of God has come near;
> repent and believe in the good news.

As this opening declaration suggests, God's reign though still future has entered history in Jesus' ministry. Jesus' parables, his other teachings, and his healing and other miracles provide glimpses and signs of this dynamic reality.

In Jesus' teaching, God's reign has both present and future dimensions. According to Luke 17:20-21, the Pharisees ask Jesus when the kingdom of God would come. In his reply, Jesus first denies that the coming of God's reign can be predicted in terms of observable signs. Then he follows with a word about the kingdom of God as a present reality: "The kingdom of God is among (*entos*) you." The exact meaning of *entos* remains elusive, as the various translations show. Did Jesus mean that the kingdom of God comes in himself (NRSV: "among you")? or that it is spiritually revealed to individual believers (NIV: "within you")? or that God's reign becomes reality within the community of Jesus and his disciples (RSV: "in the midst of you")? Most likely, Jesus himself and the community of his disciples are seen as primary channels for God's dynamic reign in the world. However, regardless of which of these understandings is correct, what Jesus announces here clearly shows that God's reign has already become manifest in the present. Yet when Jesus taught his disciples to pray, he included a clause which definitely views the kingdom as still future: "Your kingdom come" (Matt. 6:10; Luke 11:2). How then are the present and future aspects of God's reign to be correlated?

The diagrams which follow depict three classical ways of interpreting the kingdom of God. These can be labeled as the futurist, realized, and inaugurated views of the kingdom. The visual symbols represent the following:

———	History before/after Jesus' announcement of the kingdom
† †	The earthly ministry of Jesus, climaxed by his death and resurrection
|	The inbreaking of the kingdom of God
X	The present moment
. . . .	Time still to elapse until the consummation of the kingdom
!	The consummation of the kingdom
****	The reign/kingdom of God

1. In the *futurist* view, Jesus announces a future kingdom, sometimes visualized in earthly terms and sometimes anticipated as an otherworldly realm:

Futurist   ——————————† †————X .... \| !**********

2. A *realized* concept of the kingdom interprets Jesus' ministry and the community which emerged from that movement as the beginning of the actual present realization of God's reign on earth:

Realized   ——————————† †\| ****X *********************

3. According to the *inaugurated* view of the kingdom, Jesus ushered in the new reality of God's dynamic reign through his ministry and through the mission of his disciples and the church. The consummation of this reign, however, still lies in the future:

No static diagram can convey the dynamic biblical concept of the kingdom or reign of God. However, the inaugurated view most adequately communicates the fact that paradoxically God's reign is both present and future, both already realized and yet still to be consummated. The community of believers therefore lives within the tension between the "already" and the "not yet" of the reign of God. Hence Paul in 1 Thessalonians 2:12 reminds this community that as their spiritual father, he has exhorted, encouraged, and even implored them to conduct their lives in a manner worthy of God, who is calling them to enter more and more fully into God's reign and glory! *[Eschatology, p. 355.]*

THE TEXT IN THE LIFE OF THE CHURCH
Christian Character and Witness

In Mennonite and Brethren congregational life, the emphases articulated in 1 Thessalonians 2:1-12 have been correlated with passages such as 1 Timothy 3-5 and 1 Corinthians 9 in establishing ethical standards for pastors and other church leaders. Especially pertinent has been the recognition that the conduct of the preacher needs to harmonize with the message preached.

An accent on God's calling in the life of a candidate for ministerial office has frequently also led either to the rejection of an educated or a salaried ministry or at least to careful attempts to guard against clerical professionalism. Among Old German Baptist Brethren, an educated ministry has been viewed as "despising the humble, unassuming lifestyle of primitive Christianity." Accordingly, "ministers are chosen on a basis of faith, moral qualities, spiritual-mindedness, and personal life rather than on education" (BE, 2:844). Similarly, at least among some Mennonites, the education of ministers has been discouraged or prohibited.

Reasons for this suspicion of an educated clergy can easily be identified when reading the writings of early leaders within Radical

Pietism and early Anabaptism. Preachers of the gospel were expected to be people whose lives exemplified and modeled the way of discipleship as taught by Jesus. In humility as servants of the Word,
preachers were to share the gospel of Jesus Christ faithfully. Menno
Simons severely criticized his contemporaries who functioned as
priests and ministers in Lutheran, Reformed, or Catholic churches
because, as he saw it, their lives were not coherent with the gospel.
The following quotation from Menno's voluminous writings on this
subject will be sufficient to illustrate his critique:

> Since then this vocation is the true mission, vocation, and calling taught
> in the Scriptures, as has been observed, we faithfully counsel the reader
> in the pure fear of God to consider what kind of people their preachers
> are; also by whom and in what way and to what end they are called. For it
> is manifest that a portion of them are useless, haughty, immoral men;
> some are avaricious, usurers, liars, deceivers; some are drunkards, gam-
> blers, licentious, open seducers, idolators, etc., concerning whom it is
> written that they shall not inherit the kingdom of God if they do not re-
> pent. (Menno: 162)

A primary concern in the calling of persons to the ministry of the
church has therefore been to discern "what kind of people their
preachers are." Personal, moral, and spiritual qualifications have historically often been rated more highly than intelligence, education, or
eloquence. Unfortunately, the selection processes have been com-
promised. Many churches in the past and even today have discrimi-
nated against women, even though they also have gifts for ministry.
Sometimes these same churches appoint men who, while they demonstrate an ability to succeed in farming or other business, sometimes
do not have the needed spiritual gifts.

As shown by Paul's reflections on how his life and his practice of
ministry connect, the formation of Christian character is a vital aspect
of preparation for ministry. According to Paul's testimony, he and his
partners sought to model a gentle motherly yet firm fatherly style,
steeped in a humble and childlike reception of the gifts of God's
grace. That seems like a wholesome recipe for effective ministry!

What kind of discernment process can lead congregations and
denominations within the believers church to ensure that their pastors and other leaders integrate faithful theology and practice? With
the proviso that ministry is now recognized to be inclusive of women
and men, one can learn from the way the oldest extensive Mennonite
confession of faith (dating from about 1600) outlines the process of
selecting ministers of the Word:

Hence, believers who are in need, in this respect, shall, after having sought the face of God with ardent prayer, turn their eyes to a pious brother, who keeps under his own body, and brings it into subjection, and in whom the fruits of the Holy Spirit are perceived and seen. Having been chosen therefore by the voice of the Church, he shall be examined in the faith by the elder and pastors of the church, whether he, according to the Word of God, agrees with the church in every article, that he may teach others the way of truth, which he himself knows. And having been found to be sound, he may stand forth in the name of the Lord, to proclaim the will of God unto the people. (*Martyrs Mirror:* 395)

Paul makes ardent efforts in 1 Thessalonians 2:1-12 to differentiate himself from philosophical and other preachers whose motivations and practices sprang from error, uncleanness, greed, or desire for fame. This can remind the church and its leaders to exercise great care. Standards of conduct and morality need to be higher among pastors and teachers, as the epistle of James also attests (3:1), since the witness of their lives should echo and underscore the witness of their lips. Especially in North America, believers find themselves in a critical period characterized by the serious breakdown of the family. Our churches need to deal both firmly and redemptively with the perpetrators and victims of this breakdown. Perhaps most urgent is the need to provide structures and resources for pastors so that they can effectively model the Christian way and be held morally accountable when they fall into abusive or immoral behavior. Such moral failure on the part of the leaders hurts the witness of the church as a whole.

1 Thessalonians 2:13-16

Imitators in Suffering

PREVIEW

When coping with the immediate challenges of daily life, we often find it hard to view these circumstances from a broad perspective. In 2:1-12 Paul and his missionary associates have been recalling some details of their initial visit in Thessalonica. As they wrap up these particular reflections, they pause to articulate the "big picture." Ultimately the present circumstances need to be seen in light of the larger whole. After all, the Thessalonians are being called *into [God's] own kingdom and glory!* (2:12). After singing the doxology, the writers again strike the refrain in which they restate their thanksgiving to God (2:13; cf. 1:2).

In 2:1-12 we catch a glimpse of the missionary preachers proclaiming and living the message of the gospel in Thessalonica. There the concern is to document the congruence between the missionaries' message and their conduct. The focus of 2:13 rests less on the message which the evangelists have preached and more on the Thessalonians' reception of that message. In receiving the gospel, the Thessalonians have not only heard the Word. Their suffering demonstrates that they have become imitators of the Judean Christians (2:14; cf. 1:6).

The reference to the suffering experienced by both Thessalonian and Judean believers introduces a litany of the Judeans' historic and contemporary opposition to the prophets, to Jesus, and to the missionaries themselves (2:15-16a). In the climax to this paragraph, Paul

80

seems once again to reach for the "big picture." In this case, however, the focus is not on *kingdom and glory* (2:12) but on *wrath* (2:16bc). Perceptive readers will hear an echo of the theme of future *wrath* mentioned earlier in 1:10. In 2:16, *wrath* has apparently become a present reality.

It is evident that the opening thanksgiving section (1:2-10) and the present passage parallel each other in significant respects. There are also some contrasts. The parallels (in italics) and contrasts can be seen if these two thanksgiving sections are arranged in column format (adapted and expanded from Hurd: 29):

1 Thessalonians 1:2-10	*1 Thessalonians 2:13-16*
We give thanks to God always for all of you . . .	*We also give thanks to God always*
knowing . . . your election,	that receiving
for *our gospel came to you*	*the word which you heard from us*
not in word only	you accepted it *not* as a human *word*
but in power	*but* as what it really is, the word of God,
and in the Holy Spirit and with full conviction, . . .	which is at work in you who believe,
and *you became imitators* of us and of the Lord,	for *you became imitators* of the churches of God which are in Judea in Christ Jesus,
receiving the word in much *affliction* with joy inspired by the Holy Spirit,	for you also *suffered* the same things from your countryfolk as they did from the Judeans,
so that you became an example to all the believers, . . .	who killed the Lord Jesus and the prophets and drove us out and displease God and oppose all people
for your faith in God has gone out in every place. . . .	. . .
You turned toward God away from idols	by hindering us from speaking to the Gentiles
to serve the living and true God and to await his Son	so that they may be saved, . . .
whom he raised from the dead—	so that they always fill up the measure of their sins;
Jesus, who delivers us from the coming *wrath.*	but *wrath* has come upon them until the end.

Themes in the beginnings of these two sections are remarkably parallel: an expression of thanksgiving to God, the gospel preached and received as more than word, and imitators in affliction. Sharp differences emerge in the last half, with the positive example of the Thessalonian believers contrasting with the Judeans' violent opposition to God's program of reaching the Gentiles with the gospel.

OUTLINE

God's Word Received, 2:13
Imitators of Judean Churches, 2:14
Litany of Judean Opposition, 2:15-16a
Wrath Until the End, 2:16bc

EXPLANATORY NOTES

God's Word Received 2:13

Here Paul and his partners reiterate their continuing gratitude to God:

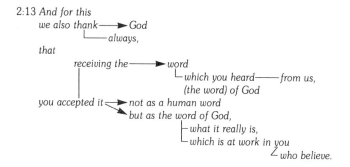

2:13 *And for this*
    we also thank───► *God*
        └───*always,*
    that
        receiving the───► *word*
            └*which you heard*───*from us,*
            (the word) of God
        you accepted it─►*not as a human word*
            ➤*but as the word of God,*
                ├*what it really is,*
                └*which is at work in you*
                    ∠*who believe.*

The phrase *for this* could refer to what has just been said, suggesting that they are thankful for God's calling (2:12); but *this* more likely points to what now follows. At the beginning of the letter the writers express their thanks to God for the Thessalonians' active *faith, love,* and *hope* (1:2), and they now expand on the reasons for their thankfulness: *we also thank God always.* The *also* has been variously interpreted by commentators. Bruce (1982:44) suggests that the Thessalonians by means of a letter or a report conveyed by Timothy have expressed their gratitude that the gospel has come to them. Paul in behalf of his co-workers therefore responds by saying, *We also* (along with you) *thank God.* Wanamaker (110) proposes that Paul here simply identifies an additional reason for thanksgiving beyond what had been specified in 1:2. Likely this latter explanation is correct. Paul and his co-workers assert, *We thank God also for this*; they then expand on their reasons for thanksgiving.

What moves Paul and his colleagues to resume their expressions of thanks? With grateful hearts they recall the way the Thessalonians responded to the gospel. In their recollections, they differentiate several aspects of the process whereby the message of the gospel has been preached and appropriated. First, the participle *receiving* is part of a technical formulation employed by Paul elsewhere to communicate that he himself has received the gospel which he preached. In 1 Corinthians 15:3 Paul articulates his dependence most clearly: "I handed on to you . . . what I in turn had received." A few verses earlier, he reminds the Corinthians of the gospel which "I proclaimed to you, which you in turn received" (15:1). The transmission of the good news therefore involves *receiving* by revelation, *handing on* through preaching, and then a dynamic process of *receiving*. Here in 1 Thessalonians 2:13, the accent rests on the final *receiving*, although the other two stages seem to be assumed. Paul and his companions know they have been entrusted with the gospel which they in turn were communicating to others (2:4).

Second, the actual content being transmitted in the preaching and the hearing of the gospel is designated by *word* (*logos*). On one hand, *word* can be recognized as human speech, delivered by the preacher and heard by the people: *the word which you heard from us.* On the other hand, Paul takes pains to point out that the preached and heard *word* is also *the word of God.* Even in the clause which describes the human process of speaking and hearing, Paul inserts a grammatically awkward phrase, *of God,* somewhat as follows: *the word which you heard from us, (the word) of God.* The divine dimension of preaching and hearing the *word* becomes explicit in this primary description of how the message has been accepted: *You accepted it not as a human word but as what it really is, the word of God.* What the Thessalonians heard when the evangelists preached the *gospel of God* (2:2, 8-9; 3:2) was heard not merely as human speech. The preached word has come to them and has been received as a profoundly transforming message from God.

The third dimension of the program of proclamation features the reception of the message. The expression *you accepted* parallels the word *receiving* used earlier, although *accepted* puts more stress on the response of the hearers. Not only was the message *heard* and *received* as *the word of God,* it has been personally *accepted.* This personal appropriation of the preached *word of God* involves both active belief and reliance on the energizing power of God within and among believers: *you accepted the word of God which is at work in you who believe.* This passage makes abundantly clear that the *word of God* is not primarily propositional truth to be accepted in faith but a dynamic power which transforms and energizes the believers and leads to their emergence as a faith community.

Indeed, already in the opening of the letter, the evangelists thank God for the Thessalonians' *work of faith*, in other words, the work which proceeds from their dynamic faith (1:2). Furthermore, the writers maintain that in their initial evangelistic preaching, *our gospel came to you not in word only but in power and in the Holy Spirit and with full conviction* (1:5). In accepting this Spirit-inspired, dynamic, and convicting message, the Thessalonians find themselves not only informed but transformed, not only enlightened but also empowered, not only inspired as individuals but also incorporated into the fellowship of the church ("God's Word Heard and Working" in TBC below).

Imitators of Judean Churches 2:14

Addressing the Thessalonians once again as *brothers and sisters* (*adelphoi*; previously 1:4; 2:1, 9), Paul and his companions offer evidence to support the claim just made:

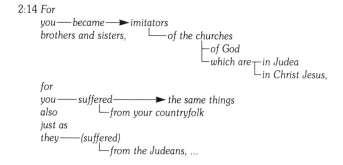

Where was the proof that the Thessalonians had genuinely accepted the gospel as the energizing word of God? Proof is found in the fact that the Thessalonians have been encountering persecution at the hands of their own people in a way reminiscent of the afflictions confronting the believers in Judea.

You became imitators, the believers in Thessalonica are told. This echoes 1:6, which also talks about imitation in suffering: *You became imitators of us and of the Lord, receiving the word in much affliction.* The fellowship of Christ's suffering has therefore been enlarged (cf. Phil. 3:10). In 1:6 this circle includes Jesus, Paul and his missionary colleagues, and the community of believers in Thessalonica. Here in 2:14 the suffering of the predominantly Gentile congregation in

Thessalonica is described as their imitation of the difficult experiences faced by the Jewish believers in Judea.

Like the believers in Jerusalem and Judea, who endured persecution in the past (as Paul the former persecutor well knows: Gal. 1:13) and again more recently (cf. Gal. 6:12), so the believers in Thessalonica were being persecuted by citizens of their own country. It was not that the Thessalonian congregation deliberately set out to copy the way the churches in Judea conducted themselves. What Paul points out is simply that the Thessalonians' experiences of persecution duplicated those of the Christians in Judea. Jewish believers in Judea and believers in Thessalonica therefore share a common allegiance to Jesus Christ in the fellowship of his suffering.

What lies behind this mention of the Thessalonians' suffering at the hands of their own countryfolk? The story in Acts reports that some Jews with help from people in the marketplace protested the missionaries' proclamation of Jesus as the Messiah, thereby creating a furor in the city. Unable to locate Paul and Silas, they attacked the house of Jason and hauled him and some of the believers before the city officials in Thessalonica (Acts 17:5-6). In all likelihood, accusations and attacks against the Thessalonian Christians continued after the evangelists were forced out of town. This would explain the repeated references to their affliction, not only in 1:6 and here in 2:14 but also in the description of Timothy's assignment for his return visit to Thessalonica (3:3-4). Second Thessalonians 1:4-6 has even more on this theme, alluding to persecutions, affliction, and suffering. All the signs point to a perilous state of affairs arising from the persecution which confronted this fledgling Christian group.

This comparison which Paul draws between the experience of Thessalonian believers and that of the Judean Christians deserves further comment. One observes a striking compilation of terms describing the Judean believers: *the churches of God which are in Judea in Christ Jesus.* The plural points to the existence of a number of congregations in Jerusalem and Judea. Elsewhere Paul also appears to use the phrase *church(es) of God* when referring especially to Jewish congregations in Judea and beyond (2 Thess. 1:4; Gal. 1:13; 1 Cor. 11:16). Here an additional qualifying phrase is added almost as an afterthought: *in Christ Jesus.* This combination of phrases recalls the salutation which addresses the believers in Thessalonica as *the church of the Thessalonians in God the Father and the Lord Jesus Christ* (1:1). This seems to be a deliberate attempt to underline the spiritual bond which unites the messianic Jews in Judea with the largely Gentile Christian community in Thessalonica. One dimension of their kinship is the fact that both groups have faced persecution at the hands of their own national compatriots. In the case of the Judean believers, this might be a reference to the persecuting activity directed by the Zealots against messianic Jews who were suspected of being in communion with Gentiles who are "lawless," not keeping the Torah in the traditional way. This type of pressure on the Jewish people to hold the line in Torah-observance had been building up during the late forties. In Judea as well as Galilee and Samaria, this Zealot fervor eventually led to open revolt against Rome in the Jewish War of 66-70 (Jewett, 1970-71:204-206). [*Historical and Political Context, p. 357.*]

Litany of Judean Opposition 2:15-16a

Mention of *the Judeans* moves Paul to accuse them of vicious behavior, both past and present:

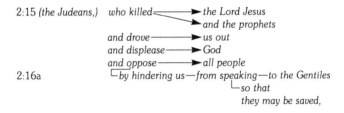

The vehemence of this litany has led Pearson to suggest that Paul could not have written these verses but that a later editor must have inserted 2:13-16 into the original letter (79-94). Schmidt argues similarly on the basis of a linguistic analysis (269-279). Those who accept these verses as coming from Paul have to confront what on the surface at least appears to be a virulent anti-Semitism, hard to reconcile with the more compassionate stance toward the Jewish people found in Romans 9–11 (Donfried, 1984). [*Relationship between 1 and 2 Thessalonians, p. 374.*]

When studying this passage, one crucial question is whether the Greek word *Ioudaioi* denotes *Jews*, as the Jewish people in general, or specifically *Judeans*, in a local or more restricted sense. Modern translations seem without exception to name *the Jews* as a whole as the guilty group. If that were the meaning Paul intended, we could conclude that he has become bitter against his own race, indeed that he is painting all Jews with the same brush. Yet we need to observe

Paul's positive though anguished identification with his Jewish kin-folk (Rom. 9:1-5) and his own past as a zealous Pharisee (Gal. 1:13-14; Phil. 3:3-6).

Hence, it is much more likely that Paul has in mind specific groups within the Jewish community whose stubborn resistance and violent opposition to God's messengers was often evident in the past. These groups included the political and religious leaders who had persecuted the prophets, the religious leaders who clamored for Jesus' death, and those who in Paul's day are opposing the proclamation of the gospel to the Gentiles. Read in this light, the litany of opposition feels less like a generalized and vindictive slur of all Jews and more like a sharply worded prophetic accusation from within the Jewish community itself concerning the activity of certain Jewish leaders.

Four participles elucidate the chronic pattern of violence perpetrated by the Judeans against God's messengers. The accusations reach a crescendo with the note that this violent activity—directed against Jesus, the prophets, and the missionaries—displeases God and in actuality opposes all people.

The Judeans are first identified as those *who killed the Lord Jesus and the prophets*. Historically, of course, the Roman authorities crucified Jesus, even though the Jewish religious leaders had been plotting for some time to do away with him. Jesus' fate therefore resembles that of the Hebrew prophets whose oracles calling for repentance and change evoked resentment and opposition and sometimes led to their deaths.

To understand the background and likely meaning of this first allegation against the Judeans, we need to examine some texts in both the OT and the NT. We can illustrate by noting one theme in Paul's anguished reflections in Romans 9-11 on the lack of response among his fellow Israelites to the gospel of Jesus Christ. In Romans 11:3 Paul cites Elijah's complaint about the official threats against his life (1 Kings 19:10). Fleeing Jezebel's search party after his confrontation with the priests of Baal on Mount Carmel, Elijah laments,

> I have been very zealous for the Lord, the God of hosts; for the Israelites have forsaken your covenant, thrown down your altars, and killed your prophets with the sword. I alone am left, and they are seeking my life, to take it away. (1 Kings 19:10)

This is reminiscent of Jesus' ironic outburst first directed specifically against Herod and then more generally at the leadership in Jerusalem:

It is impossible for a prophet to be killed outside of Jerusalem. Jerusalem, Jerusalem, the city that kills the prophets and stones those who are sent to it! How often have I desired to gather your children together as a hen gathers her brood under her wings, and you were not willing! (Luke 13:33-34)

In short, Jesus, like Elijah and other Israelite prophets before him, had faced the ire of the religious and political establishment for speaking and living God's message.

The litany continues: *and drove us out.* Having alluded to the antagonism which both the OT prophets and Jesus had faced at the hands of their own Jewish kinfolk, Paul and his missionary companions recall their own recent experiences in Thessalonica. Already in Philippi they had been persecuted and humiliated (2:2). When they proceeded to Thessalonica with their evangelistic ministry, the pattern was repeated. Acts 17:5-10 recounts that jealous Jews along with the general populace in the marketplace incited a public outcry against the evangelists, thereby forcing them to leave. Later some Thessalonian Jews even created a public demonstration against Paul and his companions during their ministry in neighboring Beroea (Acts 17:13).

So far this recital of murderous violence points to past Jewish activity against their prophets, Jesus, and the missionaries. A shift to the present tense occurs in the next entry in this list: *(the Judeans) displease God.* On the surface this smacks of slander, a piece of anti-Jewish polemic quite unbecoming to Paul. How should this be understood? Bruce throws up his hands: "Such sentiments are incongruous on the lips of Paul, whose attitude to his fellow-Jews finds clear expression in Rom. 9:1-5; 10:1-4; 11:25-32. . ." (Bruce, 1982:47). More helpfully, Best suggests that Paul here does not describe Jewish rebellion generally. Instead, Paul is commenting specifically about the activity of some Jews and "their rejection of God's will seen now (v. 16) in their attempts to hinder the spread of the gospel" (Best: 117). In other words, Paul and his co-workers put the label "displeasing to God" on the concerted attempts by some Jews to scuttle their evangelistic ministry in Thessalonica.

Why then do we have the addition of the clause *and oppose all people?* This sounds like a racially prejudiced generalization depicting all Jews as being against humanity. Strong anti-Jewish sentiments were expressed within the Greco-Roman world of Paul's day. The Roman historian Tacitus called Jewish customs "evil and disgusting." Diodorus in his world history comments concerning the Jewish race:

"They alone of all nations refused to associate with any other people and considered them all as enemies." The second century A.D. philosopher Philostratus summarizes: "For the Jews have long been in revolt not only against the Romans, but against all mankind too" (citations from Whittaker: 22, 44, 115). But, as a Jew himself, would Paul have uttered or written such racial slurs against his own people?

In the final participial clause in this series, Paul discloses the reason for the strong language used to describe the opposition he has experienced. How do the Judeans *displease God and oppose all people?* Paul declares that they have done so *by hindering us from speaking to the Gentiles so that they may be saved* (2:16a). What Paul says here can be understood if one feels the frustration of this missionary party at having been expelled from one city after another while seeking to fulfill their calling as missionaries of the gospel. Even though he has been approved by God to be entrusted with the gospel (2:4), Paul has found that, ironically, his own kinfolk in the flesh (cf. Rom. 9:3) are thwarting the free exercise of his God-given mandate as apostle to preach the gospel to the Gentiles. By obstructing God's own mission program, the Judeans—and by association the Thessalonian Jews as well—displease God and essentially oppose humanity in general by hindering the spread of the gospel to the Gentiles.

Wrath Until the End   2:16bc

This catalog of crimes against the prophets, Jesus, and the Christian missionaries concludes with a description of the end result.

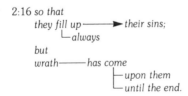

The metaphor employed here visualizes a measuring cup. As the NRSV puts it: *they have constantly been filling up the measure of their sins.* Through the various actions cataloged above, this measuring cup has been filling up with sin and is now overflowing (cf. Matt. 23:32; in OT: Dan. 8:23; in intertestamental literature: 2 Macc. 6:14). The adverb *always* attests that the pattern of defiance has been chronic. Sooner or later, therefore, the measuring cup of sin would reach its limit and *wrath* would be inflicted on those who continually perpetuate this resistance against God's redemptive plan.

The final clause in this section bristles with interpretive problems: *but wrath has come upon them until the end.* Attention will be given here to some aspects of this difficult statement, but the more complete discussion can be found later ("Wrath" in TBC below). The meaning of the word *wrath* needs to be explored in light of the other references in 1 Thessalonians: 1:10 (Jesus as the deliverer from coming *wrath*) and in 5:9 (God's intention not for *wrath* but for *salvation*). One pertinent question here is whether *wrath (orgē)* refers to a contemporary historical event or a future eschatological event.

The verb *has come (ephthasen)* can be read as an indication that a past historical event was regarded by the authors as evidence that *wrath* had already descended on the Jewish people. Or this verb could be understood to point to an event presently unfolding. Yet another option is to view it in a futuristic sense as referring to an event still future but considered to be on the verge of taking place and so certain that it can already be regarded as accomplished. In any case, the verb *has come* appears to point to an actual historical occurrence, whether already past, presently unfolding, or envisioned in the near future. This therefore seems to answer one question about the nature of *wrath*. *Wrath* is an event within history rather than exclusively an end-time phenomenon.

Most puzzling of all are the last two words, *eis telos*, a phrase which is translated in a bewildering variety of ways: *at last* (JB, RSV, NIV, NRSV), *for good and all* (NEB, REB), *finally* (Phillips), *to the uttermost* (KJV). A few additional suggestions have been put forward by commentators: *in the end, finally* (Best: 121); *fully and finally* (Marshall: 81); *fully* (Thomas: 260); *until the end* (Wanamaker: 118); *completely, for ever.*

This lack of consensus among translations and commentators reflects the basic confusion concerning whether this phrase has reference to chronology or to outcome. Does this phrase communicate a temporal meaning, that the time of *wrath* has begun or is about to begin? If temporal, does this phrase connote the everlasting nature of this *wrath*? Or does this *wrath* endure only for a time? On the other hand, might *eis telos* communicate the result or the outcome rather than the timing of *wrath*? Does it describe the completeness or finality of the judgment now descending on the Judeans? Conclusions on these and other questions await wider biblical exploration. As shown below ("Wrath" in TBC below), the most defensible readings of this text are those which view a traumatic historical event among the Judeans as an expression of *wrath* whose consequences prevail *until the end*. Nevertheless, the final word of judgment has not yet been spoken. God's final reckoning still lies in the future.

If Paul has an actual historical catastrophe in mind, which crisis might have had sufficient magnitude to warrant the conclusion that *wrath* has already descended? Several different kinds of proposals have been made in ascertaining what event Paul might have had in mind: the death of Jesus Christ on the cross, the destruction of Jerusalem in A.D. 70, and a variety of other disasters in Judea and the surrounding area between 30 and 70. Let's examine these three proposals briefly.

First, might the crucifixion event have constituted this historical expression of God's wrath? Noting that *wrath of God* within Paul's apocalyptic framework has both present and future connotations, Donfried argues that "the cross marks the culmination of God's judgment and wrath; it is the apocalyptic turning point of history." Accordingly, through the death of Christ, God's wrath has expressed itself in judgment on the people of Israel *until the end* when God's mercy will be extended to Israel (Rom. 11:25-32; Donfried, 1984:252-253).

A second possibility is that the destruction of Jerusalem in 70 was regarded as an outworking of this *wrath*. Pearson takes the verb *has come* as clearly referring to a past event, and thus he judges that the phrase *eis telos* underscores the finality of that event. He contends that only the destruction of Jerusalem in 70 could have qualified. On this basis, Pearson also concludes that 2:13-16 was not written by Paul but introduced into the text by a later editor (Pearson: 82-83).

A third perspective is represented by Jewett, who points out that apocalyptically oriented people living before the major cataclysm of 70 might have regarded other catastrophes involving the Jewish people as evidence that *wrath* had already been visited on them. Jewett specifically mentions the riot and massacre in Jerusalem after 48, in which twenty to thirty thousand Jews were killed (Josephus, *Ant.* 20.112 [20.5.3]; *War* 2.223-227 [2.12.1]). He also notes that the Theudas insurrection (44-46), the famine in Judea (46-47), or the expulsion of the Jews from Rome under Claudius (49) could have been in view. In sum, Jewett asserts "there were large-scale disasters that someone might have described in terms of wrath upon the Jews at the time of the writing of 1 Thessalonians" (Jewett, 1986:37-38). *[Historical and Political Context, p. 357.]*

All things considered, Jewett's argument most adequately explains the meaning of this text. Here Paul appears to have used the notion of *wrath* to describe some catastrophic event which has already befallen the Judeans. His underlying apocalyptic view of history leads him to regard disastrous political upheavals as expressions of divine judgment.

THE TEXT IN THE BIBLICAL CONTEXT
God's Word Heard and Working

When Paul recalls how he and his partners have preached the gospel in Thessalonica (2:13), he gives testimony to a dynamic concept of the efficacy of the word. In the Hebrew Bible, words are not just spoken and heard; they perform. More precisely, the OT writers affirm that God's word works. In the creation account, the repeated statement, "And God said" (Gen. 1:6, 9, etc.), is followed by the refrain, "and it was so" (1:7, 9, etc.).

In the sixth century B.C., a prophet often known as Second Isaiah spoke God's comforting message to the exiles in Babylon:

> Then the glory of the Lord shall be revealed, and all people shall see it together, for the mouth of the Lord has spoken. (Isa. 40:5)

The good news that God would perform a new exodus leading to the return of the exiles to Jerusalem is articulated in terms of a divinely guaranteed word:

> For as the rain and the snow come down from heaven, and do not return there until they have watered the earth, making it bring forth and sprout, giving seed to the sower and bread to the eater, so shall my word be that goes out from my mouth; it shall not return to me empty, but it shall accomplish that which I purpose, and succeed in the thing for which I sent it. For you shall go out in joy, and be led back in peace. (Isa. 55:10-12)

With eloquence and joy the prophet reassures the people in their loneliness that what God says, God also does. God would rescue them and return them to their homeland!

The slogan promises, "No sooner said than done." With respect to the hearing of the *word*, the biblical perspective might be stated: "What is truly heard is also done." In biblical categories, God's *word* invites participation in a dynamic event rather than just receiving a symbol. Action accompanies speaking. Human response to the hearing of God's *word* therefore involves obedience, if such hearing is faithful. In both biblical Hebrew and NT Greek, the verb *hear* doubles for the verb *obey*; authentic hearing of *the word* includes observing or obeying it as well.

In Deuteronomy, when Moses wraps up his extended recital about God's saving activity and the corresponding guidelines for living, he issues a reminder concerning how doable *the word* actually is:

> *Surely, this commandment that I am commanding you today is not too hard for you, nor is it too far away.* (Deut. 30:11)

Playfully eliminating heaven and the other side of the sea as places where one must go in order to *hear and observe* the commandments (30:12-13), Moses says:

> No, the word is very near to you; it is in your mouth and in your heart for you to observe. (30:14)

God's near word, spoken by mouth and internalized in the heart, energizes the community of the faithful to observe that word. It is striking that exactly this passage appears in Romans 10:8, where Paul reinterprets the near word of Deuteronomy 30:14 as "the word of faith that we proclaim." Paul adds,

> If you confess with your lips that Jesus is Lord and believe in your heart that God raised him from the dead, you will be saved. (Rom. 10:9)

The emphasis in the background text from Deuteronomy is on faithfully observing the near word of God. Hence, Paul regards the confession of the lips not as mere words but as a wholehearted commitment of one's life to God.

When Paul recalls that the Thessalonians *accepted the word*, he also adds concerning this word that it *is at work in you who believe* (2:13). More is involved in coming to faith than simple acceptance of a message. The gospel, though delivered in human speech for their hearing (cf. Rom. 10:17), has been welcomed as the word of God. This word of God in turn energizes those who believe! And this divine energy expresses itself not just within individuals but also through believers in their relationships within the community of faith.

Wrath

Even though 2:16 refers only to *wrath* (*orgē*), many translations add *God's* or the phrase *of God*, in order to make explicit that God's anger is meant. Some early copies of 1 Thessalonians specify *wrath of God*, but the earliest manuscripts simply say *wrath*. Strikingly, only three of the twenty occurrences of *wrath* in the Pauline letters use the phrase "wrath of God" (Rom. 1:18; Col. 3:6; Eph. 5:6). Elsewhere in the NT, the expression "wrath of God" appears only twice (John 3:36; Rev. 19:15). Sometimes a pronoun clarifies that it is God's wrath (Rom. 9:22; Heb. 3:11; 4:3; Rev. 11:18; 16:19; cf. "wrath of the Lamb," Rev. 6:16-17; "your anger," James 1:20). Other NT texts employ the word *wrath* in an absolute sense.

What is Paul's conception of *wrath*? First Thessalonians 1:10 seems to speak about God's end-time wrath: *the coming wrath*. However, our earlier discussion of 1:10 suggests that Jesus' rescue of believers from *the coming wrath* cannot be understood only in terms of Jesus making it possible for believers to escape God's final judgment. *Coming wrath* can also refer to judgment anticipated in the future but within history.

Is there evidence elsewhere in Paul's writings that he views events within history as manifestations of divine wrath? The clearest indication of such a theological conception can be found in Paul's discourse on "the wrath of God" in Romans 1:18-31. Paul envisions God's wrath being revealed against persons who by their godlessness and unrighteousness suppress the truth which can be known in what God has made (1:18-19). Three times in this passage, Paul laments the idolatrous exchange that humanity has made:

They exchanged the glory of the immortal God for images. (1:23)
They exchanged the truth about God for a lie. (1:25)
Their women [and men] exchanged natural intercourse for unnatural.
(1:26-27)

These exchanges, Paul declares, lead to consequences which manifest themselves in the normal course of life. Such consequences are not postponed to any end-time judgment. In a thrice-repeated refrain, "God gave them up" (1:24, 26, 28), Paul drives home the major point of his theological diagnosis: God allows humanity the freedom to trade inspired worship for idolatry, revealed truth for lies, and natural sexual relations for unnatural. The picture one gains is that God with grieved compassion allows the historical and social forces unleashed through human choices to work themselves out in "impurity," "degrading passions," "a debased mind," and various kinds of improper conduct (1:24, 26, 28-31). Against all of these, "the wrath of God is revealed" (1:18). The underlying verb *apokalup-*

tetai in 1:18 is in the present tense. Already in the present, therefore, Paul sees God's wrath expressing itself within human experience.

In Romans, Paul repeatedly also lets it be known that there will be a climactic eschatological judgment (2:5, 8, 16; 3:5; 5:9; 9:22). However, Paul's theological analysis in the opening of Romans clearly communicates his conviction that the forces of divine judgment are already unleashed within history in individuals and within communities. This theological conviction informs Paul's admonition,

> *Beloved, never avenge yourselves, but leave room for the wrath of God; for it is written, Vengeance is mine, I will repay, says the Lord. (Rom. 12:19; cf. Deut. 32:35)*

Both the law (Rom. 4:15) and the state (Rom. 13:4-5) can become instruments through which this *wrath* is expressed.

If at the time when he wrote the Thessalonian epistles, Paul held convictions similar to what he developed more fully in his later letter to Rome, the fleeting reference to *wrath* in 1 Thessalonians 2:16 can be understood as referring to historical occurrences. A catastrophic event in Judea, quite possibly the massacre which followed the Jerusalem riot in A.D. 48, could easily have been considered by Paul to be the outworking of *wrath* against the Judeans.

If this outburst against the Judeans seems anti-Semitic, the same can be said about the OT prophets. For example, in the seventh and sixth centuries B.C., the prophet Jeremiah predicts that judgment will fall on the people of Judah for the evil they have done. Reminding them that God brought their ancestors out of Egypt and established a covenant with them (Jer. 7:21-23), Jeremiah laments that the people disobeyed God and ignored the prophets whom God sent (7:24-26). Then Jeremiah utters God's word of dire warning:

> Cut off your hair and throw it away; raise a lamentation on the bare heights, for the Lord has rejected and forsaken the generation that provoked his wrath. (7:29)

This oracle calls for the people of Judah to cut off their hair in mourning and to join in chanting a funeral dirge, because they are about to feel the brunt of God's *wrath*. As the next verses make clear, this *wrath* comes at the hands of the Babylonian armies who will devastate the city and massacre its people:

> The corpses of this people will be food for the birds of the air, and for the animals of the earth; and no one will frighten them away. And I will bring

to an end the sound of mirth and gladness, the voice of the bride and bridegroom in the cities of Judah and in the streets of Jerusalem; for the land shall become a waste. (7:33-34)

Similar pronouncements can be found elsewhere in the oracles of Jeremiah (4:4, 8, 26; 17:1-4). Other prophets also portray the horror of war as expressions of God's jealous fury against the unfaithful covenant people. For example, Ezekiel like Jeremiah calls for a radical haircut as an ominous symbol of the imminent fate of Jerusalem (Ezek. 5:1-4). Ezekiel chronicles the rebellious wickedness of the people (5:5-7) and announces that God will execute judgment on them through war, pestilence, and famine (5:8-12).

Already in the eighth century B.C., Isaiah views foreign armies as instruments which God would use to punish disobedient Israel. A series of accusations against Israel (Isa. 5:8-24) sets the stage for the warning concerning God's anger:

> Therefore the anger of the Lord was kindled against his people, and he stretched out his hand against them and struck them; the mountains quaked, and their corpses were like refuse in the streets. (Isa. 5:25)

Besides this description of past devastation, perhaps through war or a natural disaster, Isaiah pictures God as a herdsman whistling for hunters or lions to come and devastate his flock:

> He (the Lord) will raise a signal for a nation far away, and whistle for a people at the ends of the earth; here they come, swiftly, speedily! (5:26)

For Isaiah, the Assyrians are the nation through whom God's anger will soon be vented on the rebellious people of Israel.

Other examples of such prophetic indictments of the people of Israel and Judah could be cited. These suffice to illustrate the way the Jewish prophets viewed recent or impending national catastrophes as expressions of God's wrath on the people who had been chosen as channels of blessing for all nations. When the chosen people violated their covenant by defying God's norms of justice and compassion, the prophets announced that God's wrath would fall on them. Wrath therefore comes as one dimension of God's steadfast love and mercy. When the people, after tasting special divine favor, responded in rebellion and disobedience, God's wounded love expressed itself in wrath, often in the form of war and other disasters. The wrath of God is not retaliatory anger, but it does allow the consequences of human freedom to be played out historically.

When narrating the tragic history of the events leading to the fall of Jerusalem in 587 B.C., the OT Chronicler includes a poignant lament. God's compassionate persistence in sending messengers to the people elicits mockery of the message and abuse of the messengers. What are the consequences? The themes in this passage sound a strikingly familiar note:

> The Lord, the God of their ancestors, sent persistently to them by his messengers, because he had compassion on his people and on his dwelling place; but they kept mocking the messengers of God, despising his words, and scoffing at his prophets, until the wrath of the Lord against his people became so great that there was no remedy. (2 Chron. 36:15-16)

Concluding this tragic saga, the Chronicler recounts the destruction of Jerusalem and the beginning of the Babylonian captivity. When the measuring cup of wrath fills up, it spills over.

Jesus similarly regards the carnage and destruction which loomed on the horizon for the people of Jerusalem in his time. Luke depicts Jesus weeping over Jerusalem as he envisions the horror about to befall this city:

> They will crush you to the ground, you and your children within you, and they will not leave within you one stone upon another; because you did not recognize the time of your visitation from God. (Luke 19:44)

Later Jesus speaks some more about these "days of vengeance" (21:22) which were about to break in upon Jerusalem:

> For there will be great distress on the earth and wrath against this people; they will fall by the edge of the sword and be taken away as captives among all nations; and Jerusalem will be trampled on by the Gentiles, until the times of the Gentiles are fulfilled. (21:23b-24)

Like the prophets before him, Jesus interprets the impending doom of Jerusalem in a way which reflects God's grieved love.

We can conclude, therefore, that Paul's utterance in 1 Thessalonians 2:16 is offered in the same spirit and with the same intent as the seemingly harsh words of the prophets and of Jesus. Elsewhere in his writings, Paul himself lashes out in frustration against Judaizers who interfere with his ministry of proclaiming the gospel to the Gentiles (Gal. 5:12). Far from being prejudicial or anti-Semitic, Paul's outburst can be heard as a compassionate and grief-stricken cry of the heart concerning the judgment of his own people by race: *Wrath has come upon them until the end.*

Until the end? Space does not allow nor does insight enable a clear explanation of how Paul envisions the final outcome of God's relationship with the ancient people Israel. In Romans 9-11, Paul demonstrates both candor and compassion as he wrestles with the ironic fact that the people of the covenant were generally rejecting the gospel. Yet, as he concludes that pivotal theological essay concerning the ongoing role of ethnic Israel, Paul vigorously denies that God has rejected this people (11:1). In his summation, Paul shares "this mystery":

> A hardening has come upon part of Israel, until the full number of the Gentiles has come in. And so all Israel will be saved. (11:25-26)

Perhaps realizing anew that all human logic and understanding fall short, Paul concludes his treatment of this most delicate theme by exclaiming,

> O the depth of the riches and wisdom and knowledge of God! How unsearchable are his judgments and how inscrutable his ways! (11:33)

In the end, and *until the end*, that is as much as any mortal can say.

THE TEXT IN THE LIFE OF THE CHURCH
Christians and Jews

When the modern state of Israel emerged in 1948, many Christians hailed this event as a major step forward in God's cosmic calendar. As a young boy at that time, I recall overhearing some excited adult conversations: "Surely Christ will soon return!" The bewilderment of the child gave way later to genuine puzzlement about the conflicting claims made by sincere believers on the basis of their study of the same Bible. During the mid-1980s, I spent a year in the Jerusalem area. This became a crucial stage in my lifelong pursuit of further understanding concerning God's special relationship with the Jewish people.

In the believers church of the latter half of the twentieth century, attitudes toward the various combatants within the ongoing Middle East conflict have generally reflected a whole range of opinions expressed in the church as a whole. I find it instructive to group these viewpoints concerning Israel into three broad categories. These need to be recognized as generalized stereotypes rather than carefully defined positions: a pro-Israel stance, anti-Semitism, and a mediating position. We'll look at each of these in turn.

Those taking a pro-Israel view remember God's promise that the land of Canaan would belong to the descendants of Abraham and Sarah as a perpetual inheritance (Gen. 17:1-8). Some Christian circles apply this promise directly to the modern state of Israel, which emerged in 1948 as a Jewish nation. Indeed, the occupation of the West Bank/Palestine following the war in June 1967 was legitimated by many Israelis as well as by many evangelical Christians on the basis that all of ancient Judea and Samaria belongs to the Jews by divine decree. A Jerusalem-based organization called International Christian Embassy (I.C.E.) illustrates this kind of pro-Israel position. In the booklet prepared for their Feast of Tabernacles celebration, we clearly detect their driving convictions:

> If it is true, as Paul says in Romans, that the fullness of Israel will be life from the dead for the rest of the world, there can hardly be a subject so important to us Christian believers as the subject of the restoration of God's people, Israel. (I.C.E., *Succot*, 1985:22)

What I.C.E. envisions is the restoration of all the world's Jews to their rightful homeland, an event which signals that history has moved forward another notch in God's timetable.

On the other end of a continuum of views concerning the Jews, some Christians still hold various anti-Semitic or anti-Judaic attitudes. A non-contextual reading of 1 Thessalonians 2:16 lends apparent support to the view that the Jews as a race deserve judgment for being Christ-killers. Another NT passage which has had a similar effect is the cry of the crowds calling for Jesus' crucifixion, as recorded by Matthew: "His blood be on us and on our children!" (Matt. 27:25). Anti-Semitism in its most vicious form during the Holocaust in the 1940s led to the death of some six million Jews in Hitler's gas chambers. Even though there were Christians among the "righteous Gentiles" (to use a Jewish designation), who risked their lives to shield Jews from the death squads, many other Christians worldwide responded with either tacit approval or indifference. In the years since World War II, the full horror of the Holocaust rightly aroused a collective sense of guilt, which in some ways paved the way in 1948 for the establishment of the state of Israel in a favorable international climate. However, the scourge of anti-Semitism still continues to surface at times even among Christians.

As I lived among both Jews and their Palestinian cousins in the Jerusalem area in 1985-86, I began to see more clearly both the shortsightedness of an unqualified pro-Israel position and the blatant injustice of anti-Semitism. In their zeal for the cause of Israel as a state, Christian pilgrims gathering for the I.C.E. Feast of Tabernacles generally had little or no contact with or even awareness of Christians living in the Holy Land. The reason soon became clear to me. Most of the Christians native to Israel/Palestine are Palestinian. Since Palestinians, including Palestinian Christians, also claim this land as their inheritance, pro-Israel Christians prefer to avoid having fellowship with the local believers.

A mediating position which is neither pro-Israel nor anti-Semitic (as defined above) can be constructed on the basis of the life and thought of the apostle Paul. His credentials as a Jew were strong (Gal. 1:13-14; Phil. 3:3-6; 2 Cor. 11:22), and his identification with and concern for the ancient people of Israel were passionate (Rom. 9:1-5). Yet Paul also knew himself to have been called, even from his mother's womb, to preach the gospel to the Gentiles (Gal. 1:15-16). When specific groups within the Jewish community both in Judea and in Thessalonica opposed the mission to which Paul had given himself, he rebuked his own people, even as the prophets and Jesus before him had done. He lamented the chronic pattern of opposition to God's messengers, a pattern recently repeated in the experiences which Paul and his missionary companions faced in Thessalonica. Thus here (1 Thess. 2:16) Paul utters the unthinkable word of judgment on these "kindred according to the flesh" (cf. Rom. 9:3): *Wrath has come upon them until the end.*

Paul speaks these harsh words as a fellow Israelite, just like Jeremiah delivered his severe message to his contemporaries:

> By your own act you shall lose the heritage that I gave you, and I will make you serve your enemies in a land that you do not know, for in my anger a fire is kindled that shall burn forever. (Jer. 17:4)

Few people would pin the label "anti-Semite" on Jeremiah or any other OT prophet or writer. Menahem Benhayim, a messianic Jew living in Jerusalem, writes that ironically the Hebrew Bible sounds more "anti-Semitic" than the NT, but the critique recorded in both testaments has a redemptive intent. With reference to 1 Thessalonians 2:16, Benhayim says that, writing in a style reminiscent of the prophets of the OT, Paul "is excoriating the people of Judea for their rebellion against the divine will, and foretelling inevitable judgment" (Benhayim: 42). In sum, therefore, God's spokespersons throughout the ages have needed to speak the truth with anguished compassion so that God's people might repent and resume their calling as channels of blessing for all the world.

What application might one find for the life of the church today? Two brief comments will need to suffice. First, the church needs to recognize that, although Jews like Jeremiah or Paul announced God's wrath on other Jews, this does not make it right for Christians (especially Gentile Christians) to perpetuate the tragic legacy of anti-Semitic attitudes and behavior which mar the history of the church.

Second, Paul's grieved compassion, glimpsed in his letters to the church in Thessalonica and articulated at length in Romans 9–11, can serve as a reminder for the church of today. God has given humanity the freedom to choose. And choices, both faithful and unfaithful, have their consequences. The message about the wrath of a loving and merciful God on human unfaithfulness needs to be communicated, even though it is painful and unpopular to do so. This message also needs to be conveyed within and to the church. Prophetic critique of unfaithful trends and tendencies within the church needs to be offered and received as a call to greater faithfulness. To what end? So that the church might more effectively serve as a channel of God's blessing to the world.

1 Thessalonians 2:17—3:10

Orphaned Yet Reassured

PREVIEW

The dynamic interaction between the missionary pastors and the new believers in Thessalonica continues!

In a spirit of gratitude to God, Paul and his colleagues begin the letter by rehearsing the story of their initial mission efforts and the Thessalonians' conversion (1:2-10). Next they review their motivations and strategies as missionaries during their first evangelistic visit in Thessalonica (2:1-12). In 2:13-16 they resume the telling of the initial experiences of the Thessalonian converts, specifically their suffering. Comparing this suffering to what the prophets, Jesus, the Judean churches, and the missionaries themselves had faced, Paul and his co-workers provide a glimpse of the eschatological reality within which this affliction can be understood: *Wrath has come upon them (the Judeans) until the end* (2:16).

At 2:17 the story line picks up again, this time from the perspective of the missionaries, who are still chafing about their premature exit from the city. An eschatological mood pervades these further personal reflections. The first of six references in the Thessalonian letters to the *coming* (*parousia*) of the Lord Jesus Christ appears at 2:19. The motifs of *glory and joy* in 2:20 echo the doxological climax earlier in the letter: *[God] calls you into his kingdom and glory* (2:12).

The theme of suffering also links this section with what precedes. Both the Thessalonians and the evangelists continue to encounter affliction (3:3-4, 7; cf. 1:6; 2:2, 14). Paul senses that their status as new believers is potentially precarious. He tells the Thessalonians that he wants to return (2:18) and is continuing to pray fervently for the opportunity to rejoin them in order to strengthen them in their newly discovered but also threatened faith (3:9-10).

In this ongoing drama involving missionary pastors and their people, three progressive episodes play themselves out on the stage. First, Paul emphatically assures the Thessalonians of his eager longing to be with them again (2:17-20). Second, since that intention has been repeatedly frustrated, Paul finally sent Timothy on an assignment back to Thessalonica (3:1-5). In the third scene, Paul expresses his relief at the good news which he heard when debriefing Timothy upon his return to Corinth (3:6-10).

This section of the letter clearly functions as a substitute for the writer's personal presence among the Thessalonians. In addition, this letter seeks to maintain and cultivate the relationship which exists between the senders and the recipients. By sharing with the Thessalonians his deep feelings toward them, and by articulating his desire for their growth in the faith, Paul prepares his readers to be receptive to the ethical guidance and the pastoral exhortation which follow in 4:1—5:22.

OUTLINE

Paul's Desire to Visit, 2:17-20
Timothy Is Sent, 3:1-5
Timothy Returns and Reports, 3:6-10

EXPLANATORY NOTES

Paul's Desire to Visit 2:17-20

Paul uses another family metaphor plus a rhetorical question and an emphatic answer to that question to express the depth of his own personal longing to make a return visit to the new believers in Thessalonica (diagram on next page).

The litany of Judean opposition in 2:15-16 documents that the missionaries themselves have been hindered from freely proclaiming the gospel among the Gentiles. Now Paul notes that he has personally also been hindered in his efforts to return to Thessalonica for a follow-up visit.

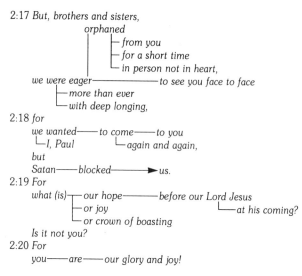

Once again, the warm personal address, *brothers and sisters*, signals a shift to the new subject (2:17). In describing their relationship to the Thessalonians, Paul and his companions employ yet another striking kinship metaphor. In 2:7 the missionaries picture themselves both as *little children* and as *nursing mother* in order to emphasize that as apostles they have been gentle and nurturing among them. In 2:11 the portrait shifts to that of an encouraging father, who also exhorts and even implores his children to live in a way that is worthy of God's reign. Earlier Paul used two images featuring the parenting roles, and now he portrays himself as an orphan.

Parenthetically, we should note that, as 2:18 shows, here Paul is speaking personally about his own feelings, apart from those of his missionary comrades. The apostle confides to the Thessalonians that, when he and his companions were expelled from their city (2:15), he felt like he had been *orphaned* (NIV: *torn away*; RSV: *bereft*) from them (2:17). To be sure, the new believers in Thessalonica had probably also felt abandoned by Paul and his team. Paul assures them, "I know the feeling. I feel like I was *orphaned from you!*" However, Paul hastens to add that this enforced separation was temporary (*for a short time*) and only physical (*in person not in heart*). In Hebraic thought, *heart* represents the personal center, the inner human core for thinking and feeling. Today Paul might say that, though physically absent, he has been with the Thessalonians in spirit.

Accompanying these expressions of the warmth of his identification with these converts, Paul declares how eager he has been to see them again: *more than ever we were eager with deep longing to see you face to face* (2:17). The phrase *with deep longing* eloquently conveys the intensity of Paul's desire for a reunion with these believers. The underlying word *longing* (*epithumia*) often refers to human desire for the forbidden or the immoral; the only other occurrence of this word in the Thessalonian letters is found in 1 Thessalonians 4:5 to describe the *passion of lust* characteristic of *the Gentiles who do not know God.* Here Paul uses this word in a positive sense to impress on the Christian group in Thessalonica that he passionately longs for more personal interaction and fellowship with them. The word usage here resembles Jesus' opening statement to his disciples during the Passover meal, as reported by Luke: "I have eagerly [literally: desirously] desired to eat this Passover with you before I suffer" (Luke 22:15).

As if to underscore the strength of his resolution to be reunited with the Thessalonians, Paul essentially repeats himself: *We wanted to come to you* (2:18). Perhaps people in Thessalonica are questioning the sincerity of Paul's determination to return. After all, Timothy has been back (cf. 3:2, 6), so why not Paul? Lest there be any doubt in the readers' minds about Paul's own determination to return to Thessalonica, he interjects, *I, Paul, wanted to come to you.* As if to reassure them that this has not just been a fleeting notion, Paul adds a note about the frequency with which that resolution has been consciously felt, literally *once and twice,* a colloquial phrase meaning *again and again.*

An explanation follows: *but Satan blocked us.* This reference to Satan's interference in the missionary enterprise reflects Paul's apocalyptic viewpoint. Behind the external forces which hinder the proclamation of the gospel, Paul sees the evil powers of the present age and the pervasive dominance of Satan, their superintendent. Another name for the leader of the forces of evil surfaces in 3:5, where Paul mentions the danger that *the tempter* might lead the new believers to deny their faith.

Examination of the larger framework of biblical teaching concerning Satan and the powers of evil can help to illumine our theological understanding of this text ("Satan, the Tempter" in TBC below). At this point we simply ask, What historical event or physical circumstance might lie behind this reference to Satan's roadblock in Paul's way? Unfortunately, we can only speculate. Suggestions have included: a police-enforced restraining order guaranteed by Jason's security bond (Acts 17:9); Jewish opposition to Paul's evangelizing activity (cf. 2:15); physical illness (cf. "a thorn . . . in the flesh, a messenger of Satan," 2 Cor. 12:7; also Gal. 4:13-14). Presumably the original readers of this letter know more clearly than do modern readers what Paul has in mind here. However, Paul definitely does shift the blame away from himself. Behind whatever external circumstances kept him from returning to Thessalonica, Paul sees the agency of Satan.

Rather than lingering for long on whatever roadblock Satan might have used to obstruct his return to Thessalonica, Paul contemplates the ultimate triumph already guaranteed by the crucified and risen Christ. Paul asks, For what is our hope or joy or crown of boasting before our Lord Jesus at his coming? He immediately responds with another rhetorical question, Is it not you? He also adds an overt announcement, For you are our glory and joy! (2:19).

With a number of code words, Paul alludes to several aspects of the climactic consummation of that which God has already done and is still doing through Christ. This is the first mention of the coming (parousia) of Christ, a topic which dominates so much of the Thessalonian correspondence (especially 1 Thess. 4:13-18; 5:1-11; 2 Thess. 1:5-10; 2:1-12). The word parousia also occurs in the wish-prayers of 1 Thessalonians 3:11-13 and 5:23 as well as in the exhortation concerning the status of the dead in Christ (4:13-18). More will later be said in general about the origin and meaning of the expectation of the (second) coming ("Parousia" in TBC for 3:11-13). At this point, we note that, in his longing to see the Thessalonians again, Paul once more takes the long view (cf. 2:12, 16).

Several other key words are associated with the parousia. Hope obviously has a futuristic ring to it. Later in the letter, Paul gives the Thessalonians further teaching concerning those who have died, so that their grief might not be like those who do not have hope (4:13). They are admonished to wear the hope of salvation like a helmet (5:8). Joy expresses the confidence of salvation despite difficult circumstances. This is already evident in the experience of the Thessalonians, who accepted the gospel in much affliction with joy inspired by the Holy Spirit (1:6). The word joy occurs twice in 2:19-20 and another time in 3:9, pointing both to exultation in the present and the inspired anticipation of a future yet to be attained.

The phrase crown of boasting comes from the practice of placing a victory wreath on the heads of victors in battle or in athletic competitions (cf. 1 Cor. 9:25). The word glory (doxa) suggestively opens up the whole panorama of God's majestic working from creation to the consummation. In sum, the believers in Thessalonica have in a profound sense become for Paul a foretaste of eschatological *hope and joy* as well as *glory*. Through their witness, Paul catches an early glimpse of that victory already assured but yet to be fully attained.

Once again (cf. 2:12, 16) Paul demonstrates that he views both setbacks and victories from within an eschatological framework. He has shared with deep feeling his desire to return to his brothers and sisters in Thessalonica and permits them to see that he regards them as his prize or reward. Accordingly, Paul longs for the Thessalonians to remain steadfast in their commitment to Christ, so that they might in the end verify his own faithfulness to his commission as minister of the gospel. Glancing ahead, we note that in 3:5 Paul expresses anxiety at the thought that his evangelistic efforts might turn out to have been in vain. Then in 3:7-8 he breathes an audible sigh of relief following Timothy's positive report about both the Thessalonians' affection and their faithfulness.

Timothy Is Sent 3:1-5

Not free to make the trip himself, Paul decides to dispatch Timothy back to Thessalonica. What was Timothy's role? his assignment?

```
3:1 Therefore
              ┌─no longer able to endure,
    we decided──── to be left behind
                            └─in Athens alone,
3:2 and
    we sent──►Timothy,
                  └─┬ our brother
                    └ and God's co-worker
                                  └─in the gospel of Christ,
              in order┬─to establish──►you
                      └─and encourage──►you
                              └─for the sake of your faith,
    3:3                  ╲that no one might be shaken
                              └─by these afflictions.

    For
    you──know──►that──we were appointed──to this,
    yourselves

3:4 for
           ┌─when we were with you,
    we told you beforehand──►that
                        we are bound──to be persecuted,
                        just as has happened,
                        and you know──►it.
```

3:5 *For this reason,*

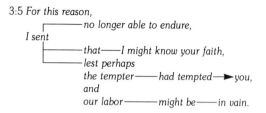

Some further dimensions of the underlying story behind this letter become evident here. In recalling his decision to dispatch Timothy from Athens back to Thessalonica, Paul also refers to some of what he has taught these converts during his evangelistic visit. Most significant perhaps are several strong hints about what Paul regards as being at stake for himself personally. Not only does Paul express his anxiety about the Thessalonians; he is also concerned about whether his investment in them will prove to be fruitful.

Paul has already bared his soul to the Thessalonians, saying that following his departure he felt like an orphan (2:17). Now he lets them know that he willingly risked further abandonment, since he was *no longer able to endure* the untimely disruption of his personal associations with them (3:1). Likely speaking primarily for himself (note the first person *I* in 3:5), Paul intimates that not knowing what was happening back in Thessalonica would be worse than being left by himself in Athens: *We decided to be left behind in Athens alone* (3:1). Luke reports that, when Paul went to Athens, Silas and Timothy stayed behind in Beroea with instructions to join Paul in Athens as soon as possible (Acts 17:14-15). Nothing is said either here or in Acts about whether Silvanus/Silas then stayed with Paul in Athens or accompanied Timothy back to Thessalonica or was situated elsewhere during this time (such as Philippi; Faw, 1993:192). Luke's narrative about Paul's evangelistic activity in Athens (17:16-34) does not mention his companions. According to Acts 18:5, Silas and Timothy arrived from Macedonia and rejoined Paul in Corinth.

Paul reports that he dispatched Timothy as his emissary back to Thessalonica: *We sent Timothy* (3:2). For reasons not indicated, Timothy apparently needed a recommendation, perhaps to reassure the congregation of Paul's full confidence in him. Paul endorses Timothy as *our brother and God's co-worker in the gospel of Christ.* The term *brother* (*adelphos*) appears frequently as a designation for the members of the Christian community in general; in this immediate context at 2:17 and 3:7, the plural *adelphoi* includes both *brothers and sisters.* Calling Timothy *our brother* here may have an additional connotation: he was viewed as a valued partner in the ministry (cf. 1 Cor. 16:20).

Textual uncertainty surrounds the second part of Paul's endorsement of Timothy. Some early manuscripts read *God's servant*; others have *God's co-worker.* The RSV reflects the former, the NRSV and NIV the latter of these two textual readings. Which of these readings might have been original? It is easier to see how scribes copying this text might have changed *co-worker* to *servant* than the other way around. Most likely, some of the scribes found it hard to imagine that Paul would have regarded Timothy as *God's co-worker,* seeming to make Timothy an equal with God. So they substituted *God's servant* instead (Metzger, 1971:631). What then does Paul mean by calling Timothy *God's co-worker?* The clue lies in what follows. Timothy (like Paul himself as well as Apollos and others; cf. 1 Cor. 3:9) is a *co-worker with God in the gospel of Christ.* Far from implying equality with God, Paul affirms that God works through human ministers such as Timothy. Through proclaiming the gospel and nurturing the community of faith, Timothy is indeed *God's co-worker! [Textual Analysis, p. 346.]*

The letter continues with a review of Timothy's assignment. Paul tells the Thessalonians: *We sent Timothy to establish and encourage you for the sake of your faith* (3:2). The verbs *establish* (*stērizai,* also translated *strengthen* or *confirm*) and *encourage* (*parakalesai*) imply that Timothy was to provide active pastoral support and teaching which would help the Thessalonians in their new relationship of faith to weather the storms of persecution now swirling around them. According to the RSV and NIV, Timothy's role was to strengthen the Thessalonians *in* (*huper*) *your faith.* NRSV gives the meaning of the underlying preposition *huper* more accurately: *for the sake of your faith.* The purpose of Timothy's presence and activity among the Thessalonian believers is not primarily to help them maintain their faith convictions but rather to give them the strength to remain faithful in their afflictions ("Faith" in TBC below).

This concern for the Thessalonians' faithfulness in the face of persecution is articulated in the ensuing purpose statement: *that no one might be shaken by these afflictions* (3:3a). Since the word *shaken* (*sainesthai*) appears nowhere else in the Greek Bible, its exact meaning is hard to ascertain. In other Greek literature, this word is used to describe the wagging of a dog's tail! On that basis some propose a gentle (puppylike) meaning such as *beguiled away* (footnote in NEB).

Most however (perhaps envisioning a more vicious dog) suggest meanings such as *unsettled* (NIV) or *shaken* (NRSV). This latter reading is more in harmony with the normal understanding of *affliction* (*thlipsis*), as the distress brought about by severe circumstances such as war or persecution.

The mention of *these afflictions* raises more questions. Whose afflictions: Paul's (3:7), or those suffered by the Thessalonians themselves (1:6; 2:14)? Were they physical or psychological afflictions? The expression *these afflictions* could be taken to refer to Paul's difficult experiences both in Thessalonica (1:6; 2:2, 15) and following his departure, including the psychological distress of being torn away from these new believers (2:17-18; 3:1, 5, 7; Malherbe, 1987:65). However, this interpretation would require us to envision that Paul sent Timothy to strengthen and encourage the Thessalonians because they were upset about what he (Paul) was enduring. A more natural reading is that Paul was concerned about how the Thessalonian converts were bearing up. Paul and his colleagues thank God for the Thessalonians' dynamic *faith, love,* and *hope* (1:3), which is already evident in the way they received the word in much affliction (1:6). Yet continuing opposition and suffering (2:14) threaten eventually to erode their faith and trust.

The death of some members of the congregation could have come as a result of persecution (cf. 4:13). The grief of the survivors is likely aggravated by the expectation, harbored at least by some in Thessalonica, that their entry into God's kingdom has made them immune to further suffering. With the collapse of some of these unrealistic expectations, their entire faith is threatened (Jewett, 1986:176-178). A Christian community, where at least some members experience this kind of confusion, needs help *for the sake of [their] faith.*

Unable to make the trip himself, Paul sent Timothy to act in his behalf. Even after Timothy's second visit, the Thessalonians still need more pastoral care *for the sake of [their] faith.* That is why Paul concludes this rehearsal of recent developments in his relationship with the Thessalonians (2:17—3:10) by expressing the prayer that he might yet see them face to face and *supply what is lacking in [their] faith* (3:10).

Having mentioned *these afflictions,* Paul digresses briefly from his comments about the nature of Timothy's mission, in order to focus further on the theme of suffering (3:3b-4). Paul urges his readers to bring to mind what he and his colleagues during their initial visit taught concerning suffering. Repeatedly in the earlier rehearsal of their missionary motivation and strategies (2:1-12), these missionary pastors appeal to what the Thessalonians already know. Similarly here: *You yourselves know, . . . for when we were with you we told you beforehand* (3:3b-4). Indeed, recent events have confirmed the accuracy of their teaching: *just as has happened, and you know it* (3:4).

What exactly had the evangelists taught concerning the Christian experience of suffering and affliction? Two largely parallel affirmations from their initial preaching are quoted here, presumably in summary form:

> We were appointed—to this [affliction] (3:3b)
> We are bound———to be persecuted (3:4)

In what sense does Paul want the inevitability or necessity of suffering to be understood? Several suggestions have been offered. Some regard this as recognizing that suffering is a normal experience for Christians living in a world that is often hostile to Christian values (Ewert, 1980:40-53). Some see this as a clear indication that in Paul's apocalyptic worldview, he thinks of himself as living in the final age; he simply reflects the conviction, often articulated in Jewish apocalypses, that in the last days there would be tribulation (Collins, 1984:191-193). Interpreters shaped by dispensationalism hasten to distinguish these afflictions from the final tribulation just before Christ's return, when only the ungodly will face the culmination of God's wrath (Thomas: 264).

Which is the correct explanation? Paul definitely views his period in history in eschatological terms. Perhaps he also thinks that the triumphant coming of Christ as Lord will occur within his lifetime. In the face of actual physical persecution (their own and the Thessalonians'), Paul and his partners have taught and are now reminding these believers that suffering normally accompanies a life of faithfulness. Suffering, therefore, should not shake them up nor demoralize them in their trust. Certainly no one should assume that a relationship with the crucified and risen Christ will usher them into a blissful realm free of pain. [*Eschatology, p. 355.*]

Paul has described Timothy's assignment in terms of what the Thessalonians needed and now admits that he had his own needs in mind as well (3:5). Significantly, Paul here uses the first person singular, *I*. First he repeats his lead statement in 3:1: *No longer able to endure, I sent [Timothy]*. Now he adds another reason for

Timothy's mission: *that I might know your faith* (3:5). As already suggested, Timothy did not rejoin the Thessalonian believers only to keep their faith convictions strong but to encourage their faithfulness in the face of persecution. Similarly here, Paul longs to know whether these new believers still continue living in the dynamic *faith, love,* and *hope* which characterized their initial response to the gospel ("Faith" in TBC below).

The next statement confirms that Paul considers the Thessalonians to be genuinely at risk: *lest perhaps the tempter had tempted you* (3:5). In 2:18 Paul blames Satan for blocking the way for his return to Thessalonica. Using another name for the head of the evil forces, Paul here expresses the fear that the Thessalonians too might already have faced interference from the evil one. Nothing is said specifically about how *the tempter* might have *tempted* them. The immediate context clearly implies that the temptations center around the Thessalonians' response to their suffering. In 3:3 Paul worries that some of the Thessalonians *might be shaken by these afflictions.* Paul senses that *the tempter* is busy seeking to sidetrack these new believers from their initial faithfulness and trust.

But Paul also lets his readers know that something is at stake for himself: *Our labor might be in vain.* In the letter thus far, Paul has alluded repeatedly to his first ministry in Thessalonica (1:5; 2:1-12). In 2:1 he calls on the Thessalonian believers themselves to acknowledge that *our coming to you was not in vain.* It is evident in 2:19 that Paul views the Thessalonian Christian community like an eschatological trophy, *a crown of boasting before our Lord Jesus at his coming.* What is at stake for Paul? Paul has been *approved by God to be entrusted with the gospel* (2:4) and desires that the Thessalonian converts might persist in their life of faith. Their continued steadfastness of faith would be proof that Paul has been faithful to the mandate he has received from God. Even though this desire for a final reward does not play a primary role in Paul's motivations, it does enter in. In addition, the Thessalonians clearly hear in these words a moving appeal to remain faithful to the gospel because of their loyalty and affection toward the apostle who has shared the gospel with them.

Timothy Returns and Reports 3:6-10

Paul does not hide his profound sense of personal relief when Timothy comes back to him with good news. Rehearsing the third phase of the ongoing drama involving the missionary pastors and these people in Thessalonica, Paul first summarizes what he has heard from Timothy (3:6) and then expresses his deep sense of relief (3:7-8). He concludes on a note of renewed thanksgiving (3:9) and intercession (3:10).

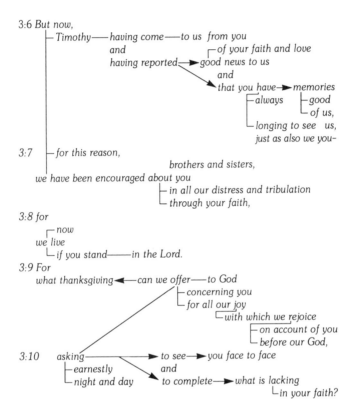

Paul apparently wrote 1 Thessalonians soon after Timothy came back to Paul in Corinth to deliver his report. Even though the details of that report are not given, Paul does provide a summary, which has two parts. In the first part Paul records the continuing response of the Thessalonians to the gospel message: *having reported good news to us of your faith and love* (3:6a). In the second half of this summary, Paul describes what he has learned about their disposition toward himself as the gospel messenger: *You always have good memories of us* (3:6b). Once again (as in 1:5, 9; 2:8), the reception of the message is closely linked to the welcome accorded to the messenger.

The expression *having reported good news* (one word in Greek: *euangelisamenou*) captures the depth of Paul's feelings of joy and gratitude for what has in fact been happening in Thessalonica. In a word, Timothy's news from Thessalonica was gospel! The noun *gospel* (*euangelion*) and the verb *evangelize* or *announce good news* (*euangelizomai*) originally had general meanings. However, these words came to be associated specifically with preaching the good news of Jesus Christ. Bruce (1982:66) thinks that Paul here uses the verb *euangelizomai* in the earlier nontechnical sense (cf. Luke 1:19, where this word is used for the angel's good news to Zechariah and Elizabeth that they would have a son). Marshall suggests that Timothy's report actually proves to be a proclamation of the gospel to Paul:

> The preaching of the gospel includes the news that Jesus Christ is proved to be a mighty Saviour in the experience of those who respond to the Christian message; knowledge of this can lead non-believers to faith and believers to thanksgiving and deeper faith. (94)

The good news concerning the Thessalonian believers has to do with their *faith and love.* Paul here alludes to only two of the three qualities mentioned in 1:3; there is no reference to *hope.* Even though there were also deficiencies in their *faith* (3:10) and *love* (4:10), Paul devotes more attention in the remainder of the letter to the problematic aspects of their *hope* (4:13-18; 5:1-11). In 3:7, it should be noted, Paul shortens the list to *faith.*

As already noted, the second half of Paul's summary of the news that he has heard from Thessalonica features the continuing positive feelings which these new believers have toward Paul. Paul sees a vital correlation between his life and his gospel. In 1:6 he affirms the Thessalonians for their imitation of both the evangelists and the Lord. In 2:8 the writers note that they have been ready to share with the Thessalonians *not only the gospel of God but also our own selves.* Given this close connection between the message and the messengers, continued faithfulness to the gospel message also invites continued affection between the gospel messengers and their people. As Malherbe puts it: "Paul did not think that his life could be distinguished from the gospel. Therefore, if the Thessalonians were tempted to forget him, their faith would be in jeopardy" (1987:68).

Paul has heard that the Thessalonians wish to see him again and hastens to reassure them that the feeling is mutual: *longing to see us just as also we you* (3:6). This desire for a reunion has already been eagerly expressed in 2:17; it also becomes the subject of a prayer report in 3:10 and the prayer itself in 3:11.

A midsentence change of subject occurs at 3:7. Paul seems to have forgotten how he began this thought. The sentence begins on a chronological note: *but now* (3:6). However, at this point Paul seems to be describing cause and effect: *for this reason*. The familiar *brothers and sisters* also suggests that this is a transition to a new thought. However, despite this interrupted flow of thought, the connection between 3:6 and this verse still works. As a result of Timothy's good report, Paul says, *we have been encouraged about you in all our distress and tribulation through your faith* (3:7).

What was Paul's situation when this encouraging news came to him? He uses the words *in all our distress and tribulation* to depict his circumstances while awaiting the news from Thessalonica. The letter has given some hints concerning the evangelists' experiences with opposition and persecution (1:6; 2:1-2, 15). According to Luke, a mob scene brewing in Beroea forced Paul to leave that city (Acts 17:13), and in Athens Paul was hauled before the council of the Areopagus to give an account of himself and his teaching (17:19; Faw, 1993:194). In his letters Paul does not say how he fared during the period immediately after leaving Thessalonica. Since Paul most likely wrote 1 Thessalonians from Corinth, where he went following his time in Athens, his comment in 1 Corinthians 2:3 may have some relevance: "I came to you in weakness and in fear and in much trembling." Bruce suggests that Paul's distress "may have been more psychological than physical" (1982:67).

In 3:2 Paul recalls for the Thessalonians that Timothy was sent *to establish and encourage you for the sake of your faith*. At this point in the letter, the Thessalonians learn that ministry has happened in both directions. They have had a similar ministry toward Paul: *We have been encouraged about you through your faith* (3:7). The Greek verb *parakalesai* here and in 3:2 can have a range of meanings, including *encourage, console, comfort*, or *exhort*. The onslaught of the tempter (3:5) not only threatened to shake the faith convictions newly held by these converts but also to sidetrack them into unfaithfulness. A ministry of encouragement which combines consolation with exhortation has helped them not only to keep the faith but also to remain faithful. Similarly, the news of the Thessalonians' faith and faithfulness despite adversity has encouraged Paul in his own experience of *distress and affliction*. Because of ongoing persecution, the Thessalonian believers were in danger of abandoning their active faith. But Timothy brought good news! These new believers turned to God with joy in the midst of their affliction and are continuing to serve God while awaiting their ultimate deliverance (cf. 1:6, 9-10).

Paul sums up his thoughts and emotions in response to the good news from Thessalonica and exults, *For now we live if you stand in the Lord* (3:8). *We live* clearly does not refer to the continuation of physical life. Using the verb *live* in a metaphorical sense, Paul (undoubtedly joined by Timothy and Silas as well) expresses his great relief and joy at the good news. Bruce paraphrases: "The news of your unwavering faith and love is the very breath of life for us" (1982:67).

Paul utilizes another metaphor (*if you stand*) to characterize the faithful perseverance of the Thessalonians. This implies a resolute or firm stance. The *if* does not suggest doubt; instead, it describes their actual status as reported by Timothy. They were standing steadfast in their Christian lives even in the face of pressure from outside and some uncertainties within their circles. The phrase *in the Lord* (like the frequent expression *in Christ* elsewhere in Paul's writings, as in 1 Thess. 4:16; 5:18) testifies to the believers' communion with the living Christ and in his body the church.

For the third time in this letter (previously 1:2; 2:13), Paul openly thanks God. Actually, he asks a rhetorical question which reveals his thankful spirit: *For what thanksgiving can we offer to God concerning you?* (3:9). The unspoken answer to this question implies that any and all expressions of thanksgiving would be quite inadequate. In the Psalms, many of the laments are stated as questions (as in 13:1-2; 42:2, 9). Yet some prayers of thanksgiving in the Psalms have a form similar to Paul's exclamation of gratitude: "What shall I return to the Lord for all his bounty to me?" (Ps. 116:12).

The story line as glimpsed in the letter thus far illustrates that these missionary pastors in their ongoing relationship with the congregation in Thessalonica oscillate between deep gratitude for past triumphs (1:2-3; 2:13) and grave anxiety concerning present perils (3:1-5). That mixture of profound thankfulness and lingering concern continues even after Timothy's positive report, as can be seen in the interface between thanksgiving and petition in 3:9-10.

Thanksgiving and petition constitute two distinct yet related movements in Paul's life of prayer. In the first place, the overflowing joy in his heart has led to adoration and praise: *In all our joy we rejoice on account of you before our God*. The expression *before our God* shows that Paul self-consciously views himself as exercising a priestly ministry in which joys as well as concerns are articulated before God. Here the dominant mood is joy. Earlier in the letter, Paul refers to the Thessalonian believers as *our hope, joy,* and *crown of boasting* (2:19), adding: *For you are our glory and joy* (2:20). Paul is like a pastor who hears good news from his beloved people and lets the joy come welling up: *We rejoice on account of you.* With joyful gratitude to God, Paul rejoices, prays, and gives thanks. He dwells for a moment on his life of prayer and thus provides another example for the people to imitate. Later in the letter, Paul and his co-workers exhort the believers in Thessalonica to cultivate a piety characterized by rejoicing, prayer, and thanksgiving (5:16-18).

The second movement in Paul's praying can be classified as petition or intercession. In this prayer-report, Paul lets his readers know what specifically he has been praying for: *asking earnestly night and day to see you face to face and to complete what is lacking in your faith* (3:10). Paul has already conveyed his heartfelt desire to see them again face to face (2:17). Now he lets the Thessalonians know the intensity and the constancy of his prayers for a reunion with them. Why does he wish to see them? Despite the Thessalonians' initial fervent reception of the gospel (1:2-10) and Timothy's encouraging news about what has happened in the interim (3:6-8), Paul continues to feel pastoral concern for these new believers. He tells them that he prays for another opportunity to return to Thessalonica in order to supply what is still lacking in their faith.

This mention of *faith* once again refers to more than a set of beliefs. The deficiencies in the Thessalonians' *faith* apparently have more to do with certain tendencies in their behavior, as suggested by the ethical and pastoral instruction which follows in 4:1—5:22. While awaiting another chance to minister in Thessalonica, Paul puts in writing some of his teaching in areas where their *faith* seems to be threatened. In the section which follows, Paul successively addresses several such areas: sexual morality (4:1-8), social relationships (4:9-12), the death of loved ones (4:13-18), the expectation of the day of the Lord (5:1-11), and life within the Christian community (5:12-22).

THE TEXT IN THE BIBLICAL CONTEXT
Satan, the Tempter

Paul blames his inability to return to Thessalonica on interference by Satan (2:18), and he expresses his anxiety about the influence of the tempter (3:5). In so doing, he reflects a perspective with roots in both biblical and extra-biblical writings. What light does this history of Israel's and the church's understanding of the evil one cast on this passage?

A figure in God's court designated as Satan or *the Satan* appears only three times in the OT. Transliterated from the Hebrew, *Satan* means "an accuser/adversary" in 1 Chronicles 21:1 and "the accuser/adversary" in Job 1-2 and Zechariah 3:1-2 (cf. 1 Kings 22:19-23, "a lying spirit"). In the introduction to the story of Job (especially 1:6-12; 2:1-6), Satan behaves like a zealous prosecuting attorney, searching for lawbreakers in order to bring them to divine justice in the heavenly court. With God's permission and within limits set by God, Satan tests Job in ways designed to prove to God that Job is not as righteous as God thinks him to be. Satan plays a similar role in one of the visions of the sixth century B.C. prophet Zechariah. There Satan stands at the right hand of an angel of the Lord to bring accusations against the high priest Joshua and by extension also against the exiled people of Israel as a whole. Quite surprisingly, the angel of the Lord conveys God's willingness to acquit and forgive instead of a readiness to condemn (Zech. 3:1-10).

In the only other OT text where Satan surfaces, the adversary seems to function as an agent of God's wrath. We cite from two parallel accounts of the census instituted during David's reign:

> Again the anger of the Lord was kindled against Israel, and he incited David against them saying, "Go, count the people of Israel and Judah."
> (2 Sam. 24:1)
> Satan stood up against Israel, and incited David to count the people of Israel. (1 Chron. 21:1)

According to the Chronicler, Satan rather than the Lord plants in David's mind the oppressive bureaucratic idea of taking a census to determine the number of soldiers available for war (1 Chron. 21:1-6). This was a sign of not fully trusting God to take care of Israel.

In blocking Paul's return to Thessalonica, Satan seems to manifest a somewhat different character. No longer a prosecuting attorney in the heavenly court, nor God's agent of judgment, Satan now works against God. As Walter Wink puts it,

> Satan seems to have evolved from a trustworthy intelligence-gatherer into a virtually autonomous and invisible suzerain within a world ruled by God. (Wink, 1986:22-23)

What has happened between the pages of the OT and the NT? Within intertestamental Judaism (300 B.C. to A.D. 100), apocalyptic writers increasingly feature both the evil one and various aligned beings. *[Apocalyptic, p. 354.]* Genesis 6:1-5 tells about sons of God from the heavenly court having intercourse with human women. This story evolved into a tradition frequently cited in several documents in the Pseudepigrapha: 1 Enoch (especially 6-16) and Jubilees (especially 5 and 10). According to this rather complex tradition, sexual unions between heavenly beings these writers call "watchers" and earthly women resulted in giants who brought widespread corruption, lawlessness, and violence. Evil spirits also emerged as a result of these lustful acts. Expelled from heaven because of their rebellion, these "watchers" and their children continue to create havoc and bring evil into the world (D. S. Russell: 249-257).

By Jesus' time, there was widespread recognition of the activity of Satan (or the devil) and various beings and forces aligned with the evil one. However, the speculation which characterizes some of the noncanonical apocalyptic writings is much less evident in the NT writings. Many different names are used for the antagonistic beings or forces which oppose God and God's people. In the interpretation of Jesus' parable of the sower, for example, Matthew records that "the evil one" immediately snatches the word from the heart (13:19); according to Mark, this is the work of "Satan" (4:15); Luke blames "the devil" (8:12). Another title is used by Matthew in the temptation narrative: "the tempter" (4:3; cf. "the devil" in Luke 4:3). Evidently a number of different yet equivalent terms are employed to designate the role of the adversary who sought to sidetrack Jesus from his mission and continues to interfere with the mission of the church.

Paul is keenly aware of evil powers at work in the world. In 1 Thessalonians 2:18 and 3:5, he says that *Satan/the tempter* obstructs his work and attempts to thwart the growth of new believers in Thessalonica. In the end-time drama, Paul envisions the intensified activity of Satan (2 Thess. 2:9). When writing to the church in Corinth, Paul warns that by various subtle designs, Satan seeks to gain an advantage over the church and its ministers (2 Cor. 2:11); indeed "Satan disguises himself as an angel of light" (2 Cor. 11:14). Yet, ultimately, faithful believers need not fear that evil will prevail, for God reigns supreme. Paul reassures the members of the house churches in Rome that "the God of peace will shortly crush Satan under your feet" (Rom. 16:20).

Some NT texts paint a picture of impersonal forces seeking to sway human affairs and to enslave the faithful. Under various labels, these include "principalities" and "powers" (Rom. 8:38, KJV; Eph.

6:12; Col. 2:15) and the "elemental spirits of the world" (Gal. 4:3, 9; Col. 2:8). Again the gospel announces that through the death and resurrection of Christ, these forces have already been arrested and rendered ineffective (Col. 2:15), although some people still allow themselves to be dominated by them (Gal. 4:8-11; Col. 2:20; cf. Berkhof; Wink, 1984-92).

When interpreting the biblical teachings about Satan and affiliated beings and forces, we can fall into one of several traps. Some people give Satan too much credit, practically regarding "the god of this world" (2 Cor. 4:4) as an equal with God. Others deny that the evil one exists. From Paul, one learns to recognize that behind those hindrances in the progress of the gospel lie evil powers of this age and the subtle influence of their leader. Yet Paul also models the joyous assurance which comes from knowing that God in Christ has already gained the victory.

Whether influences toward evil are experienced through a personal being, or as seductive forces, or both—this may in the end make little difference. With confidence, believers can pray, "Deliver us from evil/Rescue us from the evil one" (Matt. 6:13, RSV/NRSV). In both renditions of Jesus' prayer, his disciples entrust themselves to God. God delivered Jesus from death. This Jesus also *delivers us from coming wrath* (1 Thess. 1:10; "Jesus Delivers" in TBC for 1:2-10).

Faith

It should not come as a surprise that the subject of *faith* arises frequently in pastoral letters to a young congregation. Even so, the large number of references to the Thessalonians' *faith* (*pistis*) in this part of the letter (3:2, 5-7, 10) and elsewhere in these letters (1:3, 8; 5:8; 2 Thess. 1:3-4, 11; 2:13; 3:2) calls for some reflection.

When writing to Thessalonica, Paul defines neither *faith* nor the process of being "justified by faith" (Rom. 5:1). Nor does Paul in these earliest letters develop clearly how the believer's faith is related to Jesus' death and resurrection. Even though he mentions that Jesus *died for us* (1 Thess. 5:10), Paul makes no effort in the Thessalonian epistles to clarify how Jesus' death imparts salvation to those who believe. In Galatians and Romans, by contrast, Paul devotes himself extensively to that agenda.

What should we make of this difference? It is not necessary to suggest either that Paul dramatically changed his mind or that he matured theologically during the interim (whether short or longer) between writing 1 Thessalonians and composing Galatians and Romans. *[Chronology of Paul's Life, p. 369.]* Paul might have felt that, in the initial preaching of the gospel in Thessalonica, he and his coworkers had sufficiently grounded these converts on the meaning of salvation, so that the letters need not repeat this material. On the other hand, when he wrote to the church in Galatia, Paul was being challenged by some Jewish believers who insisted on circumcising Gentile converts to Christian faith. And when Paul wrote to the various house fellowships in Rome, he was preoccupied with helping these Jewish and Gentile believers to live in genuine harmony with one another (cf. Rom. 15:1-13). None of Paul's letters was written while on sabbatical. Paul was a missionary pastor whose letters address real congregational situations. Paul's more systematic reflection on what the Scriptures (our OT) teach about the relationship between *faith* and *righteousness* therefore appears in his letters to Galatia and Rome, where the congregational situations call for it.

Some of what Paul writes in Galatians and Romans about *faith* may have been conveyed during the evangelistic preaching and teaching which he and his colleagues had done in Thessalonica. On that premise, therefore, it may be appropriate to allow some of Paul's other teaching about the nature of Christian faith to inform our understanding of the frequent references to the Thessalonian's *faith*.

Two OT texts profoundly shape Paul's understanding of *faith*: Genesis 15:6 and Habakkuk 2:4. In the story concerning God's covenant with Abraham and Sarah, Abraham responds in faith to the promise that they would have many descendants:

> And he believed the Lord; and the Lord reckoned it to him as righteousness. (Gen. 15:6)

In Galatians 3:6 and Romans 4:3, 16, Paul cites this text as part of his extensive theological argument to show that those like Abraham who believe God's promises are Abraham's true descendants. To believe, therefore, is to trust God and to live confidently and obediently within the covenant offered by God. Since Abraham's justifying faith preceded the implementation of circumcision as a sign of the covenant, Paul argues that *faith* rather than the ritual of circumcision counts before God.

The other prominent text for Paul comes from the prophet Habakkuk, who was active during the rise of the mighty Babylonian empire (ca. 608-598 B.C.). Seeing his tiny nation increasingly under threat, Habakkuk laments God's seeming lack of concern: "Why do you look on the treacherous, and are silent when the wicked swallow those more righteous than they?" (1:13). In his despair about this injustice, Habakkuk experiences a vision from the Lord which he was asked to broadcast on the national billboards:

> Look at the proud! Their spirit is not right in them, but the righteous live by their faith. (2:4)

Even when their situation seems hopeless, the people of Judah are urged not to be overwhelmed by the menacing threats of the proud Babylonians but rather to trust God, for "the righteous live by their faith."

In his letter to the Christian community in Rome, Paul incorporates part of Habakkuk's reassuring vision in his thesis statement. Paul speaks of the gospel as God's power for salvation for all who believe (Rom. 1:16) and adds,

> For in it the righteousness of God is revealed through faith for faith; as it is written, "The one who is righteous will live by faith." (1:17)

Much of the rest of Romans is devoted to an explication of this theme. Because space does not allow a survey of that discussion, we can let Paul make his own summary statement, as indeed he does in Romans 3:21-26. How can people know "the righteousness of God"? According to the NRSV translation, God's righteousness is made known "through faith in Jesus Christ for all who believe" (3:22). The KJV says that God's righteousness comes "by faith of Jesus Christ unto all and upon all them that believe." In this case the KJV has captured a distinction which modern translations have included only in footnotes. God's righteousness has been disclosed to the world supremely by the faith of Jesus Christ. Not (human) faith "in Jesus Christ," but the faith and faithfulness "of Jesus Christ" provides the conclusive window on God's righteousness—God's vindicating power which brings justice and makes things right. In trust and obedience, Jesus went to the cross. Yet God vindicated Jesus by raising him from the dead! Human faith is therefore a grateful, trusting, and obedient response to this marvelous unveiling of God's redemptive justice made known in Christ.

In sum, when Paul sends Timothy to establish and encourage the Thessalonians *for the sake of [their] faith* (3:2), he does so to urge them to continue to remain faithful and trust God to preserve them in their affliction.

THE TEXT IN THE LIFE OF THE CHURCH
The Faithfulness of the Martyrs

Nothing creates more anguish in the hearts of loving parents than to know (or suspect) that their child is suffering. In 1 Thessalonians 2:7, 11, Paul portrays himself to the Thessalonians as their nursing mother and encouraging father. In 2:17 a striking change of metaphor allows Paul to show the depth of his distress at being separated (*orphaned*) from them. Paul realizes that these new believers are being persecuted and fears that these afflictions might jeopardize their faith. So he desperately wants to be with them again. This longing is fed by his fervent desire to root their faith in the faithfulness of Jesus and the trustworthiness of God.

During the first few generations of the Anabaptist movement, similar dramas played themselves out in many house churches and within numerous families. Husbands wondered about the fate of wives held captive for their faith. Wives left alone with little children longed for information about their husbands in prison.

Paul wrote letters to the Thessalonians to convey his feelings and prayers in their behalf; these letters became part of the NT. Many early Anabaptists also wrote letters, and some survive to the present. Many moving letters from this period were compiled by van Braght in the *Martyrs Mirror.*

Believers in other parts of the world often still face persecution for their faith. For most believers in North America, including those in churches tracing their roots back to the Anabaptist and radical pietist movements, the prospect of suffering for the Christian faith seems remote. In a seductive culture, whose influences shape us either subtly or overtly, we can learn by listening to the witness of fellow believers from the past, whose surrounding culture was not as tolerant as ours.

A woman named Adriaenken wrote to her husband while awaiting her execution by burning in 1572. The stirring testimony of this sixteenth-century sister illustrates both love for family and steadfast faithfulness, which characterized a host of martyrs for the faith. Adriaenken opens by saying, "I can never thank the Lord of lords enough for His daily greatness in showing His grace . . ." (cf. 1 Thess. 3:9, *What thanksgiving can we offer to God?*). Then she begins to address her husband:

> I your dearest, beloved wife and sister in the Lord, could not well forbear, but must leave your love, a few lines in remembrance of me, on account of the great love which we have had to each other, and which I hope will

abide forever, and no one shall separate us from it, and though we are separated from each other according to the eternal body, yet love remains. (*Martyrs Mirror:* 926)

Turning her attention to the riches available in Christ, Adriaenken urges her husband to share this faith with others:

But it is not expedient that we keep this joy to ourselves alone, but that we spread the same, so that you, my dearest on this earth, and all the God-fearing, if it were possible, might also rejoice, in order that you, my especially beloved husband, and all the God-fearing, may steadfastly persevere, and not be afraid. (926)

As she nears the conclusion of this moving letter, Adriaenken keeps insisting that God is faithful and true and gracious:

Herewith I will commend you my dearest husband and beloved brother in the Lord, to the Almighty God, and to the rich Word of His grace, which is able to build you up, to keep from evil and to bring you to the eternal inheritance; there I hope to see you with eternal joy, to which end the good God grant His grace. Amen. (927)

The farewell letter from Adriaenken's husband is also included in the *Martyrs Mirror* and shows their mutual affection and concern:

Farewell, and pray the Lord for me, that He may keep me in this evil time, that I may always walk in the way of the Lord. I also pray for you, that the Lord will grant you strength, that you may be an acceptable offering unto Him, and that through your bonds and through the voluntary surrender of your body into the tyrants' hands, many may come to the truth. (929)

Hearing these voices from the past, we who also seek to follow in the footsteps of Jesus are encouraged to be equally faithful in our time. This woman and her husband may well be able to supply what is lacking in our faith. Indeed, the challenges which lie before us may require that we exercise similar diligence in our battle with the wily tempter.

1 Thessalonians 3:11-13

Pastoral Prayer

PREVIEW

A cry of thanksgiving (3:9) and a prayer-report (3:10) have already introduced a prayerful mood even before the intercessory "wish-prayer" with which this part of the letter now concludes (Wiles: 52-63).

In terms of epistolary analysis, this wish-prayer serves as a transition from the letter body (2:1—3:10) to the exhortation (4:1—5:22). Within categories suggested by rhetorical analysis, there is a comparable transition from *narratio*, a narration of the grounds for thanksgiving to God, to *probatio*, which focuses on the kind of behavior which is praiseworthy for participants in God's reign (Jewett, 1986:72-76). *[Rhetorical Analysis, p. 352.]*

This wish-prayer reviews what has preceded and previews what follows:

3:11	recapitulates	2:17—3:10	return visit
3:12	recalls	2:1-12	apostolic model
	and anticipates	4:9-12; 5:12-22	love
3:13	anticipates	4:1-8	holiness
	also anticipates	4:13—5:11	the parousia

EXPLANATORY NOTES

As shown above, this wish-prayer both summarizes earlier themes
and anticipates subjects still to be addressed:

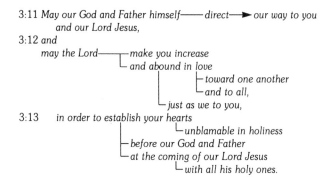

Paul addresses the first part of the prayer to God, here designated
as *our God and Father* (a frequent combination in the NT, as in
1 Thess. 1:3; 3:13) combined with *our Lord Jesus Christ* (3:11). Here
and in 2 Thess. 2:16, Paul mentions a prayer addressed to Christ.
Commentators differ on the question of whether this may point to
Paul's trinitarian beliefs:

> Either God the Father or the Lord Jesus may be the recipient of prayer,
> but this does not imply Paul held a Trinitarian or Binitarian theology.
> (Best: 147)
> There could hardly be a more impressive way of indicating the lordship of
> Christ, and His oneness with the Father. (Morris: 69)

For Paul and his co-workers, God and Jesus are viewed as dynamically one. Despite the plural subject, the verb *direct (our) way* is singular. Thus the text apparently supports an understanding of basic unity
between God and Jesus.

Paul's prayer recalls his often-stated longing to return to Thessalonica (2:17; 3:10). When he prays that God might *direct* (literally:
straighten out) *our way to you* (3:11), Paul could mean either that
God might direct his journey (cf. Rom. 1:10) or remove the obstacles
which have been preventing his return.

The second petition is addressed to *the Lord* (3:12, meaning Jesus, who is called *Lord* in 1:1, 3, 6; 3:11, 13). Paul prays that the
Thessalonian believers might *increase and abound in love*. These
two verbs cumulatively emphasize the superabundance of love which

Paul desires for these people. Paul has earlier acknowledged that the Thessalonians do love (1:3), and now he prays that their love *toward one another* might grow. Later he will urge that they express their love toward each other more and more (4:9-10).

This prayer for greater love envisions not only the Christian community itself but also the people beyond: *and to all* (cf. also 5:15). After Paul has prayed that the Thessalonians might show greater love both toward insiders and outsiders, he once again offers himself as an example: *just as we to you*. Paul's exemplary love is documented by his motherly and fatherly manner of relating to them and the sacrifice he has made in working *night and day* for his own support (2:1-12). So the imitation motif appears here once again (cf. 1:6; 2:14). How should the Thessalonian believers love? Their love should overflow toward others even as Paul loves them!

The exhortation in 4:9-12 regarding *love of the brothers and sisters* lends concreteness to this prayer for greater love. As we shall see, the members of the Christian community in Thessalonica are urged to share their resources with each other. Rather than viewing the Christian life as an ecstatic escape from responsibility, they are urged to share deeply and lovingly with each other.

The outcome for which Paul prays in behalf of the Thessalonians is that they will be firmly rooted: *in order to establish your hearts* (3:13). The *heart* in Hebraic thought connotes the whole person but especially the understanding, will, and emotion. However, the accent lies not on their inner disposition of faith but on their morality and ethics. Here Paul introduces the theme of holy living, developed in the upcoming exhortation (4:1-8). The phrase *unblamable in holiness* anticipates the agenda of *your sanctification* (or *holiness*) in 4:3. Here again (cf. 3:9) is the reminder that life is lived in the presence of God: *before our God and Father*.

But not only must life be lived in the awareness of the presence of God. The nearness of *the coming of the Lord Jesus with all his holy ones* adds urgency to the ethical appeal. The theme of the *coming (parousia) of the Lord Jesus*, introduced in 2:19, reappears here at the conclusion of the first half of the epistle (1:1—3:13). In the second half of the letter (4:1—5:28), this theme is picked up in a major way (4:13—5:11).

Who are the *holy ones* or *saints* (3:13)? Some suggest that Paul here cites Zechariah 14:5. If so, the *holy ones* are angels (as in 2 Thess. 1:7) who accompany God, the Son of Man, or the Lord Jesus during appearances to deliver or judge (cf. Deut. 33:2; Dan. 7:9-27;

8:13; Matt. 24:31; 25:31; Mark 8:38; Jude 14). However, here Paul more likely anticipates the gathering of living believers with their risen Lord accompanied by *all his saints* (NRSV), as dramatically pictured in 1 Thessalonians 4:15-17. This would agree with 2 Thessalonians 1:10, where the expression *holy ones* stands in parallel to *all the believers*.

THE TEXT IN THE BIBLICAL CONTEXT

The Parousia

Even when reviewing past events and giving counsel regarding the present, the authors of these two letters to the church at Thessalonica consistently maintain an orientation toward the future. The Thessalonian believers have been called into God's kingdom and glory (2:12), and they await God's Son from heaven (1:10). The technical term frequently employed to describe that anticipated event appears here at the climax of Paul's wish-prayer: *the coming* or *parousia* (3:13; cf. 2:19; 4:15; 5:23).

Parousia simply means *presence* or *coming*. Paul expresses his gratitude for the *parousia* or "coming" of Stephanas (1 Cor. 16:17) and of Titus (2 Cor. 7:6-7) and speaks of his own coming or presence (2 Cor. 10:10; Phil. 1:26; 2:12). In the Roman world of Paul's day, the arrival of an emperor to a city on an official visit was called a *parousia*. Since civic leaders wanted to be ready for the emperor's arrival, they urged citizens to prepare by cleaning up and decorating their city. Christians used this same word to describe their expectation of the *coming of our Lord Jesus with all his holy ones* (3:13). In Latin, the equivalent word is *adventus*. The English term *Advent* therefore appears on the Christian calendar to describe the *coming* of Christ as a child in Bethlehem. During the season of Advent, churches also typically emphasize the second Advent, the anticipated coming of Christ as triumphant Lord. *[Eschatology, p. 355.]*

In Paul's letters, the word *parousia* points to the (second) *coming* of Christ only in the Thessalonian letters (texts listed above, plus 2 Thess. 2:1, 8) and once elsewhere (1 Cor. 15:23). In 2 Thessalonians 2:9, this term also depicts the deceptive activity of Satan. In the Gospels, only Matthew reflects Jesus' use of this term. The disciples ask, "When will this be, and what will be the sign of your coming?" (Matt. 24:3). Then Jesus teaches about "the coming of the Son of Man" (Matt. 24:27, 37, 39). Elsewhere in the NT, the word *parousia* appears in James 5:7-8; 1 John 2:28; and 2 Peter 1:16; 3:4, 12.

However, the expectation of the *coming of the Lord Jesus with his holy ones* pervades most of the NT. Writers draw on other vocabulary to express this hope, including simply *the Day* or *the day of the Lord* (1 Thess. 5:2, 4; 2 Thess. 2:2). Also used is the language of epiphany: "the manifestation of our Lord Jesus Christ" (1 Tim. 6:14; 2 Tim. 4:1; cf. Titus 2:11, 13); and of revelation: "the revealing of our Lord Jesus Christ" (1 Cor. 1:7; cf. 2 Thess. 1:7). Nowhere in the NT does the adjective *second* modify *coming* or any of the equivalent expressions, although the writer of the epistle to the Hebrews comes close to the notion of a second coming:

And just as it is appointed for mortals to die once, and after that the judgment, so Christ, having been offered once to bear the sins of many, will appear a second time, not to deal with sin, but to save those who are eagerly waiting for him. (Heb. 9:27-28)

When reading the NT, we are repeatedly made aware that the early church fervently awaited the triumphant coming of Christ as Lord. The most moving testimony to this eager longing during the first few generations of the church is the fact that an Aramaic prayer surfaces untranslated in Paul's letter to the church at Corinth: *Marana tha*, which means "Our Lord, come!" (1 Cor. 16:22). In this prayer we can hear the earliest Jewish believers within the church give voice to their hope for the consummation of God's reign through the return of Christ!

In the book of Revelation, this prayer in translated form echoes throughout John's climactic concluding vision. The risen Christ alerts the faithful with the refrain: "See, I am coming soon!" (Rev. 22:7, 12). The church in turn longingly prays, "Come!" (22:17). After a final warning to those who hear these words of prophecy (22:18-19), the prophet John concludes, "The one who testifies to these things says, 'Surely I am coming soon' " (22:20a). John responds, "Amen. Come, Lord Jesus!" (22:20b).

THE TEXT IN THE LIFE OF THE CHURCH
The Pastoral Prayer and Worship

The attitude of expectation in this wish-prayer can shape the pastoral prayer as well as the worship service as a whole. When believers know they are called to live in the tension between the "already" and the "not yet" of the coming of the Lord Jesus, the gatherings for worship will also be characterized by expectancy: "Come, Lord Jesus!"

In this wish-prayer, Paul models in a beautiful way what role the pastoral prayer can play in the life of the congregation. Gathering up concerns of people in the congregation, the person offering the pastoral prayer can both recall the past and anticipate the future. In this way, people gathered for adoration and praise and for instruction and upbuilding can also be led in priestly intercession and petition.

The format of this first letter to the Thessalonian believers can serve as a guide for what happens when a congregation gathers for worship. Thanksgiving (1:1-10) and a review of the individual and collective faith stories (2:1—3:10) might precede the pastoral prayer (3:11-13). After that, there would be an occasion for further teaching and preaching designed to supply what is still lacking in their faith, love, and hope (4:1—5:22). With another prayer, the holy kiss, and a benediction (5:23-28), another congregational worship gathering would come to a close!

1 Thessalonians 4:1—5:22

Steadfastness of Hope: Pastoral Exhortation and Encouragement

OVERVIEW

Paul and his companions have been rehearsing the story of the emergence of the church in Thessalonica, giving particular attention to their relationship as missionaries to that group of believers. The mood of these reminiscences has generally been friendly and upbeat. By means of rich family metaphors, this letter conveys an atmosphere of genuine affection and concern between these missionary pastors and their people.

By the time of the writing of this letter, Timothy has already completed a return visit to Thessalonica. Paul has not yet found it possible to go. For both Paul and Timothy (and presumably also for Silvanus), the letter serves as a substitute for another face-to-face pastoral visit. The writers have devoted the first part of the letter to reestablishing personal contact with these new believers. Now they shift from recalling their past associations to offering them ethical and pastoral encouragement for situations being confronted in the present.

Traditional analyses of Paul's letters have often identified separate sections devoted respectively to doctrine and to ethics. For example, the extended theological discourse in Romans 1–11 is followed by ethical exhortation in 12–15. However, such neat distinctions between theology and ethics have been shown to be unworkable, even in letters like Romans and Ephesians. In 1 Thessalonians, a definite transition point has been reached at 4:1, but 1:1—3:13 has the character of narrative rather than doctrinal instruction. Furthermore, although the section 4:1—5:22 contains ethical and pastoral exhortation, it likely has more theological content than do the first three chapters. In addition, implicit behavioral appeal comes through in the passages with the imitation motif (especially *you became imitators of us and of the Lord*, 1:6) and with the extended discussion of missionary goals, motivations, and strategies (2:1-12).

As already mentioned, the wish-prayer of 3:11-13 provides a bridge between the letter body (2:1—3:10) and the exhortation (4:1—5:22). Paul's often-stated desire to return to Thessalonica (2:17; 3:10) is recapitulated in the wish that God might *direct our way to you* (3:11).

Several new themes introduced in the wish-prayer are now developed in the last half of the letter (4:1—5:22). After a general pastoral exhortation and a reminder of their past instructions (4:1-2), Paul and his co-workers identify a series of ethical and pastoral concerns. First they speak to some sexuality issues (4:3-8). A key word here is *holiness* (4:3-5; cf. 3:13). Next they focus on several practical aspects of their life as a Christian community, including the need to continue working, both for self-support and community maintenance (4:9-12). A key word here is *love* (4:9; cf. 3:12). A third major area is introduced with a reference to the community's grief at the death of some of their members (4:13-18); the *coming (parousia) of the Lord* receives prominent attention here (cf. 3:13). Fourth, the evangelists address the subject of *the times and the seasons* (5:1-11), teaching about the timing of *the day of the Lord* (5:2-3) and admonishing the Thessalonian believers to conduct themselves as *children of the day* (5:4-10). Finally, Paul and his partners offer a series of exhortations designed to strengthen their life and witness as a Christian community (5:12-22).

OUTLINE

4:1-8   Holiness in Relationships,
4:9-12   Love in Community
4:13-18   Always with the Lord!
5:1-11   The Times and the Seasons
5:12-22   Life and Leadership in the Community

1 Thessalonians 4:1-8

Holiness in Relationships

PREVIEW

Sex has been on the human agenda ever since the garden of Eden. First-century Thessalonica was no exception.

The first major block of material containing ethical instruction expands on one of the specific wishes articulated in the wish-prayer of 3:11-13. Apparently at least some of the Thessalonians are standing at risk in the area of sexual attitudes and conduct. One of the reasons for Paul's eagerness to return to Thessalonica seems to be to intervene pastorally in this area of their lives, as he says, *to establish your hearts unblamable in holiness* (3:13). The word *hagiasmos*, translated either *holiness* or *sanctification*, occurs three times in these eight verses (4:3-4, 7). However, this section does not describe *holiness* in general terms. The question of what *holiness* looks like in the realm of sexuality preoccupies the writers at this point in their letter.

Paul has depicted himself as a little child (2:7), a nursing mother (2:7), a father (2:11), and an orphan (2:17). Now he explicitly speaks out on issues related to sexuality, marriage, and family. The kinship theme already introduced through this rich array of metaphors is therefore amplified by a discussion of the personal and communal dimensions of holy faithfulness in sexual relationships.

This brief section begins with general exhortation (4:1-2), then moves to a specific call to sexual faithfulness (4:3-6a) and a statement concerning the motivations for ethical conduct (4:6b-8). The word *holiness* appears in the primary ethical statement in 4:3, in the exhortation of 4:4, and again in the motivation section of 4:7, thereby lending unity to this paragraph.

Once again it is apparent that Paul is not declaring or demanding anything new. As made explicit in 4:1-2, 6, the moral and ethical dimensions of the Christian life have already been addressed during the initial proclamation of the gospel in Thessalonica.

OUTLINE

A Reminder of Earlier Teaching, 4:1-2
A Call to Sexual Faithfulness, 4:3-6a
Motivations for Ethical Conduct, 4:6b-8

EXPLANATORY NOTES

A Reminder of Earlier Teaching   4:1-2

Echoes of earlier instruction can be detected throughout the pastoral exhortation section of the letter (4:1—5:22). This compares well with frequent references in the narration of 2:1—3:10 to shared experiences and convictions, often conveyed by statements like *You yourselves know* (2:1). This introductory paragraph appeals to these new converts to recall what Paul and his co-workers have taught them about conduct befitting believers:

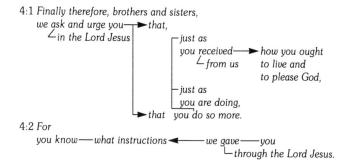

The formula *finally therefore* in 4:1 signals the transition to ethical injunctions (cf. 2 Thess. 3:1; 2 Cor. 13:11; Phil. 3:1; 4:8). For the seventh time in this letter, the writers employ the intimate familial address, *brothers and sisters*. Their affection and warmth is expressed anew at the point where they repeat some hard-hitting advice on moral issues.

Paul and his companions do not demand compliance. Instead, they extend an appeal: *We ask and urge you* (4:1). Elsewhere in the letters to the Thessalonians, the first of these verbs, *ask* (*erōtaō*), introduces the admonition concerning appropriate attitudes toward leaders within the congregation (5:12), and it begins the strongly worded warning not to get carried away by those who claim that the day of the Lord has already come (2 Thess. 2:1). The second verb, *urge* (*parakaleō*, also translated *appeal* or *beseech*) occurs repeatedly in Paul's letters to introduce personal appeals or ethical admonitions (1 Thess. 4:10; 5:14; Rom. 12:1; 15:30 16:17; 1 Cor. 1:10; 4:16; 16:15; 2 Cor. 10:1-2; Philem. 10).

A distinction Paul makes in the short letter to Philemon is instructive here. Pleading in behalf of the slave Onesimus, Paul declares that in Christ he would have the boldness to command. But then he adds, "Yet I would rather appeal (*parakaleō*) to you on the basis of love" (Philem. 9). In similar fashion, Paul and his co-workers, writing to the believers in Thessalonica, employ urgent persuasion but refrain from laying down the law. The phrase *in the Lord Jesus* clearly shows how this exhortation is conveyed. It is based on the relationship to Jesus Christ shared by these new believers and the missionaries who have communicated the gospel to them.

The writers do not immediately impart specific ethical advice. First they remind their Thessalonian readers concerning what they had already been taught (4:2). The language used here communicates the fact that moral exhortation was part of the gospel package from the beginning. The formula *you received from us* (NRSV: *you learned from us*) is reminiscent of 1 Corinthians 11:23, where Paul brings to mind the story of Jesus' last meal: "For I received from the Lord what I also handed on to you." Already in (1 Thess.) 2:13, Paul thanks God for the way in which the Thessalonians have heard the gospel message: *receiving the word which you heard from us, you accepted it . . . as the word of God.* Here in 4:1 Paul invites the Thessalonians to recall the ethical instruction which he and his partners imparted during their initial visit. Stories about Jesus (1 Cor. 11:23-25), the gospel proclamation (1 Thess. 2:13), and ethical instruction (4:1)—these are separate but related components of the rich heritage of faith transmitted by the missionaries to the people.

Here the accent lies on the ethical heritage transmitted to these new believers: *how you ought to live and to please God* (4:1). Personal acceptance of the gospel cannot be separated from the accompanying *ought*, namely a life of obedience. Even this response, however, needs to be recognized as related to the energizing word of God at work in the community of believers (as also noted in 2:13). This responsive ethic is described in two general ways. The first expression *to live* (*peripatein*, literally *to walk*), comes from Paul's Jewish background, in which halakah (from the Hebrew *halak, walk*) prescribes conduct appropriate for the covenant people. Similar language has already appeared in 2:12, where the Thessalonian believers were given fatherly encouragement to live according to the vision of God's reign: *that you walk worthy of God's kingdom and glory.*

Here in the beginning of the exhortation section (4:1-12), variations of the word *walk* occur two times in addition to the one currently under discussion. In 4:1 Paul affirms the Thessalonians for the level of faithfulness with which they already conduct themselves. Following the specific ethical advice in 4:3-8 and 4:9-12, the Thessalonians are urged to consider the impact of their Christian *walk* on outsiders (4:12). In other words, the ethical teaching in 4:1-12 has been bracketed by these reminders concerning how believers ought to live in the tension between the "already" and the "not yet" of God's reign.

Another phrase enlarges the big picture within which the ethical instruction is to be regarded. The responsive *ought* defines holy living as behavior which aims *to please God* (4:1). Having *turned toward God*, the Thessalonians have also been taught what it means *to serve the living and true God* (cf. 1:9). As Paul and his partners rehearse their motivations for preaching the gospel, they claim to be moved by a desire *to please God who tests our hearts* (2:4). Here, in introducing the subject of morality, they associate Christian conduct not with a view to attaining perfection, nor with the intention of living strictly by a set of rules, but with pleasing God, in grateful response to God's love and call.

A pastoral aside communicates the missionaries' affirmation of faithful conduct already demonstrated: *just as you are doing* (4:1). Like loving but firm parents who first compliment their children before they scold them for their behavioral shortcomings, these missionary pastors affirm their converts for signs of faithfulness and then urge them to *do so more*. By living more faithfully, they would please God more fully. At the beginning of the letter, their *work of faith, labor of love, and steadfastness of hope* has occasioned thanksgiving (1:3). Now they are exhorted to continue to grow.

A reminder of former ethical teaching follows: *For you know what instructions we gave you* (4:2). The noun *instructions* (*parangelias*), often used for military orders, refers here to ethical guidelines associated with the gospel. Elsewhere in the NT, this word occurs only in Acts 5:28, "strict orders," and in 1 Timothy 1:5, 18, "instruction(s)." The related verb *parangellō* appears frequently. Paul parallels the thought here in a letter to Corinth, as he introduces advice concerning marriage and divorce: "I give this command [*parangellō*]—not I but the Lord" (1 Cor. 7:10-11). Ultimately, the authority for these guidelines comes not from the apostles personally but *through our Lord Jesus.*

A Call to Sexual Faithfulness 4:3-6a

An exceedingly complex sentence follows. It consists of a leading general assertion concerning *the will of God*, followed by five infinitive clauses whose meanings and relationships to each other are often difficult to disentangle:

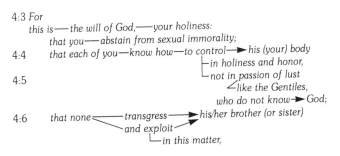

```
4:3 For
      this is——the will of God,——your holiness:
            that you——abstain from sexual immorality;
4:4         that each of you—know how—to control➤ his (your) body
                                              ├─in holiness and honor,
4:5                                           └─not in passion of lust
                                                  ⟋like the Gentiles,
                                                  who do not know➤ God;
4:6      that none⟍——transgress——➤his/her brother (or sister)
                    ⟍and exploit⟋
                         └─in this matter,
```

Scholars debate whether this section reflects general moral exhortation or whether an actual situation in Thessalonica is being addressed (Yarbrough: 65-68). If we could know what Timothy reported upon coming back to Paul after his return visit to Thessalonica, it would be easier to reconstruct the possible meaning of this instruction. Because Thessalonica had a seaport, we can surmise that prostitution and other forms of illicit sexual activity might have presented a continuing distraction or temptation for recent converts. Sexual themes were also prevalent within the mystery religions, such as the cults of Dionysus and the Cabiri, from which at least some of the converts had likely come. Some of these cults featured orgiastic rituals and promised ecstatic union with the deity through intercourse with temple prostitutes. [*Religions in the Greco-Roman World, p. 365.*] Perhaps one sign of the radicalism of a few new believers in Thessalonica was a doctrine of sexual freedom within the new age introduced by Christ.

Even without any specific reports about sexual immorality among the Thessalonian believers, Paul might have chosen to underscore earlier moral instruction. New believers could easily be tempted to return to former patterns of life. Likely Paul and his partners also feel constrained especially to help the Gentile converts gain a sense of their new identity as distinguished from their compatriots *who do not know God* (4:5).

The leading statement introduces the general theme: *For this is the will of God, your holiness* (4:3). Having characterized Christian conduct as that which pleases God (4:1), Paul now defines it in terms of *the will of God*. Those who know themselves as chosen and loved by God (1:4) and have turned to God (1:9) will also desire to serve God (1:9) and live in a worthy manner (2:12). We are reminded of the petition in Jesus' prayer, "Your will be done," which follows the hallowing of God's name and the longing for the coming of God's reign (Matt. 6:9-10).

Singled out for particular elaboration within the broad theme of God's will is the motif of *holiness* (*hagiasmos*, as also in 4:4, 7). *Hagiasmos* can mean either *sanctification*, with an emphasis on the ongoing process of becoming *holy;* or *holiness*, the outcome of this process. Normally Paul uses a related word *hagiōsunē*, also translated *holiness*, when he has the result of the process in mind (3:13; 2 Cor. 7:1; Rom. 1:4). Here in 4:3-8, Paul has in view the dynamic process of becoming holy or behaving in a holy manner in interpersonal relationships.

Significantly, the letter's concluding wish-prayer picks up this thread, utilizing the verb *hagiazō*, meaning *sanctify*: *May the God of peace sanctify you to be whole* (5:23). If Paul were asked whether God does the sanctifying or whether somehow people sanctify themselves, he would likely reply with a "both and." The God who calls people to holiness both enables them to live holy lives and invites a life of moral responsibility. Sanctification is God's work. Yet people also need to make choices toward holiness and ethical accountability in their daily lives and put forth effort to *do so more* (4:1; "Sanctification and Holiness" in TBC below).

The general assertion that God desires *holiness* introduces a series of five infinitive clauses through which the relevance of *holiness* for daily living begins to be made explicit. First: *that you abstain from sexual immorality* (4:3). People desiring to follow God's will for holy living need to refrain from *sexual immorality (porneia)*. The Greek word *porneia* can have the restricted meaning of *fornication* or sexual intercourse between a man and a woman not married to each other (so NRSV; cf. 1 Cor. 5:1; Matt. 5:32; 19:9; probably also Acts 15:20, 29; 21:25). *Porneia* can also refer to *sexual immorality* more generally, including any kind of illicit sexual relationship (so NIV; cf. possibly Gal. 5:19; 1 Cor. 6:13,18; 7:2; Eph. 5:3; Col. 3:5). In 1 Corinthians 5, Paul cites a particular case of *sexual immorality* involving a man and his father's wife, but we are not told whether an actual case in Thessalonica is being addressed here.

Although there were exceptions, Gentile standards of sexual conduct were generally lower than those prescribed within Jewish communities. Paul seems intent on impressing upon the Thessalonian converts, both Jewish and Gentile, the need to avoid any sexual activity which departs from God's norm of holiness in human relationships. The verb *abstain* occurs frequently in early ethical teaching which admonishes believers to steer clear of forbidden activities or objects (cf. 5:22; Acts 15:20, 29; 1 Pet. 2:11). One such taboo was *sexual immorality*, concerning which Paul now proceeds to make additional comments.

The second and third of the five infinitive clauses are linked together (4:4). In the NRSV this verse reads as follows: *that each one of you know how to control your own body in holiness and honor.* However, translations vary widely, because most of the key words in this verse present major puzzles. Especially difficult are the three Greek words which the NRSV renders *know how to control your own body.* To decipher this part of the sentence requires that meanings of individual words be determined on their own and in light of the contribution these potential meanings might make in the whole passage.

Here are the main possible translations of the three problematic words:

eidenai:	*to know how, know (sexually), respect*
ktasthai:	*to control, obtain, possess*
skeuos:	*vessel, wife, body, sexual organ*

What are Paul and his associates talking about here?

We begin our discussion of the disputed words by looking at the Greek word *skeuos*. At the literal level, *skeuos* simply means *object* (Mark 11:16; Heb. 9:21) or more specifically *vessel* or *jar* (Rom. 9:21). In the present passage, *skeuos* obviously has a metaphorical meaning, but which one? Three possibilities are suggested:

wife (as in 1 Pet. 3:7, where the wife is called *the weaker skeuos*, and the
husband presumably is also a *skeuos*);
body (as in 2 Cor. 4:7, where Paul asserts that heavenly treasure is stored
in his earthly *skeuos*); or
male sexual organ (as in the Septuagint [LXX] version of 1 Sam. 21:5-6,
where David when asking the priest for holy bread assures him that
his men have abstained from sexual intercourse).

In this verse, most English versions have opted for either *wife*
(RSV, TEV) or *body* (NIV, NRSV, NEB, JB) but then typically have
given the other as an alternate reading. The NAB has (*guard his*)
member. The KJV retains the literal *vessel*, thereby leaving it to the
interpreter to supply the meaning, as indeed was the case for the
original readers as well! The exegetical studies by Collins
(1984:299-325) and Yarbrough (68-87) both review the history of
interpretation and argue that *skeuos* here means *wife*. Commentators Bruce (1982:83) and Wanamaker (151-153) weigh the evidence and settle for the meaning of *body* in its sexual dimensions.

The confusion concerning the meaning of *skeuos* is not apprecia-
bly diminished by turning our attention to the infinitive *ktasthai*,
which can mean

obtain (as in Ruth 4:5, 10, LXX, where buying a field and acquiring a wife
are part of the same deal);
possess (the same general meaning but with the accent on the ongoing
arrangement between a man and his woman); or
control (in the sense of "gain mastery over," thereby taking the action to
apply to oneself rather than to another person).

Translations vary, depending in part on how *skeuos* is rendered:
RSV has *take a wife*, and TEV has *live with his wife;* while NIV,
NRSV, NEB, and NAB favor *control* or *gain mastery over*. One of the
main considerations in deciding between these several possible
meanings is whether Paul might be envisioning the wife as personal
property of the man or as an object to be used for the husband's sexual gratification. That question needs to be addressed by examining
Paul's other writings on this theme ("Wife or Body?" in TBC below).

The meaning of the leading infinitive *eidenai, know* has been less
disputed, even though several competing options have been proposed. In the OT, *know* (Hebrew *yada'*) occurs frequently as a euphemism for sexual intercourse. However, the Septuagint quite consistently employs for this a synonym also translated *know* (*gnōnai/-
ginōskein*, as in Gen. 4:1; cf. Matt. 1:25) rather than *eidenai*. Accordingly, the translation *know* (*sexually*) likely does not apply here.

Some interpreters have pointed out that in 1 Thessalonians 5:12, Paul employs *eidenai* in the sense of *respect* (for the leaders in the community) and suggest that this meaning might fit here. However, it seems best to go with the most straightforward meaning: *that each should know how*. This applies equally well to the various possible understandings outlined above.

In sum, and anticipating further discussion ("Wife or Body?" in TBC below), we propose that Paul urges the Thessalonians *that each of you know how to control his body in holiness and honor* (4:4). The masculine possessive pronoun *his* need not imply that only males are being addressed. NT language, though often male-biased, includes women as well. The NRSV appropriately renders this phrase as *your body*. For both men and women, conduct in the area of sexuality needs to be shaped by the desire to reflect God's will (4:3). Paul knows that a dynamic commitment to God-pleasing holy behavior in interpersonal relationships will result in personal *holiness*. However, not only *holiness* but also *honor* is in view (cf. Rom. 1:24-27, RSV, where Paul characterizes certain sexual activities as dishonorable).

In a further effort to depict holy and honorable sexual behavior among believers, Paul contrasts that lifestyle with general behavioral patterns often prevailing outside the church: *not in passion of lust like the Gentiles who do not know God* (4:5). Paul seems to reflect a typically Jewish caricature of pagan morality, such as portrayed in the apocryphal book Wisdom of Solomon 14:22-26. In so doing, he reminds the Gentile converts in Thessalonica that they have both *turned away from idols* and *turned toward God* (cf. 1:9). Such separation from idol worship also calls for sexual behavior which distinguishes them from those Gentiles who do not yet know or acknowledge God. Later Paul elaborates on this theme in Romans 1:18-32, where he identifies pagan idolatry as the root of degrading lustful passions (so also does Wisd. of Sol. 14:27-30).

Yet Gentiles would not necessarily recognize themselves in this Jewish caricature of their sexual patterns. For example, some Stoic philosophers also consider lustful passion to be immoral, but from a different premise. To Stoics, the fact that sexual desire does not submit readily to human reason makes it immoral. [*Philosophies*, p. 364.] For Paul, *passion of lust* is immoral not because it defies reason but because it contradicts God's will and violates the holiness which God desires in human relationships (Collins, 1984:316).

The next infinitive clause also presents ambiguities: *that no one transgress and exploit his brother in this matter* (4:6a). At issue is the phrase which is here translated *in this matter*, a reading which implies that the subject of the previous verses continues *(in the matter at hand)*. Some interpreters have insisted that the agenda has shifted to the realm of economics, in which case the text could read, *that no one transgress or exploit his brother in business*. Is Paul warning about cheating sexually or cheating financially? Most likely the agenda continues to be sexual relationships. It is hard to imagine that a new subject such as business ethics would have been introduced so abruptly into a sentence obviously dealing with sexual norms.

Because the reference here is to the exploitation of a *brother*, a few have seen this as a veiled condemnation of homosexual activity (Yarbrough: 75-76). However, such an understanding of the passage cannot be established. Most likely this verse continues to address the Thessalonians on the topic of holiness in (hetero)sexual relationships. After Paul teaches that believers must know how to exercise control over their bodies (4:4) rather than give in to lustful passions (4:5), he then mentions social implications of sexual infidelity. Adultery involves more than the two who engage in intercourse outside of a marriage covenant. When committing adultery, one also sins against the spouse of the partner in adultery.

Motivations for Ethical Conduct 4:6b-8

Paul mentions three motivations which should move the Thessalonians to abide by the moral guidelines which he has articulated: the judgment, God's call to holiness, and the gift of the Holy Spirit.

```
4:6 for
    the Lord——(is)——executor of justice
                     └—in all these things,
              just as we forewarned——▶ you
                    and testify solemnly,
4:7 for
    God———has called——▶ us
           ├─not for uncleanness
           └─but in holiness;
    4:8 consequently
      the one who disregards (this)——disregards◀ not a human being
                                              ◀ but God,
                                  └─who gives——▶ his Holy Spirit
                                         └─to you.
```

The first motivation comes immediately following the admonition concerning adultery, but the phrase *all these things* shows that this solemn reminder applies to all forms of sexual immorality: *for the Lord (is) executor of justice in all these things* (4:6b). *The Lord* can be understood to refer either to God (generally in LXX, as in Ps. 94:1, which Paul might have had in mind here) or to Jesus as God's instrument of judgment (cf. 2 Thess. 1:7-8; 2 Cor. 5:10). Likely Paul and his partners would not have made such a distinction. Jesus is depicted as the deliverer from coming wrath (1:10) but also as the one inflicting vengeance on those who do not know God nor obey the gospel (2 Thess. 1:8). Here Paul conveys the sober truth that God in Christ will ultimately judge people who act immorally or abusively in their sexual relationships.

The prospect of divine judgment on immoral behavior has also been communicated earlier during the evangelists' initial visit in Thessalonica (cf. 4:2). This reminder has a strikingly solemn tone: *just as we forewarned you and testify solemnly.* The earnestness of this clause adds to the suspicion that Timothy might have reported to Paul about one or more instances of sexually immoral behavior in Thessalonica.

After Paul has mentioned God's judgment as a warrant for maintaining holy behavior in interpersonal relationships, he approaches the subject positively. Why should a believer be careful to observe appropriate boundaries in interpersonal relationships? Paul expresses himself in terms of God's call: *for God has not called us for uncleanness but in holiness* (4:7). Earlier in the letter, Paul rehearsed his fatherly exhortation in general terms: *that you walk worthy of God, who calls you into his kingdom and glory* (2:12). Here God's calling is put more specifically. Essentially, Paul here echoes his lead assertion: *This is the will of God, your holiness* (4:3). However, he amplifies by contrasting *holiness* with what in the realm of sexual behavior is its opposite: *uncleanness.* Paul emphatically asserts that believers are called to avoid sexual immorality. Believers have not been called *for* (such) *uncleanness.* Instead, they have been called *in holiness.* The *in* conveys the notion that the Thessalonians have been called into that realm within which God's sanctifying work takes place.

With this third allusion to *holiness* in 4:3-8, Paul mentions God's Spirit, which is holy (4:8). But Paul does so as part of his final plea to the Thessalonians to conduct themselves in a God-pleasing manner.

Paul alerts his readers to the reality of divine judgment (4:6b), reminds them of God's call (4:7), and then sends another strong signal about the consequences of defying the moral guidelines he has given. In the final reckoning, the Thessalonians will not be answerable to the missionary pastors whose instructions have been conveyed in person and by letter. Ultimately, they need to deal with God: *Consequently the one who disregards this disregards not a human being but God* (4:8). The principle underlying this claim is that Paul and his companions have conveyed God's word through their preaching and teaching in Thessalonica and now also in their letter. Those who reject their message, including the instructions concerning appropriate behavior in the area of sexual relationships, actually reject God.

A note of grace emanates from this final solemn refrain. A holy God desires holiness of life and executes judgment on those who unrepentantly engage in immoral behavior. Yet God is also the gracious Giver, *who gives his Holy Spirit to you* (4:8). The Thessalonians had originally heard the gospel *in power and in the Holy Spirit* (1:5). In their initial experience as believers, the Holy Spirit inspired joy despite their affliction (1:6). Here Paul reminds the Thessalonians that, through the same Holy Spirit, God will enable them to live faithful and holy lives in their sexual relationships.

THE TEXT IN THE BIBLICAL CONTEXT
Sanctification and Holiness

A glance at the Holiness Code in Leviticus 17–26 can help to provide the larger picture within which the concern for personal holiness in 4:3-8 can be understood. At the heart of the Levitical guidelines for the people of Israel is the concern to distinguish them from their neighbors. Israel, a holy people set apart by their relationship to a holy God, must avoid certain sexual activities practiced among other peoples.

Moses receives instructions from the Lord to speak these words to the people of Israel:

> I am the Lord your God. You shall not do as they do in the land of Egypt, where you lived, and you shall not do as they do in the land of Canaan, to which I am bringing you. (Lev. 18:2b-3)

Throughout Leviticus the refrain recurs: "I am the Lord your God." For example, this formula or the shorter, "I am the Lord," appears some fifteen times in chapter 19 alone. In one case the people are reminded: "I am the Lord your God, who brought you out of the land of Egypt" (19:36).

Along with this oft-repeated identification of "the Lord your God" comes a solemn call to holiness:

> You shall be holy, for I the Lord your God am holy. (19:2; 20:26)

The God who rescued the people of Israel from oppression in Egypt and established a covenant with them at Sinai is presented as the living norm guiding the conduct of the people. However, the Israelites are not just commanded to be holy. They are assured that God also does a sanctifying work among them:

> Consecrate yourselves therefore, and be holy; for I am the Lord your God. Keep my statutes, and observe them; I am the Lord; I sanctify you. (20:7-8; cf. 21:8, 15; 22:9; Exod. 31:13)

Amid a chorus of such reminders about the identity, holiness, and sanctifying activity of God, one finds a host of prescriptions concerning holy conduct along with consequences of violating these ritual and moral guidelines. Many of these laws prohibit certain kinds of sexual relations: with members of the immediate family (Lev. 18:6-18, 20); during menstruation (18:19); male homosexual activity (18:22); intercourse with animals (18:23). Leviticus announces severe punishment for those guilty of violating these laws; the death penalty is imposed in cases of adultery, bestiality, and male homosexual relations (20:10-21).

The prophets enlarge this vision of a holy God, who calls the people to be holy, by showing that holiness goes beyond keeping oneself separate from the world and unstained by its corruption. Overwhelmed by God's holiness and his own uncleanness, Isaiah experiences God's forgiveness and then feels himself summoned to prophesy to his people (Isa. 6:1-8). Speaking to those of his generation "who have despised the word of the Holy One of Israel" (1:4), Isaiah defines holiness more in terms of justice than purity:

> Wash yourselves; make yourselves clean; remove the evil of your doings from before my eyes; cease to do evil, learn to do good; seek justice, rescue the oppressed, defend the orphan, plead for the widow. (Isa. 1:16-17)

Isaiah's contemporary, the prophet Hosea, transcends the strict Levitical code through an acted parable which dramatically demonstrates God's mercy and steadfast love. Hosea hears God's pledge of renewed betrothal with Israel, who is portrayed as an unfaithful bride:

And I will take you for my wife forever; I will take you for my wife in righteousness and in justice, in steadfast love, and in mercy. (Hos. 2:19)

To underscore this prophetic vision of God's love and mercy, Hosea takes back his adulterous wife, "just as the Lord loves the people of Israel, though they turn to other gods" (Hos. 3:1). Jesus taught his disciples to pray, "Our Father in heaven, hallowed be your name" (Matt. 6:9; cf. Luke 11:2). In Jesus' prayer for his disciples as recorded in John's Gospel, he addresses God as "Holy Father" (John 17:11). The synoptic Gospels testify that unclean spirits recognized Jesus himself as "the Holy One of God" (Mark 1:24; Luke 4:34). However, despite these themes reminiscent of the emphases in Leviticus, the Gospels generally portray Jesus' activity and teaching within the larger picture presented by the prophets. Instead of repeating the holiness formula of Leviticus ("You shall be holy, for I the Lord your God am holy"), Jesus points to God's mercy and perfection as the model and motivation for the disciple's conduct:

Be merciful, just as your Father is merciful. (Luke 6:36)
Be perfect, therefore, as your heavenly Father is perfect. (Matt. 5:48)

This call to perfection can best be understood as fullness or completeness, a virtue imparted by God and expressed through compassion, mercy, and blessing.

Yet Jesus is not silent about the need for personal holiness. One of the Beatitudes addresses "the pure in heart" (Matt. 5:8; cf. 5:28-30). However, Jesus' knowledge of God's holiness leads him to redemptive engagement with tax collectors, prostitutes, and other sinners. Jesus, confident that divine holiness has the power to transform lives, associates with the unclean, the immoral, and even the enemy, and he teaches his followers to do so as well. God's holiness calls for merciful and redemptive encounter with sinners rather than stark separation from them.

The NT pastoral letters written to congregations in cities such as Corinth and Thessalonica frequently remind new believers about the need for holiness. These believers are often called *saints* (literally: *holy ones*), even in Corinth, where Paul needs to confront blatant immorality (1 Cor. 1:2; 2 Cor. 1:1). These new converts are reminded that God calls for personal holiness and that transgression will lead to judgment (as in 1 Thess. 4:3-8). They are also taught that God sanctifies in Christ (1 Cor. 1:30; Eph. 5:26; Heb. 10:10) or by the Holy

Spirit (1 Pet. 1:2). Yet believers are not seen as passive recipients of God's gift of holiness but rather as active participants in God's sanctifying work in their lives (Rom. 6:19, 22; 2 Cor. 7:1; Heb. 12:14). In 1 Peter (1:16) a citation of the Levitical holiness code, "You shall be holy, for I am holy," serves as scriptural warrant for affirming both the grace and the demand inherent in the gospel (note especially 1:13-21). God, who calls people to holy living, both graciously empowers them to live in that way and invites them to make choices in line with God's will for holiness.

Sexuality

The beginning of the biblical narrative celebrates the creation of humankind as the climax of God's handiwork. Male and female together in relationship reflect the image of God (Gen. 1:26-27). Within the Creator's design, one aspect of this experience of community between men and women expresses itself in marriage. After recording the man's jubilant song upon being introduced to the woman (2:23), the Genesis narrative continues:

> Therefore a man leaves his father and his mother and clings to his wife, and they become one flesh. (2:24)

Both Matthew and Mark report that, when Jesus was asked about the legality of divorce, he cites both of these Genesis texts as foundational for understanding the meaning of marriage (Matt. 19:4-5; Mark 10:6-8). The "one flesh" ideal of marital unity presented in the creation account also appears in Ephesians 5:31, a discussion of the relationship between husband and wife, and in 1 Corinthians 6:16, the denunciation of sexual intercourse with a prostitute.

Following the creation story, the biblical drama as it unfolds provides glimpses into both the beautiful and the abusive dimensions of male-female relationships. On the one hand, Genesis delights the reader with the story of how Isaac meets Rebekah (Gen. 24). The book of Ruth provides fascinating details about the events which lead to her marriage to Boaz. And the Song of Solomon features the romantic poetry of playful and passionate lovers.

Yet Genesis also discloses the sordid and abusive side of sexual relationships: the threat of both homosexual rape and heterosexual abuse in Sodom (Gen. 19:1-26), a case of incest involving Lot and his daughters (19:30-38), the rape of Dinah (34), and Judah's duplicitous affair with his widowed daughter-in-law Tamar (38). King David lusts after Bathsheba, commits adultery with her, and then in an attempt to cover up this affair, arranges for her husband Uriah to be killed (2 Sam. 11). The book of Proverbs warns about both seductive women and adulterous men and depicts the consequences of becoming entrapped through lack of sexual restraint (Prov. 6:20-35). Perhaps the most notable positive model of virtuous behavior within a sexually charged situation is that of Joseph in Egypt, who resists the seductive advances of Potiphar's wife and then endures imprisonment because of her retaliatory accusations against him (Gen. 39).

These realistic biblical stories leave no doubt that the Jewish people also dealt with sexual immorality in their own midst. Gentiles were not the only ones with real life X-rated stories. Even strong separatist measures, such as Ezra's "class action" divorce of all foreign wives (Ezra 10), would not succeed in stopping the erosion of moral values.

During the Greek period, some Jews living in the diaspora viewed idolatry as the root cause of immorality among Gentiles. The Wisdom of Solomon, an apocryphal document which probably emerged in Egypt during this time, provides a graphic portrait of pagan conduct, which includes "confusion over what is good, forgetfulness of favors, defiling of souls, sexual perversion, disorder in marriages, adultery, and debauchery"(14:26). All of this is blamed on their worship of idols (14:27). Similarly, Paul in his letter to the Romans lists perversions: "impurity" and "the degrading of their bodies among themselves" (Rom. 1:24), "degrading passions" (1:26), and "every kind of wickedness" (1:29). He attributes them all to the fact that "they [the Gentiles] exchanged the glory of the immortal God for images" (1:23). However, Paul employs this traditional Jewish caricature of paganism to set a rhetorical trap whereby his Jewish readers essentially pass judgment on themselves, since (as he says) "You, the judge, are doing the very same things" (2:1). [*Judaism in the Diaspora, p. 363.*]

In their letter to the Thessalonians, Paul and his companions address a predominantly Gentile group, using language more readily understood by the Jewish minority. However, these believers, both Gentile and Jewish, are summoned to a chaste lifestyle which contrasts with the lustful passions of those *Gentiles who do not know God* (4:5). Truly to know God is also to seek to live in God-pleasing ways (4:1) and to be guided by *the will of God* (4:3). The Thessalonians have *turned toward God* and *away from idols, to serve the living and true God* (1:9). A life conformed to God's will for holy liv-

ing in male-female relationships becomes a vivid testimony to the
believer's commitment of faith.

Wife or Body?

To the church in Corinth, Paul writes at some length concerning sexual conduct. In the debate about 1 Thessalonians 4:4, certain parallels with 1 Corinthians 6–7 are often cited. Did Paul intend to exhort
the Thessalonians that *each one of you know how to take a wife for
himself?* (RSV). Or did he urge that *each one of you know how to
control your own body?* (NRSV). In support of the former, scholars
often mention parallels with 1 Corinthians 7:1-7; in agreement with
the latter, they note 1 Corinthians 6:12-20. We turn briefly to a con-
sideration of these two texts, in which Paul responds respectively to a
question from the Corinthians (7:1-40) and some disturbing reports
about sexual misconduct in that congregation (5:1—6:20).

Paul responds to a report about a case of blatant immorality in
Corinth (1 Cor. 5:1), prescribes firm discipline (5:2-5), and warns
about the insidious effect of tolerating such evil in the Christian community (5:6-8). He continues by clarifying his instructions in an earlier letter not to associate with immoral persons (5:9-13); such separation is not mandated generally but only toward "anyone who bears
the name of brother or sister who is sexually immoral"(5:11). After
dealing briefly with the issue of litigation (6:1-8), Paul returns to the
topic of sexual behavior. He warns that persons guilty of various
kinds of deviant conduct (primarily in the sexual realm) "will not in-
herit the kingdom of God" (6:9-11). What follows then is Paul's response to ways in which some Corinthians rationalize their practice
of going to prostitutes (6:12-20).

Some members of the first-century Corinthian church apparently
operate on the premise that there is nothing wrong with having intercourse with a prostitute, because in the realm of the spirit, the body
ultimately doesn't matter (1 Cor. 6:12-13). Paul counters with a
strong claim that the body indeed does matter:

> The body is meant not for fornication but for the Lord, and the Lord for
> the body. (6:13b)

Paul notes the resurrection of Christ and the future resurrection of
the believer (1 Cor. 6:14) and points to the stark incongruity of being
united in body with both a prostitute and with Christ (6:17). He
pleads:

Shun fornication! Every sin that a person commits is outside the body; but the fornicator sins against the body itself. (6:18)

As additional basis for this plea and this claim, Paul offers two further reasons and then articulates his bottom-line appeal:

Do you not know that your body is a temple of the Holy Spirit within you, which you have from God, and that you are not your own? For you were bought with a price; therefore glorify God in your body. (6:19-20)

Through the redemptive work of Christ (cf. 6:11), the believer as body, soul, and spirit belongs to God (cf. 1 Thess. 5:23). This calls for a disciplined commitment to faithfulness in the sexual realm. Thus Paul admonishes, *Control your own body in holiness and honor* (1 Thess. 4:4, NRSV).

In 1 Corinthians 7:1, Paul begins to consider several matters about which the Corinthians have written him, including an opinion expressed by some in Corinth: "It is well for a man not to touch a woman." Paul himself practices celibacy and advocates it for others as well (7:7). It is therefore likely that some members of the Corinthian community have taken this advice and are promoting sexual abstinence even within marriage. The specific cases of immoral sexual activity already mentioned, incest (5:1) and going to a prostitute (6:16), could be reflex actions of persons whose marriage partners unilaterally espouse sexual abstinence. Paul hastens to correct this misunderstanding:

But because of cases of sexual immorality, each man should have his own wife and each woman her own husband. (7:2)

Paul goes on to elaborate mutual conjugal rights of both husband and wife within marriage (1 Cor. 7:3), for which each has authority over the body of the other (7:4). Paul notes that in order to devote themselves to prayer, the couple might refrain from sexual intercourse but only by mutual consent and for a limited time; otherwise their self-control might not be adequate to resist the temptation to indulge in illicit sex (7:5).

Those who favor taking *skeuos* as *wife* in 1 Thessalonians 4:4 generally argue that Paul's counsel in 7:2 supports that understanding. However, in 7:2 Paul explicitly addresses both husband and wife rather than obliquely advising the husband to take a wife for himself. One might object that Paul undervalues marriage, since he seems to depict it as a second-rate option for those who cannot control their sexual impulses. However, Paul here vigorously promotes mutuality between husband and wife, at least in their roles as sexual partners. This militates against any reading of 1 Thessalonians 4:4 which suggests that for Paul the husband acquires a wife as his property or possesses his wife for his own sexual gratification. In their sexual relationships within marriage, both husband and wife need to exercise control over their bodies, so that each can both *have* the other and *have authority over* the body of the other when by mutual desire and consent they engage in the act of intercourse.

THE TEXT IN THE LIFE OF THE CHURCH
What Do You Think of Sex?

Myron Augsburger told a group of men on retreat about a question posed by a civic leader in a city where he had been engaged in a preaching mission: "What do you think of sex?"

"I'm for it!" Myron responded, adding, "Sex is one of God's good gifts. That is why I want to do nothing that will cheapen it."

Advertisers know that sex gets people's attention. Sex sells. The world of entertainment also capitalizes on the lure of sexual themes. One wonders, In the sexually charged atmosphere created by film and fashion, does the biblical call for holy relationships stand a chance?

But the sobering sexual realities also grab attention. Allegations of incest, sexual harassment, and various forms of sexual abuse make headlines, even in church papers. AIDS and other sexually transmitted diseases have at the time of this writing reached epidemic proportions in some areas of the world. Again one asks whether the biblical vision for holy faithfulness and mutual caring in interpersonal relationships can still catch on.

As already mentioned, the biblical stories in their realism portray both the joy and the pain of male-female relationships. The biblical drama incorporates both the sensual dance of lovers (Song of Solomon) and the scandal of a man involved in a sexual relationship with his stepmother (1 Cor. 5). The one invites celebration, the other calls for grief and repentance. In the history of the church, believers have often been reluctant to celebrate sexuality wholeheartedly as one of God's good gifts. The church's response to those whose actions cheapen this good gift has also been mixed. Sometimes the church has been too legalistic, at other times too tolerant.

A Resolution on Human Sexuality passed by the General Conference Mennonite Church during the Saskatoon conference in 1986 reflects some careful discernment concerning both biblical teachings and current realities. Neither 1 Thessalonians 4 nor any other biblical text is explicitly cited, but this statement seeks to present some of the issues. We select several in an effort to summarize briefly.

Under "Our Affirmation" the statement includes reasons that believers can joyfully celebrate their sexuality:

> We affirm that sexuality is a good and beautiful gift of God, a gift of identity and a way of being in the world as male and female.
> We affirm that sexual drives are a real part of our lives, but that the satisfaction of those drives is not the chief good in life.

This resolution also confesses and repents:

> We repent of our wrong view of the body which keeps us from speaking openly and honestly about our bodies, including our sexual nature.
> We repent of our permissiveness which too often leads to premarital and extramarital, sexual relationships.

In the preamble to a section entitled "Our Covenant" the statement includes some basic understandings concerning sexual relationships:

> We understand the Bible to teach that sexual intercourse is reserved for a man and a woman united in marriage and that violation of this teaching is a sin. It is our understanding that this teaching also precludes premarital, extramarital, and homosexual activity. We further understand the Bible to teach the sanctity of the marriage covenant and that any violation of this covenant, including spouse abuse, is sin.

In subsequent discussions of this resolution and the subject it addresses, premarital and extramarital sex has not received as much attention as homosexual activity. All these practices fall short of the biblical call to sexual holiness.

Paul's moral counsel to the believers in Thessalonica has particular relevance for the church in confronting both the glamour and the gloom of present-day sexual realities. Our sexuality is God's gracious gift. When experienced in holiness and honor, this gift can enrich and delight. When indulged in lustful passion, this gift returns to exact a penalty.

The solemn and stern biblical warnings about judgment need to be heard more clearly again, but without self-righteousness. Though God is merciful, our holy God also calls for holiness. Choices which violate God's intention will ultimately lead to judgment.

On this delicate balance between God's mercy and God's judgment, we hear a word from the sixteenth-century Anabaptist Hans Denck. He responds to a query from some Reformers:

> But did not David in the Old Testament and the Corinthian in the New, even after being enlightened, commit adultery, and were they not nevertheless received again by God, even though they had been rejected for a time?

To this suggestion that in the mercy of God, adultery and other sexual transgressions are "no big deal," Denck replies:

> Woe to him who knows God and is slave to the flesh. God is indeed merciful, and one reads that he has accepted many great sinners. But however merciful he is, one nevertheless reads of few who, after acknowledging the truth, sinned and were received back again. These are held before us as examples in order to fear, not to despise, his wrath and to praise, not sin against, his mercy. (Bauman: 139)

1 Thessalonians 4:9-12

Love in Community

PREVIEW

Having dealt with sex, Paul and his companions turn to the topic of love.

Love of the brothers and sisters (*philadelphia*, 4:9) has not been mentioned in this letter earlier. However, their *love* (*agapē*) has come up for a few comments. The Thessalonians' *labor of love* provides occasion for thanks (1:3), and the good news about their continuing *faith and love* brings profound relief (3:6). In the wish-prayer (3:11-13), which serves as bridge between the opening narration (1:2—3:10) and the exhortation (4:1—5:22), Paul mentions his desire that they might love each other more: *May the Lord make you increase and abound in love toward one another and to all* (3:12).

The introductory exhortation formula of 4:1 is echoed in a simpler form at 4:10b: *But we urge you, brothers and sisters. . . .* This is not an announcement of a new topic but rather the introduction to a heightened appeal on the topic of love in the church. Admitting that the Thessalonians have already learned to love one another (4:9-10a), Paul encourages them to do so still more (4:10b; cf. 4:1). What follow are several specific admonitions (4:11) and the rationale for heeding them (4:12).

The subjects raised in this brief paragraph receive more attention in 2 Thessalonians. In their second letter to the church in Thessalonica, Paul, Silvanus, and Timothy express gratitude that the Thessalonian believers have grown in their love for each other (1:3). However, they also feel constrained to speak more sternly to those members who apparently have not heeded their earlier more gently worded practical counsel (3:6-13).

OUTLINE

Love for Brothers and Sisters, 4:9-10a
Exhortation to Love More, 4:10b-11
Reasons for the Exhortation, 4:12

EXPLANATORY NOTES
Love for Brothers and Sisters 4:9-10a

Paul and his companions again first affirm their readers and then encourage further growth (cf. 4:1):

> 4:9 *Now concerning*——*love of the brothers and sisters,*
> *you do not need*——*(us)*——*to write*——*to you,*
> *for*
> *you yourselves*——*are*——*God-taught to love*——▶*one another,*
> 4:10 *and*
> *you do*——▶*this*——*to all the brothers and sisters*
>   └——*in all Macedonia.*

The introductory expression *now concerning* is identical to the one Paul employs on six occasions in 1 Corinthians to introduce new topics: 1 Cor. 7:1, 25; 8:1; 12:1; 16:1, 12. In the first of these, Paul refers to a letter from Corinth: "Now concerning the matters about which you wrote" (7:1). It is generally recognized that Paul in 1 Corinthians addresses successively several questions which that letter from Corinth has raised, regarding marriage, food offered to idols, spiritual gifts, the collection, and Apollos. In 1 Thessalonians, Paul uses the same formula when introducing the subjects of *love of the brothers and sisters* (4:9) and *the times and the seasons* (5:1). Hence, some writers suggest that these issues have also been raised in a letter to Paul from Thessalonica, presumably delivered by Timothy (Faw, 1952). However, no such letter is explicitly mentioned. It is equally likely that Paul here and throughout 4:1—5:22 simply addresses some of the concerns which Timothy has reported to him orally.

Outside the NT, the term *philadelphia* almost always refers to the affection between blood brothers and sisters. Intimate family language, especially *brothers and sisters*, is often used metaphorically in 1 Thessalonians to describe relationships between members of the Christian community ("Brothers and Sisters, Child, Mother, and Father" in TBC for 2:1-12). Similarly here, Paul utilizes *philadelphia* in a metaphorical sense to describe Christian *love of the brothers and sisters* (cf. also at Rom. 12:10; "Love One Another" in TBC below).

Instead of repeating the usual *as you know* or other similar reminders of their previous instruction or the Thessalonians' prior knowledge (as in 2:1, 5, 9; 4:2), Paul here says: *you do not need (us) to write to you*. Such expressions are typical of ancient letters in which affirmation of the present knowledge of the recipients becomes the basis for encouraging greater diligence in putting that knowledge into practice (Stowers: 103).

On what basis does Paul claim that the Thessalonians do not need to have anything further written to them about love within the Christian community? Paul's explanation is intriguing: *You yourselves are God-taught to love one another* (4:9). The Greek word *theodidaktoi*, literally *God-taught* (*taught by God*, NRSV), occurs here for the first time in known Greek literature. Malherbe suggests that this word may have been coined by Paul, perhaps to differentiate himself from the philosophy of Epicurus, who claimed to be self-taught (Malherbe, 1989:63-64). *[Philosophies, p. 364.]* Some commentators suggest that Isaiah 54:13, quoted in John 6:45, might have been in Paul's mind: "All your children shall be taught by the Lord" (Bruce, 1982:90; Wanamaker: 160).

Paul does not elaborate, so we can only guess what he meant. Likely he is recalling their initial preaching as evangelists in Thessalonica. This preached word, which the Thessalonians received as *the word of God* (cf. 2:13), might have included reference to Jesus' love commandment (Mark 12:31 and parallels; John 13:34; echoed by Paul in Rom. 13:9) or the OT text on which this commandment was based (Lev. 19:18). Another possibility is that Paul here anticipates his emphasis in later letters on love as one of the fruits of the Holy Spirit (Gal. 5:22; Rom. 5:5).

Paul hastens to add that indeed the Thessalonians already do love their brothers and sisters in the faith: *you do this to all the brothers and sisters in all Macedonia* (4:10a). In 1:7-8, Paul and his co-workers comment that the Thessalonians have been a positive example to the believers in Macedonia as well as Achaia, and that the word of the Lord has sounded forth from them into Macedonia and beyond. The Thessalonian converts have apparently also developed a ministry of hospitality and other practical helpfulness toward their fellow believers within their own province of Macedonia. The urban congregation in Thessalonica was well positioned to share their homes with Christian travelers visiting the city on business. Likely such visitors joined their community meals, including the love feast, during which the Thessalonian congregation celebrated the Lord's Supper (so Jewett, 1994:84-86).

Exhortation to Love More   4:10b-11

Paul has asserted that the Thessalonians have no need for further teaching about love within the Christian community. Nevertheless he proceeds to write some more on this topic anyway! Readers almost two millennia later often wish that he had written still more:

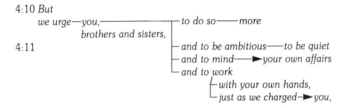

```
4:10 But
      we urge—you,——————————— to do so——more
             brothers and sisters,
4:11                              ├ and to be ambitious——to be quiet
                                  ├ and to mind——►your own affairs
                                  └ and to work
                                        ├ with your own hands,
                                        └ just as we charged—►you,
```

Further encouragement on the subject of the Thessalonians' love for each other is introduced with the formulaic expression, *But we urge you, brothers and sisters* (4:10b). This echoes and recalls the longer appeal formula with which the pastoral exhortation section begins: *Finally, brothers and sisters, we ask and urge you in the Lord Jesus . . .* (4:1).

The content of Paul's appeal is given in a succession of four infinitive clauses, the first of which simply calls the Thessalonians to a greater love for each other: *We urge you to do so more* (4:10b). This is reminiscent of 4:1, where the Thessalonians are first affirmed for how they live and please God and then exhorted to *do so more*. With regard to both holiness in sexual relationships and filial love within the Christian community, Paul first affirms and then with gentle but firm prodding urges greater faithfulness.

In the other three infinitive clauses Paul becomes more specific (4:11). First, he urges the Thessalonian believers *to be ambitious to be quiet.* Paul paradoxically calls for an ambitious pursuit of quietness! Next, Paul counsels the Thessalonians: *Mind your own affairs.*

More specific knowledge concerning the social context of this community of believers in Thessalonica would enhance our understanding of both of these admonitions. In the final infinitive clause, Paul exhorts the Thessalonians: *Work with your own hands.* These words communicate quite unambiguously, but again our interpretation of this advice is shaped by the way we envision the social situation in Thessalonica.

What circumstances within the Thessalonian Christian community might have moved Paul and his companions to admonish these believers to pursue the quiet life, tend to their own business, and to work with their own hands? How might this advice relate to the agenda of sisterly and brotherly love within the Christian community? Several other texts, both in 1 Thessalonians (specifically 5:14) and 2 Thessalonians (especially 3:6-13) directly relate to this question, because they mention *the unruly* (*ataktoi*, often called *idlers*). These texts in general and the matter of *the unruly* in particular require some preliminary attention at this point.

An interpretation of 1 and 2 Thessalonians requires some reconstruction of the circumstances which elicited these letters. The available data do not support any definitive profile of the Thessalonian congregation and its social environment. However, various attempts have been made to visualize the situation on the basis of information at hand. Factors which likely led to the writing of these two letters to Thessalonica have already been reviewed ("Why Were These Letters Written?" p. 28, above). The task here is to focus on possible reasons for this particular concern regarding social conduct and how such conduct needs to be shaped by Christian love.

The situation in Thessalonica which evoked this pastoral counsel has been reconstructed by scholars along two distinct lines: eschatological and socioeconomic.

Many commentators suggest that a group in Thessalonica had been caught up in end-time enthusiasm based in large part on their misunderstanding of Paul's apocalyptic message. Most of these interpreters (Best: 175-176; Bruce, 1982:90-91) posit an overly zealous anticipation of the coming of Christ. According to this reconstruction, enthusiasts in Thessalonica in their excitement have become boisterous and meddlesome in their expectation of Christ's imminent return. They quit working at their ordinary jobs because they anticipated that history would soon climax with the coming of Christ to usher in the kingdom. Their absence from normal work activities soon burdened the rest of the believers, who responded in Christian love by sharing their means with these people whose fanaticism made them destitute. Paul therefore urges this group to become enthusiastically quiet, mind their own business, and go back to work.

Another variant on the eschatological explanation is that a radical group in Thessalonica claims that the day of the Lord has already arrived (Jewett, 1986:168-178). Through ecstatic manifestations of the Spirit, especially prophecy, these radicals became convinced themselves and they sought to persuade others that they were already living in the new age (2 Thess. 2:2). For these enthusiasts, the old structures of everyday life no longer apply, and the standard sexual norms and the normal work ethic are no longer relevant. Apparently they expect that the Christian community will provide for their physical needs. Since they believe they are under the direct influence of the Spirit, they do not think it necessary to pay heed to any human leaders. Jewett equates this group with the *ataktoi* (5:14; 2 Thess 3:6, 11), whom he identifies not as *idlers* but as *obstinate resisters of authority*. Paul appeals to this disorderly group and to the whole congregation, which stands at risk because of their influence, to channel their ecstatic energy to be quiet, to tend to their own affairs, and to work with their hands.

Other scholars insist that the situation in Thessalonica being addressed here has to do not with eschatological views but with the social or economic background and expectations of some of the members of the congregation. These sociological analyses generally compare or contrast Paul's counsel alongside teachings of Greek and Roman moralists and philosophers. *[Philosophies, p. 364.]* Malherbe suggests that Paul employs Epicurean language to urge the believers to avoid the socially irresponsible and meddlesome behavior of the Cynic street preachers. However, Paul also calls on the converts in Thessalonica to earn the respect of the surrounding society rather than adopting the isolationist stance of the Epicurean philosophers (Malherbe, 1987:95-107).

According to Hock, the poor people in the Thessalonian congregation need occupational counseling both to keep them from dangerous or socially inappropriate vocations and to direct them into wholesome trades, especially handicrafts (Hock: 42-47). Russell's analysis also focuses on the urban poor who constitute the majority in the church at Thessalonica. He conjectures that these people have become dependent on well-to-do benefactors who are also participating in the life of the church. This frees them to engage in actively propagating their opinions and religious ideas. Accordingly,

Paul urges these idle poor recipients of Christian charity to stop troubling others but rather to tend to their own upkeep by going back to work in order to become self-sufficient and to model socially acceptable behavior among their neighbors (R. Russell). Jewett considers it more likely that the Thessalonian believers have organized tenement churches, whose gatherings often include a love feast. Food is brought in on a shared basis. Those who refuse to work are thus not able to contribute food for this common meal (Jewett, 1994:84-86).

Which of these reconstructions of the circumstances in Thessalonica is the most accurate? Given the relative lack of firm information, perhaps one simply needs to admit that both eschatological and socioeconomic factors probably have played a part. Gentile converts, who turned from idols, might well be confused at times about the practical ways in which they can serve the living and true God while awaiting God's Son from heaven (cf. 1:9-10). Paul therefore gently reminds them that serving God involves obeying the commandment to love one another. Whether for social or theological reasons or a combination of both, some Thessalonian believers have slipped into a pattern of irresponsible behavior, which left a negative witness in their communities and imposed a financial burden on members of the church. To this group, Paul in essence says that they would show their love for one another most clearly by leading a quiet life, tending to their own affairs, and working with their own hands.

Once more Paul reminds the Thessalonians that he has similarly instructed them earlier: *just as we charged you* (4:1). Of course, Paul and his co-workers have also demonstrated their own willingness to work for their keep so as not to become a burden on the community (2:9). In their second letter, this personal model of self-support is explicitly mentioned to support a strengthened appeal made necessary by apparent aggravation of the problem (2 Thess. 3:7-9).

Reasons for the Exhortation 4:12

Two reasons are given for this kind of quiet social behavior:

4:12   *in order that*
                  you might walk
                        └*properly——toward outsiders*
                  and
                  you might not have————▶ *need.*

In the first place, Paul and his companions assert that unruly and dependent behavior leaves a negative witness in the society at large.

This would be true especially in a crowded urban setting like Thessalonica, where much of daily life is quite public. [*Social and Economic Context, p. 368.*] Therefore, the missionary pastors call for the kind of decorum that will invite respect rather than ridicule from those outside the church: *in order that you might behave properly toward outsiders.* The Greek verb *peripatēte* lies behind the words *you might behave* (literally: *you might walk*). This is a typically Jewish way of describing appropriate conduct ("halakah" as faithful conduct; cf. 2:12; 4:1). However, according to Malherbe (1989:62), the word here translated *properly* echoes Greek philosophical language describing socially appropriate demeanor. In a word, the conduct of believers needs to command respect among their neighbors.

The second reason is stated in terms of the congregation: *that you might not have need.* By tending to their own concerns and working with their own hands, the Thessalonians can become self-sufficient and provide for themselves and their families as well as contribute generously to the common causes of the Christian community. For those unable to work, of course, help would be available as sisterly and brotherly love expressed itself in practical ways within the congregation. The people whose unruly defiance led to unhealthy dependence on others are urged to go back to work. One consequence is that the congregation would become better able to care for those genuinely needing assistance. After all, as recipients of God's love, they have been *God-taught to love one another* (4:9). What better way to show love than to pursue meaningful work and share the proceeds with others through the church?

THE TEXT IN THE BIBLICAL CONTEXT

Love One Another

Paul introduces the agenda of 4:9-12 by employing the term *philadelphia.* This word combines *phil-* (as in *philos,* friend, friendly; *philia,* love, friendship; *philein,* to love) with *adelphos/ē* (brother/sister), to mean *love of brothers and sisters* (NRSV). In his letter to the house churches in Rome, Paul uses this same word again, as part of his exhortation concerning behavior which conforms to "the will of God" (Rom. 12:2). Paul appeals to these believers: "Let love be genuine" (12:9). What follow are some specific prescriptions for life in the Christian community (12:9-13), including a plea for *philadelphia*: "Love one another with mutual affection "(12:10). Other items on this list of guidelines include contributions for needy saints and the practice of hospitality (12:13).

Hebrews 13 also has a list of practical admonitions concerning Christian behavior, and the headline is a call for continued *philadelphia*: "Let mutual love continue" (Heb. 13:1). This list enjoins hospitality to strangers, identification with people in prison, respect for the sanctity of marriage, and unselfish contentment regarding material things (13:2-5). Such attitudes and behaviors seem to be presented as illustrations of genuine brotherly and sisterly love. In 1 Peter 1:22 and 2 Peter 1:7, *philadelphia* connotes genuine and sincere affection among members of the Christian community; both texts also connect this affection to the dominant NT kind of *love*, which is Christlike self-giving *love (agapē)*.

In 1 Thessalonians 4:9, after announcing the subject of *philadelphia*, Paul also shifts to the distinctively Christian notion of *agapē*, the self-sacrificing *love* modeled supremely in Jesus. Specifically, Paul cites the commandment which they have been taught by God, *to love one another.*

This love commandment has clear affinities with Jesus' summation of the law, as recorded both in the synoptic Gospels and in John. When Jesus is asked, "Which commandment is the first of all?" he replies by citing two texts from the law (Deut. 6:5; Lev. 19:18): "You shall love the Lord your God," and "You shall love your neighbor as yourself" (Mark 12:28-31).

According to Luke's account, Jesus also answers a follow-up question: "Who is my neighbor?" (Luke 10:29). This question reflects an ongoing debate in Jesus' time. In Leviticus 19:18 the *neighbor* is understood to be "any [member] of your people," a fellow-Israelite. However, already in Leviticus the love commandment is made to apply more broadly as well:

> The alien who resides with you shall be to you as the citizen among you; you shall love the alien as yourself, for you were aliens in the land of Egypt: I am the Lord your God. (Lev. 19:34)

Jesus' contribution to this debate comes in the form of the parable of the good Samaritan, which understands the commandment "Love your neighbor" in terms of merciful action which transcends ethnic categories and reaches out to foreigners as well (Luke 10:30-37).

The Gospel of John records that Jesus taught his disciples a new commandment: "I give you a new commandment, that you love one another" (John 13:34a). What was new about Jesus' commandment to love? By his life, and especially through his sacrificial death, Jesus

demonstrates the kind of radical love which also needs to characterize his followers:

> Just as I have loved you, you also should love one another. By this every-
> one will know that you are my disciples, if you have love for one another.
> (John 13:34b-35)

The emphasis here and elsewhere in John's Gospel (note especially 15:9-17) is on love expressed within the Christian community.
This is also true of the Johannine letters: 1 John 3:11; 4:7, 12;
2 John 5-6. Nowhere does John specifically reflect Jesus' ethic of
love for the enemy or the alien. For John, the Christian community by
its very nature models an active and unselfish love, a love rooted in
and patterned after Christ, who laid down his life for his followers
(1 John 3:16). Both Jesus and his community of disciples demonstrate the possibility of living for others, without violence or oppression. Such unselfish sacrificial living within the community of believers both indicts and invites. According to John's writings, communities of loving disciples invite others to become God's loving children
as well, but instead, such love often evokes the world's hatred. As David Rensberger puts it, "The community of love stands as witness
against the hatred in the world, and so draws that hatred down upon
itself" (Rensberger: 129).

As already noted, Paul's letter to the house churches in Rome includes some practical guidelines for loving behavior within the Christian community (Rom. 12:9-13). What follows first are specific admonitions urging loving action toward the enemy, thereby leaving vengeance to God and potentially overcoming evil with good
(12:14-21). Second, Paul gives some guidelines on how believers
should relate to governing authorities (13:1-7). After he has elaborated on the character of genuine love within the Christian community
(12:9-13) and in relation to the often hostile world (12:14-21), Paul
returns again in 13:8-10 specifically to the theme of love. Reminiscent of the emphasis in the Gospel of John, Paul says,

> Owe no one anything, except to love one another; for the one who loves
> another has fulfilled the law. (Rom. 13:8)

Similar to the way the synoptic Gospels highlight Jesus' summation of the law, Paul cites several of the ten commandments, asserts
that these are summed up in the word from Leviticus 19:18, and concludes that love for the neighbor fulfills the law:

"Love your neighbor as yourself." Love does no wrong to a neighbor; therefore, love is the fulfilling of the law. (Rom. 13:9b-10)

In 1 Thessalonians 4:9-12, the exhortation to *love one another* seems to be stated primarily in terms of the internal life of the Christian community, like the emphasis in John's Gospel and epistles. Their reputation for hospitality and practical helpfulness is known firsthand among fellow believers throughout their province of Macedonia (4:10). As in the Gospel of John, there is awareness that relationships between members of the Christian community will be observed by the larger society. These patterns of life among believers will elicit either respect and admiration, or suspicion and even hatred. For the sake of their witness in the world around them, Paul urges the Thessalonians to avoid distracting conduct such as noisy enthusiasm or unhealthy patterns of dependency. Mutual self-giving love among brothers and sisters in Christ may also be misunderstood by outsiders, but at least not for the wrong reasons.

In his letter to the Galatians, Paul writes at greater length concerning the model and inspiration for Christian love. Along with an emphasis on freedom comes a corresponding call to exercise Christian responsibility:

Do not use your freedom as an opportunity for self-indulgence, but through love become slaves to one another. (Gal. 5:13)

The model for this love is Christ himself. "The law of Christ" (6:2), though it may be summarized in the love commandment ("You shall love your neighbor as yourself," 5:14), is embodied in Christ's self-giving, especially his death on the cross. Mutual burden bearing within the Christian community becomes a primary witness to this kind of love (6:2), although all members also need to carry their own loads (6:5). Even though God's love in Christ needs to be demonstratively shown to all, the mutual caring and love within the Christian community must come first:

So then, whenever we have an opportunity, let us work for the good of all, and especially for those of the family of faith. (Gal. 6:10)

In Thessalonica, some members have apparently become self-indulgent, expecting that their status as members of the family of faith guarantees that they would be supplied what they need. But Paul counsels them to guard the overall witness of the congregation in its social context and avoid abusing the goodwill of their fellow believers. Thus they need to moderate their expectations of what they might gain from the Christian community and become more responsible contributors themselves.

THE TEXT IN THE LIFE OF THE CHURCH
Community Life and Our Mission

In my study of 1 Thessalonians 4:11-12, I have often sensed that this counsel to the church at Thessalonica must have entered directly into the recipe for community life in the church in which I was raised. I grew up knowing that somehow we were different from *die Englische* (the English). We were "the quiet in the land," who resisted education, did not vote, and stayed away from dances, pool halls, and beer parlors. In addition, we were self-sufficient in significant ways. Mother sewed many of our clothes. More than once, although some neighbors came to help, we took up our tools and enlarged the house to provide space for a growing family. In these and in other ways we tended to our own concerns. We also worked with our hands, milking cows twice daily, seeding and weeding and then digging potatoes on an annual cycle, creating or mending with knitting needles and with hammer and saw.

I cannot recall whether any of the *Reiseprediger* (circuit preachers) who preached at the Bergthal Mennonite Church near Rosthern, Saskatchewan, preached from this text. As a teenager I did not self-consciously analyze their approach to Scripture nor their theology; I had other things on my mind. However, the value of quiet independence and hard work was certainly modeled by our church community.

The quiet and self-sufficient community lifestyle prescribed in 4:11-12 also seems particularly congenial to the way in which certain Amish and Old Order Mennonite groups view Christian faithfulness. There are several striking points of convergence between this biblical passage and the patterns of life in Old Order communities. In an article on what she calls "the rites of the redemptive process," Sandra Cronk has provided a perceptive analysis of the distinctive patterns of life in Old Order communities (Cronk: 5-11). According to Cronk, these patterns (the *Ordnung*, order) have the goal of creating a loving "brotherhood": "They provide the concrete ways in which members embody the goal of loving community" (Cronk: 6). Noting that Jesus' love, expressed through yieldedness and submission, has the power to bring about radical change, the Old Order movement seeks "to incarnate this paradoxical power of powerlessness in its communities" (Cronk: 7).

There are two closely related expressions of this yieldedness (*Gelassenheit*): in submission to God's will, and in relationships between people. First, with reference to God:

> Each person must give up self-will and self-centered desires to follow God. The death of self-will may involve both internal and external suffering. Internally there is a struggle to die to selfish desires. Externally, obedience to God's will may bring persecution. . . . Both internal and external yielding were signs of Christ's path to the cross. (Cronk: 7)

But yielding to God also involves a life of yieldedness toward others:

> The Old Order people reject any form of Christian living which emphasizes abstract belief and says nothing about the way people earn their living, raise their children or furnish their houses. (Cronk: 8)

This theological understanding leads directly to the refusal to cooperate with the military and the reluctance to rely on courts. These are regarded as coercive attempts to achieve national or personal rights. Such activities are considered to be out of harmony with the way of Christ. But this theological understanding also has implications for the community's attitude toward work. Work is not viewed primarily as a way of gaining personal wealth, power, or prestige, but rather as a means of expressing love and creating community. Cronk illustrates:

> Work on the farm creates the space for community life to take place. It provides the everyday activity which binds the family and community together into a system of sharing. Through both the self-yielding and community-building qualities of work, the economic system is transformed from a potentially competitive, self-aggrandizing process into a way of caring for others. (Cronk: 9)

Old Order communities, as analyzed by Cronk; and Old Colony and other Dutch-Prussian-Russian groups, as I have experienced them—all these have sought to maintain separation from the world through distinctive community patterns. The lifestyle advocated by Paul in writing to the Thessalonians certainly appears to provide support for the patterns of community life within some of the "conservative" branches of the Anabaptist and Brethren families.

Where then does this leave us? Personally, I still value "the quiet life," but I have not joined a church community where people shun involvement with the world. I value self-sufficiency, especially in our children, unless it becomes self-centered independence. I no longer work with my own hands, unless pecking at the keyboard of a word processor qualifies. I sometimes wonder whether my grandfather, if he were still living, would realize that he need not have cautioned me against getting an education and moving into the world as teacher and preacher. Or might he be confirmed in his fears?

The "conservers" and the "progressives" in the church, as historian John Friesen describes them, have made different decisions about how to relate to their surrounding cultures:

> From the point of view of the progressives, the conservers have frequently seemed too strongly inward looking, too closed, and lacking a vision to relate to the larger society. From the conservers' own perspective, they have attempted to emphasize the preeminence of faith for all of life, have tried to maintain the structures of community, have sensed the potentially destructive force of individualism, and have been tenacious in maintaining pacifism. ("Conservative Mennonites [Dutch-Prussian-Russian]," ME, 5:199)

Both the words of Paul to the church in Thessalonica and the historical experiences of the church teach us to try to find a healthy balance between the progressive and the conserving impulses at work within our congregations and denominations. Mission, rather than the desire to blend in, should motivate our active involvement in the larger society. A vision for a faithful inviting community needs to guide us when we choose to separate from the world.

Above all, having been *God-taught to love one another*, we need to discern new ways to live together and love each other as Christian brothers and sister. In shaping our communal experiences as congregations in a needy world, we also need to discover fresh avenues for extending hospitality, caring for the sick, and providing for needy neighbors. Will there be a revival of *philadelphia* in our midst?

1 Thessalonians 4:13-18

Always with the Lord!

PREVIEW

When new believers get hit by life's setbacks, they sometimes wonder whether they might have been duped into accepting a faith whose promises are hollow. For the believers in Thessalonica, the unexpected death of loved ones threatens to burst the bubble of their initial enthusiastic acceptance of the gospel.

This first pastoral letter to the Thessalonians here continues in the mode of exhortation (introduced in 4:1-2), but the tone shifts from ethical admonition to pastoral consolation. Having urged the Thessalonian believers to relate to each other in holiness (4:3-8) and Christian love (4:9-12), Paul and his co-workers turn to a third area of concern (4:13-18). It appears that at least some of the believers in Thessalonica are responding with hopeless grief to the death of some of their members (4:13). Instead of reminding the Thessalonians about past instructions (cf. 4:2, 6, 11), the missionary pastors address them concerning their lack of knowledge about the implications of their belief in Jesus' resurrection (4:14). Paul and his companions report a *word of the Lord* with regard to the anticipated scenario for both the living and the dead at the time of the *coming (parousia) of the Lord* (4:15-17). On this basis, they seek to impart comfort to these new believers.

The theme of *the coming of the Lord*, developed in this paragraph, was signaled in the wish-prayer of 3:11-13. Paul and his partners express the hope that the Thessalonians would be established in holiness *at the coming of the Lord Jesus with all his holy ones* (3:13). Already in 1:9-10, the missionaries gratefully rehearse the Thessalonians' conversion experience, which includes hopeful expectation, *to await [God's] Son from heaven.* Paul reviews the circumstances which made it impractical for him to return to Thessalonica and then reminds these believers that he and his fellow evangelists also have something at stake: *For what is our hope or joy or crown of boasting before our Lord Jesus at his coming? Is it not you?* (2:19).

Timothy's return visit to Thessalonica likely alerted him to the fact that these new believers have been dealt a severe setback. They were forced to deal with the stark reality of death. In 4:13-18, Paul and his team pick up this pastoral concern through further teaching about the parousia. In 5:1-11, the eschatological agenda receives further attention. These themes also dominate most of the second letter to this church, especially in 2:1-12. The evangelists are quite concerned about this dimension of the Thessalonians' Christian experience.

OUTLINE

The Grieving and the Dead, 4:13
A Creed and Its Implications, 4:14
A Word of the Lord, 4:15-17
Pastoral Exhortation, 4:18

EXPLANATORY NOTES
The Grieving and the Dead 4:13

A disclosure formula introduces the new agenda: *We do not want you to be uninformed.* Similar language is employed in Paul's other letters when he wants to communicate new or additional information to his readers (Rom. 1:13; 11:25; 1 Cor. 10:1; 12:1; 2 Cor. 1:8). When Paul expresses the wish that his readers should not be ignorant about something, he emphasizes that this is something he definitely wants them to know!

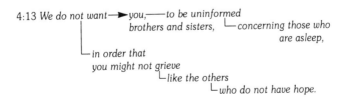

It is significant that, when approaching the tender topic of death, Paul and his missionary partners once again address their readers in familial language as *brothers and sisters.*

Instead of speaking directly about the fact that some Thessalonian Christians have recently died, Paul employs the familiar euphemism of sleep to refer to death and dying. He does not want the surviving members of this faith community to be ignorant *concerning those who are asleep,* in other words, *those who have died* (NRSV). This oblique way of referring to death is employed throughout the biblical story and in other literature as well. The use of the present tense in the phrase *those who are asleep* suggests that, while they are awaiting the resurrection, the dead are somehow in a state comparable to sleep. However, because this mention of *sleep* is metaphorical, it is not appropriate on the basis of this text to draw any particular conclusions about the nature of any "intermediate state" between death and the resurrection ("Those Who Are Asleep" in TBC below).

The missionaries show clearly that they have a pastoral reason for writing to the Thessalonians about the subject of death. They do not include the teaching in this section of the letter to satisfy the Thessalonians' curiosity about the intermediate state nor to answer their questions about the timetable of end-time events. With pastoral earnestness, Paul and his co-workers address these new converts on the topic of death. They also explain why they do so: *in order that you might not grieve like the others who do not have hope.* In their grief over the death of loved ones, the Thessalonian believers are urged to differentiate themselves from *the others.* In 4:5 these *others* are described as *the Gentiles who do not know God.* Here they are depicted as those *who do not have hope.* The text does not prohibit expressions of grief as such. However, the Thessalonian believers' grief need not be characterized by the kind of hopelessness typically felt by their nonbelieving neighbors in the face of death.

What might be the specific circumstances in Thessalonica which evoke this pastoral response? From all appearances, some members of the Christian community have died. Possibly one or more of the Thessalonian believers have died as a result of persecution. Support for this portrayal of the course of events in Thessalonica can be found in Paul's recital of his reasons for sending Timothy on a return mission to that community. Why has Timothy been sent? Paul writes to the Thessalonians explaining Timothy's mission: *to establish you and encourage you for the sake of your faith, that no one might be shaken by these afflictions* (3:2b-3a). At that point in the letter, Paul also offers a few more thoughts concerning persecution. He reminds the Thessalonians of what they have been told earlier: *We are bound to be persecuted.* Significantly, Paul adds *just as has happened, and you know it* (3:4).

It is therefore probable that the Thessalonians are grieving the death of some who have succumbed as a result of persecution. Refusal to participate in the civic cult could easily have provoked both official suppression and mob violence. Any resulting casualties will be devastating to converts who feel that, as heirs of the new heavenly kingdom, they would be spared pain and death.

If indeed these deaths have come as a result of persecution, it becomes clear why there are so many references earlier in the letter to the theme of imitation in suffering. Jesus faced persecution as well! In fact, Jesus had also died. As imitators of Jesus (cf. 1:6), Paul and his fellow evangelists and the Thessalonians themselves could therefore gain strength from the fact that Jesus not only died (cf. 2:14-15), he also rose again (1:10). The attention of the grieving Thessalonians is therefore directed toward what Paul and the other evangelists and theologians of the first century regarded as the turning point of history—Jesus' death and resurrection.

A Creed and Its Implications 4:14

The hope about which the missionaries speak is grounded in the death and resurrection of Jesus. A basic confession is cited as the foundation from which Paul and his companions offer consolation to the Thessalonians in their grief:

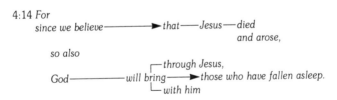

The sincerity of the Thessalonians' convictions concerning Jesus' death and resurrection appears not to have been in question. This conditional statement is best introduced by *since we believe* (NRSV) rather than *if we believe* (RSV). The Thessalonian Christians simply need to be further grounded in the dynamic implications of what they already believe: *Jesus died and arose.*

This conditional clause, *since we believe that Jesus died and arose*, may seem to imply that Jesus raised himself from the dead. However, the verb *arose* (*anestē*) in this confessional statement does not contradict the other affirmation concerning Jesus earlier in the letter: *whom (God) raised from the dead* (1:10). The early Christians had an overpowering awareness that through the resurrection God dramatically reversed Jesus' crucifixion. Thus they confess both that *Jesus arose*, using the verb *arise* (*anistēmi*) with Jesus as the subject (cf. Acts 10:41; 17:3; John 20:9), and also that *God raised him up*, using the verb *raise up* (*egeirō*), where Jesus is the object of God's action (as in Acts 4:10; Rom. 4:24; 8:11). In both cases, however, the primary agent in this dramatic action is ultimately God.

What are the benefits for those who believe that *Jesus died and arose?* With the words *so also*, Paul and his companions begin to reassure the Thessalonians about these benefits. One might expect that this description of consequences would correspond to the opening premise, perhaps as follows: "*so also* we believe that after we die we too will rise." What we have instead is an affirmation which introduces eschatological themes elaborated in the rest of this section: *so also God will bring . . . those who have fallen asleep.*

We need to unravel the theological claims expressed in this part of the sentence so we can isolate the various components and then explore how they are connected.

First of all, *God* is the primary actor in this eschatological drama. This makes explicit what is assumed in the opening conditional clause concerning the resurrection of Jesus, which is also God's act. Second, the recipients of God's anticipated dramatic action are the ones already mentioned in 4:13: *those who have fallen asleep.* The verb used here is the same as in 4:13, but the aorist (past) tense suggests that the reference here is to the actual past event of the deaths of loved ones, which resulted in them being in the state of death (*those who are asleep*: 4:13). Third, what God will do in behalf of those who have died is conveyed by the verb *will bring* (*axei*). God's dramatic action in raising Jesus from the dead also applies to *those who have fallen asleep.* In 4:15-17, the readers are told what it means that *God will bring*; they are informed how God will act in behalf of those believers who have died.

Fourth, the phrase *through Jesus* can grammatically modify either *those who have fallen asleep*, or God's action: *will bring*. If the former, this statement testifies that, at the time of their death, these persons were in communion with Jesus: *those who died as Chris-*

tians (NEB). Such a reading certainly agrees with the designation *the dead in Christ* in 4:16, although it is unclear what it might mean to die *through Jesus*. Could this be an oblique reference to their death as martyrs, through which they imitated the way of Jesus? It is more likely that the phrase *through Jesus* tells how God *will bring* the dead believers (NRSV). According to this reading, Jesus is identified as the agent through whom God will act in gathering those who have died. This view coheres with a prevailing emphasis in Paul's theology: Jesus is the instrument through whom God imparts salvation to humankind (as in Rom. 5:1; 1 Cor. 15:57).

Fifth, the phrase *with him* clearly anticipates the reassuring word with which the eschatological scenario of 4:15-17 concludes: *and so we shall always be with the Lord* (4:17). Jesus, the one who died but then was raised to life again, is presented as God's agent who gathers and accompanies those believers who have died (4:16).

In sum, the consequences of a dynamic belief in Jesus' death and resurrection may be stated as follows: *so also (we believe that) through Jesus, God will bring with him (Jesus) those who have fallen asleep.* What God has done to the crucified Jesus is therefore a foretaste and a guarantee of what God will do to the deceased believers through Jesus at his coming! ("Jesus Died and Arose" in TBC below).

A Word of the Lord (4:15-17)

An explanation follows concerning the dramatic activity projected in the words *God will bring* (4:14). However, first there is a clarification concerning the authority or basis for what the Thessalonians are about to be told:

4:15 *For*
    this ◄———*we declare*————————*to you*
        └*by a word of the Lord*
   that
   we———*shall not precede*———*those who have fallen asleep*
   ├*who are alive*
   └*who are left*
        └*until the coming*
           └*of the Lord,*
4:16 *for*
   the Lord himself—*will descend*┬*from heaven*
          ├*with a cry of command,*
          ├*with the call of an archangel,*
          └*and with the sound of the trumpet*
             └*of God,*

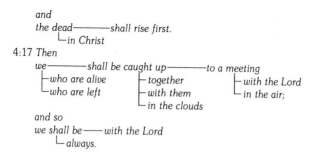

This in 4:15 does not refer back to what has just been said concerning the dynamic implications of Jesus' death and resurrection; instead, *this* points forward to what is now about to be disclosed.

What do Paul and his companions mean by this reference to *a word of the Lord*? Several suggestions have been proposed (summarized in Best: 189-193). First, this might be a saying of Jesus which has not been recorded in this form in any of the Gospels. Second, perhaps this is Paul's summary of biblical apocalyptic passages (such as Daniel 7) and Jesus' teachings on this subject (especially Mark 13:26-27 and parallels). Third, this might be a prophetic utterance inspired by the risen Christ and spoken by a Christian prophet in the early church, perhaps even by Paul himself (cf. 1 Cor. 15:51: "Listen! I will tell you a mystery!").

In the absence of any firm basis for a decision on this matter, it is best to leave the matter open. Each of the three explanations is plausible. Most important is the observation that in speaking a word of reassurance to the grieving Thessalonians, Paul and his co-workers give testimony to the divine origins and therefore authoritative grounding of their pastoral consolation. In 2:13, the evangelists gratefully note that the Thessalonians have accepted their initial proclamation in Thessalonica as *the word of God*. Similarly, here they commend what follows (in 4:15b-17) to the Thessalonians as a consoling message they should accept as *a word of the Lord*.

The first part of this divine consolation (4:15b) addresses what might be at the root of the Thessalonians' dismay and grief. When some members of their community died, the survivors apparently wondered what the status of these deceased believers would be at the coming of the Lord. In this passage Paul and his co-workers divide the people into three groups: first, *those who are asleep* (4:13-15; not the dead in general but specifically *the dead in Christ*, as named in 4:16); second, *we who are alive who are left until the com-*

ing of the Lord (4:15, 17; here the evangelists include themselves); and third, *the others who have no hope* (nonbelievers in Thessalonica, who do not share the Christian hope, identified in 4:13). As part of their pastoral ministry of encouragement, Paul, Silvanus, and Timothy speak to surviving believers about the status of *the dead in Christ*.

The survivors are designated as *we who are alive who are left until the coming of the Lord* (4:15). This text is often cited as evidence that Paul includes himself in this group and thus expects still to be alive at the time of the parousia. Later, when writing to Corinth, Paul appears to accept that he would no longer be alive at that time (2 Cor. 4:14). Paul and his fellow missionaries apparently have taught that the triumphal return of Christ as Lord is near and that they might still be alive at that time. The converts in Thessalonica have come to this conviction, and so they were surprised and upset when some members of their group died before that awaited event. We can imagine that some of these new believers are asking, "Will our loved ones who have died miss out?" Perhaps some even wonder, "Have we been deceived into accepting a gospel whose claims are empty?"

The death of some of the members has brought to light a serious flaw in the Thessalonians' understanding of the new eschatological reality introduced by Christ. At least some have apparently adopted the stance that, through ecstatic identification with the soon-coming triumphant Christ, they would be immune to misfortune and death. But misfortune did strike. Some of their Christian sisters and brothers died. For believers whose worldview had not even envisioned the possibility of such a turn of events, this kind of tragedy threatened to scuttle their faith entirely. Paul thinks they need more teaching about the apocalyptic scenario of *the coming of the Lord*. By speaking to them on their terms, he seeks to correct their flawed understanding about the new reality introduced into the world through Jesus' death and resurrection. More importantly, Paul and his partners approach their questions pastorally, by reassuring the survivors about how the dead will fare when Christ comes as Lord.

The bottom-line good news addressed to the grieving Thessalonian believers is that *we shall not precede those who have fallen asleep*. Expressed otherwise, this means that those who have died will not be left behind nor suffer a disadvantage in comparison with those alive at the time of the climactic coming of Christ. Positively stated, the outcome for those who are in Christ, both the living and the dead, will be the continuation of their communion with Christ: *and so we shall always be with the Lord* (4:17b).

How this is all to happen is explained in 4:16-17a. By means of vivid apocalyptic images, Paul and the other senders of this letter paint a lively picture of this awaited eschatological drama. These events certainly are dramatic! The future intervention of the risen Christ is projected as beginning with a breathtaking descent from heaven. Jesus has ascended into heaven (cf. Acts 1:9-11), where at the right hand of God the Father, he sits exalted (cf. Acts 2:33; Rom. 8:34; Eph. 1:20; Col. 3:1; 1 Pet. 3:22) or stands to receive the martyrs (such as Stephen, Acts 7:55-56). Now Jesus stands ready once again to come down to earth to gather his own! ("Kingdom of God" in TBC for 2:1-12; "Parousia" in TBC for 3:11-13).

A dramatic arrival of the Lord from heaven, complete with accompanying audio-visual effects, begins the series of eschatological events: *for the Lord himself will descend* (4:16). *The Lord himself* (*the Lord Jesus Christ*; cf. 1:1) appears in triumph as the one leading the ingathering of the saints, both the living and the dead. Addressing the Thessalonians in their excessive grief, the missionary pastors direct attention to the near future activity of Jesus Christ their exalted Lord. They urge the Thessalonian converts, who have *turned toward God away from idols to serve the living and true God* (1:9), to continue in their *steadfastness of hope in the Lord Jesus Christ* (1:3). Specifically, this means that, despite their affliction and their setbacks, including the deaths of loved ones, they are to continue in confident hope *to await [God's] Son from heaven* (1:10). The Thessalonians are assured that, having ascended into heaven, the risen Christ himself will also descend from heaven in order to consummate the divine program of bringing deliverance *from the coming wrath* (1:10).

According to this *word of the Lord*, three unmistakable announcements will accompany the Lord's descent from heaven. First mentioned is *a cry of command*. It is idle to speculate whether this is God's command to Jesus to descend and begin the final chapter of the redemptive plan, or whether this is Jesus' command to the dead to rise up from their graves. Perhaps this *cry* can even be identified with *the call of an archangel*, which coincides with the descent of the triumphant Lord.

What shall we make of *the sound of the trumpet of God*? In the OT, trumpets sounded for military expeditions and at festivals; the prophets mentioned the blowing of the trumpet to call Israel together and signal anticipated divine rescue or judgment (Isa. 27:13;

Joel 2:1, 15; Zech. 9:14). Elsewhere in the NT, comparable texts suggest that the blast of the trumpet constitutes the authoritative divine summons for the faithful to assemble (cf. Matt. 24:31) and the dead in Christ to rise (cf. 1 Cor. 15:51-52). All three of these phenomena (*a cry of command, the call of an archangel,* and *the sound of the trumpet of God*) create an awesome aura of majesty and authority. When Christ comes as triumphant Lord, there will be enough noise to wake the dead!

To what will this grand display lead? The eschatological drama climaxes with a twofold event, the first of which demonstrates that the resurrection of Christ foreshadows the resurrection of believers (cf. 4:14): *the dead in Christ shall rise* (4:16b). As in the early Christian confession cited in 4:14, the verb *arise (anistēmi)* appears here, this time in the future tense: *shall rise.* As Jesus himself arose from the dead (4:14), so also the dead in Christ will rise!

But there is more! The resurrection of the believers is the first act in a two-act play, as indicated by that little word *first: The dead in Christ shall rise first* (4:16b). In the second act of this cosmic play, which is signaled by the word *then,* the actors are those believers still alive at the time of the coming of the Lord (cf. 4:15): *Then we who are alive who are left shall be caught up together with them in the clouds to a meeting with the Lord in the air* (4:17a).

How should these two temporal indicators (*first* and *then*) be understood? We need to keep in mind that the missionaries' concern here is primarily pastoral. They want to reassure the surviving members of the Thessalonian Christian community that those believers who have died will not be at a disadvantage when the Lord comes. In fact, *the dead in Christ* shall actually have precedence over the believers who survive until that time: *We . . . shall not precede those who have fallen asleep* (4:15). However, even though these two events occur one after another, there is no indication that they are separated by any significant time period, such as an interim messianic reign. After the dead in Christ are raised, *then* those who have lived until that moment will have their turn ("The Timetable" in TBC for 2 Thess. 2:1-12).

What will happen to the living believers? They *shall be caught up!* The underlying Greek verb *harpazō, seize* or *snatch away,* normally describes a sudden forceful intervention. In the Septuagint, the translation of both Enoch and Elijah into heaven (Gen. 5:24; 2 Kings 2:11-12) is depicted by means of this verb. Some scholars suggest that the Thessalonian believers have come to expect that believers would be taken directly into heaven, like Enoch and Elijah (Plevnik: 274-283).

Several other occurrences of the verb *caught up* in the NT further illustrate its meaning. In Jerusalem, when Paul's life seems to be in danger because of a heated argument between the Pharisees and the Sadducees in the Jewish council, the Roman tribune orders his soldiers to "take him by force" and whisk him to safety (Acts 23:10). When Luke tells of Philip's encounter with the Ethiopian eunuch, he says that Philip was "snatched away" by the Spirit (Acts 8:39). Paul also describes for the Corinthians what likely was his own spiritual experience of having been "caught up" to the third heaven (2 Cor. 12:2, 4). From such NT uses of this verb, one learns that it depicts an abrupt transfer, either physical or spiritual. In Latin this verb is translated *rapere*, from which comes the English noun *rapture*, one of the centerpieces of dispensational theology. *[Eschatology, p. 355.]*

According to this spellbinding scenario, the living believers, having been *caught up* in the second act of this eschatological drama (4:17a), will join those believers who have been raised in the first act (4:16b). The words *together with them* communicate the restored togetherness of the dead, who have been raised, with the living, now being snatched away from the earth. Together again they find themselves *in the clouds*. In the OT, clouds frequently appear during high moments when God speaks or when God's glory is revealed to the people (Exod. 19:16; 24:15-18; 40:34-38). Clouds play a similar role in the NT. For example, when Jesus meets with Elijah and Moses on the mount of transfiguration, God speaks out of the cloud (Mark 9:7 and parallels).

However, the eschatological gathering *in the clouds*, which happens as part of Jesus' descent from heaven, can also remind us of his ascension into heaven and expectations for his return. As Luke describes it, "He [Jesus] was lifted up, and a cloud took him out of their sight." Two men in white robes say, "This Jesus, who has been taken up from you into heaven, will come in the same way as you saw him go into heaven" (Acts 1:9-11; cf. Dan. 7:13; Mark 13:26 and parallels; Rev. 1:7). In short, what the Thessalonian believers are told about the remarkable sequence of spectacular events linked to the triumphant coming of Christ as Lord is conveyed in the rich images of God's past revealing activity.

With excitement building on the cosmic stage, now occupied by resurrected and living Christians, the futuristic drama now moves to the climax, which is *a meeting with the Lord in the air* (4:17a). The word *meeting* (*apantēsis*) derives from a particular political practice in the Greco-Roman world. Whenever an emperor or other official came to a city for a formal visit, the local civic leaders normally headed a procession of its citizens so that they could meet and enthusiastically welcome the visiting dignitary to their city. Usually the meeting and formal greeting occurred outside the city gates. The leading city officials, followed by citizens, then escorted the distinguished visitor into the city for the celebrations or whatever business might be at hand. In the case of the eagerly awaited arrival of the triumphant Lord, therefore, the living and resurrected believers constitute the welcoming delegation who head out for *a meeting* with their Lord! *[Religions in the Greco-Roman World, p. 365.]*

Where do they meet? The meeting takes place *in the air.* Paul and his companions continue the use of spatial imagery: the descent of the Lord, the ascent of the believers, a gathering in the clouds, and a meeting in the air. How much of this should be taken literally? Is this all symbolic? Some interpreters, eager to fit this text into one particular eschatological timetable or another, have debated about what happens after the descending Lord meets the ascending believers *in the air.* Do the Lord and the believers who have been raised from the dead and caught up from the earth proceed together into heaven? Or does the Lord continue to move toward the earth, as a visiting emperor would enter the city after the official welcome? Is end-time fulfillment to be on a renewed earth (cf. Isa. 65:17; 66:22; Rev. 21–22)?

Within dispensational theology, the rapture of the church signals the beginning of the great tribulation. According to this view, the church escapes this seven-year period of intense suffering. At the end of this great tribulation, Christ is revealed as the triumphant Lord, and the church returns for the thousand-year reign of Christ on earth. *[Eschatology, p. 355.]* Even proponents of such a pretribulation view of the rapture recognize that neither 1 Thessalonians 4:13-18 nor any other biblical passage explicitly teaches this kind of end-time chronology of events. The sequence has been constructed from a variety of biblical texts on the basis of prior doctrinal and exegetical presuppositions (Hiebert: 205).

Speculation about these matters actually violates the pastoral intention of Paul's teaching in 1 Thessalonians 4:13-18. Paul and his missionary colleagues do not set out primarily to instruct the Thessalonian believers concerning the timetable of the end. Instead, they seek to comfort these new converts in their grief. This grief is not caused by lack of detailed knowledge about an end-time sequence of events. The surviving believers need to grasp the dynamic hope which they inherited through their faith in the crucified and risen Christ. It is this foundational hope with which these pastoral writers close this section: *and so we shall always be with the Lord!* (4:17b). These reassuring words frontally address the fears of the Thessalonian believers. All believers, whether already dead or still living, are guaranteed continuity of fellowship with the Lord, both in the present and at the time of his triumphant coming. Those who are *in Christ* while alive continue to be *in Christ* after death! Persecutions will continue, and believers will die, but life in Christ survives death!

Pastoral Exhortation 4:18

In their concluding exhortation, the missionary pastors urge the Thessalonians to minister to each other:

> 4:18 *Therefore*
> *comfort* ──────▶ *one another*
> └ *with these words.*

Paul and his fellow evangelists do not seek in the first place to provide details regarding the eschatological drama: the calendar, the sequence of events, the nature of the end-times. Their primary goal is to provide pastoral care by comforting the grieving believers. They do so by reminding these mourners that the resurrection of Jesus also has consequences for those who are in Christ! In the conclusion to this section, they urge the Thessalonians also to encourage each other with this good news.

The verb here translated *comfort (parakaleite)* recalls other uses of the same word in 1 Thessalonians. At times it means *exhort* (2:11) or *urge* (4:1, 10; 5:14). In other contexts it conveys a variety of related meanings, such as *encourage, comfort,* or *console* (3:2, 7; 5:11). Here Paul and his companions clearly intend for the Thessalonian believers to *comfort, console,* and *encourage* each other on the basis of their confession that *Jesus died and rose again* (4:14).

Even though the Holy Spirit is not explicitly mentioned here, we can assume from what Paul and his associates say elsewhere in the letter (1:5-6; 4:8; 5:19) that God's Spirit comforts and consoles the believers in their distress. According to John's Gospel, Jesus reassures his disciples by promising the coming of the Comforter (KJV) or Counselor (RSV: Greek: *paraklētos*), who consoles, teaches, and strengthens the believers (John 14:16-17, 26; 15:26; 16:7).

THE TEXT IN THE BIBLICAL CONTEXT

Those Who Sleep

The Thessalonian believers present when this letter is read would all understand the phrase *those who are asleep* (4:13). Sleep as a euphemism for death was familiar in the Greco-Roman world of their day. For example, in Homer's epic poem, *The Iliad*, the death of a young warrior is lamented:

> So there he fell, and slept a sleep of bronze, unhappy youth, far from his wedded wife. (*Iliad* 11.241-243)

Likewise, the Roman poet Catullus appeals for the devotion of his lover by reminding her that life is short and that an unending night follows:

> Suns may set and rise again. For us, when the short light has once set, remains to be slept the sleep of one unbroken night. (*Poems* 5)

The OT also refers to death as sleep. In Egypt, when Jacob anticipates his own death, he approaches Joseph with a special request:

> When I lie down with my ancestors, carry me out of Egypt and bury me in their burial place. (Gen. 47:30)

Similar language is used in Deuteronomy regarding Moses' death:

> The Lord said to Moses, "Soon you will lie down with your ancestors." (Deut. 31:16)

The death of king David is described in comparable fashion: "Then David slept with his ancestors" (1 Kings 2:10; cf. also Solomon and others: 1 Kings 11:43). More direct language concerning death is not avoided, however. After blessing Joseph's sons, Jacob says, "I am about to die" (Gen. 48:21). Deuteronomy depicts how Moses viewed the land across the Jordan and describes his death and burial: "Then Moses . . . died there in the land of Moab" (34:1-5).

In John's story about the raising of Lazarus, the disciples at first understand Jesus literally when he says, "Our friend Lazarus has fallen asleep, but I am going there to awaken him" (John 11:11). John explains that "Jesus had been speaking of his death, but they thought that he was referring merely to sleep" (11:13). John continues with the report that Jesus then moves from metaphorical to direct address: "Lazarus is dead" (11:14). The confusion of the disciples is understandable. For them, death could be described as sleep, but their minds can not easily comprehend the notion of being raised from the sleep of death.

It is clear that, when biblical writers refer to death as sleep, this is not an attempt to avoid an unpleasant topic. In a cultural context in which death was largely viewed as tragic, especially if there were no heirs, viewing death as sleep also opened the door to thinking about the possibility of some form of reawakened life after death.

In the OT, the sleep of death has a communal dimension. Death ushers people into a reunion with their ancestors, although not a joyous one. We can illustrate from several of the Psalms. Sheol, the abode of the dead, was envisioned as a shadowy underworld rather devoid of joy and hope:

> Turn, O Lord, save my life;
> deliver me for the sake of your steadfast love.
> For in death there is no remembrance of you;
> in Sheol who can give you praise? (Ps. 6:4-5)

Even though the Psalms generally portray those who have descended into Sheol as separated from God (Pss. 88:3-7; 115:17), at least one Psalm also testifies to the startling truth that even in Sheol, one cannot get away from God:

> Where can I go from your spirit?
> Or where can I flee from your presence?
> If I ascend to heaven, you are there;
> if I make my bed in Sheol you are there. (Ps. 139:7-8)

The ministry of Jesus, especially his death and resurrection, injects a radically transforming dynamic which defies the power of death. When the apostles and missionaries preach the gospel of the crucified and risen Christ, they invite their hearers joyfully to appropriate this living hope even in the face of death. Therefore, as this letter to Thessalonica affirms, those who believe that Jesus died and rose need not grieve like others who lack such hope.

No particulars about the nature of the intermediate *sleep* can be gleaned from this text. From 2 Corinthians 5:1-10, we learn that Paul envisions death as a laying aside of the earthly body, somewhat like getting undressed; in the resurrection then he anticipates being further clothed. From his prison cell, Paul later shares with the church at Philippi some of his personal thoughts as he faces the prospect of his own death:

> For to me, living is Christ and dying is gain. If I am to live in the flesh, that means fruitful labor for me; and I do not know which I prefer. I am hard pressed between the two: my desire is to depart and be with Christ, for that is far better; but to remain in the flesh is more necessary for you. (Phil. 1:21-24)

In facing his own death, Paul does not have the benefit of advance information concerning any intermediate state between his death and the resurrection. Even without knowledge concerning such details, Paul testifies to his confidence that his relationship with Christ would not be interrupted even by his death. That is also the bottom line for the Thessalonians: *So we shall always be with the Lord!* (4:17).

Jesus Died and Arose

The OT story of Job opens a window through which the human struggle with tragedy and death can be viewed. One misfortune after another strikes Job, so that he even curses the day of his own birth (Job 3). With his friends accusing him, Job contemplates his plight, oscillating between despair and faith. At one point, when reflecting on the futility of life and the inevitability of death, Job vents his feelings of hopelessness:

> As waters fail from a lake, and a river wastes away and dries up,
> so mortals lie down and do not rise again;
> until the heavens are no more, they will not awake
> or be roused out of their sleep. (Job 14:11-12)

On the basis of this outburst, one might conclude that Job does not hold any hope for life beyond Sheol. Yet Job also expresses his hope and trust in God: "For I know that my Redeemer lives, and that at the last he will stand upon the earth" (19:25).

The beginnings of a belief in the resurrection and life after death can also be identified elsewhere in the OT. The prophets Isaiah and Ezekiel speak about the return of the exiled people of Israel to their homeland as a resurrection. Isaiah eloquently prophesies concerning God's power to restore the exiles:

> Your dead shall live, their corpses shall rise.
> O dwellers in the dust, awake and sing for joy! (Isa. 26:19)

Ezekiel's vision of God breathing new life into dry bones (Ezek. 37:1-10) is followed by a metaphorical interpretation of that vision.

The bones are the people of Israel who say, "Our bones are dried up and our hope is lost" (37:11). To these despairing exiles, Ezekiel is commanded to prophesy:

> Thus says the Lord God: I am going to open your graves, and bring you up from your graves, O my people; and I will bring you back to the land of Israel. (Ezek. 37:12)

Both of these prophetic oracles testify to the confidence that God will restore life to the dead. In both cases, the prophets urge the despairing exiles to place their hope for a return to their homeland in the God who raises the dead. This hope thus centers on a corporate renewal of Israel.

A similar confidence in God comes through in the Psalms. For example, in Psalm 49, the fate of the arrogant is contrasted with the hope of the faithful:

> Like sheep they are appointed for Sheol;
>   Death shall be their shepherd;
> straight to the grave they descend,
>   and their form shall waste away;
>   Sheol shall be their home.
> But God will ransom my soul from the power of Sheol,
>   for he will receive me. (Ps. 49:14-15)

Psalm 22, whose opening cry Jesus echoes from the cross (Mark 15:34, "My God, my God, why have you forsaken me?"), ends with an affirmation that the dead who are buried in the earth acknowledge God:

> For dominion belongs to the Lord, and he rules over the nations.
> To him, indeed, shall all who sleep in the earth bow down;
>   before him shall bow all who go down to the dust,
>   and I shall live for him. (Ps. 22:28-29)

In light of God's sovereignty, which the dead have come to recognize, the psalmist declares: "I shall live for him!"

Neither the Psalms nor the prophets Isaiah and Ezekiel provide clear testimony to a belief in individual resurrection of the dead. Only Daniel in the OT unambiguously affirms such a concept of resurrection and life after death, especially for Israelites who died as martyrs:

> Many of those who sleep in the dust of the earth shall awake, some to everlasting life, and some to shame and everlasting contempt. (Dan. 12:2)

An angel tells the prophet that when Israel is delivered from the (Syrian) oppressor (12:1), those who died will be raised to share in the triumph and receive everlasting reward or punishment (Lederach, notes on Dan. 12:1-4 and the following TBC; cf. Matt. 13:43).

During the intertestamental period, especially in apocalyptic writings, this theme emerges with greater clarity (as in 2 Macc. 7:9, 23). Within the Judaism of Jesus' day, the Pharisees believe in the resurrection while the Sadducees do not. According to Acts 23:6-10, Paul manages to exploit this difference between Pharisees and Sadducees to his own benefit. When his case is being considered in the Jewish council, Paul cries out:

> I am a Pharisee, a son of Pharisees. I am on trial concerning the hope of the resurrection of the dead. (Acts 23:6)

This strategy of divide and conquer works! The Pharisees in the council begin to defend Paul, and eventually the authorities whisk him out to safety (Faw, 1993:248, 254-256).

Jesus himself expresses his clear confidence in the God who raises the dead. His own ministry on several occasions includes resuscitations of the dead: Lazarus (John 11:28-44), the daughter of Jairus (Mark 5:21-43 and parallels), and the son of the widow of Nain (Luke 7:11-17). Most significant, however, is Jesus' own resurrection. According to the Gospel accounts, Jesus predicts that he will suffer, die, and rise again. After Peter confesses at Caesarea Philippi, "You are the Messiah" (Mark 8:29), Jesus begins to teach his disciples:

> The Son of Man must undergo great suffering, and be rejected by the elders, the chief priests, and the scribes, and be killed, and after three days rise again. (Mark 8:31)

On two other occasions, according to Mark's Gospel, Jesus warns his disciples that he will suffer and die, but Jesus also assures them that he will rise again (9:31; 10:34). In Mark, the three announcements of Jesus' resurrection use the same verb as in 1 Thessalonians 4:14: *rise* (*anistēmi*). However, in the corresponding passages in the Gospel of Matthew (16:21; 17:23; 20:19), the passive form of the verb *be raised* (*egeirō*) is used, likely to underscore the fact that God raised Jesus from the dead. Certainly the apostles' sermons recorded in Acts convey that message. Thus at Pentecost Peter narrates God's decisive raising of Jesus from the dead:

But God raised him up, having freed him from death, because it was impossible for him to be held in its power. (Acts 2:24; cf. also 2:32; 13:33-37; 17:31)

When Paul writes to the church at Corinth about the topic of the resurrection (1 Cor. 15), he begins by recalling a longer form of the early Christian confession cited in 1 Thessalonians 4:14. This was the gospel which he himself has received and transmitted to them:

> That Christ died for our sins in accordance with the scriptures,
> and that he was buried,
> and that he was raised on the third day in accordance with the scriptures,
> and that he appeared to Cephas, then to the twelve. (1 Cor. 15:3-5)

Before rehearsing this gospel, however, Paul entertains a fearful thought: "unless you have come to believe in vain" (1 Cor. 15:2). As in Thessalonica so in Corinth, there appear to have been people in danger of missing the relevance of this confession. In Corinth, some of those who accept the proclamation concerning Jesus' resurrection from the dead still insist that "there is no resurrection of the dead" (15:12). After discrediting this denial of the resurrection (15:13-19), Paul reasserts both the fact that Jesus was raised and the truth that Jesus' resurrection carries positive consequences:

> But in fact Christ has been raised from the dead, the first fruits of those who have died. (1 Cor. 15:20)

The metaphor of the "first fruits" points to Jesus' resurrection as the first installment of many more resurrections to follow. After commenting that Jesus reverses the legacy of death left by Adam (1 Cor. 15:21-22), Paul explains the order of the anticipated events:

> Christ the first fruits, then at his coming those who belong to Christ. Then comes the end, when he hands over the kingdom to God the Father, after he has destroyed every ruler and every authority and power. (15:23-25)

As Paul's argument unfolds, he both acknowledges the stark reality of death (1 Cor. 15:35-50) and declares the mystery of the ultimate transformation (15:51-57):

> For the trumpet will sound, and the dead will be raised imperishable, and we will be changed. (15:52)

How does Paul conclude this grand treatise? After offering the Corinthians a majestic vision of the future transformation as guaranteed by Jesus' resurrection, Paul wraps it up with an admonition for the present:

> Therefore, my beloved, be steadfast, immovable, always excelling in the work of the Lord, because you know that in the Lord your labor is not in vain. (1 Cor. 15:58)

Those who actively put their trust in the God who raised Jesus from the dead will know that their belief (15:2) and their labor (15:58) are not in vain!

The Lord Himself Will Descend!

The Thessalonians are invited to a preview of the spectacular descent of the triumphant Lord for a meeting with the resurrected and living believers. They may not know about a similar prophecy in Daniel. Perhaps they are also unaware of what Jesus said on this subject. However, Paul and his co-workers likely recall the prophecies of Daniel and Jesus when they communicate this *word of the Lord* to the Thessalonians.

To a distressed and oppressed Jewish community, Daniel reports this vision of triumph:

> I saw one like a human being [RSV: son of man]
>   coming with the clouds of heaven.
> And he came to the Ancient of Days
>   and was presented before him.
> To him was given dominion and glory and kingship,
>   that all peoples, nations, and languages should serve him.
> (Dan. 7:13-14)

In this vision, "the Holy Ones [angels] of the Most High" and the holy people they protect are promised that they shall "possess the kingdom forever" (Dan. 7:18; cf. 7:22, 27; 2:44; Lederach: 163-168). Similarly, Jesus announces to his disciples what shall happen after a time of great suffering:

> Then they will see "the Son of Man coming in clouds" with great power and glory. Then he will send out the angels, and gather his elect from the four winds, from the ends of the earth to the ends of heaven. (Mark 13:26-27; cf. Matt. 24:30-31)

What the distressed Thessalonian believers hear from the missionaries comes with the same resounding note of triumph with which Daniel and Jesus addressed their contemporaries. What is different is that the victorious Son of Man now has been identified as Jesus Christ, the crucified one who was raised and exalted as Lord, and is to come in glory.

THE TEXT IN THE LIFE OF THE CHURCH
Grief Yet Hope

Christians have often been confused about what to make of apocalyptic passages such as 1 Thessalonians 4:13-18. Many sermons have not been helpful. Some preachers avoid such texts, others major in them. I began to experience the dynamic power of this text when I became attuned to the real-life questions which these pastoral words were designed to address. Paul and his co-workers offer this teaching not primarily to inform their readers about the timetable of the end but to console them in their unnecessarily hopeless grief.

In this case, pastoral consolation consists of the tender assurance that those who have died, likely as a result of persecution facing the community, will not face any disadvantage at the time of the coming of Christ as victorious Lord. At that time, both those believers who have already died and those still alive will be united with Christ and be with him forever!

Sermons from this passage often focus on what the apocalyptic images might mean and how the drama described here fits within some overall end-time calendar. Explanations of the rapture often go out from pulpits of fundamentalist preachers and on certain radio and TV religious broadcasts. Numerous films, videos, and paperback books also sensationalize the rapture. I am struck by an irony here. The doctrine of the rapture has grown largely out of the graphic apocalyptic imagery in 1 Thessalonians 4:13-18. As we have seen, Paul and his companions write these words to reassure the Christian community. Upset about the fact that death has separated the survivors from their loved ones, the Thessalonian Christian community hears these comforting words: *We [the dead in Christ* and *we who are alive, who are left] shall be with the Lord always!* That message is intended to console and encourage those who are anxious and upset.

Films, books, and sermons about the rapture, on the other hand, often upset and disturb people, especially children and youth. Particularly upsetting is the prospect that we might find ourselves among those alive but left when Christ comes to rescue his own. Rather than reassuring the believers with the message of the continuity of fellowship in Christ, the doctrine of the rapture succeeds in scaring them about the possibility of being left behind.

The good news being communicated in this passage is simpler and more profound than all the speculative scenarios which pious minds can build on the basis of their imaginative construal of a few highly symbolic texts. What is that message? Jesus died and arose. In Christ, those who have died will also rise. In fact, at the parousia, they will rise first. Then the resurrected saints will join the living saints, and together they will enjoy continuing communion with the Lord!

The comforting message of this text needs to be claimed and proclaimed when people die. Grief at the time of death is a universal response, but in Christ such grief need not be without hope, regardless of the circumstances which led to the death.

When ministering to the bereaved or when leading in funeral services, pastors need to let the mourners in their congregations feel their shock and grief in the face of death. However, the worship must also invite celebration of the glorious hope inherent in the gospel of the crucified and risen Lord. Mourners in our congregations can identify both with the Thessalonians' grief and this hope-inspiring message of comfort.

Such death-defying hope is often expressed most eloquently through song. One such hymn helped me to affirm this resurrection hope when my mother at age 61 succumbed to cancer:

Lift your glad voices in triumph on high,
For Jesus has risen and we shall not die!
(Henry Ware, in *Hymnal: A Worship Book*, no. 275)

Through the victory gained by Christ, those who grieve can defy even the power of death! That hopeful word from the Lord extends to us as well.

1 Thessalonians 5:1-11

The Times and the Seasons

PREVIEW

During Jesus' fateful pilgrimage to Jerusalem for the Passover, as his conflict with the temple authorities escalated, he voices the unthinkable prospect of doomsday.

"Do you see these great buildings?" Jesus asks his disciples. "Not one stone will be left here upon another; all will be thrown down" (Mark 13:2).

Then the disciples ask Jesus the calendar question, "Tell us, when will this be, and what will be the sign that all these things are about to be accomplished?" (13:4).

Ever since, people have asked, "When will this be?" The Thessalonians apparently also wanted to know.

In 1 Thessalonians 4:13-18, Paul, Silvanus, and Timothy console the grieving Thessalonian believers. They declare that Jesus' death and resurrection prepare the way for the dead and the living to be reunited at the parousia: *And so we shall always be with the Lord* (4:17b). Even though this good news has little to do with calendar, at least some of the Thessalonians still want to know, "When?"

The theme of 5:1-11 is announced as *the times and the seasons* (5:1). Following a reminder concerning the nature of *the day of the Lord* (5:1-3), the Thessalonians receive reassurance that *the day of the Lord* need not catch any of them by surprise (5:4-5). Exhortations to vigilance and faithfulness follow (5:6-8), supported by the conviction that God longs for their salvation (5:9-10). Another pastoral exhortation, similar to 4:18, brings this paragraph to a close (5:11).

In this passage the Thessalonian believers hear direct assurances and appeals, emphasized through the recurring use of the plural *you* in 5:1-2, 4-5a. The expression *brothers and sisters* at 5:1 and 4 personalizes this direct address even more. *We* and *us* language takes over from 5:5b-10, presumably since the writers include themselves with these converts as members of the community energized by *faith, love,* and *hope* (5:8; cf. 1:3). In the final exhortation, there is a concluding *you*-statement (5:11). As if to underscore the urgency of these appeals, Paul and his companions mention the *others* (5:6), who are also implied in the references to *they* and *them* in 5:3, upon whom sudden destruction will come.

This distinction between *you* (or *we*) and *them* is sharpened through the use of striking contrasts throughout this passage:

day (of the Lord)	*(thief in the) night*	(5:2)
peace and security	*sudden destruction*	(5:3)
darkness	*day*	(5:4)
children of light	*not of night*	
and children of day	*nor of darkness*	(5:5)
fall asleep	*stay awake and be sober*	(5:6)
be sober	*get drunk*	(5:6-7; 5:7-8)
night	*day*	(5:7-8)
wrath	*salvation*	(5:9)
awake	*asleep*	(5:10)
died for us	*live with him*	(5:10)

These contrasts vary in nature. Some of the images (such as *day* as well as *awake* and *asleep*) also serve double duty; their meanings within this passage shift. As later readers of this letter, we may find some of these cryptic images hard to decipher.

OUTLINE

The Day of the Lord Will Come! 5:1-3
That Day Need Not Surprise You! 5:4-5
Stay Awake and Be Sober, 5:6-8
Not Wrath but Salvation, 5:9-10
Another Pastoral Exhortation, 5:11

EXPLANATORY NOTES
The Day of the Lord Will Come! 5:1-3

A new theme is introduced by the formula *now concerning*, which was also used at 4:9 at the beginning of the advice concerning *love of the brothers and sisters*:

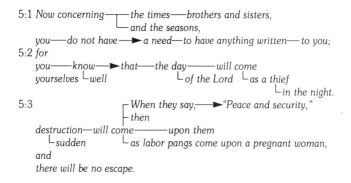

In 1 Corinthians the formula *now concerning* signals questions raised in a letter from Corinth to Paul (see 7:1), but there is no evidence that the Thessalonian congregation raised their questions in a letter. Likely Timothy had returned from his second trip to Thessalonica (3:1-10) with news about how the believers there were reacting to their suffering (cf. 3:3-4). Apparently their responses included hopeless grief in the face of the death of some of their members and some distressing questions about the nature and timing of *the day of the Lord*. Their grief is addressed in 4:13-18. In 5:1-11 we hear what Timothy, Paul, and Silvanus have to say concerning preparedness for *the day of the Lord*.

This is not new information for the Thessalonians. After announcing the topic of *the times and the seasons*, the missionary pastors insist that *you do not have a need to have anything written to you*. Nevertheless, they still do write about this subject. A similar disclaimer appears in 4:9. Ancient letters frequently employ such language to urge their readers to claim the truth of what they already know and then remind them to live accordingly (Stowers: 103). In 5:2 an emphatic *you yourselves know well* (cf. 2:1, 5, 11) lets the readers know that much of what follows is shared as a reminder concerning what they have been told previously.

What are *the times and the seasons*? Two Greek words for time lie behind this expression: *chronos* (a root for English words like *chronology* and *chronometer*), which usually signifies duration of time; and *kairos* (a loanword in English), which often conveys a qualitative meaning such as the right or opportune time. However, in actual usage, there is overlap in meaning. These two words in combination (as in LXX of Dan. 2:21; 7:12) seem to have taken on an eschatological flavor to refer to the future unfolding of the climactic events of salvation and final judgment. In Acts 1:7 the risen Christ replies to his disciples' question about the timetable, "It is not for you to know times or seasons which the Father has fixed by his own authority" (RSV). In short, the expression *the times and the seasons* occurs as a code phrase for the time of the parousia and all the events associated with it. Taking our cue from 5:2, we can also assume that concerns and questions about *the day of the Lord* lie at the root of this preoccupation with *the times and the seasons*.

The concept of *the day of the Lord* appears prominently in OT prophetic literature. In the preaching of the prophets, *the day of the Lord* can be a time of both fearful judgment and glorious hope. Both Jesus and the early church spoke about the climax of God's activity within history in these terms ("The Day of the Lord" in TBC below).

During their evangelistic preaching in Thessalonica, Paul and his companions incorporated teaching and warnings about *the day of the Lord*. It is impossible to determine exactly what they might have said. In 5:1-11 some of what they originally taught, and which the Thessalonians seemingly already *know well*, is repeated, apparently to emphasize the need for their vigilance and preparedness. Evidently further confusion and deliberate misinterpretation occurred after this first letter was read in the congregation. The second letter devotes major attention to this theme, especially to counter the arguments of some that *the day of the Lord has come* (2 Thess. 2:1-12).

At this point we need to examine what Paul and his co-workers communicate to these new believers in this first letter. By means of three word pictures, Paul and his companions bring out several of the characteristics of *the day of the Lord*. The first illustration depicts the unpredictability of that event: *the day of the Lord will come as a thief in the night* (5:2). Just as homeowners retiring for the night cannot know whether a burglar will break into their home while they are sleeping, so also *the day of the Lord* will come without advance warning. This metaphor recurs at 5:4, where the letter turns to moral exhortation. Jesus also counsels readiness by telling a parable about the impossibility of predicting when a thief will break in (Matt. 24:43-44; Luke 12:39-40; cf. 2 Pet. 3:10; Rev. 3:3; 16:15).

The second word picture has a proverbial ring to it. Jeremiah warns his contemporaries not to be lulled to sleep by prophets and priests saying, " 'Peace, peace,' when there is no peace" (Jer. 6:14; cf.

Ezek. 13:10, 16; Mic. 3:5). Paul and his coauthors alert their readers in Thessalonica to the fact that those who soothe the populace with empty promises of peace will themselves be surprised at the suddenness of the coming of *the day of the Lord: When they say, "Peace and security," then sudden destruction will come upon them* (5:3). The identity of *they* and *them* is not disclosed. However, we can safely assume that this group corresponds to *the others* mentioned in 5:6. Their condition is consistently contrasted with that of the Thessalonian believers addressed directly in the *you*-statements.

What is the nature of the *sudden destruction* which threatens to engulf *them?* Likely Paul, Timothy, and Silvanus are making a veiled reference to the fact that those who persecute the Thessalonian believers (cf. 3:3-4) will themselves be overtaken by a precipitous calamity. *"Peace and security"* may in fact be a slogan employed in the Roman empire to characterize their imperial sense of destiny as keepers of the peace (the Pax Romana). Essentially Paul and his coworkers warn the Thessalonians that the Roman peace, as gained and maintained through military conquest and rule, is a false and empty security. Ironically, while pursuing their own *peace and security* through oppressing those who confess Jesus Christ as Lord, *they* (a group including the persecutors) will face *sudden destruction.*

Later, in 2 Thessalonians 1:6-7, the Thessalonians hear this same message about God's justice in more specific form: God will afflict the afflictors and grant relief to those who are afflicted. The words *sudden destruction* may therefore refer to an imminent historical event, although *eternal destruction and exclusion* as the ultimate consequences of defying God are probably also in mind (cf. 2 Thess. 1:9). [*Historical and Political Context, p. 357; Religions in the Greco-Roman World, p. 365.*]

Another metaphor adds to this terrifying portrait of *the day of the Lord.* In addition to being unpredictable and sudden, *the day of the Lord* with its accompanying destruction is inevitable. Judgment will come *as labor pangs come upon a pregnant woman.* In a word, *there will be no escape* (5:3). OT prophets frequently utilize the birthpangs metaphor, sometimes to convey the anguish felt on the eve of a military invasion (Jer. 6:24), at other times to predict judgment on the invader (Isa. 13:8). This image also finds its way into Jewish apocalyptic writings and some of the Qumran literature. Jesus talks about wars, earthquakes, and famines as "the beginning of the birthpangs" (Matt. 24:8; Mark 13:8).

The scenario surrounding *the times and the seasons* seems more frightening than reassuring. *The day of the Lord* will be as unpredictable as a burglar, as sudden and surprising as when destruction befalls people who think they have found security, as inevitable as labor pangs for a pregnant woman. To top it off, *There will be no escape.* Does this sound like good news?

That Day Need Not Surprise You! 5:4-5

The writers, having described what will happen to *them* (the others), now remind these believers that their condition is different:

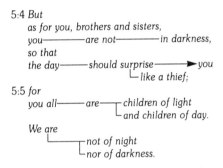

5:4 *But*
  as for you, brothers and sisters,
  you———are not———in darkness,
  so that
  the day———should surprise——▶you
        └ like a thief;
5:5 *for*
  you all——— are ———┌ children of light
              └ and children of day.
  We are
    └————┌ not of night
          └ nor of darkness.

The good news is that *the day of the Lord* need not come as a surprise. Though inevitable, sudden, and unpredictable, the *day of the Lord* will not come as a shock to those who have turned to God! The Thessalonians hearing this letter are assured that that awesome day need not catch them off guard. The *but* and an emphatic *you* plus yet another *brothers and sisters* all alert the Thessalonian believers to their status.

In 5:4-5 the main verb is the verb of being. A series of assertions beginning with *you are* or *we are* establishes a sharp contrast between *us* and *them*, the insiders and the outsiders. First, *you are not in darkness.* In other words, believers have the advantage of daylight. Thieves prefer to work under the cover of darkness. By coming at night, a burglar might catch a householder unawares (cf. 5:2). However, the Thessalonian believers operate during *the day*, so that *the day (of the Lord)* need not sneak up on them *like a thief.*

In the second and third assertions, Paul and his companions restate this truth (*You are not in darkness*) by means of parallel statements beginning with *you are* and *we are.* They do so first positively with a declaration addressed to *you all*, and then negatively with an

even more inclusive *we* statement. Both the parallelism and the variations draw attention to contrasting realms of existence:

> *You all are*   *children of light*   *and children of day.*
> *We are not*   *of night*   *nor of darkness.*

The Thessalonian converts hear assurances concerning their status
as *children of light and children of day.* (Literally, the word here is
sons, but since the Thessalonian church clearly also includes daughters, it is better to translate in an inclusive and dynamically equivalent
way, as in the NRSV, namely *children.*)

What do the evangelists mean by *light, day, night, darkness?*
Throughout this paragraph, these concepts (as well as several others
such as *asleep* and *awake,* and *be sober* and *get drunk*) are employed
primarily in a metaphorical rather than a literal sense. Even when
these terms carry metaphorical value, their meanings seem to vary,
sometimes from one verse to the next. With reference to *day,* for example, the thought associations appear to have moved from the eschatological *day of the Lord* (5:2, 4) to *day* as a spiritual and moral
category (5:5). Being *of day* or *of light* as contrasted with being *of
night* or *of darkness* speaks of the believers' spiritual status, which
also has moral implications. In both biblical and extrabiblical writings,
the motifs of light and darkness are relatively common, notably in the
Dead Sea Scrolls and in John's Gospel and epistles. Often these writings develop sharp theological distinctions between a righteous minority and the majority group ("Light and Darkness, Day and Night"
in TBC below).

Stay Awake and Be Sober 5:6-8

At 5:6 the tone shifts from reassurance to exhortation:

> 5:6 *So then*
> *let us*————*not fall asleep*
>   └ *as the others do,*
> *but*
> *let us*————┬*stay awake*
>   └*and be sober;*

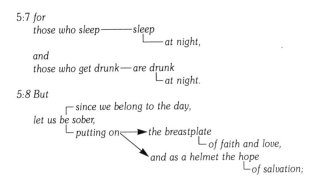

As *children of day*, these converts in Thessalonica need not dread *the day of the Lord*. But this assurance, based on their identity as believers, is also contingent on their actions and their choices. The phrase *so then* opens a series of exhortations concerning moral consequences of their spiritual condition: *So then let us not fall asleep as the others do, but let us stay awake and be sober.* Obviously the words *fall asleep* and *stay awake* need to be taken as metaphorical expressions. To *fall asleep* means to lapse into a state of moral or spiritual laxity. To *stay awake* means to be vigilant spiritually and morally. Such spiritual and moral watchfulness contrasts with the lifestyle of *the others* (perhaps equivalent to the group mentioned in 4:13: *the others who do not have hope*).

The behavior of *the others* seems to be characterized, however, not only by moral laxity but also by indulgence, as suggested in the additional admonition *and be sober*. This call for sobriety includes the need for self-control and personal discipline. Here Paul and his partners may be drawing a deliberate contrast between Christian conduct and the ecstatic orgies practiced within the mystery cults in Thessalonica. Drunkenness and sexually immoral behavior frequently occurred in these circles, from which some of the believers have come. [*Religions in the Greco-Roman World, p. 365.*]

The central concern is clear. Paul and his companions want to impress on the Thessalonian believers that how they live needs to be guided by who they are. Moral conduct must correspond to eschatological status. *Children of day* need to *stay awake and be sober*. In 5:7-8 this point is emphasized by repetition. An observation from everyday life (5:7) underscores the exhortation in 5:6 and prepares the way for this admonition to be restated and further grounded in 5:8. When do people usually sleep? *Those who sleep sleep at night*

(5:7a). When do drunkards normally indulge their craving? *Those who get drunk are drunk at night* (5:7b). Though generally true descriptions of habitual social behavior, these statements also connect with the call in 5:6 for moral vigilance and self-control: *Let us stay awake and be sober.* Evidently the thinking here flows back and forth between literal and metaphorical meanings, although the metaphorical level dominates. The admonition in 5:6 is not to be taken literally: *Let us not fall asleep.* Why would the missionary pastors advocate compulsory insomnia? However, the call to sobriety in 5:6, 8 undoubtedly includes the appeal to avoid drunkenness.

The observation in 5:7 concerning what typically happens *at night* sets the stage for an emphatic restatement of the appeal to be people whose lives echo the values of *the day: but since we belong to the day, let us be sober* (5:8a). The *we* receives emphasis, as if again to remind the Thessalonians that, just as their eschatological condition sets them apart from *the others* (5:4-5), so also their conduct and commitment need to distinguish them.

To explain what they mean by this call to vigilance and sobriety, Paul and his co-workers employ yet another metaphor: *putting on the breastplate of faith and love, and as a helmet the hope of salvation* (5:8b). The *breastplate* and *helmet* were worn by soldiers when entering battle. This military metaphor seems to be an adaptation of Isaiah 59:17, which describes God as a warrior bringing judgment on adversaries and redemption to the repentant: "He put on righteousness like a breastplate, and a helmet of salvation on his head." The imagery in Isaiah 59:17 appears also to have shaped a similar text in Wisdom of Solomon 5:17. In Ephesians 6:14-17, this warrior metaphor has been developed still further ("God's Warriors" in TBC below).

This military image raises intriguing questions. How is the sobriety of people who *belong to the day* enhanced by *putting on* this kind of armor? Does this armor enable defense, or offense, or both? Perhaps most provocative, why does Paul here recall the trilogy *faith, love,* and *hope* (1:4), and why does he substitute them for Isaiah's themes of *righteousness* and *salvation?*

The notion of *putting on* (getting dressed) appears frequently as a metaphor in Paul's letters. Baptism can be viewed in this way: "As many of you as were baptized into Christ have clothed yourselves with Christ" (RSV: "put on Christ"; Gal. 3:27). Exhortations calling for moral behavior are sometimes put in terms of taking off one set of clothes and accepting a fresh new wardrobe (Rom. 13:12-14; Col.

3:9-10, 12-14). Similar language may have been used when the converts in Thessalonica were baptized. By confessing their faith in baptism, they identified themselves with Christ and the church. The injunction to clothe themselves with the armor of *faith, love,* and *hope* essentially urges them to live in dynamic conformity to their confession and to claim the spiritual resources available to them.

At the beginning of the letter, when Paul and his co-workers recall how the Thessalonians accepted the gospel, they thank God (1:2-10). This gratitude is elicited not primarily by the Thessalonians' *faith, love,* and *hope* as such, but by their dynamic faithfulness expressed through their active love and fervent hope (1:4; "Faith, Love, and Hope" in TBC for 1:1-10). A similar premise lurks behind the military metaphor in 5:8b. *Faith, love,* and *hope* are presented as weapons in the warfare necessitated by the forces of *night* and *darkness* surrounding the *children of light* and *children of day.* Yet the *breastplate of faith and love* and the *helmet* constituted by *the hope of salvation* not only defend the believers against the onslaughts of hostile powers. In actual fact, as bearers of this divine armor, they are also summoned to take the offensive against evil through the confident and trusting exercise of *faith, love,* and *hope.* The Thessalonian believers therefore are not "passive and worried bystanders awaiting the arrival of the Lord." Their stance rather is that of "the divine combatant, ready to seize every opportunity to exercise the warfare of love" (Yoder Neufeld: 86).

The *helmet* which shields the head during this "warfare of love" is designated not just as *hope* but as *the hope of salvation.* This phrase then opens the door for an assuring word in 5:9-10 about God's intention and the source and the ultimate outcome of *salvation.*

Not Wrath but Salvation 5:9-10

As if to ground the assurances and the admonitions offered in face of *the day of the Lord,* the evangelists unequivocally declare that God intends to save rather than condemn (diagram on next page).

This reference to *wrath* within a pastoral response to questions about *the day of the Lord* (5:9) can be understood against the background of the OT. The OT prophets often associate *the day of the Lord* with *wrath* (as in Zeph. 1:14-16). Typically viewing the threat of invasion by foreign armies as expressions of imminent *wrath* on Israel, these prophets let it be known that on *the day of the Lord,* divine judgment would also fall on these foreign nations ("The Day of the

Lord" in TBC below). Yet God still intends to rescue those who repent. At times the prophets concede that only a remnant will be
saved, even though God desires that all repent.

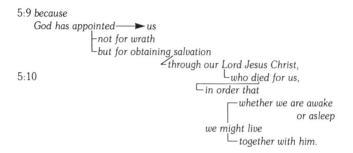

Within 1 Thessalonians, this allusion to *wrath* in 5:9 also recalls
both 1:10 and 2:16 ("Wrath" in TBC for 2:13-16). As our discussion
of those texts shows, in 1:10 *wrath* still lies in the future while in 2:16
wrath is an event either past, presently unfolding, or near. Even in
1:10, *coming wrath* may have both historical and eschatological dimensions. The Thessalonian believers were facing affliction, which
made them *imitators of us* (the missionaries) *and the Lord* (1:6).
Coming wrath likely includes the fearsome prospect that their affliction might worsen. However, the good news centers on Jesus, whose
afflictions even lead to his death. Jesus, *raised from the dead*, therefore is the one *who delivers us from the coming wrath* (1:10; "Jesus
Delivers" in TBC for 1:1-10).

Wrath is here contrasted with *obtaining salvation* (5:9). This
wording is consistent with the concept of *salvation* as a future reality,
a notion implied in the phrase *hope of salvation* (5:8). In Paul's view,
salvation can be understood as past, present, and future: a present
experience grounded in God's gracious work in Christ, an ongoing
process in which the believer participates (cf. Phil. 2:12-13), and the
anticipated outcome of that process. Here the accent lies on future
salvation, as a goal yet to be attained. ("Salvation Through Our Lord
Jesus Christ" in TBC below). A dynamic *hope of salvation* plays a vital role in the armor with which believers both defend themselves
against evil and engage in struggles for liberation.

But what does the verb *appoint* (RSV: *destine*) in 5:9 mean? Does
the assertion that *God has appointed us* imply that God destines (or
predestines) some to *wrath* and others to *obtaining salvation*? If we

draw such a conclusion from this text, we ignore how this statement fits within the overall argument of 5:1-11. Essentially, Paul here reiterates assurances stated earlier. Though *the day of the Lord* will bring *sudden destruction*, such judgment will descend *upon them* (those who bank on a false notion of *peace and security*, who live *in darkness, who sleep, who get drunk*). For *us* (*the children of day*, who heed the admonition to *stay awake and be sober*, who are clothed with the armor of *faith, love*, and *hope of salvation*), God assures *salvation*.

Throughout 5:1-11, the Thessalonian believers are summoned both to claim their identity as *children of day* and to conduct themselves accordingly. The reminder that *God has appointed us not for wrath but for obtaining salvation* seeks to instill in these converts a confidence rooted in the ultimate victory which is already assured through the death and resurrection of Jesus Christ. This confidence, however, does not permit the luxury of a passive reliance on God's omnipotent election. Those who believe also behave. True believers also actively participate in God's redemptive mission to the world ("Election" in TBC for 1:1-10).

Having alluded to *salvation* as God's ultimate intention, Paul inserts a word about what God has done to save those who commit themselves to God in faith and trust. The salvation which God grants is mediated *through our Lord Jesus Christ who died for us* (5:9-10). When Paul and his missionary colleagues first visited Thessalonica, their proclamation undoubtedly featured this foundational message. In response to that message, the Thessalonians *turned toward God away from idols* (1:9).

In a letter which he wrote later to the church at Corinth, Paul describes himself as a recipient of the good news by which those who believe "are being saved" (1 Cor. 15:1-2). In that letter to Corinthian believers, Paul summarizes in credal form the key tenets of this gospel, beginning with "Christ died for our sins in accordance with the sciptures" (15:3). Nowhere in his letter to the Thessalonians does Paul include this kind of summary of the confession of the early church. Nor does he articulate a doctrine of the atonement like he does in Romans (especially 3:24-26). However, an understanding of Jesus' death as opening the way to salvation shines through the clause in 5:10: *who died for us*. The preposition *for* (*huper*) may be taken to mean that Jesus died vicariously in our place (as our substitute), or that Jesus died on our behalf (as our representative).

References in this letter to Jesus' suffering (1:6) and death (1:10;

2:15; 4:14) show that the writers assume the Thessalonians are aware of the atoning significance of Jesus' death. Their knowledge came from hearing the good news of the crucified and risen Christ through the evangelistic preaching of the missionaries. It is not possible to replay these sermons. However, echoes of what must have been Paul's spoken witness concerning Jesus' death and resurrection can be heard in what he writes to his various churches ("Salvation Through Our Lord Jesus Christ" in TBC below; "Jesus Died and Arose" in TBC for 4:13-18).

By means of the conjunction of purpose, in order that (hina), Paul reconnects with earlier themes. What is the final outcome of Jesus' death for us? Jesus died for us in order that whether we are awake or asleep, we might live together with him (5:10b). But what do the metaphors awake and asleep mean here? In 5:6, awake and asleep have moral connotations. The injunction, stated both negatively (let us not fall asleep) and positively (let us stay awake), urges the believers to maintain a posture of spiritual and moral vigilance (5:6).

Should awake and asleep in 5:10b also be understood in this moral sense? Some interpreters have so argued: "Since future salvation has been so fully provided by Christ's finished work, it cannot be canceled by lack of readiness" (Thomas: 286). Others dismiss such a notion as blatant "moral indifferentism" (Bruce, 1982:114). Indeed, why would Paul here (and many places elsewhere) bother to admonish believers to live upright moral lives if this is a matter of indifference? To interpret the benefits of Christ's death as so sufficient that believers can bask in their assurance of eternal security, regardless of their ongoing spiritual and moral response, essentially undermines this call to spiritual vitality and moral faithfulness.

In light of the unpredictable, sudden, and inevitable coming of the day of the Lord (5:2-3), Paul appeals to Christians in Thessalonica to let their lives actively correspond to their status and identity. Because of their relationship to Christ, that day need not surprise them (5:4), but their lives must also reflect that relationship. When the day of the Lord dawns, believers are both assured and exhorted in light of the confidence and hope that they might live together with him.

As in 4:13-18, two possibilities are considered, either life or death. For both the living and the dead who are in Christ, continuity of life in Christ is envisioned. If we are awake (alive; cf. we who are alive, who are left until the coming of the Lord, 4:15, 17), Paul reassures and urges, We live together with him. If we are asleep (dead; cf. those who are asleep, 4:13, 15), Paul adds, we live together with him. As in

4:17, Paul reassures the Thessalonians that for believers, communion with Christ cannot be interrupted even by death. Nor will *the day of the Lord* undo that relationship with Christ. Therefore, believers need to watch and pray. Those who have *turned toward God* do not just passively *await [God's] Son from heaven*; in the meantime, they also are called actively *to serve the living and true God* (1:9-10).

Another Pastoral Exhortation 5:11

As at 4:18, so here at the end of this paragraph on *the times and the seasons*, Paul and his co-workers conclude on a decidedly pastoral note:

To this point, the concern has been primarily to offer assurance and guidance in light of *the day of the Lord*. Now the Thessalonian believers hear an admonition to extend such pastoral care to each other: *Therefore encourage each other.*

But the missionary pastors also nudge their sisters and brothers in Thessalonica in another way: *and build each other up*. The building image appears occasionally elsewhere in Paul's letters (especially 1 Cor. 14:3, 4, 12, 26) as he urges Christians to give careful thought about whether their worship and conduct are edifying and upbuilding. This encouragement to *build each other up* therefore serves as a natural bridge to the closing exhortations in this letter, which deal with life and ministry within the community of faith (5:12-22).

As Paul and his co-workers wrap up this part of the letter, which urges the believers in Thessalonica to console and encourage each other in light of their Christian hope, they also give credit where credit is due: *just as you are doing* (cf. also 4:1, 10). The letter begins with an expression of gratitude to God for *their steadfastness of hope in our Lord Jesus Christ* (1:3). Yet the letter also acknowledges that these new believers need to be grounded more firmly, in light of *the coming of the Lord Jesus Christ with all his holy ones* (3:13). At the end of this pastoral exhortation concerning the *parousia* and *the day of the Lord*, the recipients hear that indeed they are already consoling and encouraging each other. They just need to keep on doing so even more!

THE TEXT IN THE BIBLICAL CONTEXT
The Day of the Lord

The roots of the apocalyptic theme of *the day of the Lord* lie in the OT, particularly the prophets. Hope for divine intervention in behalf of the people of Israel was inspired by the memory of God's past mighty acts, especially the Exodus. As in the past, God would surely again avenge Israel against the nations oppressing them.

But the eighth-century prophet Amos alerts his hearers to the fact that the sword of God's judgment cuts both ways. Those who piously await the day of the Lord but do not pursue justice for others are in for a surprise:

> Alas for you who desire the day of the Lord! Why do you want the day of the Lord? It is darkness, not light; as if someone fled from a lion, and was met by a bear. (Amos 5:18-19)

The prophet Zephaniah, during the last decades of the kingdom of Judah (around 630 B.C.), also warns that "the day of the Lord is at hand" (Zeph. 1:7). This would be a day when the king and his corrupt officials would be punished (1:8). On that fateful day, the complacent would be aroused out of their groggy indifference (1:12-13). In short, this would be a season of unthinkable wrath:

> The great day of the Lord is near, near and hastening fast;
> the sound of the day of the Lord is bitter, the warrior cries aloud there.
> That day will be a day of wrath, a day of distress and anguish,
> a day of ruin and devastation, a day of darkness and gloom,
> a day of clouds and thick darkness, a day of trumpet blast and battle cry
> against the fortified cities and against the lofty battlements.
> (Zeph. 1:14-16)

The ominous threat of foreign invasion seems to be viewed as the outworking of wrath and judgment against Israel for her unfaithfulness. Nations like Assyria become God's instruments ("Assyria, the rod of my anger," Isa. 10:5), but they too will feel God's hand of judgment against them (Zeph. 2:4-15; Isa. 10:5-34). The day of the Lord therefore was to be a time of judgment on all evildoers, both in Israel as well as among the Gentiles (cf. Isa. 13:9-16; Joel 1:15—2:10).

For the humble who seek justice and for those who repent of their waywardness, the day of the Lord need not come as a surprise. Zephaniah notes that "neither their silver nor their gold will be able to save them on the day of the Lord's wrath" (1:18), Zephaniah pleads with his people:

Seek the Lord, all you humble of the land, who do his commands;
seek righteousness, seek humility;
perhaps you may be hidden on the day of the Lord's wrath. (Zeph. 2:3)

Zephaniah anticipates that a righteous remnant will repent and be forgiven, and that the Lord God ("a warrior who gives victory," 3:17) will restore their fortunes (see 3:8-20). Similar expressions of this glorious hope can be found in the oracles of other prophets as well (Obad. 15-21; Mal. 4:1-5).

In Zechariah 14, the coming day of God's judgment and deliverance is pictured as a final cataclysmic victory over the forces of evil. In the end, "the Lord will become king over all the earth" (14:9). Apocalyptic writings feature similar expectations of an event beyond history which will vindicate the righteous. [Apocalyptic, p. 354.]

Apparently Jesus also expects this kind of climactic eschatological event. According to Luke, when Jesus is asked by the Pharisees when the kingdom of God will be coming, he first denies that there would be any clearly observable signs (Luke 17:20-21). Then he teaches his disciples about "the days of the Son of Man" (17:22). Jesus describes the deceptively carefree "days of Noah" (17:26-27) and "days of Lot" (17:28-29), when judgment by flood or by fire abruptly curtailed life as usual. Then he declares, "It will be like that when the Son of Man is revealed" (17:30).

The early church confesses that "Jesus is Lord" (1 Cor. 12:3; Phil. 2:11; Rom. 10:9). Accordingly, the OT notion of "the day of the Lord" (where Lord refers to God) came to be interpreted as identical to Christ's parousia. Sometimes called "the day of the Lord" (2 Thess. 2:2; 1 Cor. 5:5; 2 Pet. 3:10), this event also came to be designated by the phrase "the day of Christ" or by similar expressions (1 Cor. 1:8; 2 Cor. 1:14; Phil. 1:10; 2:16) or simply as "the/that day" (1 Thess. 5:4; 2 Thess. 1:10; Rom. 13:12; 1 Cor. 3:13; Heb. 10:25). As implied in 1 Thessalonians 5:1-11, that day will bring calamitous judgment. However, for those who identify with Christ as crucified and risen Lord, that day ushers in the season of final salvation.

Light and Darkness, Day and Night

Apocalyptic writings typically portray sharp contrasts between opposites. As noted above (see Preview), 5:1-11 features a whole series of contrasting realities, such as light and darkness, and day and night. Our understanding of this text will be enhanced if we explore the roots and further development of this literary and theological phenomenon. We will focus primarily on *light* and *darkness*.

In the OT, *light* often denotes God's saving presence (as in Isa. 60:18-20; Job 29:3), and *darkness* the forces of adversity (Ps. 74:20; 82:5). A quotation from the prophet Micah illustrates such usage:

> Do not rejoice over me, O my enemy; when I fall, I shall rise; when I sit in darkness, the Lord will be a light to me. (Mic. 7:8)

The War Scroll (1QM), one of the documents discovered in the caves at Qumran near the Dead Sea, graphically depicts the end-time battle between "sons of darkness" and "sons of light." In this battle, which seesaws precariously back and forth, the evil forces eventually face defeat at the hands of the "sons of light," who are identified with the sectarian group at Qumran.

The Gospel and epistles of John make abundant use of the motifs of *light* and *darkness*. In Jesus himself, the light of God's salvation dispels the darkness of sin. Already in the opening prologue of the Gospel, John sounds this keynote, which reverberates throughout his writings:

> What has come into being in him was life, and the life was the light of all people. The light shines in the darkness, and the darkness did not over-come it. (John 1:3-5; cf. 3:19; 8:12; 12:36; 1 John 1:5-7)

When Paul reflects on his own personal pilgrimage and generally about the way in which God has entered into the world in the person of Christ, he also employs *light/darkness* imagery. In one case he cites from the creation story:

> For it is the God who said, "Let light shine out of darkness," who has shone in our hearts to give the light of the knowledge of the glory of God in the face of Jesus Christ. (2 Cor. 4:6)

Yet the struggle with the forces of darkness continues (2 Cor. 6:14; Eph. 6:12). This calls for deliberate strategies to guard against being enveloped by the surrounding night and to penetrate its darkness with the light of the gospel. The warrior metaphor of 1 Thessalonians 5:8 suggestively portrays such strategies.

God's Warriors

Many of the OT narratives portray a warrior God. In the Exodus and conquest stories, God dramatically intervenes in behalf of the Israelites to lead them into the land. These victories are celebrated in war hymns: the songs of Miriam (Exod. 15:21) and Moses (15:1-18), and the song of Deborah (Judg. 5). Another song of Moses (Deut. 32:1-43) reviews God's deliverance and laments the people's unfaithfulness. Numerous Psalms (such as 136) and prophetic oracles (such as Hab. 3:1-19) recall God's saving activity in the past and express a longing for a repeat performance. The warfare theology of these and other texts (see Lind: 1980; Yoder Neufeld: 1989, and his forthcoming BCBC commentary, *Ephesians*, on Eph. 6:10-20) provides the backdrop against which the military metaphor in 1 Thessalonians 5:8 needs to be interpreted.

Isaiah 59:17 appears to be the text which Paul adapts when he compares *faith and love* to a soldier's *breastplate*, and *hope of salvation* to his *helmet*. This oracle opens by lamenting that God has seemingly withdrawn because injustice and wickedness run rampant in the community (59:1-8): "The way of peace they do not know" (59:8). After the community acknowledges its plight and confesses its transgressions (59:9-15a), the Divine Warrior moves into action to redress the injustice (59:15b-20).

This portrait of the Divine Warrior includes both a description of the armor and an account of his actions:

He put on righteousness like a breastplate,
  and a helmet of salvation on his head;
he put on garments of vengeance for clothing,
  and wrapped himself in fury as a mantle.
According to their deeds, so will he repay;
  wrath to his adversaries, requital to his enemies. (Isa. 59:17-18)
And he will come to Zion as Redeemer,
  to those in Jacob who turn from transgression, says the Lord. (59:20)

Essentially, therefore, Isaiah 59 is a call to repentance. God's redemptive intervention as warrior requires that the people first repent and that they act justly in their relationships.

Strikingly, when Paul in 1 Thessalonians 5:8 adapts the military metaphor from Isaiah 59:17, he urges the believers to put on the armor! As *children of light* (5:5), therefore, the Thessalonian converts are urged to equip themselves to fight a holy war, to join the Divine Warrior in a struggle for justice and peace. Not only are they furnished military hardware to defend themselves against the forces of darkness around them. Their participation in divine warfare also calls for a radical exercise of a dynamic *faith* and self-giving *love* offered in the steadfastness and patience inspired by their *hope of salvation*. In short, with the breastplate and helmet of *faith, love,* and *hope,* believers can participate in God's redemptive work in the world.

In Romans 13:11-14 Paul employs similar imagery. As in 1 Thessalonians 5:1-11, an eschatological perspective prevails. Paul says, "You know what time (*kairos*) it is" (13:11a). Paul seeks to impress on the Roman Christians that "salvation is nearer to us now than when we became believers" (13:11b), and he urges them: "Let us then lay aside the works of darkness and put on the armor of light" (13:12). In the exhortations which follow, Paul identifies specific behaviors which need to be avoided (13:13). Positively stated, Paul simply restates the earlier injunction, "put on the armor of light," with the words: "Put on the Lord Jesus Christ" (13:14).

In the context of Romans, this final admonition recalls Paul's earlier theological reflections on baptism. In baptism, believers die with Christ so that they can be raised to newness of life in Christ (6:1-11). But baptism also has a recruiting dimension. By participating in the death and resurrection of Christ through baptism, believers enlist on God's side of the ongoing battle between wickedness and righteousness (6:12-14). Paul exhorts those who in Christ have been rescued from death and granted life: "Present your members to God as instruments of righteousness" (6:13). The word here translated *instruments (hopla),* is the one rendered as *armor* in 13:12. In both cases the translation could be *weapons.* The perspective of being baptized into God's infantry can therefore also help us to understand Romans 13 as a whole. Paul, after teaching on Christian attitudes toward the state (13:1-7) and the way of love in human relationships (13:8-10), sums up the subject by reminding believers that they have an active assignment as warriors armed with Jesus Christ himself (13:11-14)!

In Ephesians 6:10-20 we encounter the most elaborate NT development of this theme. The Christian community hears a rousing call to be empowered through taking up "the whole armor of God" (6:11). This equipment enables the church "to stand against the wiles of the devil" (6:10), whose various deputies (rulers, authorities, cosmic powers) are at work (6:12). The admonition is restated in light of the eventual culmination of this battle:

> Therefore take up the whole armor of God, so that you may be able to withstand on that evil day, and having done everything, to stand firm.
> (Eph. 6:13)

Yet more than a defensive posture is called for. Another call, "Stand therefore" (Eph. 6:14), introduces an array of metaphors which suggest an aggressive stance. Rather than passively awaiting final deliverance, the faith community finds itself summoned to fight with the weapons of truth, righteousness, the gospel of peace, faith, salvation, and the word of God (6:14-17). This proclaimed word of God is powerful in unmasking evil and working to overcome it.

First Thessalonians 5:8 therefore stands broadly within this biblical picture. God as holy warrior works for justice and fights against evil. God's people are those who repent of their own sin so that they can be fully engaged in God's ongoing liberating work in the world. Such participation in God's liberating agenda does not include the use of violence. The church as God's warriors does not engage in a Zealot-like militant fight for personal or national liberation. Nor does this stance permit passive nonengagement, simply trusting God to deliver without human cooperation. As spiritual warriors, the Christian community joins the Divine Warrior in working toward wholeness, peace, and justice. The weapons for the believers' participation in this battle are *faith and love* and *the hope of salvation.*

Salvation Through Our Lord Jesus Christ

Soteriology, the doctrine of salvation, is developed more fully elsewhere in Paul's letters, especially Romans. However, the core affirmation which lies at the heart of all views of the atonement surfaces in 1 Thessalonians 5, in the amplifying statement concerning the source of our salvation: *through our Lord Jesus Christ, who died for us* (5:9-10). Numerous other NT texts make the same claim:

> Christ died for our sins in accordance with the sciptures. (1 Cor. 15:3)
> We are convinced that one has died for all; therefore all have died.
> (2 Cor. 5:14)
> Christ died for the ungodly. (Rom. 5:6)
> Christ died for us. (Rom. 5:8)
> The Lord Jesus Christ . . . gave himself for our sins. (Gal. 1:3-4)
> The Son of God . . . loved me and gave himself for me. (Gal. 2:20)

How did Jesus' death come to be understood as being *for us?* The portrait of the suffering servant in Isaiah 53 shapes the thinking of the early church, Paul and other NT writers, and likely Jesus himself:

> He poured out himself to death,
>   and was numbered with the transgressors;
> yet he bore the sin of many,
>   and made intercession for the transgressors. (Isa. 53:12)

According to Luke, Jesus cites this text concerning himself (Luke 22:37). The Ethiopian eunuch heard Philip's proclamation of the good news about Jesus, using Isaiah 53 as a text (Acts 8:30-35). Jesus' death, therefore, is recognized as the fulfillment of the mission of the suffering servant. Yet Jesus' crucifixion is not only a historical event. Jesus' death on the cross came to be recognized primarily as a redemptive event, a powerful moment in time when God's love and grace were supremely demonstrated before a sinful and broken world.

Paul and the other NT writers utilize numerous images and symbols to try to communicate how Jesus' death imparts salvation. No single image seems to be adequate to convey the meaning of this event. Cousar, in his book dealing with the death of Jesus in Paul's letters, notes that in the history of the church, various attempts have been made to find one unifying category. Prominent among these proposals have been: justification, dying and rising with Christ, and reconciliation. However, Cousar urges that we avoid restricting ourselves to one or several ways of picturing the redemptive impact of Jesus' death (Cousar: 52-88).

Similarly, John Driver calls for a recognition of the rich legacy of images used in Scripture to describe the atonement. He catalogs these images and metaphors into ten different groups, and devotes a chapter to discuss each of them: conflict-victory-liberation; vicarious suffering; archetypal images (such as, Jesus as the last Adam); martyr motif; sacrifice motif; expiation motif and the wrath of God; redemption-purchase motif; reconciliation; justification; and adoption-family image. Driver points out that the various contexts in which the apostolic mission was carried out often dictate what kind of image is used:

> The center of the gospel proclamation was the fact of the life, death, and resurrection of Messiah and the subsequent coming upon the apostolic community of his Spirit with astonishing power. The meaning of this saving work of Christ was interpreted variously through images chosen according to the demands of particular missionary contexts. (Driver: 246)

We cannot know all that Paul or his colleagues might have preached in Thessalonica concerning the meaning of Jesus' death. However, the fleeting reference in 1 Thessalonians 5:9-10 depicts Jesus' death in most basic language as *for us*. Among Driver's categories, the phrase *for us* can be seen either in terms of vicarious suffering (Jesus died *for us*, as our substitute) or in terms of one of the archetypal images (Jesus died as our representative, as the last Adam; so Driver: 103-104; cf. "Salvation" in TBC for 2 Thess. 2:13-17).

THE TEXT IN THE LIFE OF THE CHURCH
Living in the Last Days

Christian bookstores continue to sell glossy paperbacks dealing with biblical prophecy. There is an active market for literature which claims to answer the question, "When will these things be?" Hal Lindsey's *The Late Great Planet Earth* came out in May 1970 and was into its sixteenth printing by November 1971. This book continues to sell. Why? The author portrays the future in light of biblical texts which he interprets as predictions of events now unfolding or about to occur. Most people would like to have the curtain removed so that they can view the future. The introduction to the original edition of this book states, "If you have no interest in the future, this isn't for you."

The problem with this quest for clues about the future is that it often sidetracks Christians from their mission in the present. Paul responds to the Thessalonians' concern about *the times and the seasons*, not by providing an end-time calendar, but by reassuring them about their identity in Christ and by urging them to live in harmony with their status as *children of day*. Indeed, they are summoned to be people whose identifying features are *faith, love,* and *hope of salvation*. Christians have a mission to accomplish, not just a future to await.

Before his ascension, the risen Christ was asked, "Lord, is this the time when you will restore the kingdom to Israel" (Acts 1:6)? Jesus' response to his disciples then still suffices for the church today:

> It is not for you to know the times or periods that the Father has set by his own authority. But you will receive power when the Holy Spirit has come upon you; and you will be my witnesses in Jerusalem, in all Judea and Samaria, and to the ends of the earth. (Acts 1:7-8)

The instructions Jesus left for the earliest community of his disciples still apply! During the time between Jesus' ascension and his return (1:9-11), the church has been empowered by the Holy Spirit to engage in a global mission.

When Peter begins his Pentecost sermon, he adapts Joel's prophecy concerning the "day of the Lord" (Joel 2:28-32). Peter highlights the fact that "in the last days," God is pouring out the Spirit on the expectant disciples, both women and men (Acts 2:17). Which are the last days? The last days make up the period, however long, when the church of Jesus Christ under the inspiration of the Spirit of God proclaims and lives the gospel in the world. For how long? Until "the coming of the Lord's great and glorious day" (2:20). Then "everyone who calls on the name of the Lord shall be saved" (2:21).

David Ewert has shown that this is the prevailing understanding of the concept of "the last days" in Scripture:

> Many evangelical Christians think of the last days as the final epoch just before the end. The New Testament, however, equates them with the new era introduced by Christ's work of redemption accomplished at his first advent. We can say that Christians throughout this interim have lived and are living in the last days. Believers always live, as it were, "between the times." (Ewert, 1980:17)

However, what sense does it make for a period of two thousand years or more to be classified as the last days? Ewert offers this reply:

> That this interim would last as long as it has (or may yet last) was not known to the New Testament writers, for the day and the hour of the consummation of this age was hidden in God. God is not bound by our clocks and calendars—which are human inventions. But we know on the authority of his Word, that these last days in which the church lives will come to an end. (Ewert, 1980:17)

Jesus warned his disciples that they cannot know God's calendar (Acts 1:7) and also admitted that he himself did not know "that day or hour" (Mark 13:32). Yet some people continue to try their luck at reading the signs and predicting the end. During the Gulf War in 1991, while I was teaching at Union Biblical Seminary in Pune, India, some local Christians gave me literature written by a western missionary. This tract claimed to delineate exactly how Saddam Hussein fits into biblical prophecy. My reply then was that, since only God knows how this whole enterprise will unfold, we need to be about our mission as witnesses to the good news. Our faithful engagement in God's redemptive mission is especially needed at such desperate times when nations again resort to violence rather than peacemaking as a strategy for resolving conflict.

The story of Claasz Epp illustrates how tragic such calculations of the end can become. Epp, who lived in south Russia during the nineteenth century, became passionately focused on the imminent coming of Christ. After he gathered a group of followers, in 1880 he made the trek from Russia to Turkestan to meet the Lord. This leader set the date and then revised it when it turned out to be wrong. Epp himself turned more and more fanatical, and his followers became increasingly disillusioned. Many died. Finally, Epp was excommunicated by the handful of people who had stayed with him (ME, 2:234).

Among the Brethren the story of the minister, William C. Thurman, follows a similar tragic course. In a book published in 1864, Thurman announced that the millennium would arrive on September 27, 1868. At first he gained a favorable reception. However, when the first prediction and then later when several revised dates all proved to be incorrect, the Brethren turned critical, and even his most ardent followers became disillusioned. When Thurman died in 1906, a poor and broken man, he proclaimed that the world would end in 1917 (BE, 2:1264).

Jesus' counsel deserves to be heard anew whenever anyone is tempted to try to predict the unpredictable yet inevitable *day of the Lord*:

> But about that day or hour no one knows, neither the angels in heaven, nor the Son, but only the Father. Beware, keep alert; for you do not know when the time will come. (Mark 13:32-33)

Despite assurances that they are already sufficiently informed about *the times and the seasons*, some members of the Thessalonian Christian community soon become increasingly enthralled by the misleading idea that *the day of the Lord has come* (2 Thess. 2:2). A second letter becomes necessary to warn against such deceptive claims.

Christians within the believers church tradition have sometimes also tried to outguess God and thereby been deflected from their calling to witness to God's dynamic reign, already here yet still to come in fullness.

1 Thessalonians 5:12-22

Life and Leadership in the Community of Faith

PREVIEW

In light of the imminent dawning of the *day of the Lord*, how shall the faith community live? Indeed, given the inevitable yet unpredictable coming of the Lord, how does the church organize for its life and witness in the world?

In 5:12-22, Paul, Silvanus, and Timothy advise the converts in Thessalonica about internal congregational relationships, given their eschatological situation. Their counsel to the church adds specificity to the concluding exhortation in 5:11: *Therefore encourage each other and build each other up, just as you are doing.*

Both at 5:12 and at 5:14, a verb of appeal introduces the agenda: *We ask you* (5:12), and *we urge you* (5:14). These two verbs also appear together in 4:1, where the exhortation section (4:1—5:22) begins. At both 5:12 and 5:14, the Thessalonian believers are addressed as *brothers and sisters.* On the basis of these two signals, we can divide this paragraph into two related subsections: 5:12-13 and 5:14-22. In both subsections, the *brothers and sisters* in Thessalonica hear appeals concerning their life as a Christian community. The topic addressed in 5:12-13 is their relationship to the leaders of the church. In 5:14-22 the exhortations focus on the ministering activities in which the whole church needs to be engaged. This includes the way they conduct themselves both toward each other (5:14) and toward outsiders (5:15).

The series of admonitions in 5:16-22 may be seen as a continuation of the counsel given to the whole church. Eight short exhortations concerning prayer, worship, and the exercise of the gifts of the Spirit remind the readers that the church exists as an expectant community. The church is a community which worships and serves while it awaits the coming of the triumphant Lord.

OUTLINE
Attitudes Toward Leaders, 5:12-13
The Ministry of All, 5:14-15
Worship and the Spirit, 5:16-22

EXPLANATORY NOTES
Attitudes Toward Leaders 5:12-13
Paul and his partners in the ministry introduce this section by offering some pastoral advice on attitudes toward congregational leaders:

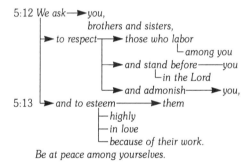

When Timothy returned from his second visit to Thessalonica (3:6), he apparently reported that the local leaders were having some trouble in the church. Among the instigators of these problems, the *unruly* (5:14; cf. also 2 Thess. 3:6-15) likely had a key role. However, Romans 12:1-21 shows that Paul can include exhortations concerning the use of ministry gifts and offer counsel about relationships within the church and the larger community, even when he has had no direct contact with a congregation. In writing to the Thessalonian congregation about their attitudes toward their leaders, Paul may be adapting general pastoral exhortations to this particular local situation.

We ask you echoes the injunction with which the pastoral exhor-

tation section (4:1—5:22) was introduced in 4:1. A largely synonymous *we urge you* (also found in 4:1) appears in 5:14. As noted earlier (*see* at 4:1), these verbs illustrate that Paul and his fellow missionaries seek to persuade rather than to issue demands. On the basis of
their common relationship *in the Lord Jesus* (4:1), missionaries, congregational leaders, and the members of the church as a whole are all
brothers and sisters.

Even though in the church all are *brothers and sisters* and all believers share the experience of being *in the Lord*, the congregation
also needs leaders who have significant functions to perform. According to Paul and his partners, such leaders deserve to be sincerely
and lovingly acknowledged for what they do. Two general attitudes
are encouraged: the Thessalonians are urged *to respect* (5:12) and *to
esteem* (5:13) their leaders.

The root of the infinitive often translated *to respect* is *know*
(*oida*), suggesting that the congregation should acknowledge those
who exercise leadership responsibilities. Who are they? The people
whom the Thessalonians are urged to acknowledge or respect are
not identified by their office or title. Instead, they are designated by a
series of three participles, all of which describe what these persons
do. The first stresses that ministry involves hard work. Church workers at Thessalonica are described as *those who labor (kopiōntas)
among you.* In 3:5, when Paul expresses his personal apprehension
that the Thessalonians' faith might not withstand persecution, he also
articulates what is at stake for himself: *Our labor might be in vain.* In
short, Paul's evangelistic ministry in Thessalonica is designated by the
word *labor* (with the same root for noun or verb; similarly in 1 Cor.
15:10). Strikingly, the same word also portrays the rigor of physical
labor: *You remember our labor and toil* (2:9; cf. 2 Thess. 3:8). Those
members of the congregation who had slipped into irresponsible
idleness (*the unruly*, 5:14) are expected to hear a subtle rebuke in
this reference to their leaders' *labor* among them.

The second description provides more specific information concerning the kind of church work which these people do. However, a
vexing translation problem makes it difficult to know exactly what
meaning is intended. Most English versions render the Greek word
proistamenous in a way which conveys the notion of leading or governing the congregation: *have charge of* (NRSV), *are over* (KJV, NIV,
RSV). Another possible meaning has been proposed by commentators on the basis of the occurrence of this same word in Romans 12:8:
caring for (Best: 224-225; Bruce: 118-119). In his study of the social

world of Paul's day, Wayne Meeks proposes another reading: These are wealthy patrons who provide protection and material resources for the members of the faith community, many of whom come from the poor working class (Meeks: 134). Wanamaker picks up Meeks' proposal and translates: *those who stand before you as protectors* (Wanamaker: 192-193).

An examination of the way the underlying word functions elsewhere in the NT can be helpful in determining its meaning here. In Romans 12:6-8 Paul lists seven different ministries which are gifts of God's grace to be used to build up the church. One of these is the *proistamenos*, which is variously translated: "he who gives aid" (RSV), "he that ruleth" (KJV), "the leader" (NRSV). In the pastoral epistles, the same word occurs on several occasions. In Titus 3:8, 14, it is used broadly in an exhortation for all believers to devote themselves to good deeds. More directly equivalent are several passages defining qualifications and compensation for various ministers. One of the required qualifications of bishops and deacons is the ability to "manage" their households well (1 Tim. 3:4-5, 12). Elders who "rule well" are deemed worthy of double honor, especially those who labor in preaching and teaching (5:17).

What then might this word mean in 1 Thessalonians 5:12? Even though meanings of compound words are not necessarily ascertained by translating their component parts, in this case such a process leads to the most likely reading: the *proistamenoi* are *those who stand before*. They have a leadership function, not in a hierarchical sense (as suggested in translations such as NRSV: *have charge of*), but as servants of the church. Rather than visualizing wealthy patrons providing for the people and protecting them, we can imagine a congregation drawn mainly from the working class, with leaders emerging largely on the basis of their gifts and abilities.

Confirmation for a nonhierarchical understanding of the work of *those who stand before you* is provided by the added phrase: *in the Lord*. The leaders and their people share in common the gift of salvation *through our Lord Jesus Christ* (5:9) and the resultant life with Christ (5:10). Hence, the leaders function not as top-down managers nor as rulers who lord it over others but rather as servants ("Those Who Stand Before You" in TBC below).

Yet another ministry activity characterizes *those who labor among you*, the ministry of admonition: *those who admonish (nouthetountas) you*. To *admonish* means to teach or nurture. However, such instruction not only informs thinking, it also offers moral guidance (Rom. 15:14; 1 Cor. 4:14; Col. 1:28; 3:16). One particular group in Thessalonica, *the unruly*, are singled out as needing to be admonished (5:14). In a situation requiring congregational discipline, the same word can have the connotation of warning (2 Thess. 3:15). Paul and his companions, possibly recognizing that most people instinctively resist guidance, urge the Christians in Thessalonica: *Respect those who admonish you.*

In 5:13 another verb heightens the appeal for respect toward leaders in the congregation: *We ask you . . . to esteem them.* The force of the word *esteem* is enhanced by the added superlative adverb, *very highly* (NRSV). The underlying word can normally be rendered by *consider* or *regard*, as in Philippians 2:3: "In humility regard others better than yourselves." In addressing the Thessalonian believers, the missionaries feel compelled to emphasize that their congregational leaders need and deserve the great *esteem* of the whole body.

This esteem is further qualified by the phrase *in love.* What might be the significance of this addition? The thanksgiving at the beginning of the letter mentions evidence of *labor of love* (1:3). The letter later expresses the prayer that the Thessalonians might *abound in love toward one another and to all* (3:12; the root of this verb *abound* is in the adverb *highly*, 5:13). The reminder *to esteem* their leaders *in love* therefore underscores the fact that church workers also (perhaps especially) need to know that the people among whom they serve love them. Indeed, *love* should be a key distinguishing mark of the Christian community. Such *love* actively expresses itself in genuine hospitality and caring and the mutual sharing of resources (4:9-12).

Another phrase qualifies this loving esteem with which the people are urged to regard their leaders: *because of their work* (5:13). Respect and esteem for leaders should be based not on ecclesiastical status but on the performance of ministry functions. Rather than feeling that they have no choice but to submit themselves to persons in authority, the people in the congregation need to regard their leaders highly as gifted persons who have been called to serve the church.

There may also be another connotation here. In referring to the leaders' *work*, Paul and his associates may be inviting the people to recall their example: *working night and day, . . . we preached to you the gospel of God* (2:9). The clause *because of their work* (5:13) hints broadly at the lifestyle being commended to all: Work hard, do not insist on your personal rights, show the self-giving love of Christ. In all these ways, you will *esteem* your leaders *highly in love because of their work.* Such *love* is shown supremely by following this example!

At this point, Paul throws in an intriguing exhortation, almost as an aside: *Be at peace among yourselves* (5:13). In the underlying text, a variant, with strong support in ancient manuscripts, leads to the alternative reading: *Be at peace with them* (the church leaders). If that were the original reading, we would have an indication that a rift has developed between the congregation and its leaders. However, on balance it is more likely that the original admonition calls for peaceable attitudes and behavior within the congregation as a whole.

Why would this call (*be at peace among yourselves*) have been added here? Again one cannot establish with certainty whether Timothy might have reported to Paul concerning a particularly contentious situation in Thessalonica. Jewett links this appeal for peace in the Thessalonian community to Paul's apology in 2:1-12. He suggests that some spiritual enthusiasts (especially the *unruly*) are resisting both the Thessalonian leaders and the ministry of Paul (Jewett, 1986:102-105). Perhaps the evangelists know about tensions within the congregation, so they address this divisiveness with an appeal for peace. Judging from Paul's letter to the house churches at Rome, appeals for peace need not be based on actual situations of conflict. Especially striking in this regard is Romans 12:18: "If it is possible, so far as it depends on you, live peaceably with all" (cf. also Rom. 14:19). This is one more of a whole series of striking parallels between Romans 12:9-21 and 1 Thessalonians 5:12-22. When Paul writes to churches about moral and other practical guidelines, he apparently follows a particular script but adapts it to each local situation.

The Ministry of All 5:14-15

The familiar formula, *We urge you, brothers and sisters* (cf. 4:1; 5:12), marks the transition to another topic:

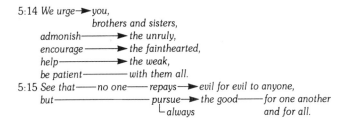

Who is being addressed here? Some interpreters suggest that, because 5:12-13 contains an appeal directed to the people concerning their attitude toward their leaders, 5:14-15 provides instructions for the leaders themselves. However, there is no evidence that *you, brothers and sisters* in 5:14 should be understood as limited to the leadership group. In both 5:12-13 and 5:14-15, Paul and his fellow missionaries appeal to the whole church. Here at 5:14 they remind the congregation as a whole that no individual or team can accomplish all the needed ministries. In a significant sense, the ministry of the church belongs to all.

The missionaries call for four different ministries, with the target groups identified in three categories plus another general one. First, *Admonish the unruly.* As noted above, admonition as instruction, nurture, and moral guidance is identified as one of the specialized ministry tasks (5:12). However, the whole church is enlisted to join the leaders in this activity. But who are the *unruly?* The Greek word *ataktoi* basically means "not in proper order," such as an out-of-step marcher (cf. the derived English word, *atactic*, "lacking regularity"). However, an analysis of the parts of this word does not help us determine the exact identity of this group in Thessalonica. Translations reflect the ongoing lack of scholarly consensus: *the idlers* (NRSV; cf. NIV, REB, TEV), *the careless* (NEB) and *them that are unruly* (KJV).

At issue are two related questions: the characteristic behavior of the *ataktoi*, and the motivations for such behavior. Some writers attribute their behavior to naive trust that their needs will be provided or simply benign laziness (hence *idlers* or *loafers*); others see this group as meddlesome, disorderly, or obstinate resisters of authority *(the unruly).* Motivation for this idleness or disorderliness is most often found in some form of spiritual enthusiasm, especially the enthusiastic expectancy among these early Christians that Christ would soon come as triumphant Lord (Jewett, 1986:104-105, 168-178). After all, why continue with the normal routines of life, especially working for a living, if the return of Christ is near? Others argue that the motivations are more social in nature. Russell envisions a situation where poor people brought into the circle of Christian love enjoy the attention they get, stop working, and increasingly become dependent on the wealthier members of the church or on those who had better work habits (R. Russell: 113).

This reference to *the unruly* needs to be seen in connection with two other passages in the Thessalonian correspondence. At 4:11 the Thessalonians are urged *to be ambitious to be quiet, mind your own affairs, and work with your own hands* (4:11). This counsel makes the most sense if a group in Thessalonica makes too much noise and generally meddles in the lives of others, in large part because they have either quit working altogether or they refuse to do manual labor. These might have been *the unruly*, who need the admonition of the congregation. In 2 Thessalonians 3:6-13, some of these themes are repeated—an indication that by this time the situation has become worse. Paul and his partners point to how they earned their own keep while in Thessalonica (cf. also 1 Thess. 2:9) and urge that the Thessalonians follow this example. Once again, even though the unacceptable behavior includes idleness, the problem is summed up in a way which points to social disorderliness: *not busy working, just busybodies* (2 Thess. 3:11).

It therefore seems best to regard the *ataktoi* as a group whose behavior is characterized both by the cessation of work and by a corresponding increase in the level of some problematic and enthusiastic religious activities. This enthusiasm proves disruptive within the congregation, leads to an unhealthy dependence, and produces an image problem for the church within its social context.

The second ministry commended to the entire congregation is also stated with the kind of brevity that elicits long-winded explanations: *Encourage the fainthearted* (5:14). Both encouragement and consolation may be included in this ministry. Again the problem comes at the point of determining the nature of the needs within this particular group. This word (literally, *the small-souled* or simply *the little people*) appears nowhere else in the NT, but in the Septuagint it characterizes fearful or grieving people (Prov. 18:14; Isa. 35:4; 54:6). Quite likely Paul and his missionary colleagues have in mind those who tend to despair in the face of their own suffering (cf. 3:4) and the deaths of loved ones (4:13). Such people, *the fainthearted*, need the comfort of brothers and sisters who have caught on that, through Jesus' death and resurrection, believers can face both life and death with hope and joy (4:13-18; 5:10).

Another group at Thessalonica also needs the pastoral care of the Christian community as a whole. The third imperative can be easily stated but less readily understood with precision: *help the weak*. The nature of this needed *help* cannot be exactly ascertained. The word can mean simply "take an interest in." But who are *the weak*, and what is the nature of their weakness? Based on usage of the underlying Greek word elsewhere in Paul's writings, *the weak* could be persons who are physically ill (1 Cor. 11:30) or beaten down by adverse circumstances (4:10-11).

However, the language of weakness also occurs extensively in 1 Corinthians 8, where *the weak* are those who have scruples about eating meat that has been offered to idols. At issue in Corinth is how those who are not bothered by this practice can avoid offending those whose consciences are upset by it. In Romans 14:1—15:6, Paul likewise refers to some members of the Jewish-Christian subgroup in Rome as "those who are weak in faith" (14:1), because they still have strong convictions about food, drink, and the observance of the Sabbath and other special days. Paul counsels the strong to take a welcoming and accepting attitude, and he enunciates a guiding principle: "We who are strong ought to put up with the failings of the weak, and not to please ourselves" (Rom. 15:1). If the situation in Thessalonica is comparable to these circumstances in Corinth and Rome, *the weak* could be persons spiritually vulnerable, perhaps easily offended or readily influenced.

Yet another interpretation suggests that the writers of this letter to Thessalonica have moral weakness in mind. According to this reading, *the weak* are threatened by moral failure, perhaps through yielding to sexual temptations (cf. 4:3-8). Without further background data about the situation in Thessalonica, we cannot be sure of our understanding of *the weak*. However, likely these converts are at risk both spiritually and morally. Persons in such circumstances are vulnerable and need the loving care of a supportive group.

The concluding charge in this series of four admonitions urges, *Be patient with them all.* Patience describes an attitude, but it also leads to action: "Love is patient; love is kind" (1 Cor. 13:4). In his list of the fruit of the Spirit (Gal. 5:22-23), Paul includes patience. The congregation's caring responses toward *the unruly, the fainthearted,* and *the weak* need to be graced by patience.

In 5:15 Paul introduces ethical guidance which has clear affinities with Jesus' teachings on love and nonretaliation (Matt. 5:43-48; Luke 6:27-36), even though he does not seem to be quoting Jesus. Likely the counsel about how to relate toward the disturbing and disturbed persons in their midst calls to mind the ethical instructions given by Jesus himself. What specifically does it mean for believers to exercise patience? Paul cites the principle which should govern relationships toward persons both within and beyond the faith community: *See that no one repays evil for evil to anyone, but always pursue the good for one another and for all.* The words *see that* introduce what amounts to a quotation of a rule for conduct among Jesus' followers. This principle features significantly in Paul's traditional ethical instruction within the churches he established.

The ethical instruction in 5:15 not only echoes Jesus' teaching; it also has clear roots in the OT (especially Prov. 20:22). Paul's later letter to the church in Rome demonstrates that he amplifies the ethical principle enunciated in 5:15. Romans 12:14-21 has particular significance as an expanded parallel to this brief passage in 1 Thessalonians. Similarly, 1 Peter teaches the way of nonretaliation, rooting it solidly in Jesus' own example (2:18-25). It seems best, therefore, to deal with the present text primarily in relation to these and other texts within the larger canonical framework ("Not Evil for Evil, But Good for All" in TBC below).

This ethical advice is given first as a prohibition and then as positive counsel. In the OT, retaliation is limited by the *lex talionis*, a law specifying that revenge should not exceed the level of damage originally inflicted: "Life for life, eye for eye, tooth for tooth" (Exod. 21:23-24). Even such limited retaliation is here prohibited: *See that no one repays evil for evil to anyone.* However, a command accompanies the prohibition. A vigorous *but* and an emphatic *always* introduce this command: *But always pursue the good for one another and for all.* The verb *pursue* occurs in a literal sense in Jesus' final beatitude to describe the effort to persecute Jesus' followers (Matt. 5:10-12, 44). Here the same verb has a similar metaphorical meaning, to portray a persistent and eager striving for *the good.*

Comparable language appears elsewhere in Paul's writings to urge his readers to strive eagerly for "love" (1 Cor. 14:1), "hospitality" (Rom. 12:13), and "what makes for peace" (Rom. 14:19). In 5:15, when urging the Thessalonians to pursue *the good,* Paul does not define what that *good* might entail in a given situation. Selfless Christian *love* likely comes closest to summarizing the moral content of *the good* which the believers are urged to pursue.

The kind of behavior which avoids retaliation and strives for *the good* is prescribed both *for one another* and *for all.* In the transitional wish-prayer at 3:11-13, a similar note is struck: *May the Lord make you increase and abound in love toward one another and to all* (3:11). Both within the Christian community (*one another*) and beyond (*all*), the believers in Thessalonica are urged actively to pursue the way of love. Within the congregation at Thessalonica, this includes *the unruly, the fainthearted,* and *the weak,* among others. In the society at large, those who persecute the church and cause suffering would be included among the targeted recipients of *the good.* In a word, the Thessalonians are hearing the radical call to love even their enemies, to seek their good rather than their harm.

Worship and the Spirit 5:16-22

Three exhortations about worship (5:16-18) and some specific instruction about the ministry of the Spirit within the faith community (5:19-22) bring the pastoral exhortation section (4:1—5:22) of this letter to a close:

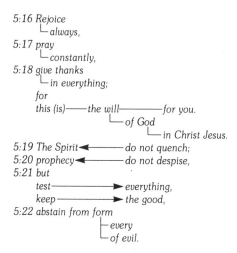

```
5:16 Rejoice
       └ always,
5:17 pray
       └ constantly,
5:18 give thanks
       └ in everything;
     for
     this (is)——the will————for you.
              └— of God
                    └— in Christ Jesus.
5:19 The Spirit◄————— do not quench;
5:20 prophecy◄————— do not despise,
5:21 but
     test——————► everything,
     keep—————► the good,
5:22 abstain from form
              ├ every
              └ of evil.
```

This succinctly worded series of guiding words concerning worship and the Spirit comes right after the radical call for the Thessalonians to love even their enemies. It provides vivid recognition of the fact that spiritual resources are available to the Christian community. Divine energy is needed when exercising patience with people within the group and striving for good even in behalf of their persecutors. A congregation can demonstrate dynamic faith, love, and hope only if it renews its inner life through worship and the empowering of the Spirit.

In 5:16-18 the Thessalonian believers hear a series of three admonitions dealing with life-giving acts of personal and corporate worship: *Always rejoice, constantly pray, in everything give thanks.*

Always rejoice! (5:16). In the opening thanksgiving (1:2-10), Paul and his colleagues mention that the Thessalonians accepted the gospel *in much affliction with joy inspired by the Holy Spirit* (1:6). The *joy* about which Paul speaks here and in many of his other letters (as in Phil. 2:17; 2 Cor. 6:10), does not require happy circumstances. This theme of joy in the midst of affliction recalls one of Jesus' beatitudes, in which he pronounces a blessing on those who experience persecution and calls on them to "rejoice and be glad" in anticipation of a heavenly reward (Matt. 5:11-12; Luke 6:22-23). For Paul, *joy* is fruit of the Spirit (Gal. 5:22), yet he also admonishes believers to *rejoice always*. An active cultivation of a joyful spirit opens the way for the Holy Spirit to empower believers for victorious living. Philippians 4:4, perhaps the closest available parallel to the terse admonition in 5:16, emphasizes the need to maintain a joyful posture in the midst of all circumstances: "Rejoice in the Lord always; again I will say, Rejoice."

Constantly pray! (5:17). Paul and his companions open the letter by reporting their unceasing prayers for the Thessalonian congregation: *mentioning you in our prayers constantly* (1:2). Now they conclude it with the reminder that their readers also should *constantly pray* (cf. also Rom. 12:12; Phil. 4:6; Col. 4:2; Eph. 6:18). The evangelists give the Thessalonians a good model to imitate, as shown by their prayer-report in 3:10: *asking earnestly night and day* (cf. also 2 Thess. 1:11). However, this responsibility to pray is a mutual and reciprocal one. Just as the missionaries pray for the church, so the Thessalonians are urged to pray for the missionaries, as seen in the admonition at the end of the letter: *Brothers and sisters, pray for us* (5:25).

In everything give thanks! (5:18). This mood of thanksgiving pervades the letter. The extended narrative (2:1—3:10), which summarizes the history of the evangelists' relationship with the congregation, is punctuated by expressions of thanks (see especially 2:13 and 3:9). Paul and his co-workers have amply demonstrated their own thankfulness and now prompt the Thessalonians also to cultivate an attitude of gratitude and to engage actively in a life punctuated by grateful prayer. Paul later amplifies this admonition when he counsels the Philippians: "In everything by prayer and supplication with thanksgiving let your requests be made known unto God" (Phil. 4:6).

The three imperatives in 5:16-18 prescribe specific orientations and activities for personal and corporate worship: *Rejoice! Pray! Give thanks!* The modifying words *always* and *constantly* and the phrase *in everything* intensify these acts. How are they to be understood? Essentially, the temporal qualifiers (*always* and *constantly*) call for the cultivation of a joyful and prayerful orientation in all of life. The phrase *in everything* conveys the importance of thanking God within all circumstances of life, even the difficult ones. In Thessalonica, these circumstances include suffering. It is important to notice, however, that Paul reminds the Thessalonians to give thanks *in everything*, not for everything.

After Paul and his companions call the Thessalonian converts to a dedicated stance of habitual thanksgiving to God in whatever circumstances they need to endure, they add, *For this is the will of God in Christ Jesus for you* (5:18). Likely *this* refers back to all three of these acts of personal and corporate worship. They call believers to conform themselves to *the will of God* by nurturing their relationship with God through rejoicing, praying, and giving thanks. The only other mention of *the will of God* in this first letter to Thessalonica comes in the introduction to the discussion on sexual morality: *This is the will of God, your holiness* (4:3). God desires holiness in interpersonal relationships. God also longs for believers to *rejoice, pray,* and *give thanks.* Indeed, we can conclude that holy and loving horizontal relationships cannot be sustained without cultivating the vertical dimension of the believer's life with God.

In 5:19-22 are several further directives dealing with how congregational worship should be conducted. They clearly suggest that the instructions of 5:16-22 apply in the first place to their worship as a faith community, although the admonitions in 5:16-18 can also be taken to apply to individual expressions of piety. In his study of worship in the early church, Ralph P. Martin has even suggested that in 5:16-24 we have the "headings of a worship service," including a call to worship (5:16-18), guidelines for listening to the prophets (5:19-22), and a closing prayer (5:23-24; R. P. Martin: 135-136; cf. Collins, 1984:140-142).

The guidelines pertain to the exercise of spiritual gifts within the congregation. First, a general rule: *The Spirit do not quench* (5:19). Keeping the word order of the underlying Greek original helps us to catch the emphasis. Envisioning the Spirit as a fire (cf. Acts 2:3), Paul cautions against doing anything that will douse the divine flame of the Spirit. The Spirit of God needs freedom to work within the gathered community.

Second, this general rule is applied to prophecy as one of the particular spiritual gifts: *Prophecy do not despise* (5:20). Even though *prophecy* has certain similarities to preaching and teaching, there are also differences. Prophets speak a word of the Lord to God's people under the inspiration of the Holy Spirit. As Paul shows in his extended treatment of this theme when writing the church at Corinth, *prophecy* functions especially to edify and strengthen the church (1 Cor. 14).

Third, the negatively worded injunctions urging the Thessalonians not to quench the Spirit nor despise prophesying, are followed by the mandate to discriminate among these gifts. Along with freedom for the exercise of spiritual gifts, Paul and his colleagues insist on some checks and balances: *But test everything, keep the good, abstain from every form of evil* (5:21-22). No criteria for testing are provided here. One needs to move to other texts in Paul's writings and elsewhere in the NT to obtain some clues about the nature of these criteria ("Worship and Prophesying" in TBC below).

A troubling congregational situation in Thessalonica has probably evoked these tersely worded instructions dealing with the ministry of the Spirit, the gift of prophecy, and the process of testing (5:19-22). Some of the troubling symptoms evident among people in the congregation likely include the tendency to favor a charismatic leadership style and a corresponding reluctance to accept the direction of established leaders. Probably *the unruly* (cf. 5:14) belong to this group. Ecstatic worship and enthusiastic expectancy of the imminent coming of the Lord also characterize this group. As seen in 2 Thessalonians 2:1-2, some prophets are later even claiming that *the day of the Lord has come.* In light of these developments, already beginning to unfold soon after the founding of the church in Thessalonica, Paul and his co-workers sense the need to intervene. The church needs both freedom for the expression of spiritual gifts and structures for testing the manifestations of the Spirit (Fee, 1994:55-62).

THE TEXT IN THE BIBLICAL CONTEXT
Those Who Stand Before You

None of the traditional descriptions of ministry nor titles for church leaders can be found in the two letters to the church at Thessalonica. Even 1 Thessalonians 5:12-22 does not refer to church workers by using any of the normal titles, such as pastor or deacon. Church leaders in Thessalonica are described simply in terms of the ministry services which they provide.

In 5:12-22, therefore, we catch a brief glimpse into one of the initial stages in the development of ministry patterns within the early church. Elsewhere in the NT, especially in the pastoral epistles, we see more clearly what ministry offices eventually emerged: "elder" (*presbuteros,* 1 Tim. 5:17) and "bishop" or "overseer" (*episkopos,* 1 Tim. 3:1-2). However, at the time when the first letter was written to the church at Thessalonica, a functional rather than institutional view of ministry still prevails.

If we reflect more broadly on 1 Thessalonians 5:12-22 within the

context of the letter as a whole and especially the pastoral exhortation section (4:1—5:22), we become aware of the theological context
for ministry. Ministry within the church is fundamentally shaped by
the eschatological tension within which the faith community exists. In
2:12, Paul and his colleagues portray their ministries in Thessalonica
as a process of calling the Thessalonians into God's *kingdom and
glory*. Though already present, the kingdom of God is also still future.
The community of believers lives in the twilight zone between the "already" and the "not yet" of the glorious reign of God ("Kingdom of
God" in TBC for 2:1-12). In 4:13-18 and 5:1-11, Paul and his co-
workers demonstrate how this eschatological situation informs their
ministries when dealing pastorally with the Thessalonian converts'
grief in the face of death and their questions about the chronology of
end-time events.

How does the eschatological situation in which the church finds
itself impinge on the nature of ministry? In his book on Paul's theology of ministry, E. Earle Ellis has a chapter entitled "Ministry for the
Coming Age." In Paul's letters, according to Ellis, Christian ministry is
viewed as part of the new work of God's Spirit which was inaugurated
by Jesus and will be consummated at the coming of Christ:

> It [Christian ministry] is regarded as a means by which the Holy Spirit me-
> diates the blessing and power of the age to come into the present age of
> sin and death. In a word, for Paul ministry is a present manifestation of
> the coming kingdom of God. (Ellis: 7)

Ministry understood in these terms features the activity of the Holy
Spirit within the life of the congregation. When the Holy Spirit energizes the body of Christ, the dramatic future reign of God invades the
present. For this reason, the church at Thessalonica is cautioned
against doing anything that would quench the Spirit (5:19).

Through baptism, individuals are incorporated into the body of
Christ. Paul testifies in his letter to the church at Corinth that "in the
one Spirit we were all baptized into one body" (1 Cor. 12:13). Similarly, Ephesians emphasizes "the unity of the Spirit," a unity symbol-
ized by baptism:

> There is one body and one Spirit, just as you were called to the one hope
> of your calling, one Lord, one faith, one baptism, one God and Father of
> all, who is above all and through all and in all. (Eph. 4:4-6)

In baptism, therefore, the individual believer identifies with the
church, which owes its being to the life, death, and resurrection of

Christ. In a profound sense, the believer is "baptized into Christ Jesus" (Rom. 6:2-4). There is no direct reference to baptism in the Thessalonian epistles, but the Christians' status in Christ (1 Thess. 4:16) or in/with the Lord (4:17; 5:10, 12) is clearly affirmed.

A crucial corollary of the Spirit-enabled incorporation of individuals into the body of Christ through baptism is that all who are baptized are thereby also called to participate in ministry. In Thessalonica, the church as a whole is summoned to engage in admonition and caregiving, as needed especially by the unruly, the fainthearted, and the weak. The church is also urged, Be patient with them all (5:14). This mention of patience can serve as a reminder of the whole fruit of the Spirit, which Paul outlines for the Galatians when he urges them to love and serve each other (cf. Gal. 5:13-15):

> The fruit of the Spirit is love, joy, peace, patience, kindness, generosity, faithfulness, gentleness, and self-control. (Gal. 5:22-23)

When the Spirit has the freedom to inspire behavior and relationships which express these values, people will be guided, nurtured, and gently corrected.

Yet baptism does not ordain all believers to the same ministry. In his letter to Corinth, Paul emphasizes both the unity enabled through being baptized in the one Spirit (1 Cor. 12:12-13) and the diversity of spiritual gifts available within the one body (12:4-11, 14-26). Two somewhat overlapping lists of ministry gifts are provided in the same chapter: 12:8-11 and 12:28-30. When these are compared with lists in Romans 12:6-8 and Ephesians 4:11, one gains a graphic overview of the diversity of ministries envisioned by Paul. [Leadership and Ministry Gifts, p. 372.]

With one exception, none of the ministering persons mentioned in 1 Thessalonians 5:12-13 as worthy of respect and esteem is explicitly included in any of the lists of ministers and ministry gifts (1 Cor. 12; Rom. 12; Eph. 4). As noted earlier, the participle translated one who stands before (5:12) is also found in Rom. 12:8, although the meaning in both places is disputed. On balance, the literal reading those who stand before seems most likely. These persons serve as leaders, and they exercise their leadership among persons with whom they have a common standing in the Lord (5:12). We can borrow the language which Paul uses in 1 Corinthians 12:13: "In the one Spirit" both the designated leaders and the other members of the church "were all baptized into one body."

The gifts of "leadership" (NRSV; RSV: "administrators") are noted in 1 Corinthians 12:28. The underlying Greek word *kubernēseis* comes from nautical jargon, where it has to do with piloting a ship; in modern technological language it has emerged as "cybernetics." These leadership gifts come close to what Paul and his colleagues likely have in mind in their reference to *those who stand before* the Thessalonians *in the Lord* (1 Thess. 5:12). As part of the dynamic interplay of unity and diversity within the body of Christ, such gifts of *leadership* are exercised by servants who lead and by leaders who serve.

One such leader in the early church is actually introduced by name at the beginning of Paul's greetings to individuals in the house fellowships at Rome (Rom. 16:1-2). Paul commends Phoebe to the church at Rome, urging them to receive her "in the Lord." Phoebe likely carried Paul's letter to Rome. Paul's commendation was designed to help clear the way for the Roman Christians to accept both Phoebe and his letter. Phoebe is described using three titles: "our sister"; "a minister [RSV: deaconess; NRSV: deacon] of the church at Cenchreae"; and "a leader [RSV: helper; NRSV: benefactor] of many and of myself as well."

My rendering of two of these descriptions of Phoebe departs from that given in most translations. The Greek word *diakonos* (for the second title) can have the general meaning "servant" (Rom. 15:8) or the more specific meaning "deacon" (Phil. 1:1; 1 Tim. 3:8, 12) or "minister" (2 Cor. 3:6; Eph. 3:7; Col. 1:7; 4:7); it is often difficult to know which word best conveys the intended meaning. Translations have tended to relegate Phoebe to the lesser role of deaconess rather than recognize her as a "minister" in Cenchreae with leadership responsibilities. The third title, "leader" (*prostatis*, the noun form of the participle *proistamenos*, in Rom. 12:8 and 1 Thess. 5:12) confirms that indeed Phoebe was a leader in her congregation and beyond. In short, Phoebe is an early example of a servant leader, "one who stands before" her people.

Not Evil for Evil, but Good for All

The church finds itself in tension between the dramatic realization that "the kingdom of God has come near" (Mark 1:15), and the eager longing expressed in the prayer, "Your kingdom come" (Matt. 6:9; Luke 11:2). This eschatological framework shapes how the church lives and worships and organizes itself for ministry. The church, a community already experiencing in its life the new work of God's

Spirit inaugurated by Jesus, still awaits the consummation of the kingdom at the coming of Christ as triumphant Lord. Living between the times (cf. 1 Cor. 10:11), the church as a community marked by *faith, love,* and *the hope of salvation* (5:8) joins in the struggle for peace and justice for all ("God's Warriors" in TBC for 5:1-11). In 1 Thessalonians 5:15, the believers are given strategy for this struggle: *See that no one repays evil for evil to anyone, but always pursue the good for one another and for all.*

These guidelines for the Christian life echo Jesus' teaching and conduct. He prohibits retaliation and advocates active goodwill toward enemies (Matt. 5:38-48; Luke 6:27-36). Jesus teaches and models this ethic in a dramatic way, but it has clear precursors in the OT. In the book of Proverbs, we read,

> Do not say, "I will repay evil";
>> wait for the Lord, and he will help you. (Prov. 20:22)
> Do not say, "I will do to others as they have done to me;
>> I will pay them back for what they have done." (24:29)
> If your enemies are hungry, give them bread to eat;
>> and if they are thirsty, give them water to drink;
> for you will heap coals of fire on their heads,
>> and the Lord will reward you. (25:21-22)

The OT includes many terrifying war stories, but there are also some episodes which demonstrate that way of love which Jesus later enunciates as the ultimate norm of behavior for his disciples. For example, Elisha the prophet, after praying for God's help, captures the Aramean army and leads them to the Israelite king in Samaria. When the king wants to kill these prisoners of war, Elisha instead urges that they be given food and drink and then be released (2 Kings 6:15-23). The story of Jonah also teaches this way of love. Jonah confesses that God is "a gracious God and merciful, slow to anger, and abounding in steadfast love, and ready to relent from punishing" (4:2). However, even to the end of this biblical story, an angry and vindictive Jonah prefers to see God destroy the godless people of Nineveh rather than forgive them. This story invites the hearers *not* to be like Jonah in their attitudes and behaviors toward their enemies.

Jesus elevates the way of love toward enemies into a bold imperative:

> Love your enemies, do good to those who hate you,
>> bless those who curse you, pray for those who abuse you.
>>>> (Luke 6:27-28; cf. Matt. 5:43-44)

After giving some practical examples of this kind of behavior, Jesus summarizes with what is called the golden rule: "Do to others as you would have them do to you" (Luke 6:31; cf. Matt. 7:12). But the Gospels show that Jesus not only teaches his disciples this way of love. He also lives the way of love, and he dies on the cross praying that God might forgive his executioners (Luke 23:34).

NT writers repeatedly portray Jesus' crucifixion as God's climactic answer to sin and evil in the world. As 1 Peter attests, Jesus' death on the cross both demonstrates the way of discipleship and atones for sin:

> To this you have been called, because Christ also suffered for you, leaving you an example, so that you should follow in his steps. (1 Pet. 2:21)
> He himself bore our sins in his body on the cross, so that, free from sins, we might live for righteousness. (2:24)

As Jesus "entrusted himself to the one who judges justly," so Jesus' followers are urged to desist from returning the abuse of their enemies (2:23; cf. 3:9).

Paul's letter to the church at Rome also depicts Jesus' death as the prime exhibit of God's love "for the ungodly" (Rom. 5:6). The apostle dramatically underscores the point that "while we still were sinners Christ died for us" (5:8), and "while we were enemies, we were reconciled to God through the death of his Son" (5:10). After reflecting at length on sin and salvation, Paul appeals to the believers in Rome:

> Do not be conformed to this world, but be transformed by the renewing of your minds, so that you may discern what is the will of God—what is good and acceptable and perfect. (Rom. 12:2)

This appeal introduces some instruction regarding ministry gifts (12:3-8) and then general guidance for church life (12:9-13); these sections are broadly parallel to 1 Thessalonians 5:12-13 and 5:14, respectively. In Romans 12:14-21, Paul moves into the subject of how to deal with enemies; this paragraph expands on what he says in 1 Thessalonians 5:15. Here we highlight those admonitions which deal directly with how believers should relate to their enemies.

First, Paul restates and expands Jesus' word about responding to persecutors: "Bless those who persecute ['you' is not in some early Greek manuscripts]; bless and do not curse them" (Rom. 12:14). Translations usually ignore the fact that this injunction broadens Jesus' instruction. Copyists likely added "you" from Jesus' sayings (Matt. 5:44; Luke 6:27-28; cf. Metzger, 1971:528). Here Paul instructs Christians to bless rather than curse persecutors generally, not just those who persecute them.

Following general counsel about identifying with "those who rejoice" and "those who weep" (Rom. 12:15) and about living in harmony and humility with others (12:16), Paul returns specifically to the question of dealing with evil:

> Do not repay anyone evil for evil, but take thought for what is noble in the sight of all. If it is possible, so far as it depends on you, live peaceably with all. (Rom. 12:17-18)

The repeated *all* stresses that this kind of behavior applies universally. But what happens when a wrong is done? Is revenge ever appropriate? Here Paul strikes a note of special tenderness, addressing the believers as "Beloved":

> Beloved, never avenge yourselves, but leave room for the wrath of God; for it is written, "Vengeance is mine, I will repay, says the Lord." (12:19)

Citing Deuteronomy 32:35, Paul points out that vengeance and vindication are God's prerogatives, not ours ("Wrath" in TBC for 2:13-16).

However, Christians have to do more than just wait for God to act. Quoting Proverbs 25:21-22 (see above), Paul prompts his readers to show hospitality and love toward their enemies, like the prophet Elisha did toward the captured enemy Arameans:

> No, "if your enemies are hungry, feed them; if they are thirsty, give them something to drink; for by doing this you will heap burning coals on their heads." (Rom. 12:20)

The reference to coals of fire on the enemies' heads need not mean the punishment of enemies at the final judgment nor the anguish of a guilty conscience, though many interpreters support such views (Zerbe: 181-184, 194-197). Rather, since hot coals for the preparation of a meal would have been carried in a container on the head (adequately insulated), this might be a symbol of hospitality. "Coals on their heads" would therefore point to a necessary preparatory stage toward a meal of reconciliation between (former) enemies (Klassen, 1984:119-121).

In Paul's vision for the church, practical helpfulness and love will transform enemies into friends! As a final word of admonition, Paul challenges his readers to trust that this can happen: "Do not be overcome by evil, but overcome evil with good" (Rom. 12:21). The faithful community, receiving its signals from the crucified and risen Christ, will trust the Spirit's power to make this vision a reality in a broken world.

Worship and Prophesying

The eschatological framework within which the church exists shapes how the church worships. When believers *rejoice, pray,* and *give thanks,* especially when they engage in these worship activities *in all circumstances* (5:16-18), they give vivid testimony to their Spirit-inspired confidence as a faith community living in the tension between the "already" and the "not yet" of God's reign. The evangelists urge the Thessalonians to *rejoice, pray,* and *give thanks* in the midst of their suffering and grief. The evangelists also advise these new believers about prophecy within the Christian community, encouraging them not to disparage the free exercise of this gift (5:20), and warning them of the need to *test everything* (5:21-22).

In 1 Corinthians 14, Paul provides more detail regarding prophecy and the testing of prophecy within the church. Paul's treatment of this theme shows that "prophesying" can more accurately be described as inspired speech (forth-telling) than as predictive utterances concerning the future (foretelling). The apostle notes both the variety and the unity of the Spirit's gifts (1 Cor. 12) and emphasizes that above all the church needs to demonstrate Christian love (13:1-13). Then he compares and contrasts the spiritual gifts of prophecy and tongues (14:1-25). Guidelines for worship follow (14:26-33a). The primary criterion for testing any act of worship, including prophecy, is whether it edifies or builds up the church: "Let all things be done for building up" (14:26b). When this kind of edifying prophecy takes place in the gathered community, outsiders and unbelievers also will worship God, declaring, "God is really among you" (14:25). Several prophets may speak in turn, while "the others weigh what is said" (14:29). The desired outcome is restated: "so that all may learn and all be encouraged" (14:31).

When Paul, Silvanus, and Timothy admonish the Thessalonians to permit prophesying (1 Thess. 5:20) but also to engage in a careful process of testing the results (5:21-22), something similar to the guidelines in 1 Corinthians 14 might be in their minds. Perhaps some teaching on this matter has been included during their initial visit in Thessalonica. When the Holy Spirit moves among believers gathered for worship, outsiders will acknowledge the presence of God, and the church will be built up. It is no coincidence that the 5:1-11 section, dealing with *the times and the seasons*, concludes with a similar admonition: *Therefore, encourage each other and build each other up, just as you are doing* (5:11).

THE TEXT IN THE LIFE OF THE CHURCH
Freedom Within Structure

Since the exhortations in 1 Thessalonians 5:12-22 concerning church leadership, caregiving, nonretaliation, and worship are eminently practical in nature, perhaps not much needs to be said about how to apply them to contemporary church life. Indeed, most of the pastoral and ethical guidance in these verses, as amplified by the biblical witness as a whole, bears directly on the life of believers today. However, differences of interpretation on these vital topics often upset the unity and jeopardize the clear witness of the church.

Our text prescribes both spontaneity and freedom as well as structure and accountability for worship and church life generally. Leaders have specific ministries to perform within an atmosphere of love and respect, yet all members are called upon to participate in caring for each other, especially for persons with special needs. During worship the Spirit needs to have freedom to move prophets to speak, yet what is said also needs to be tested.

Church of the Brethren and Mennonite congregations have in recent years experienced the impact of the "charismatic movement." "Charismatics" emphasize the baptism of the Holy Spirit and the exercise of spiritual gifts. They have often advocated greater freedom in worship, thereby upsetting some who wish to retain more traditional patterns. The overall assessment of the impact of this movement on church life seems positive, at least as reported in the articles in the respective denominational encyclopedias:

> This movement has called Christianity to examine again the intense experience of being filled with the Holy Spirit. Many people have experienced new life and new meaning in life through the transforming power of the Holy Spirit baptism. The charismatic movement has helped Christians sense the continuing divine mystery that pervades the Christian faith. (BE, 1:272)

> Some of the contributions of the charismatic movement have been renewed vigor in worship, renewed interest in releasing spiritual gifts in

congregational life, and new motivation for evangelism and missions. (ME, 5:135-136)

The instructions for the church in 1 Thessalonians 5:19-22 are still timely. Congregations need to assure that the fire of the Spirit is not quenched, but they also need to take care to test the results.

One of the criteria for testing prophetic speech has already been noted: Does it build up the body? We will let the sixteenth-century Dutch Anabaptist, Dirk Philips, provide more specific detail:

> Therefore let this new birth be powerful in you, and be eager to keep the unity of the Spirit through the bond of peace, Eph. 4:3, and do not undertake anything outside God's Word, Isa. 30:2, neither without the counsel of the Holy Spirit, and do not consider yourself all too wise, neither all too understanding, Rom. 12:3, but fear God and ask him for true wisdom. Search the Scripture diligently, understand it properly, measuring all things with the plumb line of the gospel, testing all spirits with the character, nature, and spirit of Christ. (Dyck, 1992:408-409)

This test of Christlikeness sums it up well. The church as Christ's body, living between the times and sensing the pulse of the Spirit, needs always to ask regarding life and worship: Are we reflecting the character of Christ?

1 Thessalonians 5:23-28

Benediction and Closing Instructions

PREVIEW

How might a parent conclude a letter to a child away from home? Such letters express gratitude, review recent events, and offer encouragement or advice. They usually close by expressing good wishes and by reassuring these absentee family members of their continuing thoughts and prayers.

In similar fashion, Paul, Silvanus, and Timothy thank God (1:2-10), rehearse earlier events (2:1—3:13), and exhort the congregation (4:1—5:22). Coming to the end of the letter, they articulate an intercessory wish-prayer (5:23-24; cf. 3:11-13). Adapting the typical letter-closing patterns of their day, the missionaries request prayer for themselves (5:25), invite the church to greet each other with a holy kiss (5:26), extend stern instructions about the reading of the letter (5:27), and then offer the final benediction (5:28). These tailored features reflect the fact that this letter is designed to be read when the congregation gathers for worship.

The wish-prayer of 5:23-24 recapitulates themes treated in the pastoral exhortation section of the letter (4:1-5:22):

God of peace   in 5:23 recalls 5:13, 15— *Be at peace among yourselves. Pursue the good for one another and all.*

237

Sanctify to be whole	5:23	recalls	4:3-8	This is the will of God, your holiness.
Coming of our Lord Jesus Christ	5:23	recalls	4:13—5:11	Always with the Lord. The times and the seasons.
God is faithful	5:24	echoes	4:3, 7-9, 14 5:9, 18	Will of God God calls God gives God has appointed

The exhortations concerning church life (5:12-22) repeatedly underscore the all-embracing scope of the church's outreach and worship. This emphasis is achieved through words which in the original Greek have a common root (*pant-*): *all* (5:14-15), *always* (5:16), *in everything* (5:18), *from every* (5:22). *Constantly* (5:17) uses a different word but with the same effect. The wish-prayer which immediately follows (5:23-24) also sounds this comprehensive note through two words with the prefix (Greek: *hol-*) which means *whole* or *complete*. A vision of the role of the church within God's all-encompassing purpose unites the closing exhortations with the climactic prayer.

OUTLINE

Concluding Prayer, 5:23-24
Final Exhortations and Benediction, 5:25-28

EXPLANATORY NOTES

Concluding Prayer 5:23-24

The evangelists have shared a glimpse of the cosmic scope within which the church's life and worship derives its meaning. Now they utter a prayer for God's sanctifying and sustaining presence:

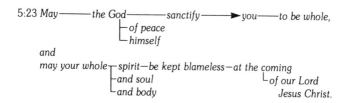

5:23 May——the God——sanctify——▶ you——to be whole,
        ⊦of peace
        ⌊himself
    and
    may your whole⌜spirit—be kept blameless—at the coming
            ⊦and soul   ⌊of our Lord
            ⌊and body   Jesus Christ.

5:24 Faithful——is the one———who calls———➤ you,
                    the one who will do———➤ this.

Here God is addressed as *the God of peace*, as also in other letter closings (Rom. 15:33; 16:20; Phil. 4:9; cf. Heb. 13:20; "the God of love and peace," 2 Cor. 13:11; *Lord of peace*, 2 Thess. 3:16). The closing prayer therefore echoes the opening greeting, *Grace to you and peace* (1:1). *Peace* comes as a gift from God. Yet, as the pastoral admonitions show, *peace* also defines a way of relating both within the fellowship of believers (5:13) and in society as a whole (5:15).

In the earlier wish-prayer, Paul and his co-workers pray that the Thessalonians might be established *unblamable in holiness* (3:13). When introducing their ethical teaching concerning appropriate sexual conduct, they highlight the need for holy behavior in this dimension of life: *This is the will of God, your holiness* (4:3; cf. 4:4, 7). This moral agenda resurfaces in the closing prayer, although here *holiness* embraces all areas of life: *May the God of peace himself sanctify you to be whole*. The verb *sanctify* (*hagiazō*) depicts the process leading to *holiness* (*hagiasmos*; "Sanctification and Holiness" in TBC for 4:1-8).

The Greek shows that *you/your* in 5:23-24 is plural. *You* in 5:23 could refer to the people who make up the congregation, so that the prayer expresses the longing for God to sanctify each individual person. *You* might also mean the church as a corporate body, with the evangelists praying for the sanctification of the whole congregation. In the pastoral exhortations (5:12-22) which precede this prayer, the writers obviously have the whole church in view. They employ the plural personal pronoun *you* (5:12, 14, 18), and the verbs of command are second person plural: *you* do this or that. The Thessalonian faith community has been unsettled by persecution (3:4), the death of some fellow members (4:13-18), and certain persons requiring special care (5:14-15). *To be whole*, the congregation as a body needs the sanctifying work of the Holy Spirit.

The second part of the prayer retains this corporate understanding but adds a personal dimension. Clearly evident again is the eschatological framework of Paul's thought. This prayer is offered in light of *the coming of our Lord Jesus Christ*. Paul views the church's life, as it were, through bifocals: his far vision glimpses the "already," while his near vision identifies the "not yet" of God's reign ("Kingdom of God" in TBC for 2:1-12). Paul and his partners see their present realities from the hope-inspiring perspective of the culmination of God's reign, and they pray for the church as a body and for the individuals who constitute this community: *May your whole spirit and soul and body be kept blameless* (5:23).

Would the Thessalonians have understood *spirit and soul and body* to identify three distinguishable components within human beings? Nowhere else does Paul or any other NT writer include a comparable listing of separable aspects of human nature, although each of these terms occurs frequently in Scripture. Jewett argues that the missionaries are combating a doctrine which regarded the *spirit* as the divine portion of the human self and the *soul and body* as the corrupt psychological and physical aspects. In response to this doctrine, Paul and his colleagues pray that the Thessalonians as whole physical, psychological, and spiritual beings might be sustained in anticipation of the triumphant coming of Christ (Jewett, 1986:107-108). Other commentators (Bruce: 129-130; Wanamaker: 206-207) suggest simply that the missionary pastors long for the Thessalonian believers as complete human beings to be preserved for the coming of Christ ("Spirit, Soul, and Body" in TBC below).

This intercession reveals the deep pastoral empathy which the writers feel toward these converts. Earlier in the letter, we sense Paul's joy and pride in the Thessalonians *before our Lord Jesus at his coming* (2:19). This closing prayer helps us to glimpse the pastor fervently interceding in behalf of his congregation to the end that they might be kept whole and blameless in anticipation of *the coming of our Lord Jesus Christ.*

A guarantee accompanies this prayer: *Faithful is the one who calls you, the one who will do this.* On what basis are the believers reassured? The God *who calls* them (5:25; 2:12; 4:7; cf. 1:4) and has appointed them *not for wrath but for obtaining salvation* (5:9) can be trusted. The God who *sanctifies* and *keeps* them (5:23) *will do this.* Ultimately, what enables believers to cope with the circumstances of life is God's faithfulness, which sustains them to the end. In their second letter to Thessalonica, Paul and his colleagues, while facing opposition, testify concerning God's faithfulness (2 Thess. 3:1-3). What the *faithful* God *will do* has as much to do with the present as with the future. Those who *turned toward God* not only *await his Son from heaven.* In the meantime, they are invited *to serve the living and true God* (1:9-10). This *living and true God* is the faithful one whose action in behalf of believers guarantees their ultimate wholeness ("Deliver Us from Evil" in TBC for 2 Thess. 2:13—3:5).

Final Exhortations and Benediction 5:25-28

A series of three exhortations and a final benediction bring this letter to a close:

> 5:25 *Brothers and sisters,*
>   *pray———for us also.*
> 5:26 *Greet———➤all the brothers and sisters*
>   └*with a holy kiss.*
> 5:27 *I solemnly charge you——to read———➤ this letter—to the brothers*
>   └*by the Lord*   · | *and sisters.*
>   └—*all*
>
> 5:28 *The grace*   *(be)*   *with you.*
>   └*of our Lord Jesus Christ*

Paul and his fellow missionaries ask for prayer (5:25), then request that Christian greetings be conveyed (5:26), and finally insist that this letter be read to the whole church (5:27).

Paul, Silvanus, and Timothy intercede for the Thessalonian Christians, but they also solicit prayer for themselves: *Brothers and sisters, pray for us also* (5:25). Prayer involves the Christian community as a whole in mutual thanksgiving, intercession, and petition in each other's behalf. The opening thanksgiving (1:2-3) and the earnest petition for a reunion between Paul and the Thessalonians (3:9-10) amply model a life punctuated by prayer. Two wish-prayers recapitulate the concerns articulated in the letter and offer them up to God in light of the eschatological context (3:11-13; 5:23-24). The missionary pastors have urged them to *rejoice, pray,* and *give thanks* (5:16-18), and now they remind the Thessalonians to pray for them as well (5:25). In their second letter, Paul and his partners state the prayer request in terms of the ongoing ministry of the word and their need for physical protection (2 Thess. 3:1-2).

The second closing admonition urges, *Greet all the brothers and sisters with a holy kiss* (5:26). Paul's letters generally end with greetings. Sometimes Paul identifies the people whom he asks the readers of the letter to greet (Rom. 16:3-15; Col. 4:15). At other times, Paul conveys greetings from persons who are with him (Rom. 16:21-23; 1 Cor. 16:19-20; Philem. 23-24; Col. 4:10-14) or more generally from the church he is with (Phil. 4:21-22) or even more universally in the name of the church as a whole (Rom. 16:16; 1 Cor. 16:19-20; 2 Cor. 13:12). In three such greeting sections, Paul includes the instruction, "Greet one another with a holy kiss" (Rom. 16:16; 1 Cor. 16:20; 2 Cor. 13:12; cf. "kiss of love," 1 Pet. 5:14). The greeting to the church in Thessalonica (5:26) emphasizes that all the members of the community should be included: *Greet all the brothers and sisters.* The particular form of greeting here is the *kiss*, an expression of kinship and friendship commonly found in the cultures around the Mediterranean region. Paul, however, nuances the significance of this common gesture within the church by calling for a *holy kiss.* The holy kiss as the mode of Christian greeting reflects the bond of love between people of whatever gender, ethnic background, or social rank who have been united in Christ ("The Holy Kiss" in TLC below).

The final instruction is strikingly stern, especially given the generally affirmative mood of the letter. Here Paul speaks for himself, using the first person *I* rather than the usual *we: I solemnly charge you by the Lord to read this letter to all the brothers and sisters* (5:27). The word translated *solemnly charge* (enorkizō; RSV: *adjure*) occurs nowhere else in the NT (though the root is in Mark 5:7; Matt. 26:63, compounded; Acts 19:13). With the phrase *by the Lord,* Paul solemnly points to the ultimate source of authority within the church. Yet the Thessalonians are also aware of the shared communion *in the Lord* which puts leaders and their people on common ground (cf. notes on 5:12).

This strict imperative needs to be understood simply in terms of what it says. First, this letter is meant to be read, presumably during a gathering for worship and instruction. This would be an innovation, since the early church followed the synagogue pattern of reading the Scriptures and hearing a homily based on them (Acts 13:13-47). Writing the Thessalonian church, Paul demands that, in addition to reading from the Scriptures, they should *read this letter.* In the later epistle to the Colossians, we see that letters specifically addressed to certain churches were circulated to be read in other congregations as well (Col. 4:16). Second, we note again the concern for inclusiveness. This letter is to be read publicly *to all the brothers and sisters.* Neither those who *work* (4:11; 5:12) nor *the unruly, the fainthearted,* and *the weak* (5:14) are to be excluded from such a meeting. Neither prophets nor those who despise prophesying (5:20) are to be favored. Whatever the contentious issues in the church at Thessalonica might be, *all the brothers and sisters* are to hear this letter and be included in processing the matters which it addresses.

The final benediction (5:28) and the wish-prayer (5:23-24) along with the opening greeting (1:1) bracket the entire letter within the framework of God's *grace and peace.* This closing benediction likely reflects worship customs in the early church: *The grace of our Lord Jesus Christ be with you* (5:28). In Colossians (4:18), the benediction is even shorter, "Grace be with you," but in Paul's other letters, it is identical (Rom. 16:20) or similar ("of the Lord Jesus," 1 Cor. 16:23; *with you all*, 2 Thess. 3:18; "with your spirit": Gal. 6:18; Phil. 4:23; Philem. 25). Second Corinthians 13:13 has the more elaborate trinitarian benediction, and Ephesians 6:23-24 has an extended impartation of divine peace.

What is the significance of the benediction? Simply put, the words *grace be with you* commend the gathered believers to God's grace as supremely revealed in Christ.

THE TEXT IN THE BIBLICAL CONTEXT
Spirit, Soul, and Body

The entities *spirit, soul,* and *body,* as described in Scripture, each merit investigation in an effort to comprehend what Paul and his colleagues mean in 1 Thessalonians 5:23, where they combine all three.

The OT sometimes refers to the human *spirit* as the locus of moral discernment. A psalm of David shows the penitent sinner pleading,

> Create in me a clean heart, O God,
>   and put a new and right spirit within me. (Ps. 51:10)

Another psalm declares blessed those "in whose spirit there is no deceit" (Ps. 32:2). A similar view of the human spirit comes through in the NT story about Jesus at Gethsemane, when he laments the sleepiness of his disciples:

> Keep awake and pray that you may not come into the time of trial; the spirit indeed is willing, but the flesh is weak. (Mark 14:38)

This reference to the willing *spirit* as contrasted with the feeble *flesh* leaves open whether this willingness can be attributed to God's Spirit or to the disciples' inner desire. Paul can speak about human self-awareness in terms of the inner spirit:

> What human being knows what is truly human except the human spirit that is within? (1 Cor. 2:11)

Generally, however, Paul views a person's spirit as divine gift, a portion of God's Spirit available for living faithfully in anticipation of the consummation of God's reign. Reassuring the Roman believers concerning their freedom in Christ, Paul says,

You are not in the flesh; you are in the Spirit, since the Spirit of God dwells in you. (Rom. 8:9)

Later in the same chapter, Paul alludes to "a spirit of adoption," whereby believers experience the witness of God's Spirit within their own spirit testifying that they indeed are God's children (Rom. 8:15-16). For Paul, therefore, the inner spirit belongs to believers without being totally distinguishable from the Holy Spirit which moves within them.

What then is the *soul?* According to Genesis 2:7, the Creator formed humanity from the dust of the earth. God's life breath caused that lump of clay to become "a living soul" (Hebrew: *nephesh;* NRSV: *a living being*). *Soul* therefore connotes the life-force within humanity which comes from God. "My soul" (similarly, "my spirit") sometimes means "I," oneself:

My soul yearns for you in the night,
my spirit within me earnestly seeks you. (Isa. 26:9)

Jesus warns his disciples not to risk losing their *soul* (*psuchē;* NRSV: *life*) in the process of seeking to gain the world (Mark 8:36-37). Paul and his co-workers give a touching show of affection for the Thessalonians when they speak of their readiness to give their *souls* (NRSV: *selves*) for them (1 Thess. 2:8). In a profound sense, each person *is* a soul. The soul cannot be isolated as a separate component within an individual.

The term *body* in the NT (*sōma*) has no one OT equivalent. In Hebrew thought, human life is viewed as a unity of body and soul. Paul also portrays human life as bodily existence, even in the resurrection (1 Cor. 15:44). A person is soul and body; one does not just have a body. Hence, human conduct in the body matters (1 Cor. 6:12-20). In his letter to the house churches in Rome, Paul introduces guidelines for Christian behavior by appealing to them to offer their bodies:

I appeal to you . . . to present your bodies as a living sacrifice, holy and acceptable to God, which is your spiritual worship. Do not be conformed to this world, but be transformed by the renewing of your minds, so that you may discern what is the will of God—what is good and acceptable and perfect. (Rom. 12:1-2)

As with *spirit* and *soul,* Paul regards the *body* not as one distinguishable component among others but as one way of regarding the whole person. Each perspective on the whole person emphasizes one particular dimension of human existence: the spiritual, psycho-logical, and physical aspects respectively. As the appeal in Romans 12:1-2 illustrates, the biblical writers also name other dimensions, such as mind, heart, conscience, and flesh. These overlap with spirit, soul, and body, but there are distinctions among them as well.

A Hebraic theological perspective which views humanity as a complex unity, rather than as a balancing act between competing spiritual and earthly parts, appears to lie beneath the wish-prayer in 5:23. Perhaps the great commandment can serve to illustrate:

> You shall love the Lord your God with all your heart, and with all your soul, and with all your might. (Deut. 6:5)

According to Mark, when Jesus quoted this commandment, he added "and with all your mind" (Mark 12:30). Within a Jewish-Christian mind-set concerning human nature, one might add *body* and even *spirit* to this list. Devotion to God should involve the whole being. Similarly, Paul and his co-workers show their deep affection for the Thessalonian converts and their zealous desire that these be-lievers might remain faithful until the end. Hence, they pray that God might sustain and preserve them as whole beings, as *spirit, soul,* and *body.*

THE TEXT IN THE LIFE OF THE CHURCH
The Holy Kiss

When we reach the end of this ancient letter, we are made keenly aware that it is written to be read aloud to the congregation at Thes-salonica. The closing prayer, the prayer request, and the benediction also help us to see that the listening church would be gathered for worship.

In our reflections on the earlier wish-prayer, we commented that the movement from thanksgiving to story to pastoral prayer can serve as a model for the beginning of a congregational worship service ("The Pastoral Prayer and Worship" in TLC for 3:11-13). This obser-vation can now be updated. Paul and his team continue by exhorting and teaching the congregation and then by offering another pastoral prayer. The offering seems to be missing, however!

Most congregations within the believers church tradition include these various components in their worship services. Prayer requests and a benediction are also familiar. But what has happened to the *holy kiss?*

Originating as a spontaneous expression of Christian unity and love, the *holy kiss* was a way of affirming the deep bond between believers. This gesture was not limited to worship settings, nor is there any evidence that social or gender differences were barriers when believers greeted each other. The *kiss* was *holy* because the ones who communicated their Christian love in this way were saints (holy ones). When criticism and misunderstanding arose, however, the church needed to decide whether to allow this practice to continue across gender lines. Clement of Alexandria, a second-century churchman, warned against shameless kissing "which occasions foul suspicions and evil reports" (Klassen, 1993:134; Clement, *The Instructor* 3.12). Eventually the holy kiss became part of a ritual often called "the passing of the peace."

In some Brethren and Mennonite churches, the holy kiss has continued to be one part of footwashing and communion services, usually with men and women in separate groups. However, my experience with the holy kiss came mainly in a community composed of believers from a wide range of denominational backgrounds. In daily gatherings for worship at the Ecumenical Institute for Theological Research near Jerusalem, we quite joyously and spontaneously embraced each other as brothers and sisters in Christ from around the world. We wished each other God's peace as we embraced and kissed, or simply clasped hands. Can such holy, joyful, and wholehearted expressions of our oneness in Christ also happen in our congregation?

2 Thessalonians

Tuning In:
Why Another Letter?

We have been listening in during the congregational reading of the first pastoral letter from Paul and his co-workers. Now we need to tune in again as we prepare to join the believers in Thessalonica in hearing what these missionary pastors say in their second letter.

First we look briefly at the circumstances in Thessalonica up to the time of the writing of the first letter. Issues needing attention in the second letter did not surface overnight. The time between the two letters might be only a few months or up to a year. In fact, the evangelistic visit, Timothy's return, and the writing of both letters may all be occurring within the span of one year. Both positive developments and problems are evident at every stage, including the time when the missionaries initially preached the gospel in Thessalonica.

Paul's preaching of the gospel of the crucified and risen Christ, whose coming as triumphant Lord might take place soon, evoked an excited response in Thessalonica. Steeped in the apocalyptic expectations inherent in Paul's gospel, some converts in Thessalonica began to take this expectation to an enthusiastic extreme. Early symptoms of such extremism may have been evident already when the evangelists were still in Thessalonica. Certainly Timothy notices them during his return visit.

These disturbing symptoms reflect both the converts' background in mystery religions (the cults of the Cabiri and of Dionysus) and their current misunderstanding of the character of the new age into which believers enter through Christ. Judging from what we hear in the first letter, at least some in Thessalonica are manifesting these symptoms, such as claims of sexual freedom (1 Thess. 4:1-8), the abandonment of daily occupations (4:9-12), a naive optimism about their immunity against misfortune and death (4:13-18), and an unwillingness to submit to the counsel of their leaders (5:12-22).

However, the confidence that their future as Christians would be marked by peace, bliss, and freedom was severely threatened by affliction. When some of their members died, likely as a result of persecution, the survivors faced a crisis of faith. The repressive forces of the civic cult punctured the balloon of their initial enthusiasm.

First Thessalonians is written in response. Rather than forthrightly attacking the worrisome trends, Paul and his partners first affirm the genuine signs of *faith, love,* and *hope* (1:3; 5:8) evident in the congregation, and then encourage greater faithfulness in several areas, including sexuality, work, and attitudes toward leaders. They also exhort the believers to claim the consequences of Jesus' resurrection by entrusting themselves and their loved ones to God, who raises the dead.

When we tune in to the follow-up letter, we immediately sense a change of mood. Further reports from the church in Thessalonica have somehow reached Paul. We are not told how this updated information came to him. There was good news as well as bad news. In the opening thanksgiving, Paul and his associates note that the congregation has grown in faith and love (2 Thess. 1:3). Furthermore, in the midst of their experiences of persecution, the members of the congregation are demonstrating steadfastness and faith (1:4).

But now for the bad news. The persecution appears to have worsened, leading some to question God's justice (1:5). Most distressing, however, is the misleading prophecy to the effect that *the day of the Lord has come* (2:2). In addition, *the unruly* are seemingly unwilling to work, although they are busy making a nuisance of themselves (3:6, 11). Certain expressions of ecstatic worship may also have characterized both the prophets and *the unruly.*

In 2 Thessalonians, the writers repeat some of the earlier material, resulting in a letter that closely resembles 1 Thessalonians in a number of ways. However, the ongoing persecution, eschatological confusion, and the lingering problem with *the unruly* lead Paul and his partners to write a letter which builds on the previous one but strongly calls for some changes in the life of this congregation.

2 Thessalonians 1:1-2

The Salutation

Apparently Paul, Silvanus, and Timothy do not wait long to write their second letter to the church at Thessalonica. Nor do they waste time reformulating the salutation. The opening of this sequel corresponds closely to the one in 1 Thessalonians:

1:1 *Paul and Silvanus and Timothy—to the church*
          ⊢ *of the Thessalonians*
          ⊢ *in God our Father*
          ⌞ *and the Lord Jesus Christ,*

1:2 *Grace—to you—from* *God the Father*
    and peace   *and the Lord Jesus Christ.*

A comparison of the two salutations reveals only two differences. In 1:1, *God our Father* (instead of *God the Father*) emphasizes the personal dimension of the relationship with God which the Christian brothers and sisters in Thessalonica have in common, both with each other and with the evangelists. The greeting expands the simple *Grace to you and peace* in the first letter to include an identification of the source of *grace* and *peace: God the Father and the Lord Jesus Christ* (1:2). This theological expansion in the customary apostolic greeting develops into the traditional greeting formula found in most of Paul's later letters (1 Cor. 1:3; 2 Cor. 1:2; Gal. 1:3; Phil. 1:2; Rom. 1:7). Likely worship services also opened with this same greeting.

251

2 Thessalonians 1:3-12

Worthy of God's Call

PREVIEW

As every pastor or parent knows, one letter, visit, or phone call may not suffice to communicate caring and offer counsel. Sometimes the message needs to be repeated. Further contact may be required, because the first efforts were not adequate or because they were misunderstood.

In their second letter, Paul and his co-workers summarize some themes from their first one, but they also expand on some new topics. The salutation (1:1-2) and the beginning of the thanksgiving section (1:3-4) repeat some material from 1 Thessalonians. However, the latter half of the thanksgiving section (1:5-10) sounds the keynote for the entire letter: *the righteous judgment of God* (1:5). While some aspects of this theme are present in 1 Thessalonians as well, it receives major attention in this follow-up letter.

The Thessalonians' *faith* and *love* again provide the occasion for thanksgiving to God. However, the Thessalonians are not commended for their *hope* (cf. 1 Thess. 3:6 also omits *hope*). Paul and his colleagues appear concerned that these believers might be sidetracked into a misguided and unfounded view of the future.

In 1:7b-10a the writers draw heavily on a number of OT texts dealing with judgment themes. Possibly this segment comes from a confession of faith or a summary of proof texts or even a sermon dealing with the last judgment. A personal comment in 1:10b reads like an attempt by the authors to stitch this older material into the flow of the letter: *because our testimony to you was believed.*

A prayer report (1:11-12) serves as the transition to introduce the upsetting problem in Thessalonica, the claim of some that *the day of the Lord has come* (2:1-2). This record of the evangelists' intercession in behalf of the community of believers functions like the wish-prayer in 1 Thessalonians 3:11-13 does in the first letter. It recapitulates what has already been said (2 Thess. 1:3-10), and it looks forward to the themes still to be addressed (2:1-12; 2:13—3:15).

The themes of *grace* and *peace* are sounded both in the greeting (1:2) and the letter's closing (3:16-18). In the two benedictions, these themes are featured in reverse order: *peace* (3:16) and *grace* (3:18). The contents of the whole letter are bracketed by the prayer that these believers might sense the embrace of God's *grace* and *peace!* It is also significant that, at the end of the prayer report which concludes the thanksgiving section of the letter, the writers invoke *the grace of our God and the Lord Jesus Christ* (1:12; cf. also the wish-prayer in 2:16).

OUTLINE

Thanksgiving for Faith and Love, 1:3-4
Evidence of God's Righteous Judgment, 1:5-10
Intercessory Prayer Report, 1:11-12

EXPLANATORY NOTES
Thanksgiving for Faith and Love   1:3-4

In comparison to the joyful mood in 1 Thessalonians 1:2-10, this thanksgiving section has a more reserved tone. An explanation for this more somber atmosphere probably lies in the nature of the agenda being introduced and the situation in Thessalonica which precipitates this second letter.

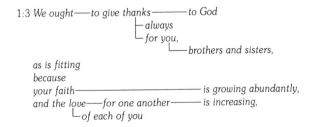

1:3 We ought——to give thanks———to God
├—always
└—for you,
  └—brothers and sisters,

as is fitting
because
your faith———————————— is growing abundantly,
and the love——for one another——— is increasing,
  └—of each of you

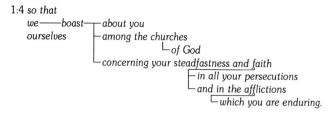

1:4 *so that*
we——boast——about you
ourselves ——among the churches
              ——of God
       ——concerning your steadfastness and faith
              ——in all your persecutions
              ——and in the afflictions
                     ——which you are enduring.

Instead of reporting to the Thessalonians, *We thank God* (1 Thess. 1:2), Paul and his colleagues assert, *We ought to give thanks to God for you, brothers and sisters* (1:3; cf. also 2:13). As they have reminded the Thessalonians earlier, God's will calls for giving thanks *always* and under all circumstances (1 Thess. 5:18). Has prayer become a duty, and thanksgiving a formality? Or might the writers be reassuring the Thessalonians that ongoing thanksgiving for them is fitting, despite their own sense that they are not worthy of the praise they received in the first letter (Bruce, 1982:144)? Paul and his co-workers do want to reassure their readers, and they give no hint that the Thessalonians are embarrassed about undeserved recognition. Instead, the writers affirm that gratitude to God is appropriate because of the affliction they are facing and the steadfastness and faith with which they are enduring it (1:4). The phrase *as is fitting* underscores the propriety of thanksgiving to God even in trying circumstances.

Two reasons for thanksgiving are cited: *Your faith is growing abundantly, and the love of each of you for one another is increasing* (1:3). Paul and his partners cannot be accused of being cool or reserved here! Growth in the Thessalonians' *faith* and *love* in the midst of their troubled situation moves the evangelists to express their thanksgiving to God.

In the first letter, the evangelists thank God for the Thessalonians' *work of faith* (1:3), despite the concern about their stamina under affliction (3:2) and the recognition that deficiencies in their *faith* need to be remedied (3:10). At the time the missionary pastors write the second letter, persecution has apparently continued, if not worsened. They praise God for the fact that in this situation, these believers model a growing *faith*, demonstrated especially in their continued faithfulness under pressure ("Faith" in TBC for 1 Thess. 2:17—3:10).

Thankful earlier for their *labor of love* (1 Thess. 1:3), and praying that their *love* might *increase and abound* (1 Thess. 3:12), Paul and his fellow missionaries now gratefully acknowledge that indeed the Thessalonians' *love of each of you for one another is increasing*

(2 Thess. 1:3). Later, in 3:6-15, it becomes apparent that further growth in *brotherly and sisterly love* (cf. 1 Thess. 4:9-12) is still needed. At this point in the second letter, the progress already made in this area of congregational life is celebrated.

As already noted, no mention is made of the Thessalonians' *hope*. In 1 Thessalonians 1:3, *steadfastness of hope* completes the trilogy, *faith, love*, and *hope*. Even in 1 Thessalonians, *hope* is not mentioned in a summary of Timothy's good news from Thessalonica (3:6). That dimension of the Thessalonians' Christian experience continues to be problematic, despite the attention given to it in the first letter (1 Thess. 4:13—5:11). This second letter has as a primary goal to address the Thessalonians' lingering questions and misunderstandings about the Christian *hope*.

Instead of recalling the Thessalonians' *steadfastness of hope*, Paul and his co-workers remember the *steadfastness and faith* which characterize these new believers while facing their *persecutions* and *afflictions* (1:4). The faithful perseverance of these new believers even moves the missionaries to boast: *We ourselves boast about you among the churches of God* (1:4). Apparently Paul and his companions still consider the Thessalonian believers as *our hope, joy*, and *crown of boasting* (1 Thess. 2:19-20). The *churches of God* include the congregations in Achaia, where Paul is located when he writes these two letters to the church at Thessalonica. The impact of the Thessalonians' faith on churches in Macedonia and Achaia has already been noted in 1 Thessalonians 1:7-8. Their faithfulness while facing persecution continues to exercise an exemplary influence on other believers.

Evidence of God's Righteous Judgment 1:5-10

Experiences of persecution inevitably raise troubling questions about whether God is in control. Oppressed people sometimes ask, "Why do the wicked prosper and the righteous suffer? Where is God's justice?"

Still thinking about the Thessalonians' faithfulness under persecution, Paul and his co-workers turn to the theme of divine justice:

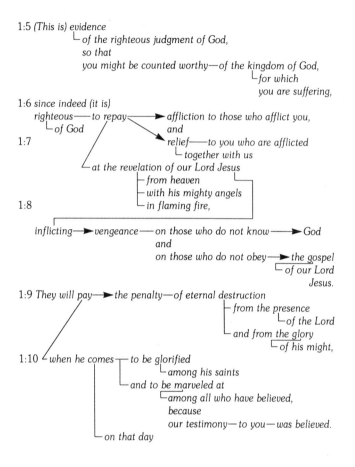

1:5 *(This is)* evidence
        └ *of the righteous judgment of God,*
        so that
        you might be counted worthy—of the kingdom of God,
                                        └ *for which*
                                           you are suffering,
1:6 *since indeed (it is)*
    righteous——*to repay* ——► *affliction to those who afflict you,*
        └ *of God*   *and*
1:7   *relief*——*to you who are afflicted*
                                        └ *together with us*
        └ *at the revelation of our Lord Jesus*
                        ├ *from heaven*
                        ├ *with his mighty angels*
1:8   └ *in flaming fire,*

    inflicting——► *vengeance* —— *on those who do not know* ——► *God*
                                    and
                                    on those who do not obey ——► *the gospel*
                                        └ *of our Lord*
                                                  Jesus.

1:9 *They will pay*——► *the penalty—of eternal destruction*
                        ├ *from the presence*
                        │   └ *of the Lord*
                        └ *and from the glory*
                            └ *of his might,*

1:10 ◄ *when he comes* ┬ *to be glorified*
                       │   └ *among his saints*
                       └ *and to be marveled at*
                           └ *among all who have believed,*
                           because
                           our testimony— to you — was believed.
        └ *on that day*

In the original text, the sentence which begins at 1:3 simply continues into 1:5 with the word *evidence*. In translating, we can begin a new sentence: *(This is) evidence of the righteous judgment of God* (1:5). What constitutes this *evidence*? Obviously something that has just been mentioned is put forward as proof that God acts justly. Three possibilities can be noted from 1:4. First, the clause *which you are enduring* can suggest that the Thessalonians' endurance provides proof of God's *righteous judgment* (Bruce, 1982:149). Second, the two phrases *in all your persecutions* and *in the afflictions* have led some scholars to argue that the afflictions themselves rather than the Thessalonians' endurance under suffering provide evidence of God's just dealings with them (Bassler, 1984; Wanamaker:

220-223). A third possibility is to understand that the *evidence* for God's *righteous judgment* is the same as the ground for the evangelists' boast: *your steadfastness and faith.*

The third of these three interpretations best accords with a straightforward reading of this passage in the context of 1 and 2 Thessalonians. These believers in Thessalonica have encountered persecution from the beginning of their experience as a Christian community. We can no longer know exactly what kind of opposition they faced, but it is most likely that political suspicions have been aroused, especially by the message concerning the *kingdom of God* and a rival *Lord.* Both civic and provincial officials in the capital city Thessalonica looked with distrust on groups that hesitated to show their full allegiance to Rome.

Already when they first accepted the gospel, the Thessalonians showed that they were ready to follow the way of suffering. The first letter emphasizes that the Thessalonians became imitators of both the evangelists and the Lord (1 Thess. 1:6). Indeed, their suffering makes them imitators of the prophets, Jesus, the churches in Judea, and the missionaries themselves (2:14-15). In a word, the faithfulness of the Thessalonians to the gospel, which appears to undermine their commitment to peace and security within the Roman empire (cf. notes on 5:2), leads to their affliction. As a community characterized by *faith, love,* and *hope,* the Thessalonian congregation has become an example to other believers (1:7). [*Historical and Political Context, p. 357.*]

But the second letter demonstrates that the exemplary character of the Thessalonian Christian community also portrays something about God. We have already read that this congregation is marked by *growing faith,* by *increasing love for one another,* and by *steadfastness and faith* in the face of the ongoing persecutions and affliction which they are enduring (2 Thess. 1:3-4). Now we learn that they dramatically show *evidence of the righteous judgment of God.*

The ensuing result clause clarifies this matter: *so that you might be counted worthy of the kingdom of God, for which you are suffering* (1:5). This clause echoes earlier themes from the first letter to the beleaguered converts in Thessalonica. At the climax of the review of their initial visit in Thessalonica, Paul and his companions remind these believers of their fatherly encouragement *that you walk worthy of God, who calls you into his kingdom and glory* (1 Thess. 2:12). After providing this glimpse into the still future though presently unfolding glorious reign of God, Paul and his colleagues immediately recall what the Thessalonian community is facing in the present. Two dimensions of their present experience as a community are singled out. First, the faith community knows the *word of God* as empowerment for a life worthy of God (2:13). And, second, this calling includes their suffering (2:14-15). In other words, having been called into God's kingdom, the community of believers in Thessalonica is sustained and empowered for its life and witness, which includes suffering.

The follow-up letter essentially repeats this emphasis. The Thessalonian believers are divinely enabled to live in *steadfastness and faith* in the midst of the persecutions which they are enduring (2 Thess. 1:4). Their *steadfastness and faith* supplies the *evidence* that indeed their lives conform to their calling. The Thessalonian Christian community has been *counted worthy of the kingdom of God* (1:5). Indeed, they are suffering in behalf of the kingdom.

Under the test of persecution, therefore, the Thessalonians' *steadfastness and faith* shows *evidence of the righteous judgment of God.* But how can this be? In 1:6-10, Paul, Silvanus and Timothy develop at some length the premise on which this assertion is based: *since indeed (it is) righteous of God to repay affliction to those who afflict you, and to you who are afflicted, relief together with us.* Ultimately, faithful endurance under persecution is rooted in the confidence that God will vindicate the faithful. Paul and his colleagues anticipate that a providential turning of the tables will occur as part of God's *righteous judgment.* Such is their confidence of relief for themselves, too, as the added phrase *together with us* shows. In this also, the Thessalonian believers become imitators. When enduring persecution in steadfastness and faith, the Thessalonians testify to the hope that in the end, God's justice will prevail. To those who afflict, God will *repay affliction* (1:6). To those being afflicted, God will grant *relief* (1:7). This is what God deems just (1:6).

Such a dramatic reversal of fortunes still lies in the future. Paul looks to the time of the parousia: *at the revelation of our Lord Jesus Christ* (1:7). Yet the consequences of this reversal reach into the present. This awareness of God's ultimate vindication inspires and empowers the faithful to endure their present distress. Even while suffering, therefore, the faith community provides evidence that God acts justly.

The coming of Christ as triumphant Lord is here described as *the revelation of our Lord Jesus Christ* (Greek: *apokalupsis;* cf. 1 Cor. 1:7). Several picturesque details follow concerning this climactic endtime moment of the execution of divine justice (2 Thess. 1:7). Jesus

Christ will be revealed *from heaven*, from which the Thessalonians are awaiting him (1 Thess. 1:10; 4:16). Furthermore, Jesus will not come alone, but *with his mighty angels* (cf. *with his holy ones*, 1 Thess. 3:13).

The onset of judgment is portrayed graphically. The words *in flaming fire* carry terror, whether associated with the revealing of Christ from heaven with his angelic host (1:7), or with the subsequent inflicting of vengeance (1:8).

Judgment is here assigned to *the Lord Jesus* as God's agent for *inflicting vengeance* (1:8; cf. 2:8 and notes thereon). Similarly, in 1 Thessalonians 4:6, when it comes to violations of God's will in the area of sexual behavior, the Lord is *executor of justice in all these things*. The consequences for the suffering believers are clear. God's righteous judgment will be exercised by Jesus as Lord, thereby freeing the Christian community from seeking vengeance. In his later letter to the house fellowships in Rome, Paul makes this point explicit:

> Beloved, never avenge yourselves, but leave room for the wrath of God; for it is written, "Vengeance is mine, I will repay, says the Lord."
> (Rom. 12:19; cf. Deut. 32:35)

The notion of divine vengeance, problematic though it might be for enlightened folks, removes revenge from the human realm and leaves judgment where it belongs—with God.

There seem to be two broad categories of people facing divine vengeance: *those who do not know God*, and *those who do not obey the gospel of our Lord Jesus Christ* (1:8). Is this one group or two? In the OT, the phrase *those who do not know God* typically refers to Gentiles (Jer. 10:25; Ps. 79:6; so in 1 Thess. 4:5), although Jews can also be described thus (Jer. 9:6; Hos. 4:1c; John 8:55). With reference to Jews, sin is often characterized as disobeying God's laws, but Paul in his letter to Rome takes pains to show that Jews and Gentiles alike have been disobedient (Rom. 11:30-32). Marshall argues that Paul and his companions envision two distinct groups: Gentiles *who do not know God*, and Jews *who do not obey the gospel* (Marshall: 177-178). It is more likely that these are two parallel ways of describing unbelieving humanity in general (Bruce, 1982:151-152). Truly to *know God* is also to *obey the gospel*. Divine judgment descends on those who refuse to acknowledge God and heed the gospel.

As part of their extended reflections on the *evidence of the righteous judgment of God*, the writers continue to ponder the final judgment and its aftermath. Still referring to *those who do not know God* and those who *do not obey the gospel*, they portray the awesome prospect which awaits such people: *They will pay the penalty of eternal destruction from the presence of the Lord and from the glory of his might* (1:9). In the earlier letter, Paul and his colleagues assure their hearers that they do not need to be surprised by the *day of the Lord*. On the other hand, people who trust the imperial Roman promise of *peace and security* will face *sudden destruction* (1 Thess. 5:3)—possibly a reference to an imminent historical event. In this second letter, the evangelists employ similar language to depict the ultimate judgment, which entails *the penalty of eternal destruction*.

Rather than dwelling on the particulars concerning *eternal destruction*, the writers articulate its most sobering aspect—exclusion *from the presence of the Lord and from the glory of his might* (1:9). In the first letter, when they address the survivors' grief in the face of death, the missionaries summarize their assurances by emphasizing that believers can anticipate unbroken communion with Christ: *We shall always be with the Lord* (1 Thess. 4:17). A similar reassurance concludes the discussion of the topic of *the day of the Lord*. Because of Jesus' death *for us*, the Thessalonians are told, *we live with him;* such continuity of life in Christ cannot be interrupted by death (5:10). In the follow-up letter, the believers hear the same message, this time stated in terms of its corollary. Those who fail to acknowledge God and heed the gospel thereby exclude themselves from both *the presence of the Lord* and *the glory of his might* (2 Thess. 1:9). God grants humanity the freedom to choose, and such choices carry consequences.

A temporal clause introduced by *when he comes* (1:10) draws renewed attention to the eschatological moment when *the righteous judgment of God* will be executed. As already noted in our discussion of 1:6-7, divine justice with reference to *those who afflict you* and *you who are afflicted* calls for God respectively *to repay affliction* and to grant *relief*. In 1:8-9, Paul and his co-workers have lingered on God's *vengeance*, to be unleashed at *the revelation of our Lord Jesus Christ from heaven* (1:7), and now in 1:10 they give the positive aspect—divine *relief* for those who believe. Rather than the fearsome prospect of *flaming fire* (1:8) and *eternal destruction* (1:9), believers can anticipate a very different scenario *when he [the Lord] comes to be glorified among his saints and to be marveled at among all who have believed* (1:10). Rather than being excluded from *the glory of his might* (1:9), the community of believers will form a holy choir glorifying the triumphant Lord!

Almost as an afterthought, Paul and his companions allude to the dynamic event behind the founding of the believing community in Thessalonica. What started the sequence of events which will lead to the marvelous eschatological drama? *Our testimony to you was believed* (1:10). In their first letter, the missionaries dwell at some length on this dramatic development (1 Thess. 1:2-10; 2:1-12). Here we have just a brief retrospective comment about those beginnings in Thessalonica. The missionaries gave witness, and the members of this congregation believed.

Another phrase dangles awkwardly at the end of the sentence: *on that day* (1:10). In the KJV these words are left at the end. However, most translations insert it earlier, often connecting it with the temporal clause at the beginning of the verse, *when he comes on that day* (RSV). The expression *on that day* clearly refers to *the day of the Lord* (cf. 1 Thess. 5:2), which becomes the main theme addressed in 2 Thessalonians 2:1-12.

What led to the afterthought and the appended phrase in the last half of 1:10? Some interpreters suggest that 1:7b-10a incorporates an early confession of faith or a thematic summary of OT texts (Bruce, 1982:148-149; Wanamaker: 232). It is also possible that the writers here include previously formed teaching material, perhaps by Paul himself, or by one of his partners, on the theme of the triumphant coming of Christ as Lord. This material draws heavily on the OT, as evident from numerous scriptural echoes and allusions. It is introduced here "because it addressed one of the major questions troubling the recipients of this letter in their time of persecution and affliction, namely, the question of God's justice" (Wanamaker: 232; "God's Righteous Judgment" in TBC below).

Intercessory Prayer Report 1:11-12

At this point, Paul, Silvanus, and Timothy include a prayer report:

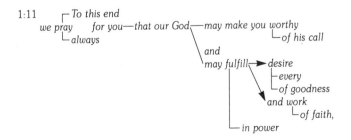

1:12 *so that*
 the name———may be glorified
  └*of our Lord Jesus* └*in you*
 and you———(may be glorified)——in him
  └*according to the grace*
            ╱*of our God*
            ╲*and the Lord Jesus Christ.*

Not only do Paul and his partners *give thanks to God always* (1:3-4; cf. 1 Thess. 5:18), they *always pray* (2 Thess. 1:11; cf. 1 Thess. 5:17). This is not a wish-prayer (as in 1 Thess. 3:11-13; 5:23-24; 2 Thess. 2:16-17; 3:5) but a report about the content of their intercessions in behalf of the Thessalonian Christian community.

Two specific requests are noted (1:11). The first recapitulates what has been said in 1:3-10: *that our God may make you worthy of his call.* Specifically, this request echoes the motif from 1:5, where Paul and his companions point to the Thessalonians' *steadfastness and faith* as *evidence* that they have been *counted worthy of the kingdom of God* (1:4-5). Recognizing the ongoing urgent need for divine enabling, the evangelists keep praying that God might continue to make them *worthy of his call* (cf. 1 Thess. 2:12).

The second request looks ahead to 2:1—3:15, with its pastoral and ethical exhortation: *(that our God) may fulfill every desire of goodness and work of faith in power* (1:11). Paul and his fellow missionaries pray not only for the Thessalonians' worthiness for the kingdom but also for their spiritual readiness and moral conduct during the interim while God's reign moves toward its consummation at the coming of Christ as Lord.

This thanksgiving section concludes on a doxological note: *so that the name of our Lord Jesus may be glorified in you and you in him according to the grace of our God and the Lord Jesus Christ* (1:12). Glory and grace emanate from the eschatological community and its triumphant Lord! Among people of *faith, love,* and *steadfastness* (1:3-4), the *name* of Christ will be lifted up in thunderous acclamation. What is the dominant theme of this cosmic chorus? The dissonant chords of *affliction* and *vengeance* and *eternal destruction* (1:5-10) recede, and the harmony of divine *grace* lifts the suffering saints and their Lord into a crescendo of praise!

Renewed by this vision of their grand destiny as persons called into God's kingdom and glory, the Christian community in Thessalonica is ready for correction concerning the nature of *the day of the Lord* (2:1-12), reassurance about their salvation (2:13-17), and instructions about how they should live in the meantime (3:1-15). To these subjects, Paul and his co-workers now turn. Undoubtedly they do so in the hope that, while pondering the dark side of their eschatological circumstances, their readers will be sustained by the uplifting chords of God's *grace.*

THE TEXT IN THE BIBLICAL CONTEXT
God's Righteous Judgment 1:5-10

When Abraham intercedes in behalf of the city of Sodom, he pleads with God, *Shall not the Judge of all the earth do what is just?* (Gen. 18:25). At stake is the question of collective punishment. Would it be just for the righteous minority to be destroyed along with all the wicked people in Sodom? In a series of interventions, Abraham proposes instead that the wicked majority receive mercy along with the righteous few. The dialogue between Abraham and God ends on the note of grace. Even if there are only ten innocent persons in the whole city, God's righteous judgment would be expressed in mercy rather than devastation (18:32). This amazing saga depicts God as a judge who shrinks from condemning the guilty. God errs, as it were, on the side of mercy.

Yet God does exercise judgment. In both testaments, God is portrayed as a judge, who rewards faithfulness and punishes disobedience. Such judgment may come through historical crises, but a final judgment also looms on the horizon ("Wrath" in TBC for 1 Thess. 2:13-16; "Day of the Lord" in TBC for 1 Thess. 5:1-11). In 2 Thessalonians 1:5-10, Paul and his coauthors reflect pastorally on *the righteous judgment of God* in light of the circumstances facing the suffering Christian community in Thessalonica. However, these pastoral reflections are also informed by awareness of OT passages dealing with divine judgment, as shown by numerous biblical echoes throughout this text.

The song of Moses in Deuteronomy 32 contains motifs which resonate in 2 Thessalonians 1:5-10. In a "lawsuit" involving God and Israel, God first prosecutes the case against this people whose chronic faithlessness threatens to break the covenant between them (Deut. 32:1-19). Contemplating their annihilation at the hands of enemy nations, God ponders a disturbing consequence of such severe action against Israel. These enemy nations quite arrogantly might think that they have gained victory because of their own superior power

(32:20-33). Consequently, God switches from the prosecution to the defense of Israel. Indeed, God presides as the judge, who both condemns the oppressor and vindicates the oppressed. Concerning the nations with designs against the covenant people, God says,

> Vengeance is mine, and recompense,
>   for the time when their foot shall slip;
> because the day of their calamity is at hand,
>   their doom comes swiftly. (Deut. 32:35)

God promises to rescue the people of Israel in their powerlessness.

> Indeed the Lord will vindicate his people,
>   have compassion on his servants,
> when he sees that their power is gone. (32:36)
> For he will avenge the blood of his children,
>   and take vengeance on his adversaries;
> he will repay those who hate him,
>   and cleanse the land for his people. (32:43)

Divine vengeance (cf. 2 Thess. 1:8) therefore takes the form of both rescue and punishment, both relief for the oppressed and pressure on their oppressors.

The prophet Isaiah communicates a similar message in an oracle announcing the day of the Lord (Isa. 2:6-22). Appearing as a refrain three times in Isaiah's speech are warnings to take refuge "from the terror of the Lord, and from the glory of his majesty" (2:10, 19, 21), "when he rises to terrify the earth" (2:19, 21). Why take refuge? The prophet predicts that the proud and the haughty will be in for a surprise:

> The haughty eyes of people shall be brought low,
>   and the pride of everyone shall be humbled;
> and the Lord alone will be exalted in that day.
> For the Lord of hosts has a day
>   against all that is proud and lofty,
>   against all that is lifted up and high. (Isa. 2:11-12; cf. 2:17)

Some of these themes reverberate in our 2 Thessalonians passage. Paul and his partners invite their readers to anticipate a turning of the tables for the afflicted and those who afflict them (1:6-7). They also foresee a time when those who refuse to acknowledge God and heed the gospel will be excluded *from the glory of his might* (1:9), whereas the saints will glorify the crucified and risen Lord (1:10). Depending on their relationship with God, people will respond to God's majesty either with terror or in worship.

Yet another text in the book of Isaiah appears to supply some of the images of judgment, especially for 1:8-9. Isaiah 66:7-16 celebrates the restoration of Jerusalem in two contrasting ways. In a series of tender maternal images, the prophet pictures God as comforting the people of Jerusalem (66:7-14). But the God who comforts the afflicted also afflicts the comfortable. This motherly God has a stern side:

> For the Lord will come in fire,
>   and his chariots like the whirlwind,
> to pay back his anger in fury,
>   and his rebuke in flames of fire.
> For by fire will the Lord execute judgment,
>   and by his sword, on all flesh;
>   and those slain by the Lord shall be many. (66:15-16)

When portraying *the revelation of the Lord Jesus from heaven* to begin the process of final judgment, Paul seems to echo the language of this text. The *Lord Jesus* will come *in flaming fire inflicting vengeance* (1:8). The sword motif from Isaiah 66:16 does not appear here explicitly, but Paul mentions *the penalty of eternal destruction* (1:9). Perhaps the gruesome scene of carnage on the battlefield as depicted in the final verse of Isaiah 66 also influences this description of the consequences of disobedience:

> And they shall go out and look at the dead bodies of the people who have rebelled against me; for their worm shall not die, their fire shall not be quenched, and they shall be an abhorrence to all flesh. (Isa. 66:24)

From this text have come some of the NT images of hell, notably Jesus' quotation and comment recorded in Mark 9:48.

Among the NT writings, the judgment themes of 2 Thessalonians 1:5-10 are echoed and expanded. According to Mark 13 (and parallels), Jesus himself teaches that there will be wars, earthquakes, and famines, all part of the birth pangs of the coming age (Mark 13:3-8). Persecution, betrayal, suffering, and false prophecy will also be characteristic phenomena of this time (13:9-23). (This sounds much like the situation confronting the Christian community in Thessalonica in A.D. 50.)

Jesus continues with a forecast concerning the climactic event:

> But in those days, after that suffering,
> the sun will be darkened,
> and the moon will not give its light,
> and the stars will be falling from heaven,
> and the powers in the heavens will be shaken.
> Then they will see the Son of Man coming in clouds with great power and glory. Then he will send out the angels, and gather his elect from the four winds, from the ends of the earth to the ends of heaven. (Mark 13:24-27)

Even though some of the details do not match exactly, the central event in Mark 13 corresponds to that depicted in 2 Thessalonians 1, particularly the coming of the Lord (in Mark, *the Son of Man*; cf. Dan. 7:13), the accompanying angels, and the power and glory.

Final judgment is not explicitly mentioned in Mark's summary of Jesus' prophecy concerning the coming of the Son of Man. However, according to Matthew, Jesus previews the last judgment in some detail (Matt. 25:31-46):

> When the Son of Man comes in his glory, and all the angels with him, then he will sit on the throne of his glory. (Matt. 25:31)

Once again we have the images of the glorious majesty of the triumphant Lord with his entourage of angels (cf. 2 Thess. 1:7, 9-10). But what the king says to the two groups gathered before him (Matt. 25:34, 41) aligns with the notion of *the penalty of eternal destruction* and exclusion *from the presence of the Lord* in 2 Thessalonians 1:9. Especially pertinent are the words of judgment addressed to those who neither recognized the Lord nor obeyed the gospel (cf. 1:8):

> You that are accursed, depart from me into the eternal fire prepared for the devil and his angels. (Matt. 25:41)

The summation at the end brings out the contrasting destinies of these two groups, whose responses to the suffering and the needy clearly reveal where their ultimate commitments lie:

> And these will go away into eternal punishment, but the righteous into eternal life. (Matt. 25:46)

Among the NT writers, Paul focuses most extensively on the theme of *the righteous judgment of God*. We will limit our examination largely to the letter which Paul wrote to the house churches in Rome. The thesis statement (Rom. 1:16-17) both introduces the main argument of Romans and announces the major theme of this letter: "the righteousness of God." Concerning the gospel, defined as "the power of God for salvation" (1:16), Paul affirms, "In it the righteousness of God is revealed through faith for faith" (1:17).

Following this theme statement is an exposé of human unrighteousness, against which "the wrath of God is revealed from heaven" (Rom. 1:18). Paul's diagnosis of the plight of sinful humanity (1:18-32) functions like a sting operation, designed to catch the culprits. Jewish hearers would readily recognize that this diagnosis condemns Gentiles as the bad guys, but Paul hastens to direct the same spotlight back on those who would judge others. Essentially, they are condemning themselves as the guilty ones (2:1-2)! The extended argument which follows in 2:1—3:31 repeatedly asserts that God shows no partiality (2:11; 3:22, 29-30). Furthermore, Paul adds that, when it comes to "righteousness," all people are in the same boat: "all, both Jews and Greeks, are under the power of sin" (3:9). Indeed, "all have sinned and fall short of the glory of God" (3:23).

The first part of Paul's discussion about God's impartiality in judgment and salvation (Rom. 2:1-16) has the most affinity with his earlier treatment of *the righteous judgment of God* in 2 Thessalonians 1:5-10. An opening series of rhetorical questions shows that God's judgment cannot be avoided (Rom. 2:3) and that God's patience should be seen as providing opportunities for repentance (2:4). Paul then adds an explicit comment about the final judgment:

> By your hard and impenitent heart you are storing up wrath for yourself on the day of wrath, when God's righteous judgment will be revealed.
> (Rom. 2:5)

Here the rhetorical thrust differs from that in 2 Thessalonians, written in part to address a suffering congregation's questions about God's justice. In Rome, the vexing congregational agenda centers on relationships between Jews and Gentiles. To the Thessalonians, Paul wishes to convey that, if not in the present, at least on the day when the victorious Lord is revealed from heaven, God's righteous judgment will be demonstrated. In the meantime, their faithful perseverance in affliction already constitutes proof of *the righteous judgment of God*. For the Roman believers, Paul seeks to establish a level playing field for Jews and Gentiles, so that they can live in harmony with one another. A reminder to Jews and Gentiles that both groups will face *God's righteous judgment* establishes their common footing before God.

Interpreters of Romans have often been puzzled by the criteria for

God's judgment according to 2:6-10. God "will repay according to each one's deeds" (2:6). "Eternal life" will be the reward for "those who by patiently doing good seek for glory and honor and immortality" (2:7). "Wrath and fury" will be the consequences for "those who are self-seeking and who obey not the truth but wickedness" (2:8). Essentially the same points are made in reverse order in 2:9-10:

> There will be anguish and distress for everyone who does evil, the Jew first and also the Greek, but glory and honor and peace for everyone who does good, the Jew first and also the Greek.

Preachers often find it easier to skip these texts, since they seem hard to reconcile with the keynote texts in Romans—1:16-17 (cited above), 3:21-26, and 5:1-11. These all emphasize faith rather than works as the way to achieve righteousness before God. However, the message of Romans 2:6-10 broadly agrees with the thrust of 2 Thessalonians 1. Judgment falls *upon those who do not know God and upon those who do not obey the gospel of our Lord Jesus* (1:8). Approval comes for those who *fulfill every desire of goodness and work of faith* (1:11).

The key to the puzzle lies in a right understanding of *faith* ("Faith" in TBC for 1 Thess. 2:17—3:10). In Romans, Paul elaborates his argument at length. The Thessalonian letters give just a few glimpses. In both, human *faith* is basically a response to Jesus' faithfulness, even unto death on the cross, and a personal appropriation of God's vindicating power, which raised Jesus from the dead and also sustains the faithful. The Thessalonians' *steadfastness and faith* while suffering persecution (1:4) provides a vivid example. Such *faith* works. Along with the missionaries and the churches in Judea, the community in Thessalonica has become imitators of Jesus, who died and was raised and now delivers believers from wrath (cf. 1 Thess. 1:6-10; 2:14). Enabled by God's grace, believers in Thessalonica endure suffering, and they are exhorted to continue to persevere, knowing that, however bleak the present, in the end such *faith* will be rewarded.

In much the same way, the dramatic witness of the Revelation of John encourages the suffering churches in Asia. We could cite texts from almost anywhere in this powerful apocalypse. Its inspiring vision of future triumph for those who align themselves with the Lamb that was slain (Rev. 5) strengthens the believers in their time of crisis. Anticipation of a final judgment provides the needed stamina, since in the end the forces of evil will be destroyed and the faithful vindicated.

Later chapters illustrate this. A funeral lamentation over Babylon (Rev. 18:1-24) has its counterpoint in the thunderous "Hallelujah!" chorus which opens the marriage celebration for the Lamb and his bride (19:1-10). Babylon represents Rome with its grandeur, wealth, and power. A funeral for Babylon? The Lamb with his bride symbolize the crucified and risen Christ with his beleaguered body, the church. A marriage celebration for Christ and his suffering church? In the vision which follows, the church though still besieged catches a further glimpse of *God's righteous judgment*, executed by a mysterious rider (representing Christ) on a white horse:

> Then I saw heaven opened, and there was a white horse! Its rider is called Faithful and True, and in righteousness he judges and makes war. His eyes are like a flame of fire, and on his head are many diadems. (Rev. 19:11-12)

In the vision, a bloody battle ensues between the rider, called "The Word of God" (Rev. 19:13), and the kings of the earth and their armies.

> From his mouth comes a sharp sword with which to strike down the nations, and he will rule them with a rod of iron; he will tread the wine press of the fury of the wrath of God the Almighty. (Rev. 19:15-16)

During this cosmic struggle, the beast and the false prophet are thrown into the lake of fire, and the army falls to the sword coming from the mouth of the rider (19:17-21, 13). With lurid detail the prophet John dramatically portrays a war ultimately won by the weak over the strong, through Christ and the proclamation of the gospel. This vision empowers and inspires the afflicted saints to remain faithful. The overwhelming forces marshaled against them will not prevail. Those who endure to the end shall be saved!

THE TEXT IN THE LIFE OF THE CHURCH
Suffering and God's Judgment

Churches in the West have often not known what to make of biblical passages such as 2 Thessalonians 1:3-12. Suffering is not a favorite theme in North American congregations, where most members live quite comfortably. Texts which emphasize God's judgment against oppressors reassure their victims that justice will ultimately prevail. But how should such biblical themes be heard among those who are living in relative comfort and ease?

As noted earlier, the same message which comforts the afflicted will often afflict the comfortable. Believers who know the "good life" need to study 1 and 2 Thessalonians realizing that the original readers faced distressing circumstances. Christians today need to identify with the suffering believers back then. The church can identify, not by seeking suffering for itself, though suffering could come as the consequence of greater faithfulness to the way of Christ. Instead, the church needs to identify with those believers who do suffer. In a word, we need sisters and brothers from African-American urban churches and from base communities in Latin America and churches in Palestine to help us understand the biblical message and discover anew what it means for us to obey the gospel of our Lord Jesus.

In this connection, we could comment about one line of interpretation of 2 Thessalonians 1:7, which promises *relief* for the afflicted at the time of *the revelation of the Lord Jesus from heaven.* Some interpreters regard this *revelation* as the first of two stages in the coming of Christ. In the first stage, Christ comes for his saints, who are taken up with him into heaven. After a seven-year period called the great tribulation, Christ comes with his saints for the final judgment. *[Eschatology, p. 355.]* This reconstruction of end-time events is based on a rather speculative stringing together of isolated texts from Daniel, the book of Revelation, the Thessalonian epistles, and other Scripture texts. Such methods of biblical interpretation usually violate the meanings of these texts in their historical and literary contexts.

Unfortunately, this type of interpretation has also misled many Christians into believing that they would be spared severe suffering. David Ewert's word of caution and his illustration from mission history apply here:

> We are ill-advised to hold out the hope to the church that, before the night of this age gets too dark, Christ will take us away from the trials of life. Missionary David Adeney, who has spent half a lifetime in Asia, observes that when tribulation came upon the church in communist China, it was caught off guard. This was the case because missionaries in China had taught that the church would be spared the tribulation. Any interpretation of biblical prophecy that exempts the church from persecution or tribulation should be rejected. (Ewert, 1980:52)

With the Christian community in Thessalonica in the first century, the church around the world today needs to be prepared for the possibility of suffering as a consequence of faithfulness. The prospect of God's final judgment carries with it the hope that ultimately justice will be done. God's righteous judgment need not elicit either dread or a gloating anticipation of revenge. Those who have entrusted themselves to God as made known in Christ can face the future with quiet confidence. They must also participate with passion and commitment in the church's mission of sharing the gospel. God desires that all might come to the knowledge of the truth. Who knows when the divine patience and the opportunity to repent will come to an end?

One way of identifying with our suffering brothers and sisters in Christ is to get in touch with the martyrs in the history of the church. The *Martyrs Mirror* has one story after another about women and men and their steadfast faithfulness even unto death. Some of these stories also testify that God's vengeance against their persecutors at times became frighteningly immediate. In 1527, Thomas Hermann, a minister of the gospel, plus sixty-seven others in Kitzbühel were put to death. Afterward, the town clerk instrumental in the executions was thrown from his sleigh by an erratic horse and died of a massive head injury (*Martyrs Mirror:* 422).

In 1528 in Moravia, five Anabaptists identified only as "three brethren and two sisters," were executed by burning. Shortly after their execution, Sir Louis, the judge who had condemned them, stepped into a hole while pursuing other Anabaptists, and sprained his ankle. Soon after this, Sir Louis "took sick unto death" and finally "he was strangled in his own blood." The narrator comments,

And thus God has often . . . checked the wicked with like examples, that thereby His work might make the greater progress among His people, to His praise, and to the salvation of many who seek that which is right, and the amendment of life; for if God had not always sustained His work, the enemy would in the course of time have extinguished it, and not have left one spark or germ of truth remain; but this [is what] God does not permit him to do. (*Martyrs Mirror:* 428)

Such testimony does not warrant the conclusion that God inflicts vengeance through accidents or illness nor that catastrophes signal God's particular displeasure with those who are struck. We can learn from these stories that God providentially sustains the church, even through severe trial. In the tug of war between God's justice and God's mercy, sometimes there are people whom God gives up to the wrath unleashed through a legacy of human idolatry and disobedience (Rom. 1:18-32). Whether within history or at the time of the end, however, judgment will inevitably come.

2 Thessalonians 2:1-17

Living in Light of the Future

OVERVIEW

With the exalted chords of glory and grace still ringing in their ears (2 Thess. 1:11-12), the Thessalonian believers quickly need to become attuned to the ominous thunder of apostasy and rebellion.

In 1 Thessalonians, a story (2:1—3:13) follows the opening thanksgiving (1:2-10). While reviewing aspects of the story of their initial visit in Thessalonica, Paul and his companions reveal some of their thoughts and feelings about that event. Paul also personally vents his own frustration and anxiety resulting from his inability to return to this congregation.

The second letter to Thessalonica follows a different track. Instead of reviewing the recent past, the evangelists confront some disturbing developments. Corrective intervention has become necessary because a false and misleading claim is being promoted among the believers—the claim that *the day of the Lord has come* (2 Thess. 2:1-2). In 2:3-15, Paul and his co-workers refute this prophecy. First they describe some phenomena which need to occur before that eschatological day, in particular *the apostasy* and various associated events (2:3-12). But they also reassure the believing community by sounding the uplifting themes again, reminding them about God's gracious gift of salvation and glory (2:13-15).

A wish-prayer (2:16-17) gathers up the evangelists' desire for the Thessalonian community and introduces closing pastoral instructions (3:1-15).

OUTLINE

2 Thessalonians 2:1-12

The Day of the Lord? Not Yet!

PREVIEW

The congregation in Thessalonica faces persecution from outside. They are also shaken up from within. Some among them are apparently claiming that *the day of the Lord* has already arrived.

In the first letter, Paul and his fellow missionaries seek to comfort grieving believers in Thessalonica by focusing on Jesus' resurrection and on the gathering of the saints with the Lord at his *coming* (4:13-18). They also include some reminders, reassurances, and exhortations concerning *the day of the Lord* (5:1-11). As evident in the opening appeal, the second letter connects with both of these themes: *the coming of our Lord Jesus Christ* and *our gathering with him* (2:1). However, the main agenda in 2:3-12 addresses some misleading claims regarding *the day of the Lord* (2:2).

The thanksgiving section (1:3-12) highlights the Thessalonians' perseverance and God's justice. The readers are consoled with the thought that at the coming of the Lord the faithful will be vindicated and the disobedient judged. But when will this be?

In 2:3-12 they hear the answer: Not just yet! Their present experiences of *oppression* resulting from the policies of the *oppressor* do not yet qualify as the end-time tribulation (2:6-7). A self-exalting and blasphemous antagonist (*the man of lawlessness*) will still be revealed in the future (2:4, 8a); then the final holy war will begin (2:8b). In the meantime, the church needs to cope with *the mystery of lawlessness* (2:7a) and guard against being deceived by Satan's false and misleading signs (2:9-10).

All of this sounds like it would frighten these new believers even more. Yet they are reassured that ultimate victory is guaranteed for those who trust God! The themes of God's grace, the believers' calling, and their ultimate glory in Christ form a comforting buffer (1:11-12; 2:13-14) around this privileged glimpse into some of the bizarre and unsettling end-time phenomena. After this graphic preview of how *the Lord Jesus will slay him* (*the lawless one*, 2:3, 8), Paul and his companions thank God—not for the fate of the wicked but for the Thessalonians' salvation (2:13).

OUTLINE

An Opening Appeal, 2:1-2
A Reminder About the Future, 2:3-5
In the Meantime, 2:6-7
And Then, 2:8-12

EXPLANATORY NOTES

An Opening Appeal 2:1-2

The appeal opens in typical fashion (cf. 1 Thess. 4:1; 5:12):

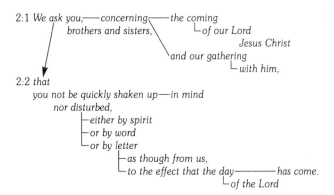

As noted above, the authors here reintroduce themes from two sections of the first letter: *the coming of our Lord Jesus Christ and our gathering with him* (cf. 1 Thess. 4:13-18), and *the day of the Lord* (5:1-11). Word has apparently come to Paul about some excitement or alarm being felt by members of the Thessalonian Christian community in relation to this *coming* and this *day*. Paul and his companions therefore urge them strongly: *that you not be quickly shaken up in mind nor disturbed* (2:2).

What is shaking up this congregation? A prophet in their midst apparently is making the claim that this anticipated near event has in fact already occurred or is presently unfolding: *the day of the Lord has come* (2:2). What is more, the proponents of this viewpoint seem to be citing Paul in support! Perhaps a prophetic utterance in the congregation (*by spirit*) or a sermon or teaching by Paul or one of his colleagues (*by word*) is being quoted in support of this conviction. Yet another possibility is also raised: *by letter as though from us* (2:2).

This mention of a previous *letter*, when seen in association with a similar reference in 2:15 and with Paul's signature at the end (*my sign in every letter*, 3:17), has aroused considerable debate. The only known earlier letter was 1 Thessalonians. Did Paul suspect that someone had forged a letter in his name? Jewett suggests that

> the eschatological excitement of the congregation caused the misinterpretation of both his teaching on the first visit and his letter in the sense that the end of time had arrived. This misinterpretation was so gross, however, that Paul could not comprehend how it might have come from his letter. A misunderstanding on this scale raised the serious possibility in his mind of an actual forgery. (Jewett, 1986:185)

Most likely the statement *by letter as though from us* simply shows that Paul and his colleagues want to disassociate themselves from the way these teachers interpret their first letter, especially 1 Thessalonians 5:1-11. [*Relationship between 1 and 2 Thessalonians, p. 374.*]

On what basis might anyone have concluded that *the day of the Lord has come*? Some scholars suspect a Gnostic spiritualized doctrine of *the day of the Lord*, perhaps similar to the notion condemned in 2 Timothy 2:18, that "the resurrection has already taken place." A different explanation is more likely. Apocalyptic writings of that time envision that the people of God would face a turbulent period of intense suffering before the end of the present age; these were sometimes called the "messianic woes" (Pobee: 38-39). The Thessalonian's suffering apparently has led some of them to conclude that they are experiencing the birth pangs of the messianic age. Probably a charismatic prophet, in the fervor and ecstasy of a worship gathering, has announced that *the day of the Lord*, which Paul and his colleagues have preached and written about, is now coming to pass. Such an announcement might well create excitement, perhaps especially among *the unruly* (cf. 1 Thess. 5:14; 2 Thess. 3:6, 11). For others, this would raise alarm and cause confusion. What are they to believe? How should they make sense of the opposition they are facing? Might their present afflictions be the tribulations of the end?

A Reminder About the Future 2:3-5

Paul and his companions feel constrained to dispel this misleading and confusing claim:

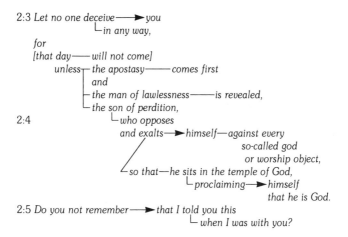

The rebuttal begins with the warning, *Let no one deceive you in any way.* Misunderstandings can occur, even in the church. However, these missionary pastors also sense that believers can be deceived. Living in the interim, while awaiting the coming of Christ as Lord, the faith community needs to realize the grave risk of deception (cf. 2:9-12).

The actual refutation begins with an incomplete sentence, perhaps reflecting the agitation or grave concern the writers feel. Most translations supply what seems to be missing in the original text (shown here by brackets): *for [that day will not come] unless. . .* (2:3). The word *unless* opens the recital of events and phenomena which must first occur before the arrival of *the day of the Lord.* In their first letter, Paul and his fellow evangelists remind the Thessalonians that *the day of the Lord*, though inevitable, sudden, and unpredictable, need not surprise them, given their status as *children of light and children of day* (5:1-5). Now they need to cool the fervor and instill some realism about what will take place first.

What must happen *first*? In the original Greek version of this text, the underlying word is *apostasia*, so one can translate: *unless the apostasy comes first* (2:3). The word *apostasia*, often rendered *rebellion* (NIV, NRSV), can refer either to a political or a religious phenomenon. The actions of the main instigator (2:4) clearly suggest that this *apostasy* has both political and religious dimensions. Paul and his associates remind their Christian brothers and sisters in Thessalonica that the time leading up to the dawning of *the day of the Lord* will include a season of grave peril. Apparently the original readers know what this means (2:5). Living under persecution, perhaps mostly precipitated by their unwillingness to do homage to the emperor within the civic cult, these new believers would readily have visualized such *apostasy*. They are personally acquainted with the blasphemous claims of divinity made by the emperors themselves or by others in the emperor's behalf. *Apostasy* of this kind clearly shows that the worlds of politics and religion intertwine. *[Religion in the Greco-Roman World, p. 365.]*

The initiator of this period of *apostasy* has various names, two of which are introduced here. One title not used in Paul's writings is antichrist, mentioned directly only in the epistles of John: 1 John 2:18, 22; 4:3; 2 John 7. To simplify our discussion of this end-time personage, we will use the general term antagonist (cf. Holland: 46; "The Antagonist" in TBC below).

First, *the man of lawlessness is revealed* (2:3; cf. *the lawless one*, 2:8). Some early manuscripts have *man of sin* (thus KJV), but the earliest Greek texts read *man of lawlessness. [Textual Analysis, p. 346.]* The category of *lawlessness* need not be understood in terms of a Jewish concept of disobedience against God's laws, but rather as general opposition to God. The one envisioned is not Satan but a historical person (*anthrōpos* in the Greek can be male or female) through whom Satan works (cf. 2:9-10). This leader of the blatant God-defying *apostasy* appears on the world stage in a way that mimics the coming of Christ for the final judgment (cf. 1:7): *the man of lawlessness is revealed*. In 2:9-10 the evangelists elaborate on ways in which the antagonist's activity will imitate the ministry of Christ. Such mimicry is clearly intended to deceive believers and beguile others into accepting a phony and dangerous substitute for God's gracious offer of salvation through Christ.

A second name for the antagonist is given: *the son of perdition* (2:3). Rather than defining the antagonist with reference to activity (*lawlessness*), this name foreshadows the eventual fate which awaits this end-time figure (cf. 2:8). Even the name sends the signal to believers that ultimately they need not fear the antics of Satan's deputy, whose doom is assured.

These antics are suggestively recounted: *who opposes and exalts himself against every so-called god or worship object so that he sits in the temple of God proclaiming himself that he is God* (2:4). We can be sure that the believers gathered for worship in Thessalonica hear these words with more insight than later readers can ever hope to attain. What might our sisters and brothers in Thessalonica have inferred from this dramatic preview?

A review of some traumatic episodes in Jewish history will help to bring us in touch with what the Thessalonian Christian community may be thinking and feeling while listening to this prediction about the provocative actions of the antagonist. Most Jews and some Gentiles (in particular the God-fearers) would have recalled some troubling stories from the past. *[Historical and Political Context, p. 357.]*

What the Syrian king Antiochus IV Epiphanes did in 167 B.C. impressed itself indelibly on the inner consciousness of the Jewish people, including Jesus himself. This king was eager to integrate the Jews into the culture of his Greek empire and probably also to identify the Greek god Zeus with himself. He erected an altar to Zeus over the altar in the court of the Jerusalem temple and there sacrificed unacceptable offerings (likely pigs; 1 Macc. 1:54-61; 2 Macc. 6:1-6; cf. 6:18-23). This came to be known as "an abomination that makes desolate" (Dan. 9:27; 11:31; 12:11), since such action defiled the temple and rendered it unclean for worship of the God of gods.

In the Gospels, Jesus employs the same language of "desolation" when predicting the desecration and destruction of the temple (Matt. 24:15; Mark 13:14; Luke 21:20). That disastrous event actually occurred in A.D. 70: after a lengthy siege of Jerusalem, the Roman general Titus and his army penetrated the defensive walls, pillaged and destroyed the city, and demolished the temple.

While Paul and his co-workers are writing 2 Thessalonians (about A.D. 50 or 51), the Jerusalem temple is still standing. Memories of Jesus' dire warnings concerning the future trauma in Jerusalem and his promise of the coming of the Son of Man in power and glory (Mark 13) are likely circulating in sermons and stories or perhaps even in an early written form.

Two other historical episodes from the time following Antiochus IV Epiphanes might have come to the minds of the readers. According to Josephus, in 63 B.C. the Roman general Pompey conquered

Jerusalem and deeply offended the temple leaders by entering the holy of holies (*War* 1.152-153 [1.7.6]). But a more recent deeply upsetting incident might be personally recalled by some people living in Thessalonica. Emperor Gaius Caligula (A.D. 37-41) preceded Claudius, emperor when these letters to Thessalonica are being written. Josephus reports concerning Gaius:

> Gaius Caesar displayed such insolence at his accession to power that he wished to be thought of and addressed as a god. . . . Indeed, he sent Petronius with an army to Jerusalem to install statues of himself in the temple; if the Jews refused them he was to execute the objectors and to reduce the whole nation to slavery. (*War* 2.184-185 [2.10.1]; cf. *Ant.* 18.257-309 [18.8.1-9])

Providentially, this order was not implemented. Gaius Caligula was assassinated before he could punish his deputy for disobeying the order. A national Jewish uprising against Rome was narrowly averted. Better said, the Jewish War of A.D. 66-70 almost broke out twenty-five years earlier. News of this close call traveled quickly to Jewish population centers throughout the Mediterranean world.

What relevance do these historical memories have for our attempt to understand what Paul, Silvanus, and Timothy mean in 2 Thessalonians 2:4? By this time, the actions of Antiochus IV Epiphanes in 167 B.C. have come to symbolize the way emperors and kings often put themselves in God's place. Pompey in 63 B.C. and Gaius Caligula in A.D. 41 used the same blueprint for their acts of blasphemous defiance. During the coming *apostasy*, Paul and his partners warn, the antagonist will follow the same script. This account detailing the activity of *the man of lawlessness, the son of perdition,* even echoes what Daniel has to say about king Antiochus, that he claimed to be "greater than any god" (Dan. 11:36-37; "The Antagonist" in TBC below; Lederach: 247-249).

Like Antiochus, the antagonist *exalts himself,* not only against the one true God but also against *every so-called god or worship object.* The antagonist's ultimate arrogant defiance expresses itself in a symbolic action: *He sits in the temple of God.* This can most naturally be taken as a reference to the Jewish temple in Jerusalem, rather than to the church as God's temple (cf. 1 Cor. 3:16-17) or to a rebuilt temple (so Thomas: 322). Along with sitting down in the temple, thereby claiming divine authority, the antagonist makes an announcement, *proclaiming himself that he is God.* What his symbolic action claims, the antagonist also openly proclaims: "I am God!"

Before shifting the focus from the still future *apostasy* (2:3-4) to the present foretaste of it (2:6-7), Paul interjects a personal question: *Do you not remember that I told you this when I was with you?* (2:5). This is one of several places in the letters to the church at Thessalonica (1 Thess. 2:18; 3:5; 5:27; 2 Thess. 3:17) where Paul specifically speaks for himself as distinct from his coauthors. This question seems to have come out of some frustration or concern. Otherwise it has the same effect as the formulas employed in the first letter (such as: *you yourselves know*, 1 Thess. 2:1; *as you know*, 2:2, 5, 11) to jog the Thessalonians' memory of Paul's first preaching and teaching in their community. Both letters assume that these converts remember some of what they have initially been taught! As later readers of these letters, we can sometimes only guess what that was.

In the Meantime 2:6-7

Scholars have done their share of (informed) guessing about the meaning of 2:6-7. Here we move into a complex sequence of assertions difficult for the modern reader to decipher. The secret code for interpreting the cryptic symbols has been lost! Even the way the adverb *now* in 2:6 connects with the rest of the sentence is disputed.

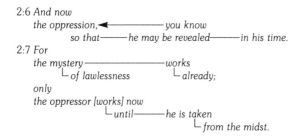

We begin by puzzling over the code word, which appears in two participles:

to katechon (2:6)	neuter	often translated: *what restrains*; my translation: *the oppression*.
ho katechōn (2:7)	masculine	often translated: *who restrains*; my translation: *the oppressor*.

Interpretations of 2:6-7 differ widely on details, but they can be divided into two broad categories, depending on how *to katechon* and *ho katechōn* are understood. In relation to the Christian community, does the *katechon/ōn* have a positive function—restraining the antagonist? or a hostile impact—oppressing the church? It should be noted at the outset that in both places, this participle does not have a stated object. Those who argue that the *katechon/ōn* holds back the antagonist, normally supply an object: *what is now restraining him* (2:6) and *the one who now restrains it* (2:7, NRSV).

Many explanations of these two verses begin with the premise that the underlying meaning of this code word is to *hold back* or *restrain* and that the one being restrained is *the man of lawlessness, the son of perdition.* What these interpretations have in common is the view that the *katechon/ōn* has the positive function of holding the antagonist in check until the end-time battle begins (2:8). Typically, interpreters then try to identify both a restraining force (*to katechon*) and a personal embodiment of that restraining force (*ho katechōn*), which/who holds the antagonist back until the right time.

But what and who restrains the antagonist? We note several attempted explanations along with one advocate of each view. In the traditional view, dating back to Tertullian (ca. A.D. 145-220), the Roman empire and the emperor through the imperial structures of law and order impose these limits on the activity of the antagonist (Bruce, 1982:171-172; Tertullian, *On the Resurrection of the Flesh* 24). Others argue that the preaching of the gospel and the apostle Paul himself have such a restraining influence, since the gospel first needs to be preached to all the nations before the end comes (cf. Mark 13:10; Cullmann: 163-166). A third position is that God through an angel or the Holy Spirit delays the final revelation of the antagonist (Hiebert: 339).

Another group of explanations begins with the premise that the *katechon/ōn* has a hostile rather than helpful intent, and that the community of believers is the victim of this hostility. None of the major Bible translations (as far as I know) has followed this line of argument, so there is no "usual translation." In actual fact, in the Septuagint the underlying verb *katechō* serves in place of seventeen different Hebrew or Aramaic words, and in the NT it has a range of meanings, such as "to lay claim, take possession, seize, oppress, suppress, hinder, restrain, or prevail." If *katechon/ōn* points to a hostile force or person victimizing the Christian community, a workable translation could be: *oppression* and *oppressor.* But, again, what/who might this be?

Several possible reconstructions along this line have been put forward. Giblin identifies the misleading prophecy that *the day of the*

Lord has come (2:2) and the frenzied false prophet who made this announcement as having a spellbinding influence in the Christian community. This prophecy (*to katechon*) and prophet (*ho katechōn*) have adversely affected the minds of the believers so that they can no longer think straight (Giblin: 167-242). Another proposed solution to this puzzle is that Paul and his co-workers are describing a rebellious force and the human or supernatural agent of Satan presently active as an occupying power holding sway in the world (Best: 301-302; Wanamaker: 252-257). A more specific version of this last explanation depicts the religious, political, and cultural power of the Roman empire and those who administer its policies as the *oppression* and the *oppressor* respectively (Krodel, 1990:440-446). In some respects, this last explanation coheres with the traditional view, which sees the Roman empire and the emperor as restraining the antagonist. The difference, of course, is that in this case the state and its representatives are recognized as hostile toward the Christian community and its claims.

All factors considered, the view espoused by Krodel is probably close to what Paul and his companions intend to convey. Using secretive language, they allude to the persecution which the Thessalonian believers are encountering as a consequence of their rejection of the civic cult and specifically their refusal to show homage to the emperor. Instead of referring directly to the policies and actions of local city politicians, the provincial officials, or even the emperor himself, the missionary pastors employ code language. The question, *Do you not remember?* (2:5), and the assertion, *You know* (2:6), function rhetorically as a kick on the shins to remind the readers that they have to decipher the code.

It is difficult for us to fathom why a code would be necessary to alert the Thessalonians to the fact that the end cannot come until the gospel has been fully preached or to remind them that a sovereign God exercises control over the end-time sequence of events. If that is the message, why not just say so openly? The symbols and secret codes must be considered essential to protect the congregation from more intense persecution, which could result from an open identification of the nature of their *oppression* and the identity of the *oppressor*.

As noted above, the Thessalonians share the widespread expectation that tribulation precedes the onset of the final messianic age. How then would a secretive allusion to their suffering persuade them to abandon the notion that *the day of the Lord has come*? Essentially, Paul and his fellow evangelists want to convey that whatever *op-pression* they experience now is just the preamble to the appearance of the later antagonist: *And now the oppression you know so that he may be revealed in his time* (2:6). Under their present circumstances, the Thessalonian believers experientially know *oppression*.

That is true *now*, but another phase will be reached when *the man of lawlessness* appears on the stage of history. They certainly are suffering in behalf of God's kingdom (1:5). Their faithfulness under *op-pression* therefore also furthers God's kingdom program, as conveyed by the purpose clause (*so that*, 1:6). *In his time*, at some point in the future, he will then *be revealed* (*the man of lawlessness, the son of perdition, the lawless one;* 2:3, 8). Usually one can infer from the passive form of the verb (*be revealed*) that God determines the *time* (*kairos*). The word *kairos* often denotes the opportune or divinely appointed *time* (cf. also 1 Thess. 5:1). In 2:9 the *coming* of the antagonist seems to be orchestrated by Satan, although, as 2:11-12 makes clear, God remains ultimately in control.

A further explanation follows concerning how the Thessalonians' present experience relates to the future revelation of the antagonist: *For the mystery of lawlessness works already* (2:7). Even though the public appearance of the *lawless one* will occur in the future, the rebellion against God acted out symbolically in the temple (2:4) already manifests itself in *the mystery of lawlessness* active in the present. In NT usage, *mystery* often pertains to the disclosure of God's purpose and work in the world (as in Rom. 11:25). Here we have a satanic counterpart. God's reign, already realized in the present, will be gloriously consummated at the coming of Christ as triumphant Lord. Similarly, the spirit of rebellion, already active, will climax in the revelation of the antagonist. Perhaps Paul and his colleagues deliberately employ *mystery* language because emperor worship is integrated into the rituals of some of the mystery cults in Thessalonica (Don-fried, 1985:353; cf. also Holland: 113-114).

This *mystery of lawlessness* or active spirit of rebellion against God already impinges on the life of the Christian community in Thessalonica. They are experiencing the *oppression* which precedes the arrival of the antagonist (2:6). But this *mystery* also comes in personified form through *the oppressor; only the oppressor [works] now until he is taken from the midst* (2:7). The word *only* hints at the limits placed on *the oppressor*. Since the sentence has no verb, the reader needs to provide one from its context, likely *works* (from 2:7a). The pronoun *he* refers back to *the oppressor*, who still *works now*, but whose jurisdiction is limited in time: *until he is taken from the midst.* What does all this mean? In their rebellion against God, the Roman empire and its representatives attempt to control or suppress the believers who confess Christ rather than the emperor as their Lord. Yet the tenure of *the oppressor* (the emperor and his provincial and local officials) will come to an end. Furthermore, *the oppressor* is just a precursor of the end-time antagonist. In Daniel 11, a succession of kings (11:2-20) precedes the arrival of the paragon of evil (11:21-35) whose defiant actions against "the God of gods" (11:36-39) foreshadow those of the antagonist (of 2 Thess. 2). Paul and his companions depict a similar sequence, but they name only two phases: first, the period when *the mystery of lawlessness* actively manifests itself through *the oppression* as perpetrated through *the oppressor*; and then, the *apostasy* associated with the revelation of *the lawless one* ("The Timetable" in TBC below).

And Then 2:8-12

Paul and his colleagues have reminded the Christian community in Thessalonica about the future *apostasy* and the appearance of the antagonist (2:3-4), and pointed out that in the meantime they need to deal with *the oppressor* (2:6-7). Now they shift attention forward to the end-time drama (diagram on next page).

We have already noted that the antagonist's revelation is a mocking imitation of the coming of Christ as Lord (2:3; cf. also 2:6). The same point is made here: *And then the lawless one will be revealed* (2:8). Yet there is no doubt about who is ultimately in charge: the lawless figure is the one *whom the Lord Jesus will slay with the breath of his mouth and destroy at the dawning of his coming* (2:8).

With the revelation of *the lawless one*, the climactic holy war begins. In a graphic picture, which recalls what Isaiah says about the messianic king (Isa. 11:3-4), Paul and his co-workers reassure the Thessalonian believers in their distress that Jesus, whom they claim as Lord, will triumph in the end. At the *dawning* (*epiphaneia*) *of his coming* (*parousia), the Lord Jesus* decisively judges the antagonist. Both verbs (*slay* and *destroy*) convey that the Lord's triumph is full and complete. The identification of the weapon as *the breath of his mouth* needs to be understood metaphorically to convey that *the Lord Jesus* wins this battle by the power of the divine word (cf. Exod. 15:8; 2 Sam. 22:16; Ps. 33:6; Isa. 11:4; Rev. 19:13, 15).

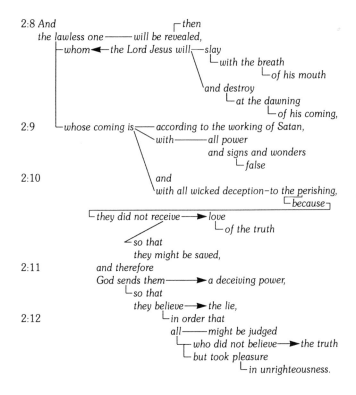

2:8 And   ┌then
    the lawless one ——— will be revealed,
    ├whom◄—the Lord Jesus will,─slay
                                   └with the breath
                                        └of his mouth
                                   and destroy
                                        └at the dawning
                                             └of his coming,
2:9   └whose coming is— according to the working of Satan,
                        with———all power
                              and signs and wonders
                                   └false
2:10   and
                       with all wicked deception–to the perishing,
                                                  └because┐
             └they did not receive—► love
                                        └of the truth
             ◄so that
             they might be saved,
2:11   and therefore
             God sends them———► a deceiving power,
                  └so that
             they believe—► the lie,
2:12   └in order that
                  all———might be judged
                       └┬who did not believe—► the truth
                        └but took pleasure
                             └in unrighteousness.

What matters ultimately—the final triumph of the Lord over the
antagonist—has been unambiguously announced in 2:8. In 2:9-12,
Paul and his fellow missionaries invite their readers to indulge in a
side glance at the deceptive antics of *the lawless one*. Without taking
their eyes off Jesus Christ, whose triumphant coming they await, the
Thessalonians are encouraged to keep the actions of Satan and his
deputies within their peripheral vision. Paul and his colleagues are
trying both to reassure and encourage the believers (more explicit in
2:13-15) as well as to alert them concerning the risk of deception
(2:9-12).

In three places within this paragraph, the writers specify that the
antagonist will *be revealed* (2:3, 6, 8). Here in 2:9, they refer to *the
coming (parousia) of the lawless one*, again suggesting that the antagonist cynically mimics Christ, whose *parousia* the Christians await
(1 Thess. 2:19; 3:13; 4:15; 5:23; 2 Thess. 2:1, 8). The antagonist's
source of inspiration and power is also disclosed: *whose coming is
according to the working of Satan* (2:9). Satan's energy moves the

antagonist into open rebellion against God; this defiance is demonstrated especially by his symbolic action and proclamation in the temple (2:4). Behind the insidious escalation of evil in the world, especially as history moves toward *the day of the Lord*, Paul and his partners detect the work of Satan. Therefore, they forewarn the Christian community not to be deceived ("Satan, the Tempter" in TBC for 1 Thess. 2:17—3:10).

Satan and his agents seek to imitate the ministries of Jesus and the church: *with all power and false signs and wonders* (2:9). Once again the intent is to deceive. God's miracles are often similarly described, especially with the expression *signs and wonders*: the deliverance of the Israelites out of Egypt (Deut. 4:34; 6:22), Jesus' healings (John 4:48; Acts 2:22), and the mighty acts done by the apostles and the early church (Acts 2:43; 4:30; Rom. 15:18-19). The *coming* of *the lawless one* will be accompanied by pseudomiracles: *false signs and wonders*. Their deceptive intent is fully unmasked in the final phrase detailing how Satan's agent works: *and with all wicked deception* (2:10).

Tragically, some will be duped by the antagonist. These are characterized as *the perishing* (from Greek, *apollumi*), perhaps because they share the destiny of *the son of perdition* (Greek: *apōleia*, 2:3), whose pretentious claims they have come to accept. In Paul's letters to the church at Corinth, "the perishing" are distinguished from "those who are being saved" (1 Cor. 1:18; 2 Cor. 2:15; 4:3). A similar contrast is developed here. The fate of *the perishing* is the result of their own choice: *they did not receive love of the truth so that they might be saved* (2:10). As can be observed in the way Paul and his partners employ the word *truth* in the sentences which follow (2:12-13), *the truth* is equivalent to *the gospel* (1:8; cf. 1 Thess. 2:2, 4, 8-9; 3:2) or more specifically, *our gospel* (2 Thess. 2:14; cf. 1 Thess. 1:5). *Love of the truth* is virtually synonymous with obeying the gospel (1:8). The gospel *truth* needs to be received as a gift. The *truth* of the gospel also evokes a responsive *love*.

Since the missionary pastors perceive that the believers in Thessalonica face the grave risk of deception, they emphasize the gospel as *truth*. They also warn against being swayed by *the lie* (2:11). Having underscored personal responsibility for the choice either to receive or reject the gospel, Paul and his co-workers remind their readers that God honors human freedom to choose. God even cooperates with human choice by adding to their delusion: *therefore God sends them a deceiving power so that they believe the lie* (2:11).

Similarly in Romans 1:18-32, Paul says that in response to human wickedness, which suppresses the truth (1:18), God gives humanity up to the results of their disobedience (1:24, 26, 28). In Romans 11:8, Paul (quoting Isa. 29:10) mentions the "sluggish spirit" which God gives those in Israel who are hardened against the gospel. The *deceiving power* from God in 2 Thessalonians 2:11 seems therefore to be God's grieved sanction for the consequences determined by human decisions to *believe the lie* rather than *love the truth.*

Even though Satan and his deputy the antagonist enchant the unsuspecting through various false wonders, God has the last word: *God sends them a deceiving power* (2:11). Ultimately, God also judges, *in order that all might be judged who did not believe the truth but took pleasure in unrighteousness* (2:12). In the final judgment, God delivers what people have ordered. Members of the Thessalonian Christian community likely recognize their persecutors in this description. Refusing to *believe the truth,* these officials of the Roman regime seem to take *pleasure in unrighteousness.* Contemplating God's final judgment, those who acknowledge the lordship of Christ can therefore anticipate that, even though they suffer now, they will finally be vindicated by God.

Heard from the perspective of the believers in Thessalonica, the primary intention behind 2:1-12 is to reassure and warn. On one hand, those who remain faithful and steadfast even under persecution are reassured that their Lord reigns and will come as righteous judge ("God's Righteous Judgment" in TBC for 2 Thess. 1:3-12). In 2:13-14, Paul and his partners thank God for these persons who continue to trust the truth. On the other hand, those being deceived by the teaching that *the day of the Lord has come* hear a warning. Though not just yet, God's righteous judgment will surely come. To those who reject *the truth* in favor of *unrighteousness,* this judgment will not be good news. In 2:15, therefore, Paul and his teammates urge the members of the Thessalonian congregation: *Stand firm and hold to the traditions which you were taught by us.* The missionaries invite those being deceived into believing the grand lie to take advantage of the extended opportunity to affirm the truth.

THE TEXT IN THE BIBLICAL CONTEXT
The Antagonist
In 2 Thessalonians 2:1-12, the end-time personage who spearheads the rebellion against God has several names: *the man of lawlessness*

(2:3), *the son of perdition* (2:3), and *the lawless one* (2:8-9). For simplicity's sake we have designated this chief rebel as the antagonist. Elsewhere in Scripture, we also hear about the antichrist, the beast, and other designations of a major adversary who opposes Christ and tests the community of believers. How does the portrait of the antagonist in 2 Thessalonians correlate with the broader biblical testimony to this menacing rebel of the end-time?

During the seventh century B.C., the prophet Ezekiel assures the exiles in Babylon that, despite appearances to the contrary, God has not abandoned them. One of the oracles which communicates such reassurance features a chief prince named Gog of the land of Magog (Ezek. 38—39). Utilizing graphic symbolism and speaking God's powerful word, Ezekiel conveys an empowering message to his fellow exiles. This oracle can be summarized in several broad strokes. Coming from the north, Gog (Babylon, cf. 26:7) attacks and captures the Israelite people. Although the armies from Magog serve God's purposes by punishing the people of Israel for their unfaithfulness, God launches a holy war against this arrogant aggressor. A cataclysmic struggle culminates in God's decisive triumph over the rebellious forces. Gog is no match for God!

Through Ezekiel's vision, the exiles in their distress hear the reminder that their gracious God can be trusted to judge the oppressor and restore the fortunes of the oppressed:

> So I will display my greatness and my holiness and make myself known in the eyes of many nations. Then they shall know that I am the Lord. (Ezek. 38:23)

As the conclusion to Ezekiel's oracle illustrates, this vision of God's triumph both reassures Israel and sends a strong signal to the nations regarding God's glory and holiness:

> Now I will restore the fortunes of Jacob, and have mercy on the whole house of Israel; and I will be jealous for my holy name. They shall forget their shame, and all the treachery they have practiced against me, when they live securely in their land with no one to make them afraid, when I have brought them back from the peoples and gathered them from their enemies' lands, and through them have displayed my holiness in the sight of many nations. Then they shall know that I am the Lord their God. . . . (Ezek. 39:25-28)

What is Ezekiel's underlying message here? The prophet communicates to the exiles that even the power of the king and the armies of mighty Babylon cannot overwhelm or destroy a faithful people whose Lord is God.

The book of Daniel, whose narrative setting is also ancient Babylon, sends a similar signal through its stories and visions. Likely written in the second century B.C., this apocalyptic work views the Syrian king, Antiochus IV Epiphanes (175-164 B.C.), as the paragon of evil. As noted above, in 167 B.C. Antiochus erected a statue dedicated to the Greek god Zeus on the altar in the Jerusalem temple. As Daniel views it, thereby the king essentially puts himself in God's place:

> The king shall act as he pleases. He shall exalt himself and consider himself greater than any god, and shall speak horrendous things against the God of gods. He shall prosper until the period of wrath is completed, for what is determined shall be done. He shall pay no respect to the gods of his ancestors, or to the one beloved by women; he shall pay no respect to any other god, for he shall consider himself greater than all. (Dan. 11:36-37)

Daniel's vision shows that this king's reign shall also come to an end (Dan. 11:40-45). Second Maccabees supplies details (2 Macc. 9). Antiochus, who claimed the name Epiphanes, "god manifest," died from worms, thereby "making the power of God manifest to all" in his death (9:8; similarly, Acts 12:22-23 reports that Herod Agrippa I died from worms after the people hailed him as a god, in A.D. 44).

As Daniel's climactic vision reveals, a time of unprecedented anguish will follow this king's defiance of "the God of gods" (12:1-13). However, God finally intervenes through the resurrection and the judgment:

> Many of those who sleep in the dust of the earth shall awake, some to everlasting life, and some to shame and everlasting contempt. Those who are wise shall shine like the brightness of the sky, and those who lead many to righteousness, like the stars forever and ever. (Dan. 12:2-3)

Even when the faithful die in their struggle against the forces of evil, God still rewards the wise and the righteous and punishes the arrogant and the wicked. The threat of death therefore need not deter God's people from living in faithful obedience. Such faithfulness unto death leads to "everlasting life." Those who follow in the footsteps of the oppressive king Antiochus, on the other hand, face "shame and everlasting contempt."

Turning to the NT portraits of the end-time personification of evil, we first note Jesus' warning:

> False messiahs and false prophets will appear and produce signs and omens, to lead astray, if possible, the elect. (Mark 13:22)

According to Jesus, not one but many will make such deceptive claims concerning themselves. Many will perform pseudowonders to try to sidetrack Jesus' followers (cf. 2 Thess. 2:9).

Similarly, the elder in the epistles of John alerts his children in the faith that "many antichrists have come" (1 John 2:18) and that "many false prophets have gone out into the world" (4:1). Among other things, these antichrists and false prophets deny that Jesus is the incarnate Christ (2:22; 4:2-3; 2 John 7). Evidently John identifies the teachers who do not acknowledge that "Jesus Christ has come in the flesh" (1 John 4:2) as symptomatic of the worldly opposition to the redemptive work of Christ during the time of the end ("the last hour," 2:18). However, the elder also anticipates that "antichrist" will still appear in the future as the supreme embodiment of this opposition (2:18). Though antichrist has yet to come, a forerunner spirit, "the spirit of the antichrist" (4:3), already exercises its influence. This spirit is reminiscent of the working of *the mystery of lawlessness* prior to the revelation of *the man of lawlessness* (2 Thess. 2:7-8).

In John's Revelation is the most elaborate portrayal of the sinister end-time characters and their behavior on the cosmic stage. One vision (Rev. 12) features the dragon (Satan) engaged in mortal combat with a woman (Mary, representing Israel), her male child (Jesus the Messiah), and her other children (the church). This vision symbolically depicts the persecution of the church as instigated by Satan.

Revelation 13 then introduces two grotesque creatures. The first one, "a beast rising out of the sea," receives his authority from the dragon (Satan), makes war against the church, and is worshiped by those people whose names are not written in the Lamb's book of life (13:1-10). The second creature, "another beast that rose out of the earth," acts in behalf of the first beast, deceiving the inhabitants of the earth through miraculous signs and demanding that all people worship the beast (13:11-18). For John's readers, these beasts symbolize the Roman empire, specifically the emperor and those who administer the imperial cult, which demands the citizens' ultimate loyalty and worship and persecutes those who refuse to conform.

In Revelation 17 the "beast," carrying a woman (symbolizing Rome), reappears. Then in chapter 19, the climactic holy war breaks out, with a rider on a white horse (Christ) arrayed against the beast. The outcome is never in doubt:

And the beast was captured, and with it the false prophet who had performed in its presence the signs by which he deceived those who had received the mark of the beast and those who worshiped its image. These two were thrown alive into the lake of fire that burns with sulfur. (19:20)

Revelation 20 finally portrays the contrasting fates of Satan, who inspires the seductive antics of the beast; and the martyrs, killed because of their witness to Jesus and their refusal to worship the beast. Satan is bound for a thousand years, released briefly, and then overthrown. The martyrs come to life, reign with Christ for a thousand years, and then in the last judgment receive their eternal reward.

The antagonist of 2 Thessalonians 2:1-12 has clear affinities with the beast in Revelation. Both symbolize the emperor. Both make the blasphemous claim of divinity, and both seek through deception or coercion to gain the allegiance of all their citizens. Yet the end-time drama which Paul and his associates portray in a series of provocative images also reflects the themes of Ezekiel 38—39 and Daniel 11—12. Through vivid word pictures and powerful images, all these biblical texts appeal to oppressed and persecuted people to remain faithful to God. God will vanquish even those most blatant perpetrators of evil of any period who seek to seduce the faithful. Even if evil seems to triumph, justice will finally be done. In the end, the forces of evil will be defeated and those who remain true will be rewarded!

The Timetable

But when will this be? In 2 Thessalonians 2, Paul and his colleagues do not answer that question. Nor do they develop a timetable outlining a sequence of end-time events. Basically they respond to the misleading prophecy that *the day of the Lord has come* (2:2). In responding to this claim, they do provide several chronological cues, but they do not offer an orderly schedule outlining the future. The chronological hints identify only two moments:

The present time: *and now* (2:6), *already, now, until* (2:7)
The end time: *unless the apostasy comes first* (2:3), *in his time* (2:6), *and then* (2:8)

The Thessalonians are essentially told that, in their present experience of *oppression* under the imperial policy of the *oppressor*, they are coping with *the mystery of lawlessness*. Still to come will be *the apostasy* led by *the man of lawlessness*. Only then *the day of the*

Lord will dawn, *the man of lawlessness* will be killed, and the final judgment will begin.

Beyond this differentiation between two periods, the present and the end, 1 Thessalonians 2:1-12 does not provide a chronological sequence. Nor can we develop a firm timetable from elsewhere in Scripture. Some books in both the OT and the NT do work with end-time schedules. The book of Daniel has long tantalized readers who enjoy speculating about the meaning of numbers. Seventy years (Dan. 9:2, from Jer. 25:11-12; 29:10) are interpreted to mean seventy weeks of years (9:24). Other calculations in Daniel include "a time, two times, and half a time" (three and a half years; 7:25; 12:7; cf. 8:14; 9:27), then 1290 days (12:11) and finally 1335 days (12:12).

The Revelation to John also includes some chronological data, notably the thousand years following the first resurrection when the martyrs reign with Christ (Rev. 20:4-6). These and other chronological data in Scripture have been read by interpreters throughout the history of the church to support a wide variety of eschatological timetables. Proponents of these particular end-time calendars are usually distinguished by labels. Postmillennialism projects that Christ will reign on earth before his final coming (*after* the thousand years, *post*millennial). Premillennialists understand Scripture to teach that Christ will come to earth with the saints, then reign for a thousand years, and finally lead the battle to defeat Satan (so Christ's coming is *before* the thousand years, *pre*millennial). Amillennialists regard the thousand years as symbolic of the entire period between Jesus' earthly sojourn and his coming as triumphant Lord. *[Eschatology, p. 355.]*

Perhaps those who espouse "*pan*millennialism" catch the real intent of the biblical writers: "It will all pan out in the end." God reigns! For those who trust God, everything will come out in the end. Scripture does not lay out the details, and Jesus himself declared that he did not know the time of the end (Mark 13:32). Hence, believers can move into the future with confidence and trust without the luxury of knowing the particulars. The times and the seasons are fixed by God's authority (cf. Acts 1:7).

TEXT IN THE LIFE OF THE CHURCH
Date-setting Usurps God's Authority

Deep dissensions often erupt within the church over the interpretation of biblical texts such as 2 Thessalonians 2:1-12. Preachers on radio and television continue to win audiences by predicting the future on the basis of the way they line up this passage with others. Congregations often emerge scarred, their energy for mission deflected into debates about an area known only to God—the future.

Cult groups at times emerge around charismatic leaders with the ability to persuade people that their construal of the future is biblical. On April 19, 1993, the standoff between the FBI and the Branch Davidians near Waco, Texas, culminated in a fiery inferno in which cult leader David Koresh and some eighty others perished. According to press reports, Koresh gained a group of followers through the force of his personality and his interpretation of the book of Revelation. Tragically, the officials who stormed the Branch Davidian compound did not comprehend the apocalyptic mentality displayed by this group. They became unwitting instruments in fulfilling the Davidians' expectation of the end of the world.

I have already alluded to Claasz Epp, who persuaded a group of Mennonites in south Russia to join him on a trek to Turkestan to meet the Lord ("Living in the Last Days" in TLC for 1 Thess. 5:1-11). Epp based his calculations of the end on his particular reading of biblical texts whose messages he correlated with events and phenomena of his time. Such point-by-point correspondences between selected Scripture texts and contemporary events continue to be proposed. I illustrate by quoting from a letter to the editor of our local paper:

> Within the next four years, I expect a global depression as we have never seen, and the new world order will be set up. It will last about seven years. For the first 3.5 years, the world will be ruled by one country. After 3.5 years, another super power will arise and invade Jerusalem. This ruler will enforce the mark of the beast, it is called, by cutting off people's heads. The world will rush to Jerusalem to defend it. This is called the battle of Armageddon. It will last 3.5 years. It will end by the sudden appearance of Christ in the heavens. The dead in Christ shall arise first, the alive in Christ shall be changed and be caught up with the resurrection to meet Christ in the sky. Then Christ will send fire from heaven and burn up the ungodly and those that don't obey the gospel (2 Thess. 1 and 2). These things must happen before Christ returns. New world order, daily sacrifice restored by the Jews, invasion of Jerusalem by the Gentiles, and the battle of Armageddon. I predict this will all happen within the next 12 years or so. (*Elkhart Truth*, 10/31/92)

We can readily see that the writer of this letter, Floyd Zimmerman, has arranged a series of biblical passages according to a chronological sequence which cannot be found in the Bible. Without regard for their context or original meaning, texts from 1 and 2 Thessalonians have been joined to others from the book of Revelation and elsewhere and then applied to contemporary events.

What is wrong with that? some ask. Besides, he might be right! Predictions like these can never be proven wrong until the time has elapsed, and by then the prophecies have been revised. Tragedy sometimes results, as noted in the examples cited above. Date-setting essentially constitutes a usurping of God's role. God knows the future, we don't. In the meantime, we have been called to live already in light of that kingdom whose full arrival we still await.

Ironically, Paul and his co-workers depict the antagonist as usurping God's authority. The landscape of church history lies strewn with the wreckage of human predictions concerning that future which is God's to determine. The above letter does not identify the antichrist, but speculation about this end-time figure has focused on many past political and religious leaders. David Ewert lists numerous candidates for the antichrist as nominated by Christian writers of the past. These include: the Roman emperors Nero and Domitian, Muhammad, various popes, Hitler, Stalin, John F. Kennedy, and Henry Kissinger (Ewert, 1980:75-79). During the tensions which preceded the 1991 Gulf War, some identified Iraqi leader Saddam Hussein as the antichrist.

The sixteenth-century Dutch Anabaptist Dirk Philips sees the spirit of antichrist active in the Catholic church and its worship. In his treatise entitled "Concerning Spiritual Restitution," Philips describes a spiritual falling away from true worship, comparable to King Jeroboam's decision to abandon Jerusalem temple worship in favor of offering sacrifices at two cult centers at Bethel and Dan (1 Kings 12):

> In like manner, the spiritual falling away from the kingdom of Christ has also taken place in the demolishing of the teaching and faith through the antichrist who has forsaken the true worship in the temple at Jerusalem and set up for himself a false worship (1 Tim. 4:1; 2 Thess. 2:3). For all that Christ has taught and commanded, that he [the antichrist] has imitated in appearance in a hypocritical manner, with his priests, altars, sacrifices, and church services; and with great pomposity he has abominably distorted the sacraments of Jesus Christ. (Dyck: 341-342)

Even though we do well to avoid such innuendo against any denomination or group, we can learn from Dirk and other early Anabaptists. The truth of the gospel sometimes becomes distorted, and worship at times turns into empty formalism. Under persecution from both Catholic and Protestant groups, the Anabaptists exposed what they considered apostate patterns of life and worship among the leaders in the churches which opposed them. Ultimately, however, they let God be the judge, as seen in the conclusion of Dirk's treatise:

> But the eternal almighty God . . . keep us in his truth through his eternal Word. . . . Through his mercy may he renew us in the inner being, and keep us in an upright life until our end, so that we may stand before the judgment seat of Jesus Christ with joy, when he shall come with the angels in his power, with the four flaming ones, to impose the vengeance upon all those who have not known God and have not been obedient to the gospel; and "to be glorified in his saints, and to appear marvelously in all the believers," 2 Thess. 1:8[-10], . . . in the resurrection and the revelation of the heavenly glory. (Dyck: 348)

As we seek to live faithfully in our time and our place, Dirk's prayer can be our prayer as well.

2 Thessalonians 2:13-17

Called to Obtain Glory!

PREVIEW

A schoolboy overhearing his teacher's stern words about the consequences of disobedience would be relieved to learn that they were not directed at him. The Thessalonians have caught glimpses of the end-time antagonist at the time of his dramatic demise; they have heard about the judgment of both deceivers and the deceived; now they are reassured, "All of that is not intended for you!"

In 2:1-12 Paul and his companions seek to document that *the day of the Lord* still lies in the future. Proof comes in a dramatic preview of the end-time spectacle, which (the readers are expected to agree) has not yet begun. In 2:13-17 the writers offer a different kind of proof. The believers in Thesssalonica, as recipients of God's grace, have been called to obtain the glory of their Lord Jesus Christ. As they stand firm within their calling, the Thessalonians testify through deed and word to Christ's present lordship, which will come to glorious fullness at the consummation of the kingdom.

Having addressed the confusion concerning *the day of the Lord*, Paul and his companions restate their thanksgiving to God, whose call to salvation and glory has reached the community of believers in Thessalonica (2:13-14). After appealing to them to stand firm (2:15), the missionaries gather up their hopes for this community in a wish-prayer (2:16-17).

OUTLINE

Renewed Thanksgiving, 2:13-14
Stand Firm! 2:15
Wish-Prayer, 2:16-17

EXPLANATORY NOTES
Renewed Thanksgiving 2:13-14

After viewing an eschatological sideshow which culminates in the defeat of *the man of lawlessness*, Paul and his fellow missionaries sum-
mon their *brothers and sisters* in Thessalonica to focus again on
God's redemptive work:

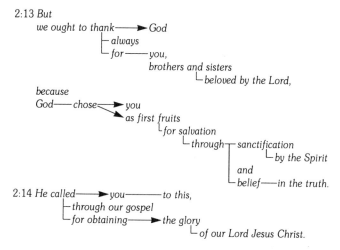

The Thessalonians learn that, at most, the deceptive ploys of
Satan need to be kept within the believers' peripheral vision. The antics of Satan can have a mesmerizing effect. Paul and his colleagues
therefore shift attention abruptly and deliberately to God's love, election, and call, as evidenced in the lives of these new believers: *But we
ought to thank God always for you, brothers and sisters, beloved by
the Lord* (2:13).

This call to thanksgiving basically repeats what the writers say in
1:3, although the phrase *beloved by the Lord* echoes 1 Thessalonians 1:4. However, the stated reason for thanksgiving is different:
*because God chose you as first fruits for salvation through sanctifica-
tion by the Spirit and belief in the truth* (2:13). In the opening thanksgiving of their first letter, Paul and his co-workers previously also

highlighted election (1 Thess. 1:4; "Election" in TBC for 1 Thess. 1:1-10). God's love and election provide the gracious backdrop against which all of history needs to be seen. This struggling group in Thessalonica is helped to see that their life as a Christian community has an important role to play within God's plan.

What is that role? There is disagreement among ancient manuscripts, with some reflecting the reading *first fruits* (*aparchēn*) and others *from the beginning* (*ap' archēs*). The NRSV accepts the former (also Bruce, 1982:190), while RSV and NIV, among others, favor the latter (similarly Wanamaker: 266). If the latter wording is original, Paul and his partners emphasize that in God's economy, the Thessalonian Christian community plays a role designated for them *from the beginning*. All factors considered, however, the original text likely read *first fruits* (Metzger, 1971:636). *[Textual Analysis, p. 346.]*

The concept of *first fruits* derives from the practice of bringing the first of the harvest as a thank offering to God during the Jewish harvest festivals (Deut. 26:1-11). The *first fruits* therefore represent the larger harvest which will follow. Elsewhere, Paul employs the *first fruits* metaphor (with *aparchē*) to designate individuals who were "the first converts in Achaia" (1 Cor. 16:15) and "the first convert in Asia" (Rom. 16:5). He also refers to the risen Christ as "the first fruits of those who have died" (1 Cor. 15:20, 23); this harvest will be completed when the dead in Christ are raised. Yet another use of the *first fruits* metaphor occurs in Romans 8:23, where the reassuring presence of the Holy Spirit is seen as the first installment of the greater glory still to come.

What then might be the significance of *first fruits* language in 2 Thessalonians 2:13? Since the Thessalonian congregation was not the first to be established in Macedonia, their status as *first fruits* likely has a generic meaning. The harvest in Thessalonica, which resulted in the emergence of a community of faith, promises that an abundant harvest will follow! Indeed, as Paul and his missionary associates testified earlier, the impact of the Thessalonians' faith and faithfulness is being felt throughout Macedonia and beyond (1 Thess. 1:8). Their faithful witness verifies their status as God's chosen ones.

Specifically God has chosen them *for salvation*. In the only previous references to *salvation* within the letters to Thessalonica, Paul and his colleagues allude to the *hope of salvation* (1 Thess. 5:8) and also its source: *salvation through our Lord Jesus Christ, who died for us* (5:9-10). In these texts, *salvation* clearly has a futuristic connotation, as most likely also here in 2 Thessalonians 2:13. However, the community of believers experiences the present in light of the glorious future, and lives already as a saved people ("Salvation" in TBC below).

How is *salvation* actualized in human experience? The authors point first to what God does through the Holy Spirit. *Salvation* is effected *through sanctification by the Spirit.* The sanctifying work of the Spirit in the life of the community is also featured in the earlier letter (1 Thess. 3:13; 4:7-8; 5:23). However, the ministry of the Spirit does not unilaterally bring *salvation.* A response is required from the human side: *and belief in the truth.* As noted in our discussion of 2:10, 12, *the truth* means *the gospel,* which invites *belief.* And *belief* implies more than mental assent. The community of faith manifests *belief in the truth* when they respond in gratitude, trust, and obedience to God's love and call as supremely made known in Christ.

With reference to *salvation,* Paul and his companions add: *to this he called you through our gospel* (2:14). The expression *our gospel* points to yet another aspect of the dynamic process of *salvation*—the preaching of the gospel. Similarly in 1 Thessalonians 1:4-5, election, missionary proclamation, and human response to the gospel are viewed in a dynamic relationship with each other. God calls people to experience salvation. Paul and his partners refer to their message as *our gospel,* since they have proclaimed and embodied God's gracious invitation to the people of Thessalonica.

To what end does God call the Thessalonian believers? The evangelists help them view the present with its conflict and uncertainty in light of that glorious future which God still has in store for them. God has called them *for obtaining the glory of our Lord Jesus Christ* (2:14). Believers already glimpse this *glory,* but they still need to await its fullness (cf. 1 Thess. 2:12, God *calls you into his kingdom and glory*). The word *obtaining* also points to the anticipated full attainment of that dynamic reality which the believing community already experiences partially in the present. This word also occurs in 1 Thessalonians 5:9: *God has not appointed us for wrath but for obtaining salvation through our Lord Jesus Christ* ("Kingdom of God" in TBC for 1 Thess. 2:1-12).

The prospect of *obtaining the glory* stands in sharp contrast with what lies in store for those who reject *love of the truth* (cf. 2:10-12). For those who know *salvation through sanctification by the Spirit and belief in the truth* (2:13), the future looks infinitely glorious!

Stand Firm! 2:15

The anticipation of *obtaining the glory of our Lord Jesus Christ* calls for more than passive waiting:

2:15 *So then,   brothers and sisters,*
stand firm
and
observe ——▶ *the traditions*
                    which you were taught,
                              ⌐*either by our word*
                              ⌐*or by our letter.*

For much of this second letter to the church at Thessalonica, Paul and his partners have been focusing their readers' attention on the end-time scenario, with its fearsome and reassuring aspects. There have been hints all along that this eschatological emphasis has implications for the present as well as the future. The missionaries appeal to their readers to live now in light of future glory.

The opener, *So then, brothers and sisters,* signals the transition to a brief exhortation concerning how they should conduct themselves: *Stand firm and observe the traditions which you were taught.* The instruction, *stand firm,* reminds us of Paul's personal comment in 1 Thessalonians 3:8. After he hears Timothy's reassuring report concerning the Thessalonians' faithful perseverance under persecution, Paul exclaims, *Now we live, if you stand in the Lord.* Given their continuing affliction (2 Thess. 1:4) and the risk of being shaken by the prophetic word that *the day of the Lord has come* (2:2), the Thessalonian community receives strong encouragement: *Stand firm.* This calls for a resolute commitment to Jesus Christ as Lord.

More specifically, Paul and his associates urge their converts in Thessalonica, *Observe the traditions which you were taught.* The biblical word *tradition* (*paradosis*) requires some explanation, since the modern conception of tradition differs significantly. *Paradosis* refers to that sacred memory which is passed on from one person or group to another. This inherited memory includes stories about Jesus, the key points of the gospel message, and guidance about how Jesus' disciples should live. The first letter to Thessalonica does not employ the word *paradosis*, but it does use some standard language to describe the process of transmitting the sacred memory. Paul and his missionary colleagues know that they have themselves received and then passed on both the gospel message itself (1 Thess. 2:13) and the ethical teachings associated with the gospel (4:1). This same understanding of *tradition* operates here in 2 Thessalonians 2:15 (also at 3:6). In light of potential threat to the Thessalonians' steadfastness and faith, the missionaries appeal to them to *observe the traditions* which they have been taught.

The gospel has been transmitted to the Thessalonians in two ways: *by our word* and *by our letter*. *Our word* refers to what the missionary pastors have communicated orally in preaching and teaching while present with them. *Our letter* can most naturally be taken as a reference to 1 Thessalonians. According to 2:2, the deceptive teaching concerning *the day of the Lord* has been conveyed *either by spirit or by word or by letter as though from us*. Here in 2:15, Paul and his co-workers appeal to the Thessalonians not to be sidetracked from those *traditions* they have originally been taught.

Wish-Prayer 2:16-17

A wish-prayer brings the extended eschatological discourse (2:1-15) to an end. Like the two wish-prayers in the first letter (1 Thess. 3:11-13; 5:23-24), this one gathers up some of the previous concerns and serves as a transition to the next part of the letter.

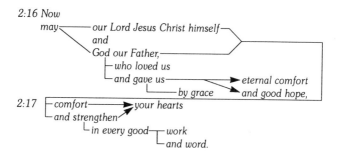

This wish-prayer begins by addressing and identifying God. Actually, the prayer invokes *our Lord Jesus Christ himself and God our Father*. Naming *Jesus* first is somewhat unusual (cf. 1 Thess. 3:11, which begins with *our God and Father*), although this occurs elsewhere in Paul's writings as well (Gal. 1:1; 2 Cor. 13:13). For Paul, God and *Jesus* function in dynamic unity.

God is further identified in ways that expand on the theme of *salvation: who loved us and gave us eternal comfort and good hope by grace*. God's saving activity through Christ is communicated by means of a few key words: *By grace, God loved and gave!* Two of

God's gracious gifts are mentioned: *eternal comfort*, needed by victims of persecution (cf. 1:3-12); and *good hope*, especially pertinent in the face of the false hope expressed by the prophecy that *the day of the Lord has come* (cf. 2:1-12). The phrase *by grace* consciously expands the portrait of *salvation* beyond that which the human mind can comprehend. God's tender mercy embraces all who open themselves to it. No doctrine of *grace* is expounded in this rather severe letter to the Thessalonians. However, the opening greeting (1:2), the final benediction (3:18), and the prayers (1:11-12; 2:16-17) show that everything in this letter needs to be heard from the underlying theological assumption that God *by grace* reaches out to all people. Robert Jewett appropriately entitles his article on the theology of 2 Thessalonians, "A Matrix of Grace" (Jewett, 1991).

The actual petitions in this wish-prayer anticipate the exhortation section which follows (3:1-15): *Now may God . . . comfort and strengthen your hearts in every good work and word* (2:17). This prayer for *comfort* continues the assurance of *eternal comfort* already mentioned (2:16). The request that God might *strengthen* them connects with the assurance in the next section: God *will strengthen you and guard you from evil* (3:3). In desiring a community witness which reflects an authentic integration of *good work and word*, the writers clearly anticipate the issue of *the unruly*, addressed in 3:6-15. The Christian community needs to embody Jesus' way, in which word and deed harmonize.

THE TEXT IN THE BIBLICAL CONTEXT
Salvation

If the eschatological scenario sketched in 2:1-12 can be described as a sideshow, what constitutes the main feature? Front and center on stage throughout Satan's pretentious activity (2:3-10) is the drama of *salvation* (2:13-14)! Ironically, however, in 2 Thessalonians the main drama seems to receive less attention than the sideshow. We need to go elsewhere in Scripture to see and hear more fully the exciting story of salvation.

In our earlier essay on this theme, we noted the variety of ways in which scriptural writers portray the atonement ("Salvation Through Our Lord Jesus Christ" in TBC for 1 Thess. 5:1-11). Human language proves inadequate for conveying the significance of the central event in the salvation story—the life, death, and resurrection of Jesus Christ. Hence, biblical writers and especially Paul employ various metaphors and word pictures in an attempt to communicate both the salvation story and its meaning.

A particularly dramatic NT metaphor pictures Jesus' death on the cross as the public unmasking and defeat of the evil powers. We can illustrate from the epistle to the Colossians. New life, the forgiveness of sin, and the cancellation of various kinds of legal demands are all linked to what God has done through the death and resurrection of Jesus Christ:

> And when you were dead in trespasses and the uncircumcision of your flesh, God made you alive together with him, when he forgave us all our trespasses, erasing the record that stood against us with its legal demands. He set this aside, nailing it to the cross. He disarmed the rulers and authorities and made a public example of them, triumphing over them in it. (Col. 2:13-15)

Vivid word pictures in this passage help us visualize the drama of salvation: the dead are raised, the record is erased, legal demands are nailed to the cross, rulers are disarmed and publicly paraded through the streets. Each of these sensational and dramatic scenes invites grateful reflection by those who through belief and baptism have joined the community of the redeemed (cf. Col. 2:12). Perhaps the most gripping image is that of the disarming of the authorities. When Jesus died on the cross, he gained a victory over those who crucified him! Jesus' crucifixion put the authorities on public display—as when prisoners of war from conquered nations were marched through the streets of Rome in triumphal procession! (E. Martin: 113-117, 126-127).

In his study of the atonement, John Driver identifies a number of texts, including Colossians 2:13-15, which feature what he calls the "Conflict-Victory-Liberation Motif" (Driver: chap. 3). Since 2 Thessalonians 2:3-10 depicts the escalating end-time conflict which culminates in the climactic defeat of *the lawless one*, the story of *salvation* underlying 2:13-14 must have been equally dramatic.

In the OT, God engages in a titanic struggle in behalf of the enslaved Hebrews in Egypt. Through annual Passover celebrations, the covenanting descendants of these slaves continue to dramatize God's victory over the oppressive powers (Exod. 12). This struggle against wickedness and injustice continues, but the good news is that through the death and resurrection of Christ, ultimate victory has been assured. As Driver puts it,

The chief significance of the work of Christ was that he won the decisive battle, the turning point in God's struggle with the forces of opposition. This struggle was waged throughout the Old Testament. It continued in the early church and is still being waged in our time. It is the war of the lamb against all the principalities and powers of Satan's kingdom. (Driver: 74)

Jesus expels demons and evil spirits, and he empowers his disciples to do so as well. When the seventy report about their experiences during their mission, Jesus exclaims, "I watched Satan fall from heaven like a flash of lightning" (Luke 10:18). During Jesus' earthly ministry, the proclamation of the kingdom of God, accompanied by casting out evil spirits and healings, foreshadows Satan's eventual defeat!

This struggle against Satan reaches a climax at Calvary, where Jesus in his death delivers the fatal blow. Yet the conflict will continue until all the enemies have been subdued. This is how Paul in his letter to Corinth describes the final victory, as guaranteed by Jesus' death and resurrection:

> Then comes the end, when he hands over the kingdom to God the Father, after he has destroyed every ruler and every authority and power. For he must reign until he has put all his enemies under his feet. The last enemy to be destroyed is death. (1 Cor. 15:24-26)

In this victory, all believers will finally share. In the meantime, the message of the cross is foolishness to the perishing, but to those being saved it is the power of God (1 Cor. 1:18).

God's gracious gift of salvation is described in the NT in other ways as well. Whether salvation is described in law-court language as justification (Rom. 5:1) or in terms of atoning sacrifice (Rom. 3:25), or whatever other image, this gift invites humble gratitude and praise to God the Giver. Paul's outburst of praise in 1 Corinthians 15:57 can appropriately give voice to the church of all ages and in all circumstances as it ponders this indescribable gift: "Thanks be to God, who gives us the victory through our Lord Jesus Christ!"

THE TEXT IN THE LIFE OF THE CHURCH

Tradition

Challenges confront the church in every age. For the Christian community in Thessalonica, persecution from without and confusion about eschatology from within created the need for pastoral encouragement and guidance.

In 2 Thessalonians 2:13-17, Paul and his missionary companions demonstrate an important pastoral principle. When dealing with a crisis in the congregation, it is helpful to get back to the basics. What could be more foundational for the life of the church than God's love and call and salvation as communicated in the gospel (cf. 2:13-14)? All this is part of the tradition within which the Thessalonians are urged to stand firm (2:15).

People in congregations within the believers church family tend to have an uneasy relationship with tradition. For one thing, traditions are sometimes defined in terms of customary foods (such as shoofly pie or *vereneki*), styles of dress, or other observable distinctions. Such traditions may be respected or rejected, depending, among other things, on whether people view themselves as set apart from their surrounding culture.

Of course, a distinction needs to be made between tradition and traditionalism. Tradition energizes, while traditionalism often stifles. I have heard this distinction stated as follows:

Traditionalism is the dead voice of the living.
Tradition is the living voice of the dead.

As we mentioned in our discussion of 2:15, the word *tradition* in the NT refers to that which is passed on, including the stories about Jesus, the gospel message, and normative ethical guidance for believers. This dynamic memory, the living voice of our Lord and his apostles, constitutes the authoritative center from which believing communities are urged to derive inspiration and guidance for their lives.

A revitalizing rootedness in the living *tradition* defined in this way is needed by the church of every age. The Scriptures as a whole, and in particular the story of God's saving activity as revealed supremely in Jesus Christ, define the life-giving baseline from which all the contingencies of life need to be addressed.

2 Thessalonians 3:1-15

Pastoral Instructions

OVERVIEW

When the preacher says "finally," the sermon is nearing its end, maybe. With Paul, Silvanus, and Timothy, the word *finally* introduces the concluding section of their second letter to Thessalonica (3:1-15). Yet they still have some important things to say. This section consists of pastoral instructions, both general (3:1-5) and specific (3:6-15).

In their first letter to this congregation, the missionaries begin their exhortations in a similar fashion (1 Thess. 4:1). There too they still have plenty to share with the church. The exhortations in 1 Thessalonians deal mainly with holiness in sexual conduct (4:1-8), loving relationships within the community (4:9-12), grief at the death of church members (4:13-18), the day of the Lord (5:1-11), and life and leadership within the faith community (5:12-22). This section is largely commendatory in tone, although the evangelists also encourage their readers to keep on growing (as in 1 Thess. 5:11).

One item on the agenda picks up a concern from the exhortation section in 1 Thessalonians. Gentle reminders concerning *love of the brothers and sisters* (1 Thess. 4:9-12) give way to stern instructions on this same theme in (2 Thess.) 3:6-15. Two short wish-prayers, a greeting, and the benediction (3:16-18) bring the letter to a close.

OUTLINE

3:1-5   Confronting Evil
3:6-15   Conduct in the Community Faith

2 Thessalonians 3:1-5

Confronting Evil

PREVIEW

A teacher who gently commends her students gets better results than one who shouts commands.

The missionary pastors have just expressed the wish that God might *comfort and strengthen your hearts in every good work and word* (2:17). Rather than proceeding directly with some advice and commands concerning *good work and word*, they reach out to the Christian community in Thessalonica in several bridge-building ways. The missionaries request prayer for themselves (3:1-2) and, after asserting that the Lord is trustworthy (3:3), they express their confidence in the Thessalonians' present and future performance (3:4). A wish-prayer again wraps up this section (3:5).

This commendation functions as encouragement toward faithfulness. For this reason, we can classify 3:1-5 as part of the exhortation section. These verses also prepare the way for the stern instructions concerning relationships with the *unruly* in the congregation (3:6-15).

OUTLINE

A Call for Prayer, 3:1-2
Expressions of Confidence, 3:3-4
Another Wish-Prayer, 3:5

EXPLANATORY NOTES
A Call for Prayer 3:1-2

In 1 Thessalonians 5:25, Paul and his partners request prayer without specifying any particular concerns. At this point in the second letter, they again ask for prayer, but this time they become specific:

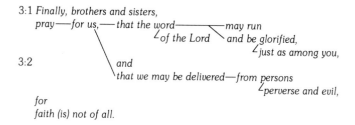

3:1 *Finally, brothers and sisters,*
pray—for us,—that the word——may run
of the Lord and be glorified,
just as among you,
3:2 *and*
that we may be delivered—from persons
perverse and evil,
for
faith (is) not of all.

There are two requests. First they invite intercession in behalf of the progress of the missionary enterprise: *Pray for us that the word of the Lord may run and be glorified, just as among you* (3:1). Writing from Corinth, Paul and his companions solicit prayer for their mission in that region and elsewhere. *The word of the Lord* refers to the gospel (cf. 1 Thess. 1:8). Paul occasionally describes his own apostolic endeavors using the imagery of a footrace (Gal. 2:2; 1 Cor. 9:24, 26; Phil. 2:16). Likely Paul and his readers are aware of competitions involving Olympic runners and other athletes. Possibly Paul also liked to run to keep himself physically fit! Here he uses the verb *run* (*trechō*) as a metaphor to describe the speedy spread of the gospel (cf. Ps. 147:15). But Paul wants the gospel not only to run but also to win! The verb *be glorified* (*doxazō*) may have athletic associations, since the winner is glorified through receiving the prize (hence RSV translates with the verb *triumph*).

The second prayer request focuses on the evangelists' concern for their own personal safety: *that we may be delivered from perverse and evil persons* (3:2). It is not clear whether the Thessalonians know the nature of the peril facing Paul and his co-workers. As later readers of this letter, we cannot identify these *perverse and evil persons*. The account in Acts 18 depicts active Jewish opposition during Paul's ministry in Corinth, but nothing in our text suggests that this is what Paul has in mind here. As 1 Thessalonians 2:16 demonstrates, Paul becomes particularly agitated toward those who obstruct him in his primary calling—the preaching of the gospel to the Gentiles. As apostle to the Gentiles, Paul encounters both opposition to his message and personal suffering. Paul's comments in some of his letters (cf. Gal. 5:2-12; 1 Cor. 4:10-13; 2 Cor. 11:21-33) suggest that Jews or Judaizers as well as Gentiles at various times opposed the gospel and persecuted him.

An explanation for such hostility is given here in 2 Thessalonians 3:2: *for faith (is) not of all.* In other words, not all people respond to *the word of the Lord* with *faith (pistis).* Paul and his fellow missionaries sadly and realistically note that not all people believe the gospel or trust the Lord. In their own apostolic experience, they have discovered that people who do not respond in *faith* sometimes actively oppose both the gospel and those who proclaim it ("Faith" in TBC for 1 Thess. 2:17—3:10).

The theme of deliverance recalls a key clause from the first letter, where Paul and his associates summarize the gospel which the Thesssalonians have accepted. Jesus, whom God raised from the dead, *delivers us from the coming wrath* (1 Thess. 1:10). As noted in our discussion of this confession, Jesus' ministry as the delivered Deliverer has implications for believers both within history and eschatologically ("Jesus Delivers" in TBC for 1 Thess. 1:1-10). Here in the second letter to the Thessalonian congregation, the evangelists seek deliverance in the face of present and looming peril. The one who delivers the faithful from wrath is also able to intervene by rescuing them from their enemies.

Expressions of Confidence 3:3-4

Paul and his partners have requested prayer and now express their confidence:

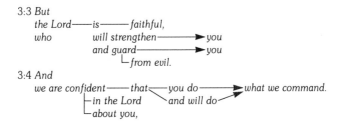

The regrettable absence of *faith* (*pistis*) among some people contrasts sharply with the character of God: *But the Lord is faithful* (*pistos*). Instead of despairing about the lack of *faith* among people, Paul and his associates gratefully acknowledge the faithfulness of the

Lord. A similar affirmation concludes the final wish-prayer in the first letter: *Faithful is the one who calls you, the one who will do this* (1 Thess. 5:24). Some people choose not to believe the gospel or trust God, but the fact remains: God can be trusted!

Paul and his co-workers articulate their confidence in God in order to undergird their call for intercessory prayer (3:1-2). However, on the same basis, they also reassure the Thessalonian believers, who are coping with affliction as well. God's faithfulness ensures strength and protection to those who trust God: *[The Lord] will strengthen you and guard you from evil* (3:3). The phrase *from evil* could with equal validity be translated *from the evil one* (Satan), but by association with the previous allusion to *perverse and evil people* (3:2), this is likely also a general reference to *evil*. But then again, such a distinction may not be needed, since Paul recognizes the activity of Satan behind those factors which hinder the progress of the gospel (1 Thess. 2:18; "Satan, the Tempter" in TBC for 1 Thess. 2:17—3:10).

Confidence that *the Lord is faithful* (3:3a) stands behind the prayer for deliverance (3:2) and the promise of strength and protection (3:3b). The language here is reminiscent of Jesus' prayer, especially the petition, "Deliver us from evil" (Matt. 6:13, RSV; NRSV: "the evil one"). Jesus' prayer may have been in the minds of the writers. Certainly the rich legacy of biblical testimonials to the trustworthiness of God underlies this expression of confidence in God ("Deliver Us from Evil" in TBC below).

However, Paul and his partners also communicate confidence in their readers: *And we are confident in the Lord about you that you do and will do what we command* (3:4). Here commendation prepares the way for the commands that will follow in 3:6-15. The confidence conveyed here is rooted *in the Lord*. Implicitly, this statement also appeals for an obedient response to instructions, since they are given *in the Lord*. Compliance is assumed for the present and anticipated for the future: *you are doing and will go on doing the things that we command* (3:4, NRSV).

Another Wish-Prayer 3:5

Yet another wish-prayer (cf. 1 Thess. 3:11-13; 5:23-24; 2 Thess. 2:16-17) marks the transition to the more specific exhortations in 3:6-15.

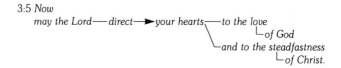

3:5 *Now*
may the Lord — direct → your hearts — to the love
└of God
└and to the steadfastness
└of Christ.

The other wish-prayers generally summarize what has preceded and point forward to themes yet to come in the letter. This prayer has a more general thrust. The Thessalonians are commended to God's love and Christ's steadfastness as spiritual resources for their daily lives and as motivations for their conduct.

THE TEXT IN THE BIBLICAL CONTEXT
Deliver Us from Evil

The Psalms repeatedly express the hope that God will rescue, strengthen, and protect the faithful during times of distress. Even a glance at the concordance reveals that many psalms feature the verbs *deliver* and *guard*. In private prayer and corporate worship, God's people continually voice their confidence in God's ability to rescue them from peril. The request for prayer and the expressions of confidence in 2 Thessalonians 3:1-5 demonstrate the same trusting attitude.

Psalm 34 amply demonstrates such trust. After an opening hymn of praise (34:1-3), the psalmist testifies,

> I sought the Lord, and he answered me,
>   and delivered me from all my fears.
> Look to him, and be radiant;
>   so your faces shall never be ashamed.
> This poor soul cried, and was heard by the Lord,
>   and was saved from every trouble. (Ps. 34:4-6)

The psalmist continues (34:7-10) with further testimony to how God delivers the needy and with eloquent invitations for others also to experience God's protection.

> The angel of the Lord encamps around those who fear him,
>   and delivers them.
> O taste and see that the Lord is good;
>   happy are those who take refuge in him. (Ps. 34:7-8)

As the Psalm progresses, the worshiper hears the reminder that those who trust God do not just passively wait for God to act. Such trust also includes active participation in the Lord's program of peace and righteousness (34:11-14).

> Depart from evil, and do good;
>   seek peace, and pursue it. (Ps. 34:14)

The rest of the Psalm (34:15-22) affirms that God both rescues the righteous and condemns the evildoers.

> The eyes of the Lord are on the righteous,
>   and his ears are open to their cry.
> The face of the Lord is against evildoers,
>   to cut off the remembrance of them from the earth. (Ps. 34:15-16)

A similar confidence in God surrounds the last petition in Jesus' prayer: "And lead us not into temptation, but deliver us from evil" (Matt. 6:13, RSV; "the evil one," NRSV). This confidence is put to the test in Jesus' own pilgrimage as he faces his death. At Gethsemane he wrestles in prayer before God, asking that, if possible, the cup of suffering might be taken from him (Matt. 26:36-46). But Jesus needs to trust God all the way to the cross. On Golgotha, as he hangs on the cross, Jesus is taunted by chief priests, scribes, and elders, who quote from one of the Psalms:

> He trusts in God; let God deliver him now, if he wants to;
> for he said, "I am God's Son." (Matt. 27:43)

This is a mocking quotation from Psalm 22:8, the same Psalm from which Jesus cites the opening lament while he breathes his last: "My God, my God, why have you forsaken me?" (Matt. 27:46; cf. Ps. 22:1). The reader of the Gospel knows, of course, that Jesus' confidence in God remains firm. Even his final cry from the cross can be heard as a prelude to the statements of assurance found later in the Psalm (especially 22:3-5, 28, 31). Jesus' obedience unto death is rewarded. He is raised from the dead (Matt. 28:1-10)! When he meets with the eleven disciples on the mountain in Galilee, the risen Christ speaks these words: "All authority in heaven and on earth has been given to me" (28:18).

We cannot determine whether Paul consciously uses the language of the psalmist or cites from Jesus' prayer. However, Paul echoes the same spirit of confidence and trust as he faces opposition and when he invites his churches to intercede for his ministry. Some time after writing the letters to the church at Thessalonica, Paul shares with the Corinthian congregation about a life-threatening circumstance which he encountered in Asia (2 Cor. 1:8-11). No details are given concerning this desperate situation. Paul simply gives testimony to his past and anticipated future experiences of divine rescue.

> Indeed, we felt that we had received the sentence of death so that we would rely not on ourselves but on God who raises the dead. He who rescued us from so deadly a peril will continue to rescue us; on him we have set our hope that he will rescue us again. (2 Cor. 1:9-10)

Similar themes are sounded near the end of Paul's letter to the house churches in Rome (Rom. 15:30-32). Paul informs them about his upcoming plans to go to Jerusalem, and he invites them to pray "that I may be rescued from the unbelievers in Judea" (15:31).

From the Psalms, Jesus, and Paul, we hear the testimony of those who pray, "Deliver us from evil." In the spirit of this trusting prayer, Paul, Silvanus, and Timothy urge the Thessalonian believers to intercede for them and to trust God for strength and protection in their own lives.

THE TEXT IN THE LIFE OF THE CHURCH

In God We Trust

For the last (almost) half of my life, I have made purchases and paid expenses with dollar bills which include a confession of faith. The paper currency in the United States announces to all the world, IN GOD WE TRUST. During my earlier years in Canada, I did not witness to my faith in quite the same way each time I pulled out my wallet.

For the most part, I do not pay much attention to any of the fine print on these bills. Usually I focus only on what the big number says! There are times, however, when the fine print looms large for me. A high percentage of the income tax dollar in the U.S. goes to support the military. If we trust in God, why invest in bombs? How can we justify spending IN-GOD-WE-TRUST dollars on armaments?

The historic peace churches have sought to negotiate exemptions from the military wherever their members have migrated. However, the U.S. and Canada and most other countries continue to conscript tax dollars for military purposes. Some people have chosen to witness to their faith in God through refusing to pay the war tax. In the U.S., at the time of this writing, a proposed Peace Tax Fund is slowly gaining support among some legislators.

Most early Anabaptists followed Jesus' teaching on peace and the way of nonresistance to evil. However, Thomas Müntzer of Germany was an exception. In 1525 Müntzer threw his support behind the Peasants' Revolt, and called on others to join this struggle for social and economic justice. In the letter in which he issued the rallying call, Müntzer assumes that even a trustworthy God needs some human fighters:

> I tell you this, that if you are unwilling to suffer for the sake of God, then you will have to be martyrs for the devil. So watch out, don't be downcast or negligent, or flatter any longer the perverted phantasts, the godless evil-doers; make a start and fight the fight of the Lord. It is high time; keep all your brothers at it, so that they do not scorn the divine testimony and perish as a result. (Matheson:140-41)

According to Müntzer, those who seek to be liberated from "godless evil-doers" need to trust God by joining in a violent struggle for change:

> Even if there are only three of you whose trust in God is unperturbable and who seek his name and honour alone, you need have no fear of a hundred thousand. So go to it, go to it, go to it! The time has come, the evil-doers are running like scared dogs! (Matheson: 141)

Just before signing the letter as "a servant of God against the godless," Thomas Müntzer quotes excerpts from 2 Chronicles 20:15-18.

> This is what God says, "You should have no fear. You should not shrink from this great host; it is not your fight, but the Lord's. It is not you who fight; stand up like men. Above you, you will see the Lord helping." (Matheson: 142)

Müntzer was evidently influenced by certain kinds of apocalyptic expectation. He anticipated that, if the faithful few confront godless tyranny in God's name, God would act decisively to usher in the just kingdom. That is not what happened. About a month after this letter was written, the uprising was severely suppressed. Müntzer was imprisoned, tortured to make him recant, and eventually executed.

There has been considerable debate about possible associations between Müntzer and early Anabaptist leaders. Martin Luther tended to characterize Anabaptism generally as fanaticism, largely on the basis of Müntzer's role in the ill-fated revolt. Churches within the believers church stream typically try to distance themselves from this colorful leader. Anabaptist historian Werner Packull (ME, 5:607-609) has a word worth hearing:

Müntzer misread the signs of the times. He failed to see that an armed defense of the future kingdom inevitably led to new coercive structures in the present. But despite these delinquencies, or perhaps because of them, Müntzer deserves a fair hearing and a rightful place in the all-too-human story of the Reformation and of Anabaptist beginnings. (ME, 5:609; also see "Müntzer, Thomas," ME, 3:785-789)

At stake is the question, What kind of human participation is needed in confronting evil in the world? Or to put the question in another way, What role do people have in the work of God's kingdom? As noted in our earlier discussion of the divine warrior theme, believers are invited to be actively engaged in God's struggle for peace and justice ("God's Warriors" in TBC for 1 Thess. 5:1-11). However, the weapons to be used in this battle are not guns nor bombs but faith, love, and hope.

2 Thessalonians 3:6-15

Conduct in the Community of Faith

PREVIEW

What might be the single most important factor moving Paul and his co-workers to write the second letter to the church in Thessalonica? After all, not much time has passed since the first letter. The excitement and anxiety created by prophets announcing the arrival of the day of the Lord (2:2) could be the stimulant. Perhaps even more irritating, however, might be the restless idleness of the *unruly* (3:6-13). These two circumstances may have somehow been connected.

The statement of confidence in 3:4 sets the stage for the specific exhortations in 3:6-15: *We are confident in the Lord about you that you do and will do what we command.* This verb *command* (3:4), appearing earlier in these letters only at 1 Thessalonians 4:11, occurs in the present section three times (3:6, 10, 12). On other topics, Paul and his colleagues *ask* (1 Thess. 4:1; 5:12; 2 Thess. 2:1) or *urge* (1 Thess. 2:12; 4:1, 10; 5:14; cf. 2 Thess. 3:12) the Thessalonian community to conform to certain patterns of behavior. Only when addressing issues related to the *unruly* do they *command*: 1 Thess. 4:10b-12; and the present passage. Evidently the issue of the *unruly* touches an apostolic nerve.

Prominent among the concerns raised in this section is the fact that some members of the Thessalonian community of believers are no longer willing to work for their support (3:11). Paul and his associates address this concern in several ways. They remind the congregation about their earlier teaching (3:10), recall their own pattern of self-support (3:7-8), urge that this example be imitated (3:9), address the *unruly* with a firm imperative to get back to work (3:12), encourage the rest of the congregation not to become weary of doing good (3:13), and prescribe a process of discipline (3:6, 14-15).

First Thessalonians alludes briefly to the earlier teaching on the topic of work (4:11), but it says more about how Paul and his companions supported themselves while in Thessalonica (2:9) and the call for the believers to imitate the missionaries' example (1:6; 2:14). The imperative to get back to work and the demand for disciplinary action are new to the second letter, an indication that the situation has apparently deteriorated and more firm action has become necessary.

OUTLINE
What to Do with the Unruly? 3:6
Previous Instructions and Example, 3:7-10
The Renewed Charge, 3:11-12
Disciplinary Action, 3:13-15

EXPLANATORY NOTES
What to Do with the Unruly? (3:6)
Confident of the Thessalonians' present and future obedience (cf. 3:4), Paul and his colleagues begin to articulate their demand:

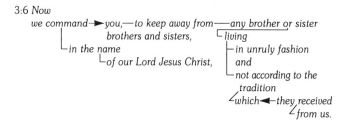

This command is given from the same basis as the earlier statement: *We are confident in the Lord* (3:4). That premise is formulated more fully here: *Now we command you, brothers and sisters, in the name of our Lord Jesus Christ* (cf. also 3:12). Authority for the instructions being transmitted rests not with Paul nor with any of his associates but rather in Christ. As the opening greeting specifies, the members of the Christian community in Thessalonica are being addressed throughout this letter on the basis that they share with the missionaries a common relationship in *the Lord Jesus Christ* (cf. 1:1-2). From this assumed shared commitment, Paul and his co-workers admonish their *brothers and sisters* on a topic of major concern within the congregation.

Before commenting on the command itself, we need to try to identify the group within the church whose conduct elicits this concern. It is difficult to determine what attitudes and behavior characterize this group. One side of the puzzle centers on the meaning of several words, all with the same Greek root (*atakt-*, which literally means "not in proper order"). This word-group appears in the NT only here in 1 Thessalonians 5:14 and in 2 Thessalonians 3:6-15. Since these three words occur nowhere else in the NT and only once in the Septuagint (3 Macc. 1:19), we are largely restricted to the clues contained within these two epistles.

In 1 Thessalonians 5:14, the congregation is urged: *Admonish the unruly.* The adjective *ataktoi*, employed as a plural noun, is often translated *the idlers* (NRSV) or *those who are idle* (NIV), but the KJV has *them that are unruly.* I have already argued (notes on 1 Thess. 4:11 and 5:14) that this group cannot be characterized simply as idle or lazy. In addition, they seem to have been socially disruptive, perhaps also resisting instruction and guidance given by the leaders or the congregation generally. Hence my translation: *the unruly.*

Another word with the same root appears both in 2 Thessalonians 3:6 and 3:11. The adverb *ataktōs* modifies the participle *living* (*peripatountos*, literally: *walking*). Proposed translations include: *living in idleness* (NRSV), *living a lazy life* (TEV), and *that walketh disorderly* (KJV). In harmony with the argument given above, I suggest that Paul and his partners here identify people who are *living in an unruly fashion.*

The third word with the root *atakt-* is the verb *ētaktēsamen* in 3:7b. The missionaries issue a disclaimer about how they behaved during their initial visit in Thessalonica. Again the translations fall into categories similar to those indicated above: *We were not idle* (NRSV); *We were not lazy* (TEV); *We behaved not ourselves disorderly* (KJV). My proposal: *We were not unruly among you.*

We return to the command itself. Paul and his missionary partners ask the other members of the congregation to stay aloof from the *unruly* members: *Keep away from any brother or sister living in unruly fashion.* This call for avoidance is rephrased in 3:14, although with different terminology: *do not associate.* That verse gives detail about this process and explains the desired outcome (*see* notes below).

The problematic behavior which calls for such firm action is defined negatively: *and not according to the tradition which they received from us.* Those *living in unruly fashion* are guilty of nonobservance of the theological and moral *tradition* which they had received from the missionaries. As noted in our discussion of the injunction in 2:15 (*stand firm, and observe the traditions*), the word *tradition* as employed here refers to the inherited memory (stories, confessions of faith, and moral guidance) passed on by the missionaries to their churches.

Previous Instruction and Example 3:7-10

This *tradition* has been transmitted to the Thessalonians through both teaching and example. In 3:7-9 the evangelists recall what they have modeled, and in 3:10 what they have taught concerning work.

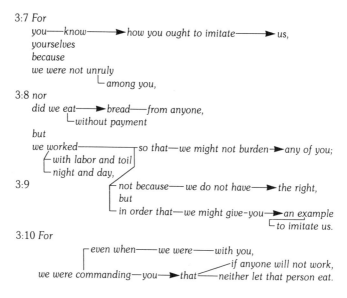

3:7 *For*
   you——know———▶how you ought to imitate———▶us,
   yourselves
   because
   we were not unruly
            └ *among you,*
3:8 *nor*
   did we eat——▶bread——from anyone,
      └ *without payment*
   but
   we worked————————┬so that—we might not burden—▶any of you;
    ┌ *with labor and toil*
    └ *night and day,*
  3:9   ┌ *not because— we do not have——▶ the right,*
            but
       └ *in order that—we might give-you—▶an example*
                      └ *to imitate us.*
  3:10 *For*
      ┌ *even when——we were——with you,*
      │   ┌ *if anyone will not work,*
  we were commanding—you—▶that◁*—neither let that person eat.*

The familiar formula, *you yourselves know* (cf. 1 Thess. 2:1; 3:3, 4:2; 5:2), jogs the memory of the Thessalonian Christian community. All the members of this community, but especially the recalcitrant *unruly* members, are urged to call to mind that the missionaries have lived in a way worthy of imitation. Even the lifestyle of the messengers who have preached the gospel to them communicates a moral direction: *You yourselves know how you ought to imitate us* (2 Thess. 3:7). This use of the imitation motif recalls specific references in the earlier letter to the fact that the Thessalonian converts have become imitators of the missionaries and the Lord (1 Thess. 1:6; 2:14). In addition, the recital concerning the evangelists' motivations and conduct while preaching the gospel (1 Thess. 2:1-12) carries with it an implicit appeal. Here that appeal is made explicit: *You ought to imitate us.*

Paul and his colleagues single out one fact as particularly relevant to the situation that has developed in Thessalonica: during their evangelistic visit, they worked to provide for their own material needs. The missionaries did not rely on the congregation for that support (cf. 1 Thess. 2:9-12). They invite the Thessalonian believers to remember that Paul and his company did not model the kind of behavior which now characterizes *the unruly*: *we were not unruly among you* (3:7). A more specific disclaimer follows: *nor did we eat bread from anyone without payment* (3:8). The expression *eat bread* has a general meaning here (cf. also at 3:12). The Septuagint uses similar language in telling how David pledged lifelong maintenance of Jonathan's physically handicapped son Mephibosheth (2 Sam. 9:7). Paul and his co-workers are not saying that whenever they were offered a meal, they felt constrained to pay for it. They are declaring that they did not expect or accept gratis food and lodging on a continuing basis from people among whom they shared the gospel.

Instead of receiving their room and board, as would have been their right (cf. 3:9), Paul and his companions supported themselves through manual labor: *with labor and toil we worked night and day* (3:8). This statement echoes much of the language of 1 Thessalonians 2:9. Use of the two synonymous terms, *labor* and *toil*, emphasizes that Paul, Silvanus, and Timothy worked hard. Similarly, the expression *night and day* puts the accent on the level of exertion required in their effort to remain materially self-sufficient.

The missionaries' motives for maintaining themselves are stated in a way that is also reminiscent of 1 Thessalonians 2:9: *so that we might not burden any of you* (3:8). Paul and his co-workers may want to differentiate themselves from some itinerant philosophers who abuse their right to hospitality (cf. 1 Thess. 2:3-10). The *unruly* members apparently are taking advantage of the Christian love and practical helpfulness available in the congregation. By pointing to their desire not to be a burden to any people in the church, Paul and his associates implicitly rebuke *the unruly* for living in a way that increases rather than lessens the burden of caring for the truly needy in their midst.

The writers continue by noting that they could have exercised their right to receive support. Working to maintain themselves, the missionaries have essentially waived their right to receive financial support. They did so in order to provide their converts with a model of responsible conduct: *not because we do not have the right but in order that we might give ourselves as an example to imitate* (3:9). Their personal commitment to self-support not only modeled self-sufficiency; it also showed that they were concerned for the welfare of the congregation. On both counts, the church members whose lifestyle earned them the nickname of *the unruly* need to take heed. Here is their model, *an example to imitate*.

When writing to the church at Corinth, Paul argues in a similar fashion about his apostolic right to be supported by the church (1 Cor. 9:3-14) and his decision not to make use of that right (9:15-27). In support of his claim that those who proclaim the gospel have the right to make their living in this way, Paul quotes Moses (Deut. 25:4) and alludes to a saying of Jesus (likely Luke 10:7; Matt. 10:10). We will examine these and other texts later, to explore further both the apostolic right to receive church support and possible reasons for renouncing that right ("Ministry and Support" in TBC below).

Still recalling their initial ministry in Thessalonica, Paul and his associates rehearse what they taught at that time: *For even when we were with you, we were commanding you: if anyone will not work, neither let that person eat* (3:10). Other references to their previous teaching appear throughout the two letters (1 Thess. 2:11-12; 3:4; 4:1-2, 9, 11; 5:2; 2 Thess. 2:5). On the topic of *work*, the injunction in 1 Thessalonians 4:11 reviews earlier instructions and urges more faithful compliance: *to be ambitious to be quiet, to mind your own affairs, and to work with your hands, just as we charged you.* Judging from both 1 Thessalonians 4:11 and 2 Thessalonians 3:10, already during their first visit in Thessalonica, the missionaries discerned the need for some explicit teaching concerning attitudes and commitments toward *work*, and in particular, toward manual labor. As we have seen, these circumstances also led Paul and his partners to be intentional about how they took care of their own upkeep.

Here in 2 Thessalonians 3:10, we as later readers of these letters hear a "sound bite" from the teaching which Paul and his co-workers offered while in Thessalonica. Instead of a formal gathering of the converts for a teaching session, we imagine a workshop setting where these itinerant missionaries worked alongside artisans and crafts-people from Thessalonica. Using informal opportunities for preaching and teaching in that setting, Paul and the others would also have conversed with those who gathered around out of curiosity or interest. Among other things, they apparently shared the maxim: *If anyone will not work, neither let that person eat.* The verb *we were commanding you* (imperfect tense) implies that this command was spoken on several occasions rather than just stated once.

What might be the background of this command? Some scholars suggest that this citation reflects an ancient Jewish or Hellenistic proverb (Best: 338-339). Connections with the Genesis creation account have also been proposed. God's words in the garden after the man and the woman eat from the tree of knowledge also have to do with working and eating (Gen. 3:17-19; Menken: 277-278). We will deal with this larger biblical picture later ("On Working and Eating" in TBC below).

Let us note several things about this command. The conditional clause refers to willingness to work: *if anyone will not work.* This therefore does not include the unemployed seeking work or persons physically unable to work for their own keep. The meaning of the prohibition which follows is less clear: *neither let that person eat.* A pattern of community meals is likely implied. Some reconstructions of the social world of the Christian communities in cities like Thessalonica posit that these believers are meeting in homes owned by wealthier members, and that these gatherings often include a communal meal (Meeks: 75-77, 102-103). In Thessalonica the converts seem to come from the working class. No names of heads of house churches (such as in Rom. 16) are given in the Thessalonian epistles. Perhaps communal meals in Thessalonica are organized along the lines of a potluck, with everyone bringing food to share with others (so Jewett, 1994:77-84). Some of these meals may also have included the celebration of the Lord's Supper. *[Social and Economic Context, p. 368.]*

Under circumstances such as these, the prohibition against letting the nonworkers eat can be understood. The *unruly* appear unwilling to work both to support themselves and to contribute to the common cause by sharing their food with the community. Paul and his co-workers therefore instruct the rest of the community to exclude these members from the meals which they regularly share together.

The Renewed Charge 3:11-12

After these recollections about what they have modeled and taught while in Thessalonica (3:7-10), Paul and his partners speak directly to the *unruly*. First the missionaries report what they have been hearing about this group (3:11). Next they solemnly charge these members to change their ways (3:12).

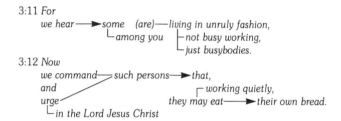

3:11 *For*
   we hear ──► *some   (are)*──*living in unruly fashion,*
           └*among you* ├*not busy working,*
                    └*just busybodies.*
3:12 *Now*
   we command──*such persons*──►*that,*
   and   ┌*working quietly,*
   urge   *they may eat*──►*their own bread.*
   └*in the Lord Jesus Christ*

News has apparently traveled to Corinth, where Paul is involved in evangelistic ministries and from which these letters to Thessalonica are being written: *For we hear some among you (are) living in unruly fashion* (3:11). This description of the group echoes the language of 3:6. In both places it is apparent that these persons are still considered to be Christians affiliated with the congregation: *any brother or sister* (3:6), *some among you* (3:11).

In 3:11 the portrait of this group is expanded through a vivid wordplay. Such verbal wit usually loses force through translation, though in this case an idiomatic English expression both conveys the meaning and introduces a similar wordplay. Paul and his partners have heard that these persons are *not busy working, just busybodies*. This brief additional glimpse into the behavior of these persons shows that they are not just lazy and inactive. They are also inclined toward disorderly conduct. Perhaps they are meddling inappropriately in the private lives of other members or engaged in certain forms of offensive propagandizing. In addition to being economically irresponsible, therefore, these persons have developed some socially obnoxious patterns of behavior. Their lifestyle not only upsets the community of believers from within; it also tends to invite ridicule in their social contexts.

After Paul and his associates play back what they have heard about those *living in unruly fashion*, they address this group with a solemnly worded charge: *Now we command and urge such persons in the Lord Jesus Christ* (3:12). The solemnity of this command is underscored by the double injunction: *we command and urge*. The phrase *in the Lord Jesus Christ* also communicates the seriousness of the situation. As noted with reference to the comparable expression *in the name of our Lord Jesus Christ* in 3:6, this formula reflects the fact that the authority behind the command lies ultimately not with the apostles but in Christ. The missionaries and their people together share that relationship under their common Lord.

The charge itself calls on these people to become quietly productive by working rather than noisily meddlesome while idle: *that working with quietness they might eat their own bread* (3:12). The adverbial phrase *with quietness* echoes the verb in 1 Thessalonians 4:11, where the Thessalonians were urged *to be ambitious to be quiet*. Not only are the *unruly* commanded to work. They are also challenged to direct their restless energy into productive activity. Likely the reasons stated in 1 Thessalonians 4:12 still apply, only with greater urgency: to gain the outsiders' respect for the Christian community, and to assure that personal and community material needs are met.

Disciplinary Action 3:13-15

After appealing directly to the *unruly* members of the congregation (3:11-12), the writers share a general admonition (3:13) and some specific directives (3:14-15) for the rest of the congregation.

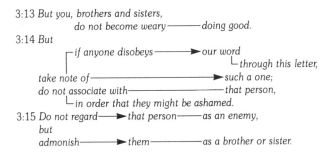

3:13 *But you, brothers and sisters,*
    do not become weary —— doing good.
3:14 *But*
   if anyone disobeys —▶ our word
                      through this letter,
  take note of ——————▶ such a one;
  do not associate with————— that person,
    in order that they might be ashamed.
3:15 *Do not regard —▶ that person —— as an enemy,*
  but
  admonish ——▶ them ———— as a brother or sister.

Before outlining a procedure for dealing with persistent noncompliance, Paul and his companions offer a word of encouragement: *But you, brothers and sisters, do not become weary doing good* (3:13). This final *brothers and sisters* (*adelphoi*) in the letter again signals a transition. Some translations (notably NRSV, NIV) attach 3:13 to the preceding paragraph. Others (such as REB, TEV) have rightly recognized that 3:13-15 constitutes a unit of material advising the church about how to respond to this delicate situation.

Perhaps some of the responsible members of the congregation are becoming tired or feeling resentful toward those who do not carry their share of the load. Even though their acts of brotherly and sisterly love seem to be taken for granted, these faithful members are urged to continue *doing good*. One aspect of Christian love is to call erring members of the community of faith back to faithfulness.

Disciplinary action may become necessary in the life of a caring congregation. If reminders about the evangelists' past teaching and example (3:7-10) and strongly worded further instructions (3:11-12) and the continuing generosity of the community (3:13) do not lead to change, then some form of social avoidance (3:6) may be needed.

In 3:14 the missionaries outline a disciplinary process and define the anticipated outcome. When should firm action be taken by the congregation? Basically, the circumstance calling for disciplinary action is the persistent lack of regard for the Christian tradition as conveyed by the life and teaching of the evangelists: *But if anyone disobeys our word through this letter*. The present tense of the verb *disobeys* points to the unrelenting continuation of the offending behavior, despite various reminders and appeals. *Our word* as conveyed *through this letter* encompasses the received *tradition* (see comments on 3:6), as taught and modeled by the missionaries and now rehearsed for the second time in a letter. This is not the heavy-handed exercise of apostolic authority (cf. Bruce, 1982:209-210) but the next step in a loving and firm congregational process. The church's goal is to win erring members back into full fellowship through faithful observance of the inherited tradition.

In this particular case, the *unruly* manifest a pattern of irresponsible behavior which departs from what the missionaries have taught. With reference to such persons, they advise the congregation: *Take note of such a one* (3:14). Benign tolerance will not do. When believers depart from the gospel and the way of life correlated with the gospel, they require a caring and firm response.

But what type of response? On the surface the injunction sounds harsh and punitive: *Do not associate with that person* (3:14). This reiterates the instruction in the opening sentence of this section: *Keep away from any brother or sister living in unruly fashion and not according to the tradition which they received from us* (3:6). Two different verbs are used in these two verses, apparently synonymously: *keep away from* (3:6) and *do not associate with* (3:14). The latter verb appears twice in 1 Corinthians 5:9-11, where Paul corrects a misreading of his earlier letter:

But now I am writing to you not to associate with anyone who bears the name of brother or sister who is sexually immoral or greedy, or is an idolater, reviler, drunkard, or robber. Do not even eat with such a one. (1 Cor. 5:11)

In Corinth the problem is immorality, while in Thessalonica it is disorderly idleness. Despite these differences, the congregational situation in Thessalonica broadly corresponds to what develops later in Corinth. The *unruly* in Thessalonica also bear the name of *brother or sister*, yet their behavior does not conform to the ethical norms of the gospel as delivered to them by Paul and his missionary partners. Under both sets of circumstances, the mandated action is the same: *Do not associate with that person.*

The nature and extent of this prescribed avoidance cannot be established with any kind of confidence. Various suggestions have been put forward. Some interpreters suggest that the *unruly* are to be excluded from community meals. This would be one way of enforcing the ruling: *If anyone will not work, neither let that person eat* (3:10; Best: 343; Jewett, 1994:80-84). Others propose that avoidance is prescribed for those community meals when they celebrate the Lord's Supper (Wanamaker: 289). Still others posit general avoidance, with church members refusing to initiate social contacts but using unplanned encounters as opportunities to admonish them (Marshall: 228).

The purpose statement shows that, whatever form this avoidance is to take, it has a redemptive intent: *in order that they might be ashamed* (3:14). The missionaries hope that a member of the congregation receiving such treatment will feel the kind of shame that leads to repentance and change and therefore also opens the way for full restoration.

The command, *Do not associate*, does not call for complete social ostracism nor total exclusion. The final qualifying instructions make this quite clear: *Do not regard that person as an enemy, but admonish them as a brother or sister* (3:15). Even though Paul and his co-workers urge the Thessalonian believers to take firm action, their ultimate goal is to restore rather than condemn these persons whose behavior deviates from the normative tradition.

In the history of the Christian church, 2 Thessalonians 3:14-15 and other texts have been examined for possible guidelines for church discipline. Jesus' teaching about binding and loosing in the community of his disciples (Matt. 18:15-22) provides a framework within which these other texts can be understood. In his study of discipling in the church, Marlin Jeschke takes Jesus' steps as outlined in Matthew 18 as successive stages in a redemptive process. Jeschke reads the prescription for avoidance in 2 Thessalonians 3:6, 14 as a call for the excommunication of the offending individual. However, in his view, excommunication does not involve social ostracism:

> Avoidance is the adoption of an especially discreet relationship with excommunicated persons that brings home to them the truth about their spiritual condition. . . .
> Avoidance must say two things simultaneously, first, that a given person has forsaken the way of discipleship; and second, that he or she has a standing invitation to return to it. (Jeschke: 95)

We will refer to Jeschke's study further in our reflections on the meaning of this text for the life of the church ("Discipling in the Church" in TLC below).

THE TEXT IN THE BIBLICAL CONTEXT
Ministry and Support

While in Thessalonica, Paul and his missionary companions deliberately followed a strategy of maintaining themselves rather than depending on support from the people among whom they preached the gospel. Even though they recognized that they had the right to expect such support (1 Thess. 2:7; 2 Thess. 3:9), they chose to remain self-sufficient and did not accept patronage (1 Thess. 2:9; 2 Thess. 3:7-8).

We have already mentioned (notes on 2 Thess. 3:9) that, when Paul writes to the church at Corinth, he develops a theological rationale for apostolic support (1 Cor. 9:3-14) and then proceeds to explain why he renounced that right (9:15-27). He makes several points in defense of these apostolic rights. In a series of rhetorical questions, Paul attempts to establish his case. Would not his right to support be equal to that of the other apostles (9:5-6)? Or to a soldier, farmer, or shepherd (9:7)?

Having argued by drawing several analogies, Paul moves to a series of other arguments: from the law of Moses (1 Cor. 9:8-10), the temple service (9:13), and the memory of Jesus' teaching (9:14). Paul cites a precept from Deuteronomy 25:4, "You shall not muzzle an ox while it is treading out the grain" (1 Cor. 9:9). Using a rabbinic exegetical technique which expands the relevance of biblical principles beyond the surface meaning, Paul asks, "Is it for oxen that God is concerned? Or does he not speak entirely for our sake?" (9:9-10). Paul concludes,

> It was indeed written for our sake, for whoever plows should plow in hope and whoever threshes should thresh in hope of a share in the crop. (9:10)

Paul applies this principle to his own situation by raising another question:

> If we have sown spiritual good among you, is it too much if we reap your material benefits? (1 Cor. 9:11)

Clearly the readers are expected to answer, Yes, apostles and missionaries have the right to material benefits from the people among whom they preach the gospel.

Paul turns next to an analogy that seems more comparable to his own situation. Temple priests help themselves to the sacrificial food itself (1 Cor. 9:13; cf. Lev. 2:2-3; 7:28-36). A missionary pastor should therefore also have a similar right. Gentiles would understand this as well, since priests in various Hellenistic temples followed this same practice. Such privilege could be abused, as the story of Eli's scoundrel sons illustrates (1 Sam. 2:13-17); they reserved the choicest portions of the offerings for themselves (2:29).

The clincher in this series of defenses of the apostolic right to receive support is a word from Jesus:

> In the same way, the Lord commanded that those who proclaim the gospel should get their living by the gospel. (1 Cor. 9:14)

Here Paul reflects Jesus' instructions to his disciples when he sends them out on a mission (Matt. 10:5-16; Luke 9:2-5; 10:1-12). Jesus asks them to travel light. They trust God for protection from danger, and they rely on their hearers to provide for their needs. Especially pertinent is Jesus' rationale for such reliance on the hospitality of people receptive to the message of the kingdom of God:

> Remain in the same house, eating and drinking whatever they provide, for the laborer deserves to be paid. (Luke 10:7)

> For laborers deserve their food. (Matt. 10:10b)

Both Jesus and Paul clearly establish the principle that preachers of the gospel can anticipate receiving maintenance from those among whom they work. In 1 Timothy 5:18 we find another statement of this policy for elders (bishops, pastors), in this case supported by the same citations from Moses (Deut. 25:4) and Jesus (Luke 10:7). Why then does Paul renounce this right for himself?

In Thessalonica, Paul and his co-workers sense that they need to be extra careful to model social and economic responsibility for this young congregation. They do not want to be confused with those itinerant philosophers who speak for material gain (1 Thess. 2:5). They also do not want their lifestyle to give the *unruly* in Thessalonica any encouragement to indulge further in their irresponsible and noisy idleness (2 Thess. 3:11).

In Corinth, Pauls's renunciation of the right to receive material support is motivated by his understanding of Christian freedom and apostolic urgency. Paul announces, "We endure anything rather than putting an obstacle in the way of the gospel of Christ" (1 Cor. 9:12). He therefore determines to proclaim the gospel "free of charge," a sign of God's grace in his own ministry (9:18). That gospel brings him its own blessing (9:23). In refusing to demand or accept patronage, Paul preserves his apostolic freedom from inappropriate control of his ministry (9:19).

In both Thessalonica and Corinth, therefore, Paul makes a pastoral assessment of the situation in the congregation and the social context for these new believers. As a consequence, he relinquishes certain freedoms and rights, so that the mission of the church can be furthered. (For TLC discussion, see "The Unsalaried Ministry" in Faw, 1993: 223-224.)

On Working and Eating

The maxim in 2 Thessalonians 3:10 eloquently upholds the virtue of hard work and self-sufficiency: *If anyone will not work, neither let that person eat.* This saying definitely undergirds a work ethic, but the conditional clause refers to willingness rather than ability to work. Wrongly applied, it has provided justification for discrimination against welfare recipients. Some people quote this saying to encourage diligence and productivity, but others who worry about a theology of righteousness by works might wish to downplay this text.

How should this saying be understood? Fundamentally, it deals with the relationship between working and eating. We turn, therefore, to a brief survey of what the Bible as a whole teaches about that relationship.

In the Genesis creation story, the man is placed in the garden of Eden to till and keep it (Gen. 2:15). Along with this assignment comes the guarantee of food, although with limits:

> You may freely eat of every tree of the garden; but of the tree of the knowledge of good and evil you shall not eat. (2:16-17)

As events unfold, the man and the woman, prompted by the serpent, ignore this prohibition (Gen. 3:1-13). Consequently, the wily serpent is condemned to slither on its belly (3:14-15) and both the woman and the man are punished for conspiring to disobey God's command (3:16-19). A curse is put on the ground, with the result that the man is consigned to the hard work of cultivating the soil for food. God says to the man concerning the ground:

> In toil you shall eat of it all the days of your life;
> thorns and thistles it shall bring forth for you;
> and you shall eat the plants of the field.
> By the sweat of your face you shall eat bread
> until you return to the ground. . . . (Gen. 3:17-19)

The biblical story of beginnings therefore establishes a clear connection between working and eating. More sweat and toil seem to be needed after the fall into disobedience than earlier. But work and food are linked even before the act of human defiance which leads to the ground being cursed (Gen. 2:15).

Israel's prophets sometimes picture her future restoration as a return to the conditions of Eden (Isa. 51:3; Ezek. 36:35). Apocalyptic writings frequently portray future paradise in similar terms, on the premise that God will reverse the curse and provide another fertile garden requiring next to no tending. We can illustrate from a Jewish apocalypse known as 2 Baruch.

> And it will happen in those days that the reapers will not become tired, and the farmers will not wear themselves out, because the products of themselves will shoot out speedily, during the time that they work on them in full tranquility. (2 Bar. 74:1, from Charlesworth, 1:646)

In one of the concluding visions of the Revelation of John, the angel shows him an Eden-like scene featuring "the river of the water of life," and beside it, "the tree of life with its twelve kinds of fruit, producing its fruit each month" (Rev. 22:1-2). With conditions like these, why work to provide food for yourself? According to one reading of the situation in Thessalonica, the *unruly* in the congregation believe that paradise has returned, and so the old order which requires hard work has been annulled (Menken: 287).

But the teaching cited in 2 Thessalonians 3:10 also has some affinity to OT wisdom writings. A number of Proverbs warn against sloth (Prov. 6:6-11; 15:19; 19:15; 21:25; 24:30-34). One of the best known of these proverbs urges lazybones to learn from the ant: "It prepares its food in summer, and gathers its sustenance in harvest" (6:8). This proverb continues by warning that people who fail to learn from the ant will slip into poverty (6:10-11). Those who refuse to work will eventually have nothing to eat.

The book of Ecclesiastes also reflects on the relationship between working and eating. On the one hand, work is valued and recognized as fulfilling:

> There is nothing better for mortals than to eat and drink, and find enjoyment in their toil. This also, I saw, is from the hand of God; for apart from him who can eat or who can have enjoyment? (Eccles. 2:24-25)

On the other hand, Ecclesiastes also takes a cynical view of work:

> All human toil is for the mouth, yet the appetite is not satisfied. (6:7)

In other words, even those who work and eat often crave for more.

Jesus speaks about human toil and the gift of food in yet another way. In the Sermon on the Mount, Jesus points to the birds of the air, that "neither sow nor reap nor gather into barns"; and the lilies of the field, "that they neither toil nor spin." These are evidence that God can be trusted to provide for the needs of the body (Matt. 6:26, 28-29). Jesus chides his disciples about their tendency to worry about such things:

> Therefore do not worry, saying, "What will we eat?" or "What will we drink?" or "What will we wear?". . . Your heavenly Father knows that you need all these things. But strive first for the kingdom of God and his righteousness, and all these things will be given to you as well. (Matt. 6:31-33)

Human efforts ultimately do not produce food. God does! As they seek God's kingdom and righteousness, Jesus' disciples therefore need not be anxious. What they need for their daily sustenance will be provided as well.

Yet Jesus' parables assume that people do need to sow, reap, and gather. Jesus, "the carpenter's son" (Matt. 13:55), undoubtedly knows firsthand that those who do not work will not have food to eat.

An exhortation in Ephesians provides another perspective on the significance of work. Thieves are urged to stop stealing from others and start working to benefit others: "Let them work honestly with their own hands, so as to have something to share with the needy" (Eph. 4:28). Titus 3:14 has a similar thrust. Believers pursue productive and meaningful work, motivated by the desire to share with others and not just by the goal of self-sufficiency.

THE TEXT IN THE LIFE OF THE CHURCH
Discipling in the Church

"Are you willing to give and receive counsel from the members of this congregation?" The baptismal candidate says "I am," and the congregation responds by pledging to support and nurture her in the faith. After a prayer and a few more remarks, she is baptized in the name "of the Father and of the Son and of the Holy Spirit" (Matt. 28:19), and then received as a member of the church.

But is the congregation ready and willing to give counsel? If that member departs from the faith which she confessed at the time of her baptism, does the congregation love her enough to take the steps to call her back to faithfulness?

Some congregations within the believers church have in times past acted in legalistic ways. Such church discipline seems primarily concerned to preserve the purity of the church. Other congregations have slid into benign tolerance toward diverse forms of belief and conduct. Such lack of church discipline reflects respect for individual freedom even when that freedom tarnishes the witness of the church in the world.

Paul and his partners personally confront church members and urge the congregation to confront members who depart from the normative gospel tradition. We have traced this process in relation to the church in Thessalonica. Other NT epistles also include guidelines for firm yet loving church discipline (especially 1 Cor. 5:1-13; Gal. 6:1-5; Rom. 16:17-20). But Jesus' instructions as reported in Matthew 18 have had the most impact on the practice of church discipline in the life of the church.

As already noted, Marlin Jeschke's book *Discipling in the Church* follows the steps outlined in Matthew 18 in an effort "to portray systematically what discipline based on the gospel looks like, from beginning to end, from recognition of a problem of sin to its resolution in forgiveness or excommunication" (Jeschke: 19).

Already in the early stages of the Swiss Anabaptist movement, the procedure spelled out in Matthew 18 was considered to be the normative process for discipling in the church. The Schleitheim Confession of 1527 expresses the following consensus concerning the ban:

> The ban shall be employed with all those who have given themselves over to the Lord, to walk after [Him] in His commandments; those who have been baptized into the one body of Christ, and let themselves be called brothers or sisters, and still somehow slip and fall into error and sin, being inadvertently overtaken. The same [shall] be warned twice privately and the third time be publicly admonished before the entire congregation according to the command of Christ (Matt. 18). But this shall be done according to the ordering of the Spirit of God before the breaking of the bread, so that we may all in one spirit and in one love break and eat from one bread and drink from one cup. (Yoder: 37)

The occasion for church discipline, simply put, is sin—in particular, a persistent pattern of sinning. Disorderly idleness had become a problem in first-century Thessalonica. In later generations of the church, other sins have marred her witness in the world: greed, immorality, and abuse, to name a few. Out of concern both for the spiritual health of the individual and the integrity of the congregation, loving confrontation and admonition need to occur. Ignoring sin does not show love. Hence, the Thessalonian believers as a group are admonished not to grow weary in well-doing, even when that includes disciplining some members of their group. In his tract of 1527, "Concerning True Love," the Anabaptist leader Hans Denck writes:

> For whoever loves someone other than through God's truth and Love, hates him; but whoever for the sake of God's Love hates someone, loves him more than the former. Yet, for the sake of Love, one cannot hate anyone beyond the intention of earnestly admonishing him and, with heartfelt sorrow shunning him, if he does not wish to hear: this also is called being truly loved. (Bauman: 195)

The goal of church discipline is not to punish but to restore an erring brother or sister. Like evangelism, discipline is a redemptive ministry of the church, inspired by God's grace and motivated by God's love. Menno Simons admonishes the church to expel those who do not repent after admonition and rebuke. However, even this is to be done in order that the excommunicated brother or sister whom we cannot convert by gentle services may by such means be shamed unto repentance and made to acknowledge to what he has come and from what he is fallen. In this way the ban is a work of great love, notwithstanding it is looked upon by the foolish as an act of hatred. (Menno: 413)

The practice of avoidance therefore does not cut off communication. It is a last-ditch attempt to communicate the gospel with its offer of forgiveness to those who repent of their sin. As Jesus amply demonstrates, tax collectors and other sinners and even enemies can know God's love through those who relate lovingly toward them while also calling them to repent.

2 Thessalonians 3:16-18
Personal Greeting and Benediction

PREVIEW

After confronting those we love, what better than to wish for God's peace and grace to be upon them all? In this letter, Paul and his co-workers first thank God for the Thessalonians' *faith, love,* and *steadfastness* amid ongoing affliction (1:1-12). Next they correct some misleading teachings about *the day of the Lord* (2:1-12) and reassure the believers of their calling to salvation (2:13-17). Exhortations general (3:1-5) and specific (3:6-15) conclude the main body of the letter. As noted, instructions about how the church should deal with the *unruly* call for loving but firm admonition, with the possibility of avoidance. The letter closes with two brief wish-prayers (3:16), a personal greeting and autograph (3:17), and a final benediction (3:18).

OUTLINE

Concluding Wish-Prayers, 3:16
Greeting, 3:17
Benediction, 3:18

EXPLANATORY NOTES
Concluding Wish-Prayers 3:16

These prayers remind us of the wish-prayer that wraps up the first letter to Thessalonica (1 Thess. 5:23-24) and also stresses *peace.* There God is addressed as *the God of peace,* here as *the Lord of peace.*

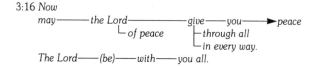

The evangelists articulate their longing that all the members of the community of believers (note the plural *you*) might experience peace: *Now may the Lord of peace himself give you peace*. Instead of recapitulating earlier themes in the letter, like 1 Thessalonians 5:23-24 does, this wish-prayer alludes more generally to the subjects addressed in this second letter. The evangelists wish for these converts to know *peace through all in every way*. Perhaps the phrase *through all* (NRSV: *at all times*) recalls the eschatological concerns of 2:1-17 and the phrase *in every way* points to the congregational disciplinary agenda addressed in 3:1-16. Both phrases would also appropriately apply to those whose experiences of affliction have led them to question God's justice (1:1-12).

A second wish-prayer follows: *The Lord (be) with you all*. Undoubtedly *you all* means what it says. Included would be those whose faithfulness and steadfastness continue during persecution, but also the prophets and the *unruly* whose eschatological teaching and lifestyle have upset the community. Behind both of these brief wish-prayers stands the priestly benediction of Numbers 6:24-26, with its rich themes of *peace* and *grace* ("Peace and Grace" in TBC below).

Greeting 3:17

Ancient letters usually included greetings. Paul's adaptations of this practice were noted briefly in the discussion of 1 Thessalonians 5:26. Here Paul personally appends a written greeting to the letter:

> 3:17 The greeting——(is)——in my hand,
>   ├——Paul,
>   which is (my) sign——in every letter.
> So——I write.

This is essentially Paul's autograph, designed to personalize his greetings in a letter which comes from Silvanus and Timothy as well. Along with several comparable texts in Paul's letters (Gal. 6:11; 1 Cor. 16:21; Col. 4:18; Philem. 19), this reference demonstrates that Paul dictates his letters. In Romans, Tertius identifies himself as the scribe and sneaks in a personal word of greeting (Rom. 16:22).

As the dictation session ends, we can visualize Paul asking his assistant for the quill and writing this greeting. But he seems to be interested in more than adding a personal touch. In our explanatory note on 2:2, we mentioned that Paul seems to wonder whether someone has forged a letter in his name (*by letter as though from us*, 2:2). By calling attention to his handwriting and signature, Paul signals the authenticity of this particular letter: *which is (my) sign in every letter. So I write*. If the original letter is ever found, we would have a sample of Paul's personal handwriting. As it is, even the oldest available editions of this letter are copies.

Benediction 3:18

The final benediction echoes the one which concludes the first letter:

> 3:18 *The grace ———— (be) —— with you all.*
> └ *of the Lord Jesus Christ*

There is one small but significant expansion in the word *all*. Paul and his missionary companions genuinely desire that *all* of the members of this faith community might experience God's *grace* anew!

THE TEXT IN THE BIBLICAL CONTEXT
Peace and Grace

On several occasions in our study of these two epistles addressed to the community of believers in Thessalonica, we have become aware that these letters were written to be read aloud. Specifically, they were drafted for use in worship. Certainly the concluding benedictions are suitable to use when the congregation gathers for worship.

The themes of *grace* and *peace* in the wish-prayers and the benediction echo the letter's opening greeting: *Grace to you and peace from God the Father and the Lord Jesus Christ* (1:2). A matrix of God's *grace* or unmerited favor provides the large picture within which believers can make sense of all their experiences. *Peace* combines the dual aspects of God's gift and God's expectation for faithful discipleship. Knowing God's *grace* as manifest supremely in Jesus Christ, believers can both experience personal *peace* and work for *peace* within the church and in the world.

A prayer for *peace* connects Christians profoundly with Hebrew prayers for *shalom*, such as the one in Numbers 6:24-26:

The Lord bless you and keep you;
the Lord make his face to shine upon you, and be gracious to you;
the Lord lift up his countenance upon you, and give you peace.

Like the prayers and benediction ending 2 Thessalonians, this priest-ly blessing combines *grace* and *peace*. It also voices the wish that the people might know God's presence (God's *face*) in their daily lives.

In his discussion of *peace* in the greetings of Paul's letters, Mauser suggests that the formula *grace and peace* has the power of a bless-ing which communicates a message originating from God. What Mauser says in general about Paul's letters certainly applies to the way in which the prayer and the benediction at the end of 2 Thessa-lonians invoke God's *peace* and *grace:*

> The address clarifies the ground on which the entire letter is built, and it sets the tone in which the letter as a whole is to be understood. This ground and tone are the grace and peace that come from God. The letter, whatever it may contain, is ultimately brought about by a divine act of re-creation in which the enmity between God and human beings is over-come, and it imparts a blessing in which the restoration to a filial trust and obedience is initiated and nourished. (Mauser: 108)

THE TEXT IN THE LIFE OF THE CHURCH
The Message of Peace

In his "Reply to False Accusations," Menno Simons summarizes the gospel in terms of the message of peace (Menno: 554):

> The Prince of peace is Christ Jesus; his kingdom is the kingdom of peace, which is his church; his messengers are the messengers of peace; his Word is the word of peace; his body is the body of peace; his children are the seed of peace; and his inheritance and reward are the inheritance and reward of peace. In short, with this King, and in his kingdom and reign, it is nothing but peace. Everything that is seen, heard, and done is peace.

What the church needs is a renewed commitment to this message of peace! Even in churches within the historic peace tradition, every generation needs a revival rooted in God's gift of peace through our Lord Jesus Christ. Congregations deeply rooted in God's peace will also embody the message of peace in their families, their local com-munities, and the world.

Outline of
1 Thessalonians

The Salutation 1:1

Work of Faith: You Turned Toward God	1:2-10
Thanksgiving for Faith, Love, and Hope	1:2-3
God Has Chosen You!	1:4
How the Gospel Came	1:5
Imitators of Us and the Lord	1:6-8
Turned Toward God to Serve and Await	1:9-10

LABOR OF LOVE: THE STORY OF PASTORS	
AND PEOPLE	2:1—3:13
Gentle Nurse and Encouraging Father	2:1-12
From Philippi to Thessalonica	2:1-2
Motivations for Preaching the Gospel	2:3-4
Behavior and Strategy: Like a Nursing Mother	2:5-8
Strategy and Goals: Like an Encouraging Father	2:9-12
Imitators in Suffering	2:13-16
God's Word Received	2:13
Imitators of Judean Churches	2:14
Litany of Judean Opposition	2:15-16a
Wrath Until the End	2:16bc

Outline of
2 Thessalonians

Abbreviations

Names of biblical books in parentheses or essays are abbreviated to the first letters, as with 1 Thess. for 1 Thessalonians, Gen. for Genesis, etc.

A.D.	anno Domini, in the year of the Lord
B.C.	before Christ
BCE	before common era
BE	*The Brethren Encyclopedia* (see Bibliography)
ca.	circa, approximately
CE	common era
cf.	*conferre*, compare
e.g.	*exempli gratia*, for example
JB	*Jerusalem Bible*
KJV	*King James Version of the Holy Bible*
LXX	Septuagint, Greek Old Testament
ME	*The Mennonite Encyclopedia* (see Bibliography)
NASB	*New American Standard Bible*
NEB	*New English Bible*
notes	Explanatory Notes in each section
NIV	*New International Version*
NRSV	*New Revised Standard Version*
NT	New Testament
OT	Old Testament
REB	*Revised English Bible*
RSV	*Revised Standard Version*
TBC	The Text in the Biblical Context, after notes in each section
TEV	*Today's English Version* (*Good News Bible*)
TLC	The Text in the Life of the Church, after TBC in each section

Journals

CBQ	*Catholic Biblical Quarterly*
JBL	*Journal of Biblical Literature*
MQR	*Mennonite Quarterly Review*
NTS	*New Testament Studies*

Ancient Sources

Also see Index of Ancient Sources. Quotations from Josephus, *War*, are taken from the translation by Gaalya Cornfeld, *Josephus: The Jewish War* (Grand Rapids: Zondervan, 1982). Other ancient sources are cited from the Loeb Classical Library, Harvard University Press. Paragraph numbering for the Whiston translation of Josephus is added in square brackets.

Catullus	*The Poems of Gaius Valerius Catullus*
Josephus	
Ant.	*Antiquities of the Jews*
War	*The Jewish War*
Homer	
Iliad	*The Iliad*
Philo	
Embassy	*The Embassy to Gaius*
Suetonius	
Claudius	*Lives of the Caesars,* book 5: *The Deified Claudius*

Essays

BIBLICAL STUDY METHODOLOGIES

All interpreters of the Bible bring methodological assumptions to their reading and study of the text, whether they are aware of them or not. This is also true of the expositor whose work is contained within the pages of this commentary.

The study of letters like 1 and 2 Thessalonians calls for prayerful engagement with the text. When believers in Christian community read these letters, the Holy Spirit illumines their meaning and their contemporary relevance. The "Author's Preface" freely acknowledges the insights of others, which helped to shape this interpretation of the Thessalonian correspondence. A careful and faithful reading can also be enhanced through several specific methodologies and approaches. We briefly describe four of these approaches: textual analysis, epistolary analysis, grammatical analysis, and rhetorical analysis.

For more on these and other biblical studies methodologies, see Bibliography for the works by: Roetzel, Schreiner, Fee (1993), Hayes and Holladay, and Perry Yoder.

TEXTUAL ANALYSIS None of the original manuscripts of biblical documents has survived. Only copies of these manuscripts have been discovered in modern times. Fortunately, scribes who copied biblical texts have left a rich legacy of materials, and most of their dedicated work was done with devotion and care. As one might expect, however, changes were introduced during the copying process, some accidentally, others intentionally. As a result, there are divergent readings of some biblical passages among the various available manuscripts. This is the case with 1 and 2 Thessalonians as well.

The discipline of textual analysis (or textual criticism) has the goal of determining what the original text said. By means of a variety of procedures, scholars weigh the available evidence and seek to establish the most probable original wording. When evaluating divergent textual data, textual scholars consider both external and internal criteria. External criteria include such things as the age of the manuscript; in general, the readings in the oldest manuscripts are to be preferred over more recent ones. Internal criteria also need to be considered. For example, generally the shorter reading is correct, since scribes tended to add to the text rather than omit material. Also, the more difficult reading is usually to be preferred, because scribes were more likely to simplify texts than to make them more complex.

The textual apparatus on each page of the Nestle-Aland *Novum Testamentum Graece* summarizes the underlying textual history. Pastors and scholars familiar with this apparatus are able to evaluate the external and internal evidence for themselves. The United Bible Societies edition of *The Greek New Testament* also provides information about variant readings, although only more-significant ones are included. *A Textual Commentary on the Greek New Testament* reports some considerations which led the editors to decide on particular readings (Metzger, 1971).

Those who rely on English translations of the NT are frequently alerted to the existence of textual variants, usually in a footnote which says something like, "Other ancient authorities read. . . ." However, data and background are not generally provided.

For 1 and 2 Thessalonians, no major doctrine is in jeopardy because of these textual variants, but a number of them do make significant differences in our understanding of these letters. We note several (as discussed in Metzger, 1971:629-638). These examples also serve to illustrate the kinds of judgments which need to be made through the discipline of textual analysis.

1. First Thess. 2:7. Were the missionaries *little children?* or *gentle?* Two different words alternately appear in the ancient manuscripts. Did Paul and his partners say that they have been *little children* (*nēpioi*) or that they have been *gentle* (*ēpioi*) among the Thessalonians during their initial visit? In the Greek the only distinction between these two words is the presence of the *n* in *nēpioi*. The previous word in the sentence ends in *n*. Since scribes often copied from dictation, it would have been hard for them by ear to determine where the *n* belongs: only with the preceding word or also with this word.

External evidence weighs in favor of the reading *little children* (*nēpioi*). On the basis of internal criteria, however, most translations and commentators opt for the less-supported *gentle* (*ēpioi*). For example, the NRSV has *gentle* but includes a footnote: "Other ancient authorities read *infants*." Within the flow of the argument in 1 Thess. 2:1-12, it seems quite natural that the missionaries would emphasize their gentleness to distinguish themselves from some itinerant philosophers (2:3, 5-6). However, as our discussion of 2:7 suggests, the reading *little children* also fits the rhetoric of this passage and is therefore to be preferred. It is characteristic of Paul, who in other letters uses it ten times. In the NT, *ēpion* otherwise appears only in 2 Tim. 2:24.

2. First Thess. 3:2: Is Timothy God's *co-worker?* or God's *servant?* The strongest manuscript testimony supports the reading *servant* (*diakonon*). However, given the many other variants which have crept into this text, it is likely that scribes intentionally introduced changes because they found the original reading theologically problematic. For Paul to have described Timothy as God's *co-worker* (*sunergon*) seemed to some scribes to elevate him to a status of equality with God. In this case, the more difficult reading *co-worker* (NRSV) or *fellow worker* (NIV) is to be preferred over *servant* (RSV). Yet, instead of implying equality with God, this description testifies to the truth that God works through human channels such as the young man Timothy. In fact, Paul elsewhere describes both Apollos and himself using both terms: "Servants" and "God's fellow workers" (1 Cor. 3:5, 9, RSV).

3. Second Thess. 2:3: *Man of lawlessness?* or *man of sin?* If we follow the principle of majority rule, the first name given in 2 Thess. 2:3-12 for the antagonist is *man of sin* (so KJV); more manuscripts read *man of sin* than *man of lawlessness*. However, the earliest manuscripts read *man of lawlessness* (NIV; cf. NRSV: *the lawless one*). Probably some scribes who copied this material substituted the word *sin* for the less frequently used *lawlessness*, and it was *sin*, therefore, that came to be more widely used in later copies of the letter. The original reading most likely was *man of lawlessness*.

4. Second Thess. 2:13: Were the Thessalonians chosen *as first fruits?* or *from the beginning?* External evidence seems to favor the reading *from the beginning* (*ap' archēs:* KJV, RSV, NIV), although the reading *as first fruits* (*aparchēn:* NRSV) also has respectable manuscript support. Once again, it would have been difficult for scribes copying from dictation to hear the difference between these two expressions. A judgment concerning which was the original reading needs to be made on the basis of internal criteria. Metzger cites several factors; the most weighty is that the notion of *first fruits* (*aparchēn*) often occurs elsewhere in Paul's letters. Most likely, therefore, Paul here testifies that the Thessalonian congregation has been chosen by God as *first fruits* showing the promise of an abundant harvest yet to come.

For more on textual analysis, see Metzger, 1971; Ewert, 1983.

EPISTOLARY ANALYSIS Readers of 1 and 2 Thessalonians need to recognize that these are letters, not Gospels or essays or sermons. The fact that these are letters has implications for the process of interpreting these biblical texts. In epistolary analysis, the interpreter focuses on how the biblical writers use and adapt the standard letter-writing conventions of their day.

Formal studies of ancient letters have been made possible because of some dramatic discoveries of letters, mostly on papyri, preserved in the dry desert sands of Egypt. These studies reveal a standard format: the letter opening, a statement of thanksgiving or a health-wish, the letter body, and the letter closing. The following brief letter dated 154 B.C. illustrates this format (cited by Doty: 13):

> Serapion to his brothers Ptolemaeus and Apollonius greeting. If you are well, it would be excellent. I myself am well. I have made a contract with the daughter of Hesperus and intend to marry her in the month of Mesore. Please send me half a chous of oil. I have written to you to let you know. Goodbye. Year 28, Epeiph 21. Come for the wedding day, Apollonius.

Though short and to the point, this letter includes an opening, a health-wish, the main letter body consisting of an announcement and a request, and a closing. The fact that this letter has been adapted for a particular purpose is evident from the postscript, which invites one of the two brothers to come to the wedding!

Paul in his letter writing follows the prevailing epistolary patterns but shapes his letters so that they suit his specific pastoral intentions. This is also evident in 1 and 2 Thessalonians:

1. The Salutation: 1 Thess. 1:1 and 2 Thess. 1:1-2
The salutations with which the letter opens typically contain three elements: the name(s) of the sender or senders; the person or group to whom the letter is addressed; and the greeting.

In both of the letters to the church at Thessalonica, three senders are named: *Paul, Silvanus, and Timothy.* Unlike later letters, which include some further identifying information such as "an apostle of Christ Jesus" (1 Cor. 1:1) or "a servant of Jesus Christ" (Rom. 1:1), these earliest NT letters simply give the names of Paul and his missionary companions.

The greeting in contemporary Hellenistic letters is often limited to the word "greetings," or some other near equivalent to "hello" or ".hi." In 1 and 2 Thessalonians, Paul enlarges this usual opening greeting by means of two words which have rich theological significance for his converts: *grace* and *peace.* The simplest greeting in 1 Thess. 1:1 is elaborated in 2 Thess. 1:2 and in the later letters to note the source of *grace* and *peace: God the Father and the Lord Jesus Christ.*

2. The Thanksgiving Section: 1 Thess. 1:2-10 and 2 Thess. 1:3-12
In all of his letters except Galatians, Paul includes a thanksgiving section, which serves as the transition between the traditional letter opening and the main body of the letter. Contemporary Greek letters usually contained a wish for the good health of the recipients and/or an expression of thanks for health or prosperity. In Paul's letters, the thanksgiving section typically provides a general preview of some of the themes and concerns addressed in the

main letter body. For example, the triad in 1 Thess. 1:2-3 seems to announce the major themes of the letter: *work of faith, labor of love,* and *steadfastness of hope.* In 2 Thessalonians the thanksgiving section signals a shift of focus toward the themes of *steadfastness and faith* in the midst of the Thessalonians' afflictions (1:4) and an accompanying concern about *the righteous judgment of God* (1:5).

3. The Letter Body: 1 Thess. 2:1—5:22 and 2 Thess. 2:1—3:15

In the Hellenistic letter quoted above, after the customary opening and wish for good health, the writer turns to the main reason for his letter: to announce his upcoming wedding and to make a request. Similarly, Paul begins to address the primary issues after opening his letters with the salutation and thanksgiving. In epistolary analysis, this section of the letter is normally called the letter body.

Paul's pastoral and theological agenda and the needs of the churches largely determine the scope and content of the main body of his letters. The letter to Philemon and the epistle to the Romans respectively illustrate how brief (Philem. 8-22) and how extensive (Rom. 1:16—15:33) this part of the letter can be.

Most letters include a section of ethical exhortations and pastoral instructions. These can be regarded as part of the letter body, although some epistolary analyses put them into a separate category.

4. The Letter Closing: 1 Thess. 5:23-28 and 2 Thess. 3:16-18

Hellenistic letters regularly concluded with two or three conventional formulas: another health wish for the recipient of the letter, a word of farewell, and sometimes a word of greeting (Doty: 39).

Paul adapted these usual closings to his missionary concerns in relation to these fledgling churches. The situation in the congregation again shaped the content of this part of the letter. Following are some of the components in these letter closings, along with occurrences in the Thessalonian letters, or other examples lacking there:

Travel plans	Rom. 15:22-29
Wish-prayer, specifically a peace wish	1 Thess. 5:23; 2 Thess. 3:16
Commendation of fellow workers	Rom. 16:1-2
Prayer requests	1 Thess. 5:25
Greetings	Rom. 16:3-16; cf. 1 Thess. 5:26
Final instructions and exhortations	1 Thess. 5:27
Holy kiss	1 Thess. 5:26
Autographed greeting	2 Thess. 3:17
Benediction	1 Thess. 5:28; 2 Thess. 3:18

In sum, epistolary analysis directs the interpreter's attention to the particular medium of communication being employed in the ongoing interaction between the missionary pastors and their congregations. The letter serves as the medium for continuing a pastoral conversation when separated from their congregations. As apostle to the Gentiles, Paul adapted the letter form in effective ways to communicate pastorally both to churches he was instrumental in planting (such as at Thessalonica) and later to other churches as well (for example, at Rome). These letters came to be read more broadly in other churches and eventually were incorporated into the NT canon. For more epistolary analysis, see Roetzel: 59-71; Stowers; Doty.

GRAMMATICAL ANALYSIS　The reader seeks to determine what a given text actually communicates after establishing the original text (textual analysis) and noting ways in which the customary letter form has been pastorally adapted (epistolary analysis). A key step in this process involves the analysis of the syntax and grammar of the passage.

A sentence-flow diagram can often serve as a helpful window into the world of meaning conveyed by a particular biblical text. The Explanatory Notes in this commentary include sentence-flow diagrams for the section of 1 and 2 Thessalonians under discussion. Their purpose is to help the reader visualize the flow of thinking and the progression of the argumentation in each unit of text.

Ideally these sentence-flow diagrams should be based on the text as it was originally written. Since the NT was written in Greek, it is necessary to translate the text. Translations of the NT from the original Greek into the various English versions (whether NRSV, RSV, NIV, KJV, or any other) squeeze the message into English sentence structures, which differ somewhat from those employed in the Koine Greek of the NT. Any translation therefore introduces some subtle or more major changes in meaning. The translations of 1 and 2 Thessalonians in the sentence-flow diagrams in this commentary were done by the author. Most of these translations are rather literal, in order to present as much as possible the syntax and grammar of the original text. However, all translation also involves interpretation. For some passages, I have attempted to provide dynamically equivalent, less-literal readings.

The grammatical analysis employed in developing each sentence-flow diagram includes several steps. The first stage is to identify the main verb, its subject, and its object, if it has one. After noting the leading thought in the sentence, the second step involves identifying the modifiers (adjectives, adverbs, prepositional phrases, subordinate clauses) and showing how they are connected to the main verb or its subject or object. A final process requires the identification of coordinating conjunctions and other linking words to determine how they connect each part of the sentence with what precedes or follows it.

To illustrate this method, we turn to the thanksgiving section of 1 Thessalonians (1:2-10).

First, we identify the leading verb and its subject: *We give thanks* (one word in Greek). In the Greek, this verb is followed by the noun *God* in the dative case, usually translated with the English preposition *to*. The dominant thought of the whole thanksgiving section is, therefore:

We give thanks to God

Next we note the modifiers. In this case, no adjective or adjectival phrase or clause modifies the noun *God*. However, an adverb (*always*) and an adverbial phrase (*for all of you*) and then a series of three participial clauses (beginning with the participles *mentioning, remembering,* and *knowing*) modify the verb *we give thanks*. These connections are shown by means of lines, as follows:

Each participle also has an object, as the lines and arrows demonstrate. The participles *mentioning* and *remembering* also have adverbial modifiers.

A mild disclaimer may be in place here. Not all the modifiers have been identified as such in the sentence diagrams. For example, in the diagram above, *our, your,* and the phrases *of faith, of love,* and *of hope* all function as modifiers. These words and phrases all could be diagrammed accordingly. To keep the diagrams relatively simple and compact, I have chosen not to go into such detail.

The third stage calls for an examination of how the coordinating conjunctions connect the subsequent assertions to the leading statement. In 1 Thess. 1:5 the conjunction *for* introduces the narration of the events which evoke the missionaries' thanksgiving: the coming of the gospel to Thessalonica and the response of the Thessalonians to the gospel. A series of conjunctions link the narrative statements which tell this story. These conjunctions introduce statements which first depict the basis or grounds for thanksgiving and then provide explanations or state consequences. Instead of drawing lines to join these conjunctions to each other, the sentence-flow diagrams generally put them near the left margin on a line by themselves or wherever they fit in the flow of the argument.

1:2	*We give thanks to God . . .*	
1:5	*for*	Basis
	our gospel came . . .	
	just as	Explanation
	you know what kind of persons . . .	
1:6	*and*	Further explanation
	you became imitators . . .	
1:7	*so that*	Consequence
	you became an example . . .	
1:8	*for*	Explanation
	the word has sounded forth . . .	
	so that	Consequence
	we have no need to say anything . . .	
1:9	*for*	Explanation
	they report . . .	

For details, the reader is referred to the full sentence-flow diagrams included with the notes for 1 Thess. 1:5-10.

For more detailed discussion of grammatical analysis, see Schreiner: 77-126; Fee, 1993:65-80.

RHETORICAL ANALYSIS   Rhetoric, the art of oratorical persuasion and argumentation, flourished within the Greek empire and also in the Roman world in which the church emerged. Politicians, philosophers, and educators used their skills in oratory to move their audiences. Handbooks were written to describe differing approaches to this art. The fourth-century B.C. Greek philosopher Aristotle prepared a highly influential guidebook *On Rhetoric,* which organized the current knowledge of the art of persuasion for use in teaching and practicing effective speech.

Paul the diaspora Jew was raised in a Hellenized environment in which undoubtedly he frequently heard public speeches. Likely he also studied rhetoric. Accordingly, biblical scholars have increasingly given attention to the kind of rhetoric which Paul employs in his letters.

Three factors can shape the kind of persuasive strategy being employed by an orator or writer in the communication process: ethos, pathos, and logos. We define each of these briefly (adapted from Mack: 35-36) and give an example from 1 and 2 Thessalonians:

1. Ethos (the character of the speaker): Just to gain a hearing, the speaker needs to be perceived as trustworthy and knowledgeable. In 1 Thess. 2:1-12, Paul persuades the readers regarding his own credibility and implicitly urges them to imitate his model of faithfulness.

2. Pathos (affection of the audience): Knowledge of the audience, its convictions and mood, helps the orator to move them emotionally and cognitively. In 1 Thess. 2:17-20, Paul "plays to the audience," calling the believers in Thessalonica *our glory and joy.*

3. Logos (the context of the argument): The logic of the argument also needs to persuade the audience or readers. Letters like Romans display developed theological arguments. Yet this dimension is not missing in the Thessalonian correspondence. For example, in 2 Thess. 2:3-12, Paul and his companions enumerate a series of proofs indicating clearly that indeed *the day of the Lord* has not yet come.

Rhetorical analyses of Paul's letters have often tried to determine the genre of the rhetoric in a given letter. Three broad categories of rhetoric as outlined in the ancient handbooks are distinguished from each other: judicial, deliberative, and epideictic (ep-i-DĪK-tik: demonstrative). These distinctions can be characterized as follows (adapted from Mack: 34-35):

Judicial speech   occasion: a trial
                             time: past
                             audience: judge and jury
                             issue: fact and legality (Is one guilty or not?)
                             example: Galatians

Deliberative speech   occasion: a public debate
time: future
audience: critics in council or assembly
issue: expediency (Better to do this or that?)
example: 2 Thessalonians

Epideictic speech   occasion: memorial
time: present
audience: spectators
issue: question of honor (What are the grounds for
praise or blame?)
example: 1 Thessalonians

In our two letters, 1 Thessalonians employs epideictic rhetoric and 2 Thessalonians uses deliberative rhetoric (Jewett, 1986:71-72, 81-82). In 1 Thessalonians, Paul seems intent on persuading his readers to reaffirm and strengthen their present stance. Basically, the Thessalonian believers are on the right track. Jewett's rhetorical analysis of 1 Thessalonians sees the argument unfolding in the following way (Jewett, 1986:72-76):

Exordium (introduction)	1:1-5
Narratio (narration of grounds for thanksgiving)	1:6—3:13
Probatio (proofs, showing praiseworthy behavior in present, with encouragement to continue)	4:1—5:22
Peroratio (conclusion)	5:23-28

The tone and style of 2 Thessalonians are somewhat different. Jewett suggests that the emphasis on the obligation of thanksgiving (*we ought to give thanks*) in 1:3 and 2:13 conveys a sense of dissatisfaction and concern regarding developments in Thessalonica. Paul also confronts the aberrant eschatological teachings (2:2-3) and the lifestyle of *the unruly* (3:6-13) with the kind of vigor not found in the first letter. The rhetorical genre of 2 Thessalonians is, therefore, deliberative, since the writers are seeking to persuade the readers to take corrective action in the future (Jewett, 1986:81-82). Jewett outlines 2 Thessalonians along the following lines (82-85):

Exordium (introduction)	1:1-12
Partitio (identification of false teaching needing to be refuted)	2:1-2
Probatio (refutation of false teachings and proof of the truth)	2:3-3:5
Exhortatio (exhortations and instructions)	3:6-15
Peroratio (conclusion)	3:16-18

For more on using rhetorical analysis in the study of the Pauline epistles, see Mack; Jewett, 1986:63-87; Hughes; Schreiner: 31-36.

GENERAL BACKGROUND

APOCALYPTIC The term *apocalyptic* derives from the Greek word *apokalupsis*, meaning *revelation* or *unveiling*. It describes both a genre of literature and a theological mind-set. Even though Paul's letters cannot be described as apocalyptic literature, like Daniel in the OT or the Revelation of John in the NT, Paul's theology is shaped by Jewish apocalypticism.

Apocalyptic writings within the Jewish community often surfaced during times of national crisis, such as the Maccabean War (167-164 B.C.), the Roman conquest of Judea (63 B.C.), the Jewish War with Rome (A.D. 66-70), and experiences of persecution under emperor Domitian, A.D. 81-96. The theological themes featured in these writings also influenced other writings, including Paul's letters.

One of the characteristic features of apocalyptic thought is the dualistic doctrine of two ages: this present age is passing away, and the age to come is about to begin. Such dualism also manifests itself both in the way apocalyptic writings depict the inner personal struggles between good and evil and in their portrayal of the cosmic tug-of-war between God and Satan. However, writers of apocalyptic envision that in the end God and good will triumph over Satan and evil. In fact, history moves relentlessly toward the time when God will win the victory. The faithful therefore just need to be steadfast until the end. Through a future cataclysmic act of divine intervention, God will judge the wicked and vindicate the faithful.

We can illustrate this from a Jewish apocalypse roughly contemporary with the writings of the NT. In 2 Esdras, the divine messenger declares:

> This present world is not the end; the full glory does not remain in it; therefore those who were strong prayed for the weak. But the day of judgment will be the end of this age and the beginning of the immortal age to come, in which corruption has passed away, sinful indulgence has come to an end, unbelief has been cut off, and righteousness has increased and truth has appeared. (2 Esd. 7:112-114, Apocrypha)

The primary intention of 2 Esdras is to reassure the Jewish people, still reeling from the fall of Jerusalem and the destruction of the temple at the end of the Jewish War (A.D. 66-70). Despite present indications to the contrary, God is still in control, and justice will ultimately prevail.

In his letter to the Galatians, Paul describes his life-transforming experience on the way to Damascus as "a revelation (*apokalupsis*) of Jesus Christ" (Gal. 1:12; cf. 1:16). The opening greeting of the same letter depicts the impact of the death of Jesus Christ in apocalyptic terms: "who gave himself for our sins to set us free from the present evil age" (Gal. 1:4). On the basis of these and related texts, there is a growing consensus that Paul's theology derives to a significant extent from Jewish apocalyptic. NT scholar J. Christiaan Beker, who has helped to shape this consensus, can be cited to illustrate these conclusions concerning Paul's theology. In a book entitled *The Triumph of God*, Beker describes the significance of apocalyptic for Paul under two points:

> The significance of apocalyptic for Paul may be outlined as follows:
> 1. The enduring center of Paul's gospel is his conviction that Christ's death and resurrection have opened up a new future for the world. This

future will reach its climax when the reign and triumph of God are made manifest and the whole created order attains its wonderful perfection according to God's promises to Israel.

2. The apocalyptic framework of the gospel also corresponds to the manner in which Paul proclaims it. The gospel concerning the future reign of God is brought to expression in such a way that, analogous to the incarnation of God in Christ, it embodies itself in the concrete and varied circumstances of human life. In this way Paul enables his churches to discern already in the present time signs of God's future glory. Moreover, Paul's churches are empowered by God to participate in redemptive praxis in the world, which aims at preparing the whole creation for its future glory. (Beker, 1990:20)

According to Jewett, in Thessalonica Paul's apocalyptic message was interpreted by some radicals within the Christian community along the lines of the cult of the Cabiri. Within this particular mystery cult, the redeemer figure was expected to return to defend the rights of laborers and establish a realm of bliss and freedom (Jewett, 1986:176-178). If this reconstruction is correct, the millenarian radicalism of *the unruly* (2 Thess. 2:2-3; 3:6-13), though rooted in the apocalyptic expectation of the triumphant return of Christ, was significantly shaped by the mystery religions as well. *[Religions in the Greco-Roman World, p. 365.]*

ESCHATOLOGY   The word eschatology itself does not occur in the NT. It derives from a combination of two Greek words: *eschaton*, meaning *the last thing*, and *logos*, meaning *word* or *teaching*. Eschatology has therefore become a technical theological term for the doctrine concerning final events. Related themes include the *parousia* or coming of Christ, the resurrection of the dead, the judgment, and final rewards and punishment.

However, biblical eschatology deals with more than the future or the end of history or an otherworldly realm beyond this life. Jesus' preaching and teaching centers on the imminence of the "kingdom of God" (Mark 1:15). This "kingdom," though present (Luke 17:20-21), still remains future: "Your kingdom come" (Matt. 6:10; Luke 11:2).

Much of Paul's teaching reflects this eschatological tension between the "already" and the "not yet" of the arrival of God's kingdom. According to Paul, believers find themselves living within the dynamic interplay of the present and the future. A key text in this regard is 1 Thess. 2:12, where Paul and his partners urge their readers to let the future (God's *kingdom and glory*) shape how they live in the present ("Kingdom of God" in TBC for 1 Thess. 2:1-12).

Biblical texts such as 1 and 2 Thessalonians are often interpreted in support of *dispensational* theology. The details vary, but generally a dispensationalist view of the end-times envisions a sequence of the following events:

• The rapture of the church, both the living and the dead in Christ, brings the present age to a close.
• Continuing residents of the earth experience the great tribulation, a seven-year period when Satan and his emissary the antichrist oppress Israel and the nations.

• However, some premillennialists put the rapture after the great tribulation. In this view, the church lives through the tribulation.

• The church returns to earth with Christ, thereby setting the stage for the conversion of Israel and a thousand-year reign of Christ from Jerusalem (the millennium; cf. Rev. 20:1-4).

• At the end of the millennium, Satan and his followers join in a final revolt against God, and the forces of evil are decisively defeated.

• Then comes the final judgment, followed by eternal life for believers and eternal punishment for nonbelievers.

Dispensationalism constitutes one expression of the theological and social phenomenon called millennialism. Its followers typically try to correlate current historical events with a presumed timetable for the end of history and the return of Christ. In addition to the *premillennial* scenario outlined above (Christ's return *before* the millennium), there are various *post*millennial constructs of the future (Christ's return *after* the millennium). Essentially, postmillennialists expect the church to remain on earth during the millennium, when the reign of Christ will increasingly lead to peace and justice. At the end of this time, Christ will return in glory.

Given the various subtle interpretive moves required to sustain both the pre- and postmillennial positions, many Christians have chosen to position themselves with *amillennialism* (*no* literal millennium). In this understanding of biblical eschatology, the reign of Christ began with his initial coming, and the millennium symbolizes that whole present interim period during which believers who realize both the "already" and the "not yet" character of Christ's reign await its final consummation.

Proponents of premillennialism (likely the dominant view among evangelicals in North America) also acknowledge that 1 and 2 Thessalonians do not expressly portray this particular chronological sequence of end-time events. For example, D. Edmond Hiebert, who holds the premillennial view, says:

The view one accepts will be determined largely by doctrinal and exegetical presuppositions. (Hiebert: 218).

With reference to the timing of the rapture, Hiebert pleads for an attitude of sincere openness toward contrary views:

Equally devout and sincere students of Scripture will doubtless continue to hold different views on the question of the time of the rapture. Advocates of their respective views must avoid attributing unworthy motives or insincerity in exegesis to each other because they do not agree. (219)

Hiebert also makes a further plea regarding efforts to establish a chronology of end-time events:

It is appropriate and proper that diligent efforts should be given to the study of the evidence for a chronology of end-time events. But these efforts must not be allowed to lead to a preoccupation with uncertain details so that the sanctifying power of this blessed hope for daily living is lost sight of. (219)

Hiebert's concluding admonition harmonizes with the pastoral character of Paul's eschatological teaching in 1 and 2 Thessalonians. Holy living and faithful engagement in the mission of the church need to take priority. Efforts at deciphering chronological clues in Scripture can sidetrack the church from the mission which God desires to accomplish in the world.
Recommended for further study: Ewert, 1980.

HISTORICAL AND POLITICAL CONTEXT The Thessalonian correspondence should be read in the light of what can be known about the political history of Thessalonica. Political developments in the rest of the Greco-Roman world must also be considered. We must reckon with Paul's own background as a diaspora Jew, the existence of a Jewish community in Thessalonica, and the presence of a Jewish minority in the young Thessalonian congregation. In addition, we must give some attention to how this political context would be understood by Paul and by the Jewish population in this community. This essay is designed to sketch the historical and political developments as they impinge on our interpretation of 1 and 2 Thessalonians.

Thessalonica emerged as a politically prominent city during the Greek empire. During the period of Roman dominance, this city grew in its political importance. In what follows, we focus on some key developments locally, provincially, and internationally. These are selected with particular attention to those events deemed especially significant to Christians, both those (like Paul) whose roots lie within Judaism and those Gentiles who *turned toward God away from idols to serve the living and true God and to await his Son from heaven* (1 Thess. 1:9-10).

The Greek Empire 336 B.C. The city of Thessalonica and the province of Macedonia feature prominently in the dramatic emergence of the Greek empire in the fourth century B.C. In 336 B.C., Alexander the Great, the son of Philip of Macedon, became king of Macedonia after his father was assassinated. Within a period of five years, Alexander and his armies gained supremacy over the Persian empire. Hellenistic culture and Greek religions were introduced to the subject peoples through the establishment of Greek cities throughout the Mediterranean region, including Palestine. In 323 B.C. Alexander died and the empire was divided among his generals.

316 B.C. One of Alexander's generals, Cassander, founded the city of Thessalonica and named it in honor of his wife, Thessalonike, the stepsister of Alexander. The earlier city, Therme, and about twenty-five other towns or villages in the area became incorporated into this new city. The Gulf of Thessalonica provided a fine natural harbor for this city, thereby assuring convenient links for commercial, cultural, and military traffic.

167 B.C. The region of Palestine had also become part of the Greek empire after Alexander's armies won a crucial battle over the Persians at Issus (near Tarsus of Cilicia) in 333 B.C. Greek cities with their theaters, gymnasiums, and schools introduced Hellenistic ideas and practices among the Jews and other peoples in Galilee, Samaria, and Judea. Eventually the encroachment of Greek culture and religion into the Jewish way of life provoked a violent reaction. The Maccabean Revolt, which began in 167 B.C. in Palestine, significantly shaped the collective psyche of the Jewish people, including those living in the diaspora. This revolutionary movement began after the Seleucid king, Antiochus IV Epiphanes of Syria (175-164 B.C.), introduced a policy forcing the Jews and other subject peoples to become Helle-nized. This is how the author of 1 Maccabees describes the king's command:

> The king sent letters by messengers to Jerusalem and the towns of Ju-dah; he directed them to follow customs strange to the land, to forbid burnt offerings and sacrifices and drink offerings in the sanctuary, to pro-fane sabbaths and festivals, to defile the sanctuary and the priests, to build altars and sacred precincts and shrines for idols, to sacrifice swine and other unclean animals, and to leave their sons uncircumcised.
> (1 Macc. 1:44-48)

A short time later, according to 1 Maccabees, the king's officers "erected a desolating sacrilege on the altar of burnt offering. They also built altars in the surrounding towns of Judah" (1:54). These provocative actions finally in-cited open revolt, led by the priest Mattathias and his sons from the village of Modein (1 Macc. 2). This uprising eventually succeeded in establishing a peri-od of relative independence for the Jewish people.

Through the festival of Hannukah, the OT book of Daniel, and 1 and 2 Maccabees, the memory of this liberation movement remained alive. This story continued to shape Jewish self-awareness, despite the fact that the kingdom which the Maccabeans established ended in 64 B.C., when the Ro-man general Pompey conquered Syria, including Palestine. Diaspora Jews, including those in Thessalonica, also remembered this event.

The Roman Empire   Ever since the third century B.C., Rome had become increasingly ascendant in the Mediterranean region. Eventually the Roman empire absorbed all of the area previously ruled by the Greeks.

146 B.C.   Rome came to dominate both Macedonia and Achaia by about 148 B.C. In 146 Macedonia became a Roman province, with Thes-salonica as its capital and the center of Roman administration in this region.

64 B.C.   Syria, which included Palestine, came under Roman control. During the next year, general Pompey arrived in Jerusalem and even entered the holy of holies in the temple (Josephus, *Ant.* 14.54-79 [14.4.1-5]). A la-ment by the pious Jew who writes the Psalms of Solomon clearly demon-strates the horror felt by the Jewish community in response to this desecra-tion of the temple:

> Arrogantly the sinner broke down the strong walls with a battering ram and you did not interfere. Gentile foreigners went up to your places for sacrifice; they arrogantly trampled it with their sandals. (Ps. of Sol. 2:1-2, from Charlesworth, 2:651-652)

42 B.C.   During the Roman Civil War and before the decisive battle of Philippi, the city of Thessalonica publicly supported Mark Antony and Oc-tavian, who defeated Brutus (cf. Shakespeare, *Julius Caesar*). As a conse-quence of this support, Thessalonica in 42 B.C. gained the status of a free city, which included immunity from the payment of tribute and the right to es-tablish its own city government. City officials called "politarchs" (Acts 17:6, NRSV note) were named to govern the city. To cultivate continued good re-lationships with Rome, city officials initiated games in honor of Roman vic-tors, minted coins commemorating Roman emperors, and promoted the civ-ic cult. *[Philosophies, p. 364; Religions in the Greco-Roman World, p. 365.]*

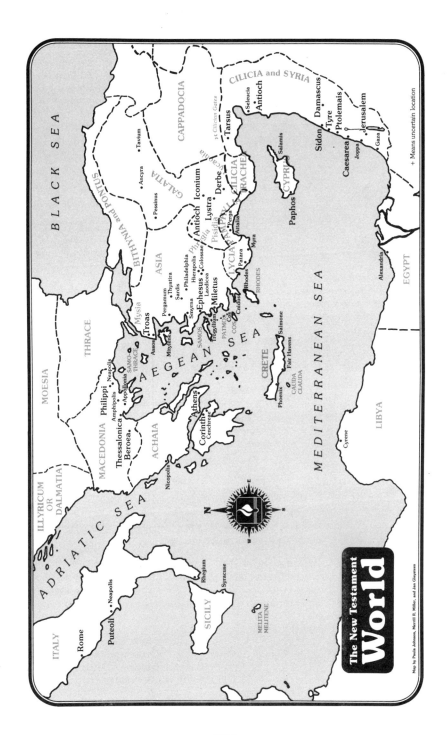

The New Testament World

Map by Paula Johnson, Merrill R. Miller, and Jan Gleysteen

+ Means uncertain location

359

27 B.C.—A.D. 14 Octavian, later renamed Caesar Augustus, reigned as Roman emperor when Jesus was born (Luke 2:1). A temple of Caesar was built in Thessalonica during his reign. Coins acclaiming Julius Caesar as a god were minted in Thessalonica in about 27 B.C. During this time, the head of Augustus displaced the head of the Greek god Zeus on coins.

A.D. 14–37 Tiberius Caesar ruled as emperor when Jesus conducted his ministry (Luke 3:1) and Pontius Pilate was governor of Judea (A.D. 26-36). Tiberius actively discouraged the cult of the living emperor. In fact, he did not accept divine honors when they were extended to him.

A.D. 37-41 The reign of Gaius Caligula. Up to this point, the emperor was deified only after his death (Julius), or divine honors were accepted with a degree of modesty during the emperor's lifetime (Augustus), or deification and divine honors were resisted (Tiberius). Gaius, however, pursued divinity with vigor and passion. Josephus reports that "Gaius Caesar displayed such insolence at his accession to power that he wished to be thought of and addressed as a god" (*War* 2.184 [2.10.1]). Josephus goes on to say that Gaius ordered the Syrian governor Petronius to proceed to Jerusalem with an army to install statues of himself in the temple.

From Philo, a contemporary Jew (born ca. 13 B.C.) from Alexandria in Egypt, we have vivid testimony concerning how much this development upset the Jewish people, both in Palestine and throughout the Jewish diaspora. Philo participated in a delegation which sought to intervene directly with the emperor. From *The Embassy to Gaius*, we cite some emotion-laden excerpts. First, the quotation of a statement by King Herod Agrippa I (A.D. 40-44) concerning the depth of the diaspora Jews' emotional ties to Jerusalem and the temple:

> While she, as I have said, is my native city, she is also the mother city not of one country Judaea but of most of the others in virtue of the colonies sent out at various times to the neighbouring lands Egypt, Phoenicia, the part of Syria called the Hollow and the rest as well and the lands lying far apart, Pamphylia, Cilicia, most of Asia up to Bithynia and the corners of Pontus, similarly also into Europe, Thessaly, Boeotia, Macedonia, Aetolia, Attica, Argos, Corinth and most of the best parts of Peloponnese. (*Embassy* 281)

When news arrived about Gaius's plan to erect a statue of himself in the Jerusalem temple, the people in Alexandria cry out,

> Our temple is lost, Gaius has ordered a colossal statue to be set up within the inner sanctuary dedicated to himself under the name of Zeus. (188)

When finally Philo and the other ambassadors from Alexandria manage to present their case to the emperor, they are dismissed as fools. However, their trust in God prevails, even during the mockery of a hearing:

> Since we all the time expected nothing else but death, in our deep distress our souls had passed from within us and went forth to supplicate the true God that he should restrain the wrath of the pretender to that name. (366)

Philo does not describe the eventual outcome of this crisis. Josephus, however, reports that Petronius did not implement Gaius's order. Before he could punish his deputy for disobeying the order, Gaius himself was assassinated (*War* 2.199-204 [2.10.5—11.1]). News of this close call traveled quickly to centers throughout the Mediterranean world where there were Jewish populations. This would undoubtedly have included Thessalonica.

A.D. 41-54 The reign of Claudius Caesar. Claudius reversed the oppressive policy of his predecessor Gaius. He returned to the form of the emperor cult established by Augustus. We illustrate by quoting from Claudius's edict:

> Kings Agrippa and Herod, my dearest friends, having petitioned me to permit the same privileges to be maintained for the Jews throughout the empire under the Romans as those in Alexandria enjoy, I very gladly consented, not merely in order to please those who petitioned me, but also because in my opinion the Jews deserve to obtain their request on account of their loyalty and friendship to the Romans. In particular, I did so because I hold it right that not even Greek cities should be deprived of these privileges, seeing that they were in fact guaranteed for them in the time of the divine Augustus. It is right, therefore, that the Jews throughout the whole world under our sway should also observe the customs of their fathers without let or hindrance. I enjoin upon them also by these presents to avail themselves of their kindness in a more reasonable spirit, and not to set at nought the beliefs about the gods held by other people but to keep their own laws. (Josephus, *Ant.* 19.287-291 [19.5.3])

Even though Jews and other religious groups were granted more freedom than they experienced during the tenure of Gaius Caligula, Claudius also let it be known that there would be limits to such tolerance. As seen in the last sentence of the above quotation, Claudius specifically urges the Jews to be tolerant toward others and not to test the limits of their own privileges. We can readily detect a degree of imperial edginess toward the Jewish populations in the empire.

From the Jewish side, especially in Palestine, restlessness about Roman rule and outrage at any imperial claims of divinity continued to create instability. Josephus recounts that when some young men erected an image of Caesar in the Jewish synagogue of Dora, possibly as a prank, governor Petronius of Syria, wishing to avoid giving the Jews any occasion to proceed with desperate measures, acted quickly to denounce these young men and to remind them of the edict of Claudius (*Ant.* 19.300-310 [19.6.3]).

Several other crises erupted in Judea during Claudius's reign, when Cumanus served as procurator in Judea (A.D. 48-52). We mention one which could have been fresh in Paul's mind when in A.D. 50 he writes concerning the Judeans, that *wrath has come upon them until the end* (1 Thess. 2:16). An obscene gesture by a Roman soldier, stationed in Jerusalem during the Feast of Unleavened Bread, led to an open riot (*War* 2.223-227 [2.12.1]; *Ant.* 20.105-112 [20.5.3]). When Cumanus sent for troop reinforcements, panic ensued.

When these troops poured into the porticoes, the Jews were seized with uncontrollable panic and turned to fly from the Temple courts into the city. So violently did the dense mass struggle to escape through the exits that they were trodden underfoot and, crushing one another, more than thirty thousand people died. Thus the Feast ended in total distress to the nation and mourning in every household. (Josephus, *War* 2.227 [2.12.1])

Even if one allows for some exaggeration by Josephus (his parallel account in *Ant.* 20.112 [20.5.3] estimates the number of deaths at twenty thousand), this was a catastrophe of gigantic proportions. This disaster could easily have led to the deaths of members of diaspora Jewish families on pilgrimage in Jerusalem for the Feast.

Several other catastrophes to strike Judeans might have had a similar impact on diaspora Jews. One was the insurrection led by Theudas in A.D. 44-46 (*Ant.* 20.97-99 [20.5.1]; cf. Acts 5:36). The other was the famine in Judea in A.D. 46-47 (*Ant.* 20.101 [20.5.2]; cf. Acts 11:28). These catastrophes could also have been interpreted as expressions of divine wrath (Jewett, 1986:37-38).

Another event during Claudius's reign undoubtedly sent shock waves throughout the Jewish communities around the Mediterranean. Claudius issued an edict expelling Jews from Rome. This expulsion is mentioned by Luke in an aside about Paul's initial meeting with Priscilla and Aquila:

There [Corinth] he [Paul] found a Jew named Aquila, a native of Pontus, who had recently come from Italy with his wife Priscilla, because Claudius had ordered all Jews to leave Rome. (Acts 18:2)

The Roman historian Suetonius also alludes to Claudius's decision to banish the Jews from Rome:

Since the Jews constantly made disturbances at the instigation of Chrestus, he expelled them from Rome. (*Claudius* 25.4)

This event has generally been dated in A.D. 49, based on the testimony of the historian Orosius, who refers to "the expulsion of Jews by Claudius in his ninth year" (Orosius, *History* 7.6.15, cited by Murphy-O'Connor: 130). Some scholars question Orosius' accuracy and posit a date earlier in Claudius's reign, A.D. 41 (Luedemann: 164-171; Murphy-O'Connor: 130-140). However, we continue to locate this event in A.D. 49 because of the more congenial attitude toward the Jews in the edict earlier in Claudius's reign (cited above), the alignment of Acts 18:2 with the historical references in Suetonius and Orosius, and the further corroborative data regarding Gallio (Acts 18:12 and an inscription at Delphi; Faw, 1993:209; Jewett, 1979:36-38).

Likely "Chrestus" in Suetonius's statement means Christ. What kinds of disturbances were instigated because of Christ? The Jewish communities in Rome were divided over whether to regard Jesus as the Messiah. There might also have been differing judgments on the extent to which the Jewish synagogues in Rome should identify with the growing Zealot movement in Palestine and its mood of rebellion (cf. Rom. 13:1-7). Either or both of these issues could possibly have become contentious enough within the Jewish population in Rome to provoke the Emperor Claudius to expel the Jews from the city.

A.D. 54-68 During the reign of emperor Nero, the Zealots and other revolutionaries opposed to Roman rule in Palestine began their open revolt. The Jewish War of A.D. 66-70 culminated in the devastation of the city of Jerusalem and the desecration and destruction of the Jewish temple.

Literature dealing with the historical and political context is voluminous. The above material is based on articles and books such as Donfried, 1985; Bruce, 1977: ch. 21; Hendrix; Jewett, 1986: ch. 7; Puskas: ch. 1; Koester, 1: sect. 1, 6.

JUDAISM IN THE DIASPORA Paul was a diaspora Jew. According to the story in Acts, Paul gave a speech in Jerusalem detailing his origins:

> I am a Jew, born in Tarsus in Cilicia, but brought up in this city at the feet of Gamaliel, educated strictly according to our ancestral law, being zealous for God. (Acts 22:3)

This opening I-statement deftly depicts some of the realities facing Jews living in the diaspora. Jews who were more or less permanently settled outside Palestine confronted the perennial question of when to adapt to the surrounding dominant culture and when to maintain the boundaries prescribed by the law.

Meeks estimates that in the first century A.D., some five to six million Jews were living in the diaspora. This movement of the Jewish people to various lands in the Mediterranean region came as a result of both political factors, such as the deportations during the Babylonian exile of the sixth century B.C., and economic forces, especially the search for commercial opportunities. Meeks asserts:

> Consequently there was a substantial Jewish population in virtually every town of any size in the lands bordering the Mediterranean. Estimates run from 10 to 15 percent of the total population of a city—in the case of Alexandria, even higher. (Meeks: 34)

These Jews, like some other immigrant populations, typically resided in neighborhoods among their own kind of people. Unlike some groups, however, the Jews exhibited a cohesiveness and solidarity which sometimes created problems for both local officials and the Roman imperial authorities.

Typically, synagogues served as rallying places for Jewish communities, not only for the study of Scripture and for prayer, but also for a variety of social gatherings. No extrabiblical or archaeological evidence for the existence of a synagogue in Thessalonica has been found. However, Luke testifies that first-century Thessalonica had a synagogue and that Paul began his Thessalonian ministry there (Acts 17:1).

In synagogues of the diaspora, the scriptural readings generally came from the Greek version known as the Septuagint (LXX). According to a pious story in the Letter of Aristeas, the Hebrew Bible was translated into Greek in Egypt during the reign of Ptolemy Philadelphus (284-247 B.C.) by seventy-two scholars who completed their work in seventy-two days. The emergence of a Greek translation of the Hebrew Scriptures in Egypt testifies to the fact that Jews in the diaspora were gradually becoming assimilated into the Hellenistic culture. They were losing touch with Hebrew and needing the Scriptures in Greek for worship and study.

Among diaspora Jews, the developments which preceded the catastrophe of A.D. 70 created significant internal pressures, especially on questions related to associations with Gentiles. As apostle to the Gentiles, Paul was particularly suspect on this score, since he had ongoing contact with Gentile communities. Formerly also a zealous persecutor of the church (Gal. 1:13-14), Paul himself faced persecution at the hands of messianic Jews who yielded to Zealot pressure to hold the line on Torah-observance (Jewett, 1970-71:204-206).

PHILOSOPHIES Among the educated within the Greco-Roman world, philosophy often played a more crucial role than religion. During the Greek and Roman periods, several philosophical schools exercised considerable influence, not only on the educated elite but in a popularized form among the general populace as well. The letters of Paul show that he was familiar with several of these philosophies. Luke's account of Paul's ministry in Athens includes a reference to his dialogue with Stoics and Epicureans (Acts 17:18).

In this essay, we note the main characteristics of three of these philosophies: Epicureanism, Stoicism, and Cynicism. We also comment specifically about how Cynicism has shaped what Paul and his companions say about the motivations and strategy for their mission in Thessalonica.

Epicureanism was founded by Epicurus (e-pi-KYUR-us), who lived in Athens (342-270 B.C.). Although the Epicureans did not deny the existence of gods, they regarded any gods that might exist as irrelevant to human life. It is up to each individual to achieve happiness here on earth, since death marks the end. Pleasure is the chief goal of life. However, such pleasure is not hedonism but freedom from disturbance. A quote from Epicurus illustrates this conviction:

> By pleasure we mean the absence of pain in the body and of trouble in the soul. . . . It is sober reasoning, searching out the grounds of every choice and avoidance, and banishing those beliefs through which the great tumults take possession of the soul. (from L. Martin: 38)

The epithet, "Let us eat, drink and be merry, for tomorrow we die" (cf. 1 Cor. 15:32; Luke 12:19-20), is popularly attributed to the Epicureans. However, this is a caricature rather than an accurate portrayal of the main thrust of this philosophy. When the missionaries advocate the quiet life (1 Thess. 4:11-12), they articulate a perspective which has some similarities to Epicurean philosophy. However, the emphasis on being God-taught (4:9) clearly differentiates the Christian ethic from Epicureanism, in which Epicurus claimed to be self-taught (Malherbe, 1987:101-106).

Stoicism originated with Zeno of Citium (Cyprus; 336-263 B.C.), who taught in the Stoa Poikile, a public hall in Athens that gave its name to this school. Stoics viewed the universe as an ordered and closed system, centered in the "logos," eternal principle, reason, or purpose. Since a spark of this universal law can be found within all of nature, the human task is to live in harmony with it. Each person must listen to the voice within (cf. Rom. 2:14-16, God has written his law on the hearts of all). The inner self is the true self. Everything else, including the body, is really of no ultimate importance. Therefore, in cultivating the inner life, a person has to ignore external attractions or distractions. Paul's awareness of Stoic thought likely comes through when he says, "I have learned to be content with whatever I have" (Phil. 4:11). Unlike the Stoics, however, Paul finds his inner peace through Christ.

Cynicism in Thessalonica evoked more of a response from Paul than either Epicureanism or Stoicism. This philosophical movement was rooted in the life and teaching of Diogenes of Sinope (ca. 400-325 B.C.). The name came from Diogenes being called *kuōn* (dog) and his followers *kunikoi* (doglike), Cynics, because he and his followers manifested certain kinds of shameless behavior in public. Cynics were wandering moralists with a lifestyle of simplicity and voluntary poverty. They tried to attain a sense of detachment from society through such activities as using coarse language, wearing filthy clothes, and performing natural acts such as sexual intercourse in public (cf. 1 Thess. 4:5). Their public lectures and discussions were characterized by boldness of speech (cf. 1 Thess. 2:2). Finances often came from their followers or through public begging (cf. 1 Thess. 2:5).

In Thessalonica, Paul took steps to differentiate himself from some of these traveling philosophers, as seen in 1 Thess. 2:1-12. Malherbe has shown that in this passage, Paul's language strikingly parallels how the orator and philosopher Dio Chrysostom (A.D. 40-ca. 120) describes the ideal Cynic:

> But to find a man who with purity and without guile speaks with a philosopher's boldness, not for the sake of glory, nor making false pretensions for the sake of gain, but who stands ready out of good will and concern for his fellowman, if need be, to submit to ridicule and the uproar of the mob—to find such a man is not easy, but rather the good fortune of a very lucky city, so great is the dearth of noble, independent souls, and such the abundance of flatterers, charlatans and sophists. (Malherbe, 1989:45)

From Dio Chrysostom, therefore, we learn that within the Cynic philosopher group itself, at least some members recognized the need to distinguish between the good and the bad preachers of Cynic morality.

For more on these and other Greco-Roman philosophies, see Roetzel: 38-44; Ferguson: 275-302; Malherbe, 1989:11-24, 35-48; L. Martin: 35-40.

RELIGIONS IN THE GRECO-ROMAN WORLD In addition to Judaism and Christianity, numerous religions sought adherents in first-century Thessalonica. After a comment about the status of traditional religions, we examine several mystery religions whose impact can be discerned in our reading of the epistles to the Thessalonians. We will also explore more fully the nature of the civic cult.

Traditional religions, which featured Zeus and the other Greek and Roman gods and goddesses who supposedly inhabited Mt. Olympus, had lost some of their earlier appeal by the first century A.D. Some of the Thessalonian converts may be among those who have grown disenchanted with these religions. Paul and his partners are able to report: *You turned toward God away from idols* (1 Thess. 1:9). From a Jewish perspective, of course, the category of "idol worship" would apply equally well to other forms of religious expression in the Hellenistic world.

Mystery religions increasingly attracted the allegiance of the people. Many of these mystery religions were introduced by artisans and tradespersons to geographical areas where they traveled on business. One result of this mobility was that religions from various regions of the Mediterranean intermingled with each other. The cult of Serapis in ancient Thessalonica, for example, has origins in the worship of Isis and Osiris in Egypt.

Several common characteristics of these religious movements can be noted. They feature a myth, usually about a dying and rising deity. Through rites of initiation, individuals were thought to be brought into a special relationship with the god or goddess. The central concern of the mysteries was to gain personal salvation through direct identification with the deity. By means of regular ceremonies, the myth was ritually reenacted by the initiates within the cult. In some mystery religions, sexual union in a cultic setting such as a temple promised ecstatic identification with the god or goddess.

Two mystery religions in Thessalonica have special significance for our understanding of the Thessalonian epistles. The cult of Dionysus (also called Bacchus) was known, among other things, for its sexual symbolism and for its wild and frenzied celebrations, at which wine flowed freely. Paul may have the sensually provocative Dionysian orgies in mind when exhorting the Thessalonians to maintain concerning sexual morality (1 Thess. 4:3-8) and when using the metaphor of drunkenness to depict the risk of spiritual laxity (1 Thess. 5:5-7).

Another mystery religion, the cult of the Cabiri, featured similar orgiastic rituals. Its foundational myth tells how one Cabirus was murdered and his head was wrapped in a royal purple cloth for burial at the foot of Mount Olympus. Later, this Cabirus figure returns to life to assist manual laborers, perform magic for the needy, free slaves, and offer sexual fulfillment. Jewett suggests that, as the Cabiri became increasingly absorbed into the civic cult in Thessalonica, the working class in that city became disenchanted with the cult of the Cabiri and were receptive to the Christian gospel. He sees striking parallels between that dying-and-rising Cabirus figure and the apocalyptic picture of Christ as proclaimed by Paul. This made it easier for disillusioned devotees of Cabirus to accept the gospel of Jesus Christ (Jewett, 1986:126-132).

Civic cults in first-century Thessalonica arose from historical developments during the Greek and Roman periods and events that shaped this city. *[Historical and Political Context, p. 357.]* Because of well-placed political support for the winning side in a major battle during the Roman Civil War, Thessalonica was granted the freedom to run its own civic affairs (42 B.C.). However, the city officials in Thessalonica also found it politically expedient actively to cultivate the goodwill of the Roman emperors, especially since Thessalonica in 146 B.C. had been made capital of the Roman province of Macedonia. Through games, monuments, a temple of Caesar, the minting of coins, and various public rituals, the city politicians ("politarchs," Acts 17:6, NRSV note) endeavored to cultivate and maintain the enthusiastic allegiance of the population toward the Roman imperial power. Local officials wanted to keep the population in harmony with the aims of the empire and help them identify dissidents. Hence, they likely administered an oath of allegiance similar to one used elsewhere in the empire during the reign of Caesar Augustus:

I swear . . . that I will support Caesar Augustus, his children and descendants, throughout my life, in word, deed and thought, . . . that in whatso-
ever concerns them I will spare neither body nor soul nor life nor children, . . . that whenever I see or hear of anything being said, planned or
done against them I will report it, . . . and whomsoever they regard as enemies I will attack and pursue with arms and the sword by land and by
sea. . . . (from Donfried, 1985:343)

Traditional Greek and Roman religions effectively integrated politics and
religion. With the decline of the traditional religions, there was pressure on
the mystery religions and other religious groups to conform to the civic cult
and to cultivate popular support for the emperor and the empire. As already
mentioned, Jewett thinks that the cult of the Cabiri, which had been popular
with the working class, became increasingly co-opted into the civil religious
life of the city of Thessalonica, with the result that these lower-class people
looked elsewhere in their longing for liberation (Jewett, 1986:131-132).

A central tenet among the rituals of the civic cult was the exaltation of the
emperor. Even when the emperor himself resisted deification, local and provincial leaders found that their own political goals were furthered through
promoting the emperor cult. The following announcement of birthday celebrations for Caesar Augustus illustrates this tendency:

Whereas Providence that orders all our lives has in her display of concern
and generosity in our behalf adorned our lives with the highest good: Augustus, whom she has filled with virtue for the benefit of humanity, and
has in her beneficence granted us and those who will come after us a Sav-
ior who has made war to cease and shall put everything in peaceful order.
. . . (adapted from Hendrix: 114)

Hendrix comments about a significant religious shift which took place in
Thessalonica during the first centuries B.C. and A.D.:

In this period, the city's assembly began to issue many of its decrees no
longer on its own but in association with an official Roman group. "Roma
and Roman Benefactors" were added to the cultic patrons of the gymnasiums, the city cult of "the gods." In the pecking order of civic religious in-
stitutions, the priesthood of "the gods" descended gradually until it dis-
appeared entirely in the second century CE. Ascending in the pecking order was a new civic religious office established at the city in the last quarter of the first century BCE, a "priest and agonothete [judge, director] of
the Imperator Caesar Augustus son of god." (Hendrix: 114-115)

When we grasp this background of the developing civic cult in Thessalonica, with its decrees, oaths, temples, games, rituals, and monuments, we
find it easier to understand certain events behind the epistles to the Thessalonians. While the city officials trumpeted the *peace and security* of the Roman empire, Paul and his associates classified the forces of the empire on the
side of *darkness, sleep, drunkenness,* and *wrath* (1 Thess. 5:1-11). As Luke
puts it, while the city officials sought to administer "the decrees of the
emperor," the missionaries proclaimed the subversive message of "another
king named Jesus" (Acts 17:6-7).

The **NT letters** show Paul and his companions boldly adapting political language to describe the believers' hope in the future *coming* (*parousia*) of Christ and their anticipated *meeting* (*apantēsis*) with *the Lord* (*kurios*) *in the air* (1 Thess. 4:13-18). The Thessalonian readers would recognize the word *parousia* as signifying an official visit of the emperor or some other official, *apantēsis* as referring to the citizens' formal meeting with the dignitary along the parade route, and *kurios* as one of the formal titles used for the emperor.

Once we recognize the subversive nature of this gospel, which calls on the people to acknowledge Jesus Christ as Lord, we can comprehend why believers suffered persecution (1 Thess. 1:6; 2:14; 3:4; 2 Thess. 1:4, 6). We can also understand why the missionaries used cryptic code language when they wrote about the empire and the emperor: *the oppression* (*to katechon*) and *the oppressor* (*ho katechōn*, 2 Thess. 2:1-12). Possibly the mention of *the mystery of lawlessness* (2 Thess. 2:7) can be traced to the fact that emperor worship had been integrated into the rituals of some of the mystery cults in Thessalonica.

For more on Greco-Roman religions in first-century Thessalonica and generally, see Donfried, 1993:12-27; Jewett, 1986:126-132; Roetzel: 19-46; Koester, 1:164-204, 362-389; L. Martin.

SOCIAL AND ECONOMIC CONTEXT In this essay we focus on a few of the social and economic factors which influenced the emergence and life of the Christian community in Thessalonica: the urban situation, the work environment, and the household.

As apostle to the Gentiles, Paul targeted the cities of the Greco-Roman world, including Antioch of Syria, Antioch of Pisidia, Ephesus, Philippi, Thessalonica, Athens, Corinth, and Rome. These major cities on Paul's itinerary were linked by a system of roads and marine navigation routes. Artisans and business people traveled widely by both land and sea.

Situated on the Via Egnatia, a major east-west Roman road (built ca. 130 B.C.), and adjacent to an excellent natural harbor on the Thermaic Gulf of the Aegean Sea, Thessalonica became a major trade and commercial center. Among the many travelers to this ancient Macedonian city was the artisan (Acts 18:3, tentmaker) and missionary Paul.

Studies of the urban centers of that time have shown that generally the residential areas were crowded, but up to one-fourth of the land space was devoted to general public use (Meeks: 28-29). Though most of the people in these cities endured crowded conditions at home, they could enjoy the more spacious public areas, which they shared with their neighbors and with travelers. In this kind of environment, news or rumor spread rapidly, and riots and public uprisings erupted easily. When Paul's preaching in Thessalonica is interpreted as being "contrary to the decrees of the emperor" (Acts 17:7), a crowd gathers spontaneously in the marketplace, and hostilities soon break out against the missionaries and their followers.

People with common ethnic origins or socioeconomic characteristics tended to settle in particular neighborhoods among their own kind of people. Likely Thessalonica had a Jewish quarter. Trade and professional associations also formed and established themselves near each other. Street names reflect such clustering of tradespeople and artisans. For example, Meeks mentions a group in Thessalonica called the Purple-Dyers of Eighteenth Street (Meeks: 32). Guilds or trade associations came to serve a social function among the participants, since the members shared meals together and likely discussed politics and religion in addition to their common business concerns.

As an artisan himself, Paul would naturally have located alongside other people engaged in a similar craft. His leatherworking shop served as a setting not only to ply his trade but also to engage both clients and curious bystanders in conversation about politics and religion. Like some philosophers who engaged in manual labor while teaching, Paul used his workshop as a place from which he could share the gospel (Malherbe, 1987:17-20; Hock: 37-42; cf. Acts 18:1-4).

In addition to the workshop, the household served as a context for establishing congregations. Luke mentions the house of Jason as a meeting place for the believers in Thessalonica (Acts 17:5). Sometimes whole households converted to Christianity. These homes, and especially the larger homes of the wealthier members, provided the physical space for worship and other congregational gatherings. In what has come to be called "love patriarchalism," some of the traditional hierarchical family structures were perpetuated in the church family:

> This love-patriarchalism takes social differences for granted but ameliorates them through an obligation of respect and love, an obligation imposed upon those who are socially stronger. From the weaker are required subordination, fidelity, and esteem. (Theissen: 107)

However, the gospel also challenged these hierarchical structures. Men and women, Jews and Gentiles, and slaves and free people alike found themselves children of God, united through Christ (Gal. 3:26-28). In the church, social patterns which embodied this drive toward egalitarian relationships began slowly to emerge. Jewett may be on target in his suggestion that the tenement building rather than individual houses served as the setting for early church life in Thessalonica. In what he has termed "love communalism," believers met regularly to share meals together in love feasts. A less hierarchical congregational structure also came as a result (Jewett, 1994:77-86).

SPECIFIC BACKGROUND

CHRONOLOGY OF PAUL'S LIFE In our treatment of introductory questions, we claimed a consensus for the date of 1 and 2 Thessalonians, especially among those scholars and commentators who regard 2 Thessalonians as a genuine Pauline letter. Most agree that these letters were written in A.D. 50 from Corinth ("When Were These Letters Written?" p. 28) Our purpose here is to place the writing of these letters more broadly into the context of Paul's life and ministry. It is also necessary to qualify the consensus.

There are two sources of information about Paul's life: his letters (the primary source) and the Acts of the Apostles (a secondary source). Scholars disagree on the question of how these two sources of data should be utilized in the process of reconstructing the chronology of Paul's life. This question is especially acute when the reader is confronted with seemingly contradictory information. For example, following his conversion, did Paul go to Jerusalem after many days (Acts 9:23, 26) or after three years (Gal. 1:15-20)?

We can identify three different approaches to this process of using the available primary and secondary sources to sketch the time line for Paul's life and ministry. In each case we also mention one or two books which exemplify that approach:

1. Acts tells the story of Paul's conversion and his missionary travels. Hence, data from the letters can be harmonized with the sequence of events as narrated in Acts. Examples: Bruce, 1977; Faw, 1993.
2. The letters come directly from Paul, so priority needs to be given to data provided by these letters. But information from Acts can be carefully appropriated as well. Example: Jewett, 1979.
3. The letters come directly from Paul. The writer of the Acts of the Apostles has mainly theological rather than historical goals in mind. Even when Acts gives chronological data, a chronology of Paul's life needs to be based totally on evidence from the letters. Example: Luedemann.

A first step in this process of establishing a chronology is to establish a relative sequence of events, without attempting to assign dates. In the sequence of the chart, we utilize data from both the letters and Acts (chart on next page adapted from Campbell).

The next challenge in this process involves the assigning of dates. In attempting to determine the actual dates of some of the events identified in this sequence, two kinds of data have been utilized: autobiographical statements in the letters, and several references in Acts which can be correlated with extrabiblical historical records. The chronological clues in Acts tend to be quite general (e.g., 9:23: "after some time had passed") and therefore not very helpful, although there are exceptions (e.g., 18:11: Paul stayed in Corinth *a year and six months*).

Paul's autobiographical allusions in Gal. 1:15—2:1 provide a basic framework for a chronology of his life up to the time when he wrote Galatians. Beginning with the revelation of God's Son to him, Paul refers to several of his geographical movements and notes the amount of time which elapsed between them:

I went away at once into Arabia, and afterwards I returned to Damascus. (1:17)
Then after three years I did go up to Jerusalem to visit Cephas [Peter] and stayed with him fifteen days. (1:18)
Then I went into the regions of Syria and Cilicia. (1:21)
Then after fourteen years I went up again to Jerusalem. (2:1)

By utilizing these chronological clues, we have the beginning of a framework for fourteen or seventeen years of Paul's life. Whether the years add up to fourteen or seventeen depends on whether or not the "fourteen years" of 2:1 include the "three years" of 1:18.

Some absolute dates can be determined from two texts in Acts 18 mentioning events and persons which can be correlated with extrabiblical historical and archaeological data:

A.D. 49: Emperor Claudius's expulsion of the Jews from Rome, mentioned by Suetonius, and dated by Orosius in the emperor's ninth year, surfaces in Luke's account of Paul's ministry in Corinth: "Claudius had ordered all Jews to leave Rome" (Acts 18:2).

Events and Places in Paul's Life	Mentioned in Acts	Mentioned in Paul's Letters
Paul's life within Judaism	9:1-2; 22:3-6; 26:4-11	Gal. 1:13-14; Phil. 3:4-6
Paul's conversion and call	9:3-25; 22:6-12; 26:12-23	Gal. 1:15-16; 1 Tim. 1:12-14
Arabia		Gal. 1:17
Damascus		Gal. 1:17; 2 Cor. 11:32-33
First Jerusalem visit	9:26-29	Gal. 1:18
Caesarea	9:30	
Syria and Cilicia	9:30; 11:25	Gal. 1:21
Antioch of Syria	11:26	
Second Jerusalem visit	11:29-30; 12:25	Gal. 2:1?
First missionay journey	13:1—14:28	
Third Jerusalem visit; Conference	15:1-29	Gal. 2:1?
Second missionary journey:	15:30—18:22a	
Antioch to Troas	15:30—16:10	Antioch: Gal. 2:11
Philippi	16:11-40	1 Thess. 2:2; Phil. 4:15
Thessalonica	17:1-9	1 Thess. 2:2; Phil. 4:16
Beroea	17:10-15	
Athens	17:16-34	1 Thess. 3:1
Corinth	18:1-18	1 Cor. 1:14-16; 2:1; 3:5-6; 2 Cor. 11:7-9
Ephesus	18:19-21	
Caesarea	18:22a	
Fourth Jerusalem visit	18:22b	
Third missionay journey	18:22c—21:14	1 Cor. 16:8; 2 Cor. 2:12-13; 9:4; Rom. 15:19
Fifth Jerusalem visit	21:15—23:30	Rom. 15:25-27
Journey to Rome	23:33—28:14	
Rome	28:14-31	Rom. 15:28-32

A.D. 51-52: An inscription found in Delphi provides data concerning Gallio's tenure as proconsul, thereby yielding another peg on which to hang a chronology of Paul's life. Paul's eighteen months in Corinth (18:11) overlap with the time "when Gallio was proconsul of Achaia" (18:12). *[Historical and Political context, p. 357.]*

Because judgment calls need to be made concerning a number of matters, including the basic question of how much to utilize data from Acts, scholars have come to differing conclusions when seeking to supply actual dates. The following chart, summarizing chronologies developed by the scholars whose works are noted above, represents three different perspectives on the use of Acts as a source: Bruce, Jewett, and Luedemann (cf. Faw, 1993:309-310). Luedemann's chronology generally cites two possible dates, because of the uncertainty which surrounds the dating of Jesus' death and resurrection (likely either A.D. 27 or 30); Paul's conversion occurred some time after this event.

For our purposes, we continue the story line only through the Thessalonian ministry, including the writing of the letters to the congregation in Thessalonica, and the Jerusalem Conference (chart on next page).

A few observations are in order. Bruce and Jewett agree on dating 1 and 2 Thessalonians in A.D. 50. Bruce holds that this occurred after the Jerusalem Conference, which he dates in A.D. 49. Jewett places the Apostolic Conference in Jerusalem in A.D. 51, shortly after the writing of 1 and 2 Thessalonians. Bruce suspects that Galatians was written in A.D. 48, before the Jerusalem Conference (so also Faw, 1993:169-170), whereas Jewett thinks Galatians was written after the Apostolic Conference, likely in A.D. 53.

Luedemann's conclusions differ on several counts. He argues that Claudius's edict expelling the Jews from Rome was issued early in his reign (A.D. 41) rather than in A.D. 49. *[Historical and Political Context, p. 357.]* On this basis, and on a number of judgments with regard to other external and internal data, Luedemann proposes that 1 Thessalonians was written in A.D. 41. If this were correct, 1 Thessalonians would have been written within eight or eleven years of Paul's conversion and six or nine years before the Jerusalem Conference. Luedemann does not consider 2 Thessalonians to come from Paul, and so he does not propose a date for that letter.

While it is not possible to be definitive in these matters, the later date (A.D. 50) seems more plausible. This date is based on evidence from both Acts and the letters. Furthermore, this date is supported by the external data regarding Claudius's expulsion edict (A.D. 49) and Gallio's tenure as proconsul of Achaia (A.D. 51-52), both of which are mentioned in connection with Paul's eighteen months in Corinth (Acts 18:1-22). The issues of circumcision and the law, so prominent in Galatians, do not seem to enter into the epistolary interactions with the Thessalonians. Hence, the Jerusalem Conference and the writing of the letter to the Galatians likely both occurred after the writing of 1 and 2 Thessalonians.

LEADERSHIP AND MINISTRY GIFTS   In the letters to the church in Thessalonica, Paul does not expand on the nature of his calling as apostle. Only in 1 Thess. 2:7 does Paul use the phrase *apostles of Christ*, a description which he appears to apply both to himself and to his co-workers. An *apostle* (literally: *one sent*) serves as a missionary, an ambassador, a representative serving in behalf of another (such as Christ, Lord of the church).

Nor does Paul in 1 and 2 Thessalonians articulate a developed view of ministry within the church. Various leadership tasks are described in 1 Thess. 5:12-13, but the emphasis rests on ministry functions rather than on defined roles. The purpose of this essay is to show how the offices and functions of ministry are developed in Paul's later letters.

Chronologies of Paul's Life

Bruce	Jewett	Luedemann
ca. 33: Conversion	34:Conversion 34-37: Activities in Arabia, return to Damascus	30 (33): Conversion, stay in Arabia, return to Damascus
ca. 35: Paul's first post-conversion Jeru- salem visit	37: First Jerusalem journey	33 (36): Paul's first visit to Jerusalem
35-46: Paul in Cilicia and Syria 46: Paul's second Jerusalem visit	37-51: Activities in Syria and Cilicia	34 (37): Journey to Syria and Cilicia
47-48: Paul and Barnabas in Cyprus and Galatia ?48: Wrote *Galatians*	43-45: Cyprus, Pamphylia, and south Galatia	34 (37): Mission to Syr- ia and Cilicia, and south Galatia
	46-48: Expedition through north Galatia to Troas 48-49: Philippian min- istry	From ca. 36 (39): Paul's independent mission in Europe: Philippi, Thessalonica
	49: Thessalonian min- istry 50-51: Corinthian ministry 50: Wrote *1 and 2 Thes-* *salonians*	Ca. 41: Paul in Corinth. 41: Wrote *1 Thes-* *salonians*
49: Council of Jerusalem	51: Apostolic confer- ence	47 (50): Second visit to Jerusalem: Jerusalem Conference
49-50: Paul and Silas travel through Asia Minor to Macedonia and Achais 50: *Letters to the* *Thessaloninas*		
	53: Wrote *Galatians*	50 (53): Wrote *Galatians*

In his letter to Corinth, Paul emphasizes both the unity enabled through being baptized in the one Spirit (1 Cor. 12:12-13) and the diversity of spiritual gifts available within the one body (12:14-26). Baptism does not ordain all believers to the same ministry. Two somewhat overlapping lists of ministry gifts are provided in the same chapter: 12:8-11 and 12:28-30. When these are combined with comparable lists in Rom. 12:6-8 and Eph. 4:11, one gains a graphic overview of the diversity of ministries envisioned by Paul:

Ministries Named by Paul

1 Cor. 12:8-11	1 Cor. 12:28-30	Rom. 12:6-8	Eph. 4:11
	apostles		apostles
prophecy	prophets	prophecy	prophets
			evangelists
			pastors
		ministry	
	teachers	teacher	teachers
		exhorter	
utterance of wisdom			
utterance of knowledge			
faith	deeds of power		
gifts of healing	gifts of healing		
working of miracles	work miracles		
	assistance	giver	
	leadership	leader	
		compassionate	
discernment of spirits			
various kinds of tongues	various kinds of tongues		
interpretation of tongues	interpret [tongues]		

With one exception, none of the persons mentioned in 1 Thess. 5:12-13 as worthy of respect and esteem is explicitly included in the above lists. That exception: "the leader," one who stands before (Rom. 12:8; 1 Thess. 5:12).

RELATIONSHIP BETWEEN 1 AND 2 THESSALONIANS

Interpreters of 1 and 2 Thessalonians have long noticed that these letters are remarkably similar and yet quite different. Great similarities exist between the two letters, both in words, phrases, and concepts, as well as in their structure, which differs in some respects from the standard Pauline letter form. Yet 2 Thessalonians seems to be less personal and intimate than 1 Thessalonians, and it has been seen as teaching a different eschatology. How then does one explain both the major linguistic and structural similarities and the differences in tone and content?

A previous letter is mentioned in several places in 2 Thessalonians. According to 2:1-2, some upsetting eschatological teaching was being conveyed either by spirit or by word or by letter, as though from us. Is this letter 1 Thessalonians? Or a forged letter written in the name of Paul? Or an indication that 1 Thessalonians was apparently being misinterpreted? The wording of Paul's autograph greeting in 3:17 has been taken to communicate a concern to assure the Thessalonians of the authenticity of this letter. Why was this concern expressed in the second letter and not in the first? Some interpreters read this as an indication that 2 Thessalonians was pseudonymous. In 2:15 the writers exhort the Thessalonians: *Stand firm and observe the traditions which you were taught either by our word or by our letter.* A similar reference in 3:14 (usually translated *this letter*) can be read to refer either to a previous letter (1 Thessalonians) or to the letter being written (2 Thessalonians).

The most plausible reading of these references, as argued in the Explanatory Notes for these texts, is that the *letter* mentioned in 2 Thess. 2:2, 15; 3:14 is 1 Thessalonians. In 2:2 the qualifying phrase *as though from us* suggests that Paul found the claim that *the day of the Lord has come* so disturbing that he even considers the possibility that another letter has been circulating in his name (Jewett, 1986:181-186).

Scholars have also made several other proposals for resolving the puzzling question of the relationship between these letters. We examine three of these hypotheses briefly (summarized from Jewett, 1986: chaps. 1-3; Best: 7-59): separate recipients, reversed sequence, pseudonymity of 2 Thessalonians.

Separate recipients for the two letters have been suggested by several scholars. Harnack argued that there were Jewish and Gentile factions in the congregation at Thessalonica, and that 1 Thessalonians was addressed to the Gentile majority group and 2 Thessalonians to the Jewish minority. Goguel proposed that 2 Thessalonians had originally been written to a congregation in Beroea, the city which Paul visited following his expulsion from Thessalonica (Acts 17:10-15). E. Earle Ellis posits that 1 Thessalonians was written to the congregation as a whole, and 2 Thessalonians was targeted for the congregational leaders. None of these separate recipient hypotheses has found wide acceptance among scholars and commentators.

Reversed sequence of these letters has recently been proposed by Charles Wanamaker: 2 Thessalonians preceded 1 Thessalonians (Wanamaker: 37-45). Since canonical order of the NT books is not based on chronological order, the present order in the NT does not rule out this hypothesis. But what is the evidence? We name a few arguments for 2 Thessalonians being written first and some counterarguments (chart on next page).

All things considered, the arguments for 2 Thessalonians being written first are not persuasive. There are strong reasons for believing that indeed 1 Thessalonians came first, and the reasons include references in 2 Thessalonians to a previous letter (see above). The story about how Paul and his companions went about their ministry and how they were welcomed in Thessalonica seems appropriate in a first letter (1 Thess. 1:5-10; 2:1-12). A reference to the growth of the Thessalonian congregation (2 Thess. 1:3-4) fits quite naturally in a sequel.

The pseudonymity of 2 Thessalonians is another explanation for the combination of striking similarities and major differences between 1 and 2 Thessalonians. This proposal has gained widespread academic support. A survey of articles given at a 1988 colloquium dealing with the Thessalonian correspondence reveals that among scholars, the advocates of Pauline authorship of 2 Thessalonians are definitely in the minority (Collins, 1990).

Arguments for 2 Thess. Earliest	Arguments for 1 Thess. Earliest
Persecutions are present in 2 Thess. 1:4-7 but past in 1 Thess. 2:14.	Persecutions are also a present reality in 1 Thess. 3:3.
The problem with the *unruly* appears to be new in 2 Thess. 3:11-15, but well-known in 1 Thess. 5:14.	The problem existed even during the initial visit. First Thess. 4:11 shows it has not disappeared, so Paul mentions it in 5:14; since the problem is later becoming more acute, Paul provides more detailed instruction in 2 Thess. 3:6-15.
The emphasis on the genuineness of the letter in 2 Thess. 3:17 is most appropriate in a first letter.	Paul apparently fears the possibility of a forgery, which is more likely only after a first letter.
In 1 Thess. (5:1) there is no need for instruction about *times and seasons* since the Thessalonians already have 2 Thess. 2.	Oral teaching about *times and seasons* has been given during the missionaries' initial visit.

According to an increasingly dominant view, 2 Thessalonians was not written by Paul. Some scholars suggest a date shortly after Paul's death, when the destruction of Jerusalem and the temple elicited apocalyptic excitement and the setting of dates; this letter was written to defuse such eschatological enthusiasm (Beker, 1991:80-83). Other scholars, notably Wilhelm Wrede, propose that a writer around A.D. 100 wrote 2 Thessalonians in Paul's name to oppose the notion, which seemed to be rooted in the eschatology of 1 Thessalonians, that the parousia had already occurred (Wrede's position summarized by Jewett, 1986:5-10).

As indicated in the introduction ("Who Wrote These Letters?" p. 25), the present commentary is based on the premise that Paul, Silvanus, and Timothy were coauthors of both 1 and 2 Thessalonians, with Paul having the primary hand in writing these letters. Complete certainty about such matters may not be possible, and so the debate continues. To introduce some of the issues, we enumerate several arguments and counterarguments regarding pseudonymity and Pauline authorship (chart on next page).

Arguments for Pseudonymity	*Arguments for Pauline Authorship*
Vocabulary and style: Word choice and stylistic features distinguish 2 Thess. from 1 Thess.	The range of unusual words and expressions and distinctive styles is not wider than that in other letters.
Tone: 2 Thess. seems more cool and formal than 1 Thess.	The second letter is less personal in tone because of the aggravated situation being addressed.
Form: 1 and 2 Thess. share some unusual formal features (such as an opening thanksgiving followed later by renewed thanksgiving), suggesting that 2 Thess. is a pseudonymous letter patterned after 1 Thess.	Departures from standard letter format occur in other letters as well; for example, Galatians lacks a thanksgiving section entirely. The circumstances shape the form.
Theology: In 2 Thess. the gospel, the Christian life, and the mission of the church are viewed in ways that seem to reflect a postapostolic era.	Judgments about apostolic and postapostolic theology are chronically difficult to make because of the circular reasoning which often goes into such judgments.
Eschatology: In 1 Thess. the coming of Christ as Lord is viewed as near, sudden, and without warning, whereas 2 Thess. introduces a timetable of signs and events preceding this event.	Early Christian expectation of the coming of Christ maintained an emphasis on both surprise and signs (Mark 13:14-37). Rather than developing a timetable, 2 Thess. 2:1-12 and 13-15 provide proofs that *the day of the Lord* has not yet come.

In sum, the arguments favoring pseudonymous authorship are not convincing. All of the real or perceived differences between the two letters (vocabulary and style, tone, form, theology, and eschatology) can be interpreted in light of the situation which developed in Thessalonica. This included heightened persecution, misleading eschatological teachings, and the irresponsible lifestyle of *the unruly.*

Another variable may have been the role of an amanuensis or secretary in writing these letters. It is evident from Paul's letters that he employed the services of an amanuensis, either to take direct dictation or to actually draft the letter based on written or oral instructions. Depending on the level of freedom given the amanuensis for this assignment, that secretary could have shaped the vocabulary, style, and even content of the letter to a signficant extent (Richards). In the case of 1 and 2 Thessalonians, of course, one or both of the coauthors with Paul could have drafted one or the other of these letters.

For more discussion of the relationship between 1 and 2 Thessalonians, including the question of the authorship of 2 Thessalonians, see Jewett, 1986:3-46, 181-192; Best: 37-59; Wanamaker: 17-45; Roetzel: 83-86, 144-148; Donfried, 1993:83-89.

Bibliography

Aus, Roger
1984   "II Thessalonians." In *1-2 Timothy, Titus, 2 Thessalonians.*
        Augsburg Commentary on the New Testament. Minneapolis:
        Augsburg.

Bassler, Jouette M.
1984   "The Enigmatic Sign: 2 Thessalonians 1:5." *CBQ* 46:496-510.
1991   *Pauline Theology,* vol. 1: *Thessalonians, Philippians, Galatians,
        Philemon.* Minneapolis: Augsburg Fortress.

Bauman, Clarence
1991   *The Spiritual Legacy of Hans Denck: Interpretation and Transla-
        tion of Key Texts.* Studies in Medieval and Reformation Thought,
        47. Leiden: Brill.

BE
1983   *The Brethren Encyclopedia.* Vols. 1-2. Elgin, Ill.: Brethren Press.

Beker, J. Christiaan
1980   *Paul the Apostle: The Triumph of God in Life and Thought.* Phil-
        adelphia: Fortress.
1990   *The Triumph of God: The Essence of Paul's Thought.* Trans. by
        Loren T. Stuckenbruck. Minneapolis: Fortress.
1991   *The Heirs of Paul: Paul's Legacy in the New Testament and in
        the Church Today.* Minneapolis: Fortress.

Benhayim, Menahem
1985   *Jews, Gentiles and the New Testament: Alleged Anti-Semitism
        in the New Testament.* Jerusalem: Yanetz.

Berkhof, Hendrik
1977   *Christ and the Powers.* Trans. by J. H. Yoder. Scottdale, Pa.:
        Herald Press.

Best, Ernest
  1972 A Commentary to the First and Second Epistles to the Thes-
        salonians. Harper's N. T. Commentaries. London: A. & C. Black.

Bosch, David J.
  1979 A Spirituality of the Road. Institute of Mennonite Studies, Mis-
        sionary Studies, no. 6. Scottdale, Pa.: Herald Press.

Bruce, F. F.
  1977 Paul: Apostle of the Heart Set Free. Grand Rapids: Eerdmans.
  1982 1 and 2 Thessalonians. Word Biblical Commentary, 45. Waco,
        Tex.: Word Books.

Campbell, Thomas H.
  1955 "Paul's Missionary Journeys as Reflected in His Letters." JBL
        74:80-87.

Charlesworth, James H., ed.
  1983-85 The Old Testament Pseudepigrapha. 2 vols. New York: Dou-
        bleday.

Collins, Raymond F.
  1984 Studies on the First Letter to the Thessalonians. Bibliotheca
        Ephemeridum Theologicarum Lovaniensium, 66. Leuven: Uni-
        versity Press.
  1990 The Thessalonian Correspondence. Bibliotheca Ephemeridum
        Theologicarum Lovaniensium, 87. Leuven: University Press.
  1993 The Birth of the New Testament: The Origin and Development
        of the First Christian Generation. New York: Crossroad.

Cousar, Charles B.
  1990 A Theology of the Cross: The Death of Jesus in the Pauline Let-
        ters. Overtures to Biblical Theology, 24. Minneapolis: Augsburg
        Fortress.

Cronk, Sandra
  1981 "Gelassenheit: The Rites of the Redemptive Process in Old Order
        Amish and Old Order Mennonite Communities." MQR 55:5-44.

Cullmann, Oscar
  1962 Christ and Time: The Primitive Christian Conception of Time
        and History. Rev. ed. Trans. by Floyd V. Filson. London: SCM.

DeWind, H. A.
  1955 "Anabaptists in Thessalonica." MQR 29:70-73.

Donfried, Karl P.
  1984 "Paul and Judaism: 1 Thessalonians 2:13-16 as a Test Case." In-
        terpretation 38:242-253.
  1985 "The Cults of Thessalonica and the Thessalonian Correspon-
        dence." NTS 31:336-356
  1993 The Theology of the Shorter Pauline Letters. New Testament
        Theology. New York: Cambridge University Press.

Doty, William G.
1973 *Letters in Primitive Christianity.* Guides to Biblical Scholarship, New Testament Series. Philadelphia: Fortress.

Driver, John
1986 *Understanding the Atonement for the Mission of the Church.* Scottdale, Pa.: Herald Press.

Dyck, Cornelius J., William E. Keeney, and Alvin J. Beachy, eds.
1992 *The Writings of Dirk Philips.* Classics of the Radical Reformation, 6. Scottdale, Pa.: Herald Press.

Elias, Jacob W.
1992 " 'Jesus Who Delivers Us from the Wrath to Come' (1 Thess 1:10): Apocalyptic and Peace in the Thessalonian Correspondence." In *Society of Biblical Literature 1992 Seminar Papers,* 121-132. Atlanta: Scholars Press.

Ellingworth, Paul, and Eugene A. Nida
1976 *A Translator's Handbook on Paul's Letters to the Thessalonians.* New York: United Bible Societies.

Ellis, E. Earle
1989 *Pauline Theology: Ministry and Society.* Grand Rapids: Eerdmans.

Ewert, David
1980 *And Then Comes the End.* Scottdale, Pa.: Herald Press.
1983 *A General Introduction to the Bible: From Ancient Tablets to Modern Translations.* Grand Rapids: Zondervan.

Faw, Chalmer
1952 "On the Writing of First Thessalonians." *JBL* 71:217-232.
1993 *Acts.* Believers Church Bible Commentary. Scottdale, Pa.: Herald Press.

Fee, Gordon D.
1993 *New Testament Exegesis: A Handbook for Students and Pastors.* Rev. ed. Louisville: Westminster/John Knox.
1994 *God's Empowering Presence: The Holy Spirit in the Letters of Paul.* Peabody, Mass.: Hendrickson.

Ferguson, Everett
1987 *Backgrounds of Early Christianity.* Grand Rapids: Eerdmans.

Frame, James E.
1912 *A Critical and Exegetical Commentary on Paul's Letters to the Thessalonians.* The International Critical Commentary. New York: Scribner's.

Friedmann, Robert
1955 "Christian Sectarians in Thessalonica and Their Relationship to the Anabaptists." *MQR* 29:54-69.

1959   "Thessalonica." ME 4:708-709. *See below*, ME.

Gaventa, Beverly Roberts
1986   *From Darkness to Light: Aspects of Conversion in the New Testament*. Overtures to Biblical Theology, 20. Philadelphia: Fortress.

Giblin, Charles H.
1967   *The Threat to Faith: An Exegetical and Theological Reexamination of 2 Thessalonians 2*. Analecta Biblica, 31. Rome: Pontifical Biblical Institute.

Gundry Volf, Judith M.
1990   *Paul and Perseverance: Staying In and Falling Away*. Wissenschaftliche Untersuchungen zum Neuen Testament, ser. 2, vol. 37. Tübingen: J. C. B. Mohr (Paul Siebeck); Louisville: Westminster/John Knox.

Harder, Leland, ed.
1985   *The Sources of Swiss Anabaptism*. Classics of the Radical Reformation, 4. Scottdale, Pa.: Herald Press.

Hayes, John H., and Carl R. Holladay
1987   *Biblical Exegesis: A Beginner's Handbook*. Rev. ed. Atlanta: John Knox.

Hendrix, Holland Lee
1991   "Archaeology and Eschatology at Thessalonica." In B. Pearson, ed., *The Future of Early Christianity*, 107-118. Minneapolis: Augsburg.

Hiebert, D. Edmond
1992   *1 and 2 Thessalonians*. Rev. ed. Chicago: Moody.

Hock, Ronald F.
1980   *The Social Context of Paul's Ministry: Tentmaking and Apostleship*. Philadelphia: Fortress.

Holland, Glenn S.
1988   *The Tradition That You Received from Us: 2 Thessalonians in the Pauline Tradition*. Tübingen: J. C. B. Mohr (Paul Siebeck).

Hughes, Frank Witt
1989   *Early Christian Rhetoric and 2 Thessalonians*. JSNT, Supplement Series, 30. Sheffield, U.K.: Sheffield Academic Press.

Hurd, John C.
1986   "Paul Ahead of His Time: 1 Thess 2:13-16." In Peter Richardson, ed., *Anti-Judaism in Early Christianity*. Studies in Christianity and Judaism, 2. Vol. 1: *Paul and the Gospels*, 21-36. Waterloo, Ont.: Wilfred Laurier University Press.

Jeschke, Marlin
  1988   *Discipling in the Church: Recovering a Ministry of the Gospel.* 3d ed. Scottdale, Pa.: Herald Press.

Jewett, Robert
  1970-71 "The Agitators and the Galatian Congregation." *NTS* 17:198-212.
  1979   *A Chronology of Paul's Life.* Philadelphia: Fortress.
  1986   *The Thessalonian Correspondence: Pauline Rhetoric and Millenarian Piety.* Foundations and Facets, New Testament. Philadelphia: Fortress.
  1991   "A Matrix of Grace: The Theology of 2 Thessalonians as a Pauline Letter." In Jouette M. Bassler, ed., *Pauline Theology*, vol. 1: *Thessalonians, Philippians, Galatians, Philemon*, 63-70. Minneapolis: Fortress.
  1994   *Paul the Apostle to America: Cultural Trends and Pauline Scholarship.* Louisville: Westminster/John Knox.

Juel, Donald H.
  1985   "1 Thessalonians." In *Galatians, Philippians, Philemon, 1 Thessalonians.* Augsburg Commentary on the New Testament. Minneapolis: Augsburg.

Kemmler, Dieter Werner
  1975   *Faith and Human Reason: A Study of Paul's Method of Preaching as Illustrated by 1-2 Thessalonians and Acts 17:2-4.* Supplements to Novum Testamentum, 40. Leiden: Brill.

Klassen, William
  1984   *Love of Enemies: The Way to Peace.* Overtures to Biblical Theology, 15. Philadelphia: Fortress.
  1993   "The Sacred Kiss in the NT: An Example of Social Boundary Lines." *NTS* 39:122-135.

Kloppenborg, John S.
  1993   "*Philadelphia, Theodidaktos* and the Dioscuri: Rhetorical Engagement in 1 Thessalonians 4:9-12." *NTS* 39:265-289.

Koester, Helmut
  1982   *Introduction to the New Testament.* Vol. 1: *History, Culture, and Religion of the Hellenistic Age.* Vol. 2: *History and Literature of Early Christianity.* Philadelphia: Fortress.

Krodel, Gerhard
  1978   "2 Thessalonians." In Gerhard Krodel, ed., *Ephesians, Colossians, 2 Thessalonians, The Pastoral Epistles*, 73-96. Proclamation Commentaries, The NT Witnesses for Preaching. Philadelphia: Fortress.
  1990   "The 'Religious Power of Lawlessness' (*Katechon*) as Precursor of the 'Lawless One' (*Anomos*). 2 Thess 2:6-7." *Currents in Theology and Mission* 17 (1990): 440-446.

Lederach, Paul M.
    1994   *Daniel.* Believers Church Bible Commentary. Scottdale, Pa.:
          Herald Press.

Lind, Millard C.
    1980   *Yahweh Is a Warrior: The Theology of Warfare in Ancient Israel.*
          Scottdale, Pa.: Herald Press.

Luedemann, Gerd
    1984   *Paul, Apostle to the Gentiles: Studies in Chronology.* Trans. by F.
          Stanley Jones. Philadelphia: Fortress.

Lyons, George
    1985   *Pauline Autobiography: Toward a New Understanding.* SBL Dis-
          sertation Series, 73. Atlanta: Scholars Press.

Mack, Burton L.
    1990   *Rhetoric and the New Testament.* Guides to Biblical Scholarship,
          New Testament Series. Minneapolis: Augsburg Fortress.

Malherbe, Abraham J.
    1987   *Paul and the Thessalonians: The Philosophic Tradition of Pasto-
          ral Care.* Philadelphia: Fortress.
    1989   *Paul and the Popular Philosophers.* Minneapolis: Augsburg
          Fortress.

Marshall, I. Howard
    1983   *1 and 2 Thessalonians.* New Century Bible Commentary. Lon-
          don: Marshall Morgan and Scott.

Martin, Ernest D.
    1993   *Colossians, Philemon.* Believers Church Bible Commentary.
          Scottdale, Pa.: Herald Press.

Martin, Luther H.
    1987   *Hellenistic Religions: An Introduction.* New York: Oxford Uni-
          versity Press.

Martin, Ralph P.
    1964   *Worship in the Early Church.* London. 1975 rev. ed., Grand
          Rapids: Eerdmans.

Martyrs Mirror
    1938   *The Bloody Theater or Martyrs Mirror of the Defenseless Chris-
          tians.* Compiled by Thieleman J. van Braght. Trans. by J. F. Sohm
          from the 1660 Dutch edition. Scottdale, Pa.: Herald Press.
Matheson, Peter, ed., trans.
    1988   *The Collected Works of Thomas Müntzer.* Edinburgh: T. & T.
          Clark.
Mauser, Ulrich
    1992   *The Gospel of Peace. A Scriptural Message for Today's World.*
          Louisville: Westminster/John Knox.

ME
   1955-59 *The Mennonite Encyclopedia*. Vols. 1-4. Scottdale, Pa.: Men-
           nonite Publishing House, Herald Press, et al.
   1990   *The Mennonite Encyclopedia*. Vol. 5. Scottdale, Pa.: Mennonite
           Publishing House, Herald Press, et al.

Meeks, Wayne A.
   1983   *The First Urban Christians: The Social World of the Apostle
           Paul*. New Haven: Yale University Press.

Menken, M. J. J.
   1992   "Paradise Regained or Still Lost? Eschatology and Disorderly Be-
           haviour in 2 Thessalonians." *NTS* 38:271-289.

Menno Simons
   1956   *The Complete Writings of Menno Simons c. 1496-1561*. Scott-
           dale, Pa.: Herald Press.

Metzger, Bruce M.
   1971   *A Textual Commentary on the Greek New Testament*. New
           York: United Bible Societies.
   1992   *The Text of the New Testament: Its Transmission, Corruption,
           and Restoration*. 3d ed. New York: Oxford University Press.

Morris, Leon
   1959   *The First and Second Epistles to the Thessalonians*. The New In-
           ternational Commentary on the New Testament. Grand Rapids:
           Eerdmans.

Murphy-O'Connor, Jerome
   1983   *St. Paul's Corinth: Texts and Archaeology*. Good News Studies,
           6. Wilmington: Michael Glazier.

Patte, Daniel
   1983   *Paul's Faith and the Power of the Gospel: A Structural Introduc-
           tion to the Pauline Letters*. Philadelphia: Fortress.

Pearson, Birger A.
   1971   "1 Thessalonians 2:13-16: A Deutero-Pauline Interpolation."
           Harvard Theological Review 64:79-94.

Plevnik, Joseph
   1984   "The Taking Up of the Faithful and the Resurrection of the Dead
           in 1 Thessalonians 4:13-18." *CBQ* 46:274-83.

Pobee, John S.
   1985   *Persecution and Martyrdom in the Theology of Paul*. *JSNT*,
           Suppl. series, 6. Sheffield, U.K.: Sheffield Academic Press.
Puskas, Charles B.
   1989   *An Introduction to the New Testament*. Peabody, Mass.:
           Hendrickson.

Rensberger, David
1988 *Johannine Faith and Liberating Community.* Philadelphia: Westminster.

Richards, E. Randolph
1991 *The Secretary in the Letters of Paul.* Wissenshaftliche Untersuchungen zum Neuen Testament, ser. 2, vol. 42. Tübingen: J. C. B. Mohr (Paul Siebeck).

Rideman [Riedemann], Peter
1970 *Confession of Faith: Account of Our Religion, Doctrine and Faith.* Rifton, N.Y.: Plough Publishing House.

Roetzel, Calvin J.
1991 *The Letters of Paul: Conversations in Context.* 3d ed. Louisville: Westminster/John Knox.

Russell, D. S.
1964 *The Method and Message of Jewish Apocalyptic: 200 BC—AD 100.* SCM/Westminster.

Russell, R.
1988 "The Idle in 2 Thess 3:6-12: An Eschatological or a Social Problem?" *NTS* 34:105-119.

Schatzmann, Siegfried
1987 *A Pauline Theology of Charismata.* Peabody, Mass.: Hendrickson.

Schmidt, Daryl
1983 "1 Thess 2:13-16: Linguistic Evidence for an Interpolation." *JBL* 102:269-279.

Schreiner, Thomas R.
1990 *Interpreting the Pauline Epistles.* Guides to New Testament Exegesis, 5. Grand Rapids: Baker Book House.

Segal, Alan F.
1990 *Paul the Convert: The Apostolate and Apostasy of Saul the Pharisee.* New Haven: Yale University Press.

Stowers, Stanley K.
1986 *Letter Writing in Greco-Roman Antiquity.* Library of Early Christianity. Philadelphia: Westminster.

Theissen, Gerd
1982 *The Social Setting of Pauline Christianity: Essays on Corinth.* Trans. by John H. Schütz. Philadelphia: Fortress.

Thomas, Robert L.
1978 "I and II Thessalonians." In *Expositor's Bible Commentary,* 11:229-337. Grand Rapids: Zondervan.

Wanamaker, Charles A.
  1990   *The Epistles to the Thessalonians: A Commentary on the Greek Text.* The New International Greek Testament Commentary. Grand Rapids: Eerdmans.

Whittaker, Molly
  1984   *Jews and Christians: Graeco-Roman Views.* Cambridge Commentaries on Writings of the Jewish and Christian World, 200 BC to 200 AD, 6. New York: Cambridge University Press.

Wiles, Gordon P.
  1974   *Paul's Intercessory Prayers.* Society for NT Studies, Monograph Series, 24. Cambridge: Cambridge University Press.

Williams, David J.
  1992   *1 and 2 Thessalonians.* New International Biblical Commentary. Peabody, Mass.: Hendrickson.

Wink, Walter
  1984   *Naming the Powers: The Language of Power in the New Testament.* The Powers, 1. Philadelphia: Fortress.
  1986   *Unmasking the Powers: The Invisible Forces that Determine Human Existence.* The Powers, 2. Philadelphia: Fortress.
  1992   *Engaging the Powers: Discernment and Resistance in a World of Domination.* The Powers, 3. Minneapolis: Fortress.

Yarbrough, O. Larry
  1985   *Not Like the Gentiles: Marriage Rules in the Letters of Paul.* SBL Dissertation Series, 80. Atlanta: Scholars Press.

Yoder, John H., trans., ed.
  1973   *The Legacy of Michael Sattler.* Classics of the Radical Reformation, 1. Scottdale, Pa.: Herald Press.

Yoder, Perry
  1982   *From Word to Life: A Guide to the Art of Bible Study.* Scottdale, Pa.: Herald Press.

Yoder Neufeld, Thomas R.
  1989   "God and Saints at War: The Transformation and Democratization of the Divine Warrior in Isaiah 59, Wisdom of Solomon 5, 1 Thessalonians 5, and Ephesians 6." Dissertation, Harvard University Divinity School.

Zerbe, Gordon
  1992   "Paul's Ethic of Nonretaliation and Peace." In Willard M. Swartley, ed., *The Love of Enemy and Nonretaliation in the New Testament,* 177-222. Louisville: Westminster/John Knox.

Selected Resources for Personal and Group Study

Four types of resources are listed here for 1 and 2 Thessalonians: general introductions (including interpretive methodologies), commentaries, books on Paul's theology, and several focused studies in relevant subject areas.

General Introductions

Jewett, Robert. *The Thessalonian Correspondence: Pauline Rhetoric and Millenarian Piety*. Foundations and Facets, NT. Philadelphia: Fortress, 1986. Stimulating survey of scholarly treatment of these letters. Analyzes circumstances eliciting them.

Malherbe, Abraham J. *Paul and the Thessalonians: The Philosophic Tradition of Pastoral Care*. Philadelphia: Fortress, 1987. How Paul established and nurtured the church in Thessalonica against the background of contemporary philosophy and culture.

Meeks, Wayne A. *The First Urban Christians: The Social World of the Apostle Paul*. New Haven: Yale University Press, 1983. Major social-world analysis of Greco-Roman society in which Paul established churches in first-century cities.

Roetzel, Calvin J. *The Letters of Paul: Conversations in Context*. 3d ed. Louisville: Westminster/John Knox, 1991. Introduces Paul in his cultural and religious context and focuses on the letters as pastoral conversations with communities of believers.

Schreiner, Thomas R. *Interpreting the Pauline Epistles*. Guides to New Testament Exegesis, 5. Grand Rapids: Baker, 1990. Practical guide to exegesis and interpretation of the Pauline letters.

Commentaries

Bruce, F. F. *1 and 2 Thessalonians.* Word Biblical Commentary, 45. Waco, Tex.: Word Books, 1982. In series presenting "the best in evangelical critical scholarship for a new generation."

Marshall, I. Howard. *1 and 2 Thessalonians.* New Century Bible Commentary. London: Marshall Morgan and Scott, 1983. Thorough but readable. By scholar from University of Aberdeen.

Wanamaker, Charles A. *The Epistles to the Thessalonians: A Commentary on the Greek Text.* The New International Greek Testament Commentary. Grand Rapids: Eerdmans, 1990. This NT scholar from South Africa includes provocative social analysis.

Books on Paul's Theology

Bassler, Jouette M., ed. *Pauline Theology,* vol. 1: *Thessalonians, Philippians, Galatians, Philemon.* Minneapolis: Augsburg Fortress, 1991. Articles summarizing scholarly discussion of the theology of these letters in the Pauline Theology Group, Society for Biblical Literature annual meetings, 1986-88.

Beker, J. Christiaan. *Paul the Apostle: The Triumph of God in Life and Thought.* Philadelphia: Fortress, 1980. *The Triumph of God: The Essence of Paul's Thought.* Trans. by Loren T. Stuckenbruck. Minneapolis: Fortress, 1990. Both treat Paul's apocalyptic theology with its emphasis on God's triumph through the death and resurrection of Jesus Christ. The 1990 book summarizes the former.

Bruce, F. F. *Paul: Apostle of the Heart Set Free.* Grand Rapids: Eerdmans, 1977. Treats the life, teaching, and mission of the apostle Paul. The main themes in Paul's theology are set in their historical framework and illustrated from his letters.

Focused Studies

Cousar, Charles B. *A Theology of the Cross: The Death of Jesus in the Pauline Letters.* Overtures to Biblical Theology, 24. Minneapolis: Augsburg Fortress, 1990. An analysis of major texts in Paul's letters dealing with Jesus' death and the gift of salvation.

Ewert, David. *And Then Comes the End.* Scottdale, Pa.: Herald Press, 1980. A biblical treatment of Christian hope.

Jeschke, Marlin. *Discipling in the Church: Recovering a Ministry of the Gospel.* 3d ed. Scottdale, Pa.: Herald Press, 1988. Helpful background for disciplinary action advocated in 2 Thess. 3:6-15.

Index of Ancient Sources

The Author

Jacob W. Elias grew up on a farm near Rosthern, Saskatchewan. His family was affiliated with the Bergthaler Mennonite Church of Saskatchewan. He pursued an education at the University of Saskatchewan in preparation for a high school teaching career. While there, Elias became involved in the First Mennonite Church of Saskatoon, where he was baptized and encouraged to consider leadership ministry in the church.

For three years Elias taught high school mathematics and science in Viscount, Saskatchewan, and Thompson, Manitoba. Then he studied at Mennonite Biblical Seminary, Elkhart, Indiana, from which he graduated in 1968. For the next six years, he served as pastor of the Mountainview Mennonite Church in Vancouver, B.C. In 1974 he began studies at the Toronto School of Theology and completed his Th.D. degree in 1978.

From 1977 Elias has served at the Associated Mennonite Biblical Seminary, as lecturer in New Testament (1977-78), director of field education (1978-81), dean (1981-90), associate professor (from 1981) and then professor of New Testament (from 1995). A sabbatical year at the Ecumenical Institute for Theological Research near Jerusalem (1985-86) provided the opportunity for travel in Turkey and Greece, to places where Paul planted churches, including Thessalonica, now called Thessaloníki. He also taught at Union Biblical Seminary, Pune, India, for one term in 1991.

Jacob and his wife, Lillian, are active members of the Hively Avenue Mennonite Church in Elkhart. In 1991-93 Jacob served as president of the Central District Conference of the General Conference Mennonite Church. He has written many articles, primarily for church papers. This commentary is his first book.

Family life for Jacob and Lillian now centers around the comings and goings of their three adult children. Laurel and her husband, Mark Crawford, live in Australia. Morlin resides in Washington, D.C. Joylin, her husband, John Ykimoff, and daughter, Amber, make their home in Michigan. When Jacob and Lillian manage to get their family together, they usually plan outdoor activities such as bicycling, cross-country skiing, or backyard croquet.